Catholicism in
Social and Historical
Contexts

Catholicism in Social and Historical Contexts

An Introduction

Curt Cadorette

ORBIS BOOKS
Maryknoll, New York 10545

Founded in 1970, Orbis Books endeavors to publish works that enlighten the mind, nourish the spirit, and challenge the conscience. The publishing arm of the Maryknoll Fathers and Brothers, Orbis seeks to explore the global dimensions of the Christian faith and mission, to invite dialogue with diverse cultures and religious traditions, and to serve the cause of reconciliation and peace. The books published reflect the views of their authors and do not represent the official position of the Maryknoll Society. To learn more about Maryknoll and Orbis Books, please visit our website at www.maryknollsociety.org.

Library of Congress Cataloging-in-Publication Data

Cadorette, Curt, 1948–
    Catholicism in social and historical contexts : an introduction / Curt Cadorette.
        p.   cm.
    Includes bibliographical references.
    ISBN 978-1-57075-872-0 (pbk.)
    1. Church history. 2. Catholic Church – History. 3. Christian sociology – Catholic Church. 4. Church and social problems – Catholic Church.   I. Title.
BR145.3.C33 2009
282.09 – dc22   2009034125

Contents

Preface

When I arrived at the University of Rochester in 1994 I wanted to teach a course on Catholic social teaching. There were two principal reasons. I had been hired to teach Catholic studies and the topic was one that I was passionate about. It turned out, however, that I was in a bit over my head. Although I knew a fair amount about the Catholic Church's position on many social issues because of my experience in Peru and graduate studies in Toronto, I was still something of an amateur. Like a lot of other professors, there were occasions in which I was "winging it," something we academics do all the time but are loath to admit. To a degree my lack of knowledge has been remedied over the years as I have pored through texts and tried to gain insight into the Christian, and particularly the Catholic, tradition of social thought that has its origins in Jesus' vision of the Reign of God and continues to be applied and expanded to this day. Perhaps I have moved from an amateur level to an intermediate one, but that assessment is best left to the students I have taught these last fifteen years.

One of the things that struck from the outset was the general lack of awareness about the Catholic Church's social teaching in general. When I would ask students about their knowledge of Catholic teaching at the beginning of a semester, they would often refer to the church's position on sexuality and reproductive issues, rarely aware that there is a rich tradition that focuses on economics, politics, and social structures. Invariably, my response would be: "Yes, you're right, but there is a lot more to it than that." And I would hasten to add that this "other stuff" could be galvanizing and prophetic. Admittedly, much of the formal material that comes from the church is dry and complex, but working through it can provide an alternative vision to the day-to-day assumptions that we take for granted. These assumptions are often the reason behind so much injustice and oppression in the modern world.

I decided to write this book to help students better grasp the long and rich history behind the church's position on social issues, from Jesus to modernity. Naturally, this is an impossible range of material, but this book is predicated on providing a few good morsels that will hopefully whet readers' appetites. The problem with this type of approach is that there is never enough time to cover a topic adequately. The number of books about

Jesus' social vision, early Christianity, Augustine, Aquinas, John Paul II, or any similar topic is enormous. I expect to be criticized for missing some crucial points along the way. As we used to say in the old Latin Mass, *mea culpa*, in other words, I bear full responsibility.

One of the things that can't be done and shouldn't be done when writing a book like this is to keep one's passion at bay. That doesn't mean reckless statements are acceptable, but certainly questions of social justice are about life and death. They are not armchair considerations. So you will sense some intensity in this discussion. As a historical and social institution, the Catholic Church sometimes gets it right, and sometimes gets it wrong. Its actions are consequential. The good news is that the church is at the forefront of the struggle for justice. It has a special perspective that needs to be appreciated.

I hope that the discussion in the book leads to further questions. Without being overly technical, I have tried to generate notes with references to many excellent works. For some of you, that may be the next step. I certainly hope so.

Acknowledgments

The author of a book never works alone. There are always many people behind the cover. That is certainly true of this work as well. I didn't write it alone. It required support, inspiration, and patience from a number of other people.

First, I would like to thank Bill and Barbara, along with the Newman Community at the University of Rochester for having established an academic chair in Catholic Studies in the early 1990s. Without their generosity I would not have the great job that I do.

Second, I would like to thank the students I have taught here. It is a rare privilege to interact with so many gifted young people, many of whom have gone on to be of service to others in an array of professions. They embody what this book tries to communicate through their actions and commitment to create more just societies.

Third, the people of Peru loom large in everything that I have written. I had the honor of working with them for several years in the southern highlands. Suffering and hope commingled in an incredible way. There was great pain and injustice, but there was also hope and joy. Life in the *altiplano* was often like the light shimmering on Lake Titicaca. It was an ineffable spectrum — sometimes dark and other times brilliant.

Finally, many thanks to dear friends who have provided me with unstinting support as I have worked on this text over the past several years, particularly Molly Grave and Mary Hembrow Snyder, those two people in my life who share my love of Latin America and a passion for justice.

Chapter One

Jesus, Justice, and God's Reign

Before Jesus Became the Christ

Few parts of the world can match Palestine in terms of historical and religious richness. Nor can many equal it in terms of political and social turmoil. Ironically, there is a link between Jesus' first-century Jewish world and the contemporary Middle East. Perhaps no part of the earth has given birth to as many religions — Judaism, Christianity, and Islam, among others, each with internal problems and infighting, not to mention hostility toward each other. The number of armies that has trod through Palestine is equally impressive. In the ancient world, an approaching army was a portent of enormous suffering. Egypt, Assyria, Babylon, Greece, Rome, Byzantium, Turkey, and, most recently, Great Britain have all garrisoned soldiers on this narrow strip of land. Today Jews and Palestinians fight over whether this is the new State of Israel or an Arab nation with its own right to self-determination. One of the principal reasons for all this cultural, political, and social unrest lies in the geographic position of Palestine. It is a natural bridge, and, in antiquity, imperialistic nations simply marched over less powerful people who were in their way. The Jewish community, then and now, was in possession of a piece of land with enormous geopolitical and military importance. Politically and militarily insignificant as a small nation-state, it was easily conquered and bullied by the most recent invaders, most of whom saw Jews and Judaism as odd and even contemptible.

In Jesus' day the northern region of the Galilee, like the rest of the Jewish nation, could be a hellish place.[1] Herod the Great, and later his sons, acted as Roman agents, extracting everything they could from impoverished peasants who were lucky if they lived to be forty. Large numbers of peasants were rendered destitute and landless because of exorbitant taxes.[2] And for those who raised their voices in protest, there was the prospect

---

1. Richard A. Horsley has written a number of excellent books on the social, political, and religious forces at play in Jesus' lifetime. Several are cited at the end of the book.

2. Jewish peasants paid the equivalent of 35 percent of their income in taxes, 20 percent in support of the Temple in Jerusalem while the rest went to Herod and Rome.

1

of crucifixion, a commonplace form of execution sometimes inflicted on thousands of victims simultaneously. What solace there was resided in family and faith, two integrally connected dimensions of human life that for Jesus and his contemporaries were nearly one and the same. In the small synagogue of Nazareth Jesus prayed with his family and learned what it meant to be a Jew. In the confines of this small Jewish town, Jesus and his fellow Galilean Jews had a modicum of dignity. In the larger scheme of things, however, they had no social significance. In the eyes of the Jewish aristocracy and pious laity for whom Jerusalem was the center of the world, they were considered uncouth and ignorant peasants with no real knowledge of Judaism. Romans saw them as despicable, uncultured barbarians who spoke no Greek or Latin and subscribed to a bizarre religious tradition that required circumcision, fasting, strange dietary customs, and general avoidance of non-Jews.[3]

By the end of the first century early Christians had constructed varied accounts of Jesus' life in Nazareth. In Matthew and Luke we are offered a picture of a precocious child whose father and mother are hard pressed to understand him. In some of the Gnostic gospels Jesus performs all sorts of magical feats, some of which are less than edifying.[4] Pious imagination aside, however, it is doubtful if life for Jesus, or any one else in Nazareth, was so enchanted. His parents, about whom we actually know very little, gave him a popular Jewish name. The name Jesus is as commonplace as John or Michael in contemporary culture. If his father was, in fact, a carpenter, his life might have been slightly more comfortable than those of the local peasantry, but everyone's existence was precarious. Subsistence agriculture is a dangerous way to live. Too much or too little rain, hail, or wind can spell disaster. Taxation had reached destructive levels. Failure to pay the Temple tithe resulted in ritual impurity. The penalty for not paying the Herodian and Roman taxes was confiscation of a family's land. There was political and religious hostility in the air. Herod the Great, and later his sons, were thoroughly despised. They lived in luxurious and heavily fortified palaces throughout Palestine. Roman troops were garrisoned in Caesarea and Jerusalem and often went out of their way to enrage the Jewish population, mocking ancient religious and social customs. Revolts, although suicidal, were inevitable, with the greatest and most catastrophic taking place from 66 to 70 C.E.

---

3. There is, of course, a vast amount of literature that focuses on the historical Jesus. An eminently readable work is by Marcus Borg, *Jesus: Uncovering the Life, Teachings, and Relevance of a Religious Revolutionary.*

4. The Gnostic gospels circulated widely in Egypt and the Middle East. They were rejected by the mainline catholic church in the second century because of their otherworldly understanding of Jesus.

Daily life in Nazareth, however, was most likely relatively tranquil, at least when tax collectors and Roman troops were not in the area. As peasants do to this day, they measured time by the sun, moon, and rainy and dry seasons. The natural world was immediate and well known. Mind and matter worked together far more intimately than they do for us moderns. Everyone was religious and assumed the existence of a supreme deity, angels, and demons. In fact, the world itself was understood religiously. The synagogue and Jewish liturgical year were enormously important for achieving a sense of identity and purpose. Undoubtedly, Jesus spent a great deal of time in the local synagogue, where he mostly likely learned to read Hebrew. He would hear commentaries on Torah and the prophetic texts of the Bible given by adult males in the local dialect of Aramaic, the Semitic language that most Palestinian Jews spoke on a daily basis. He would learn that fidelity to God entails compassion and justice toward one's neighbors. Quite likely, he, his parents, and his siblings, following the traditions of their people, would visit a *mikvah*, or ritual bath, to insure their compliance with the laws of purity.[5] Diet and food preparation would follow the rules of *kashrut* — kosher regulations. Yet if the word for religion existed in first-century Aramaic, and it did not, Jesus and his fellow citizens would have been baffled. Religion as a discreet, personal phenomenon would have made little or no sense to them. Religion was both an individual and collective reality. There were holy people, but the Jewish nation itself was holy to the extent that it was faithful to its God. Torah was seen as a way of life, a way to exist as a human being in relationship to the divine and one's neighbors, all bound to each other in a covenantal relationship. In the small synagogue of Nazareth Jesus became a "Torah Jew" impassioned by his faith and deeply committed to his own people, whose suffering was becoming unbearable.

From Nazareth to Jerusalem

Sometime in his late twenties, Jesus of Nazareth seems to have begun a search for a deeper and more consequential understanding of his Jewish beliefs. Ultimately, this search would lead him to redefine Judaism in a theologically and socially radical way. Jesus started a reform movement that challenged the religious and social order of his day. Fraught with tensions, the Jewish community responded to Roman oppression in different ways, from acquiescence to overt confrontation. Oppression, especially of

---

5. Recent University of Rochester archaeological excavations in Yodefat, a town close to Nazareth, uncovered a significant number of *mitzvoth* (pl.), an important discovery in understanding how Judaism was lived among Galilean Jews in the early first century of the Christian era.

an entire culture and nation, is bound to generate diverse responses. Frequently this divergence is exploited by the oppressors themselves. By the time of Jesus' life, the Romans had been involved in imperialistic wars of expansion for several centuries. They knew instinctually that the most effective way to conquer and maintain their control was to exploit existing divisions. Victims victimize themselves in internecine struggles, thus minimizing the danger of concerted opposition.

Some of this tension is visible in the four canonical Gospels that make up the bulk of the New Testament. It is understandable to look to them for a reliable description of first-century Judaism and Jesus' place in that turbulent world. Matthew, Mark, Luke, and John, however, are problematic resources. None of the texts is historical in the contemporary sense of the term. Each, in different and sometimes contradictory ways, is an apology — an attempt to convince the reader that Jesus of Nazareth is the Christ and the founder of the emerging Christian community. All were written after the civil war of 66–70, when the religious and social world Jesus knew had been thoroughly shattered by brutal Roman legions. Also, to varying degrees, there are anti-Jewish biases woven into parts of the texts whose connection with Jesus is highly questionable, if not frankly erroneous. This is particularly the case with Matthew and John, whose diatribes against the Pharisees and the Jewish people in general are often vitriolic and, tragically, a source for subsequent anti-Semitism. In terms of the Gospels, it is important to remember that they were written at a precise historical moment. The Jewish community had recently endured the catastrophe of a war that was as much civil and internal as it was a war of liberation from Rome. It led to tens of thousands of deaths, Jew killing Jew, and Romans killing anyone they captured. The greatest tragedy was the destruction of the Temple by Vespasian's son, Titus, who, like his father, would eventually become emperor. What was left of the Jewish religious tradition after 70 C.E. was essentially Pharisaic. Jews who considered Jesus to be the messiah were an intolerable threat, a wedge that threatened more division. Followers of Jesus claimed to be the truest version of Judaism and the cornerstone of a New Israel. They insisted that they were a legitimate Jewish community and should be afforded the legal protections granted to Jews by the Roman senate. As Crossan points out in *The Historical Jesus*, "By the end of the first century two great religions, rabbinic Judaism and early Christianity, were emerging from a common matrix. Each claimed to be its only legitimate continuation, and each had texts and traditions to prove it."[6] What is construed in the Gospels as a debate between Jesus and other representatives of Judaism about their respective understanding

---

6. Crossan, *The Historical Jesus*, 422.

of religion and society is, then, a late first-century fight far removed from Jesus' own life and times.

In terms of discerning what was transpiring in the Palestinian Jewish community in the early first century, there are, however, some resources. One comes from the writings of Philo of Alexandria, a contemporary of Jesus and a Platonic Jew who attempted in his prolific writings to explain Jewish belief and politics to his Greco-Roman contemporaries. Arguably more important is the work of Josephus, a Pharisee and want-to-be general who surrendered the Jewish garrison at Yodefat to Vespasian, the Roman general sent by Nero to quell the Jewish revolt in 66. In one of the great ironies of history, not only did Josephus avoid crucifixion, he was adopted into Vespasian's Flavian family and spent the rest of his life in Italy, where he wrote *The Antiquities of the Jews* and *War of the Jews*. Like Philo, he was attempting to explain the religious and social history of the Jewish community to less than sympathetic Greeks and Romans. Josephus dedicates a few sentences to John the Baptist and may have written a few lines about Jesus, although some scholars consider the remarks later Christian interpolations. What follows is a brief synopsis of these two writers' description of the political and theological factions of Jesus' day, combined with the insights of contemporary scholars. The academic literature on the questions of Second Temple Judaism is complex and vast and is marked by a mixture of speculation and scholarly debate.[7] Still, it is possible to come up with a schematic and generally agreed upon description of the principal social and theological "schools" in Jesus' day.[8] Each viewed Judaism and the dangerous social world it inhabited in different ways.

The Sadducees

It is hard to imagine a group whose understanding of Judaism and the social order was more contrary to Jesus' vision than that of the Sadducees. Affluent social and religious conservatives, they controlled the high priesthood and the operation of the Temple in Jerusalem and generally functioned as the Jewish people's interlocutors with Roman authorities. The Sadducees were an aristocratic, priestly class that resided exclusively in Jerusalem. The high priest, whose appointment was carefully monitored by Rome, was drawn exclusively from their ranks. Most were presumably bilingual, speaking both Aramaic and *koine* Greek, the common language of the eastern half of the empire. For centuries a debate

---

7. The term "Second Temple" refers to the period of the reestablishment of the Jewish state as a province of the Persian empire in the sixth century B.C.E. until the destruction of the Temple by Rome.

8. Sanders, *Paul (Past Masters)*, 8–18, 84–100.

had been raging among the Jewish population of Palestine about the surrounding Greco-Roman world with its different philosophies and religions. Some, like the Sadducees, proposed a realistic tolerance while more radical groups, like the Essenes, advocated a hostile rejection of everything connected with the Hellenistic world. What little we know about the Sadducees comes from Josephus, a Pharisee who was highly critical of the Sadducees for their elitism, theology, and role as colonial lackeys. He describes them as having "none but the rich on their side."[9] Surely, there were good and pious Sadducees despite Josephus's characterizations. They were, however, part of an oppressive social and religious system that produced poverty and unrest for the majority of the Jewish people.

Living in comfortable homes in Jerusalem, the Sadducees derived their income from rent from their landholdings and especially the half *shekel* tax that was forwarded to the Temple by all pious Jews. They used the income to maintain the Temple, but also to support the small army of priests that staffed it. To use a contemporary analogy, they were in charge of the national treasury. The residents of Galilee also had to fill the coffers of Herod Antipas, one of Herod's four sons, all of whom were named after their father. In Jesus' day Herod Antipas had launched enormous and costly building projects in the Galilee, creating Hellenized towns with lavish baths and theaters mimicking the glories of Rome. Between the rents and taxes, peasants were pushed to the point of desperation.[10] If they were unable to come up with the annual taxes, peasants would borrow money on the hope that the next harvest would be abundant. In a system of subsistence farming, such a hope is easily dashed. Too much or too little rain, an early frost, or any number of vagaries could mean a poor crop with inevitable hunger and misery. In addition, failure to pay the Temple tax made a Jewish peasant unobservant and impure. Failure to pay Antipas's taxes could lead to expulsion from one's land. In an agrarian society like that of first-century Palestine, losing ancestral land was the greatest of disasters. Land had belonged to families for generations and was seen as sacred, as part of the nation of Israel.

Both the Sadducees and Herod Antipas were the beneficiaries of an unjust economic system and the allies of Rome, who kept a close eye on this turbulent piece of colonial real estate infamous for its obstinacy and tendency to revolt. Like other empires before it, Rome used local elites to govern in its name if at all possible. Colonial systems work more efficiently when controlled by surrogates who know the language and culture of an oppressed people. Any sort of opposition or resistance can be more

---

9. Josephus, *Antiquities of the Jews*, xiii, 10, 6.
10. Horsley and Silberman, *The Message and the Kingdom*, 22–42.

readily detected and dealt with by local powers than by a Roman procurator who, in the case of Palestine, would know no Aramaic and have little or no knowledge of the religious and social mores of the Jewish population. Political realists, the Sadducees did Rome's bidding and were rewarded for their efforts with money and prestige. For more than a century they kept the lid on a veritable pressure cooker, finally losing control in 66 C.E. Ironically, they disappeared from Jewish history in the civil war, destroyed by political and religious extremists who, according to Josephus, slaughtered their fellow Jews in prodigious numbers in Jerusalem, as conditions in the besieged city deteriorated, with factions fighting each other like so many cornered rats. Those who tried to escape the hellish conditions inside the sacred city were almost invariably caught by the Romans and crucified outside the city walls. Josephus tells of hundreds of crosses set up with crucified Jews facing the city walls. Titus was a master of terror, and the situation in Jerusalem became utterly chaotic, with fanaticism winning the day. The cool rationality of the Sadducees no longer held sway and they were now the victims of the very disorder they had tried to avoid.

The greatest power that the Sadducees wielded was their control of the Temple and the myriad religious rituals that took place within its confines. Headed by the high priest, a small army of priests performed sacrifices and purifying rituals that were a central part of Jewish religious practice. One of the assumptions behind the Temple, and one that Jesus would challenge, was that expiation or atonement had to be made to an otherwise angry and punitive deity. The Temple, which had been expanded and embellished by Herod the Great, was infinitely more than a building. It was a place of divine residence and unimaginable holiness. Jews through the Greco-Roman world dutifully supported the Temple and whenever possible went to Jerusalem, particularly for the feast of Passover each spring. In a world in which the social and religious were fused, the Temple embodied Jewish belief and identity. Whereas a synagogue, and there were many in Jerusalem itself, was and still is considered a mere building, the Temple exuded sacredness. The Sadducees, therefore, controlled the most powerful building and piece of land in the whole of the Jewish world. They claimed a special access to the divine, and their use of ritual in a manipulative and magical way was inevitable. Both the Pharisees and Jesus criticized them for doing just that. Josephus notes their arrogance as the religious and social elite of Jerusalem. The Sadducees subscribed to a frozen, ritual-based understanding of Judaism that served them well. They were affluent, well-connected sophisticates whose political talents and age-old rituals were consumed in the fury of an uprising of unprecedented ferocity.

The Pharisees

The first thing that must be addressed when discussing the Pharisees is a long history of misperception and bias on the part of Christians that is rooted in the gospel narratives themselves. As an adjective, the word "Pharisaic" has the connotation of someone duplicitous and self-righteous. The Pharisees were neither. We must be careful of our sources. First, Josephus may well exaggerate their numbers and popularity given his membership in their ranks. The Gospels, on the other hand, construe the Pharisees as Jesus' principal and most malicious opponents. Matthew is shrill and obsessive in his denunciation of them, and John is not much kinder. Although there were obvious differences between Jesus' approach to Judaism and that of the Pharisees, it stretches the imagination to have the former constantly vilifying the latter. Jesus shared many of the theological concepts central to Pharisaic Judaism. The origins of the Pharisees are not absolutely clear, but they seem to have emerged as a religious reform movement during the reign of the Hasmonean king John Hyrcanus (d. 104 B.C.E.), who ruled from Jerusalem and expanded Jewish control and communities outside of Judea itself, especially in the northern area of Galilee. There is some debate about the meaning of the term "Pharisee." The more general consensus is that it means something like "the separate ones." Perhaps they originated as a protest party over the politics and religious policy of the Sadducees. The two groups were not necessarily pitted against each other, but there were social and religious differences that set them apart. Still, they shared power in the Sanhedrin, the governing body of the Jewish people. To use a contemporary analogy, the two groups were not unlike different political parties vying for power in a common political system.

In terms of status, the Pharisees were members of the laity, not the priesthood. They had no inherent sacral or religious qualities, although they strove for holiness as great as that of the priests through their careful observance of Torah. Contemporary socioeconomic terms can be misleading, but the Pharisees might be described as an urban middle class, far more comfortable than Jewish peasants or villagers, but less affluent than the privileged Saducean families with their land and recourse to the Temple's revenues. Whereas the Sadducees generally accepted the trappings of Hellenistic culture, the Pharisees rejected it in all its forms, seeing the Greco-Roman world as a threat to the integrity of Judaism. They certainly disliked their Roman oppressors, but unlike groups such as the Essenes and Zealots, they were not interested in picking a fight. They were religious exclusivists and political pragmatists who knew that a war with Rome was collective suicide. When Titus breached the walls of Jerusalem, they managed to broker a deal with him and reestablish

Jewish communities outside of the city. In fact, all forms of contemporary Judaism have their roots in the Pharisaic or rabbinic tradition. Committed scholars, they kept Jewish knowledge and religious practice alive at a time in which it was threatened with extinction. Tragically, the Jewish-Christian struggle for legitimacy and recognition toward the end of the first century would lead to mutual recriminations and excommunications, with Christians blaming the Pharisees for perverting Judaism and rejecting Jesus as the messiah. For their part, Pharisaic rabbis surely saw Christians as heretics with a divisive message that threatened a badly mauled Jewish community.

The Pharisees did not reject the Temple or its rituals. In fact, they stressed personal piety and the strict performance of Jewish rituals as indispensable for salvation. In terms of interpreting Torah they held a more expansive view than the Sadducees, putting stock in its oral dimension as revelatory as well. Herein lies the beginnings of the Talmudic tradition with its rabbinic commentaries on scripture which are seen as second only to the Torah as a divinely inspired work. Their belief in oral revelation allowed them to incorporate new theological ideas not found in the text of scripture itself, such as the notion of life after death and human resurrection, ideas that the Sadducees rejected as scripturally unfounded. They saw the Sadducees, with their affinity for Hellenistic culture and many political deals with Rome, as a negative influence on the Jewish faith and people. Like any sectarian, reformist movement, they insisted on the exclusivity of their religious insights, but they were willing to interact with the Sadducees as need required. What they aspired to do was to live life in complete holiness while winning back the impure and nonobservant Jews of their day to their version of Judaism. The Gospels present the Pharisees in a negative light, as ones who imposed religious burdens on the majority of the Jewish people, the *'amme ha-arets*, or "people of the land," who were neither Sadducees nor Pharisees, but rather peasants and villagers. The Gospels accuse them of disdain for those who were socially inferior and less knowledgeable about Torah. Yet many of the *'amme ha-arets* seemed to have admired and respected the Pharisees, especially rabbinic teachers who were renowned for their compassion, holiness, and wisdom. It is not so far-fetched to imagine Jesus being taught by a Pharisee in Nazareth, even if he eventually rejected their particular interpretation of Torah.

The Gospels also condemn the Pharisees for externalism and imposition of scrupulosity on an already oppressed people. They are deemed hypocrites and self-deluded liars. In all likelihood, few were. In a secular world, whether we are believers or not, we find it hard to understand the intensity of Pharisaic Judaism. It seems compulsive and overwrought. But the Pharisees, like most committed religious people, were driven by

a vision. They had a mission: making Israel holy so that it could survive the brutal yoke of Roman rule. If the Romans could not be expelled,
and the Pharisees knew they could not be, then one could at least live a
life of thoroughgoing, Torah-based holiness. The seeming compulsivity of
their version of Judaism is expressive of an intense desire to survive as
individuals and a nation in a ruthless world. Unlike the Sadducees, who
actually collaborated with Rome, the Pharisees lived and preached a type
of passive resistance. Of course, their beliefs did little or nothing to ame-
liorate the living conditions of most Jews, other than providing them with
psychological and religious comfort — no small achievements in such a
hostile world. The tension between Jesus and the Pharisees was not about
the nature of Torah, which both saw as revealed truth. Their perceptions
of the God revealed in Torah, however, were different. Jesus stressed a
God who was accepting and compassionate. The Pharisees emphasized
a God who was more demanding and concerned with religious behavior.
Both views are legitimate conclusions that one can draw from the pages of
the Hebrew Bible. Different theologies, however, lead to different behaviors. The Pharisees' political strategy vis-à-vis Rome made them cautious
and conservative. Their theology provided them with a sense of religious
mission and purity that helped ward off the collapse and dissolution of
Palestinian Judaism. Jesus' vision was more concerned with creating an
inclusive Jewish nation based on compassion and justice that he referred
to as the Reign or Kingdom of God.[11] He objected to the notion that God
could be placated by religious rituals or impressed by scrupulous religious
behavior. Still, there is little evidence to indicate that he rejected Temple
ritual per se or the personal piety of the Pharisees, despite inferences to
that effect in the Gospels. His mission was to purify the Temple, to make
it a place of worship in which rituals were acts of thanksgiving and a
person's religious beliefs led to greater acceptance of others and social
justice.

The Essenes

At a very early age, all of us learn that compromise is essential and
inevitable. For a tiny minority of people, however, compromise is seen
as failure, or even a sin. Such an exacting group existed in Second Temple
Judaism. Around 130 B.C.E., a number of disgruntled priests who served
in the Jerusalem Temple concluded that the high priest and even most of
their fellow priests were compromised and therefore sinful. Rather than

---

11. Henceforth the term "Reign" rather than "Kingdom" will be used. Not only is the
word more inclusive, it is arguably as good a translation of the Greek term from which it is
derived.

risk being contaminated by the rampant impurity and immorality they saw around them, they entered into self-imposed exile. They took up residence in a desolate area near the Dead Sea known as Qumran, where they formed a sectarian, ultra-orthodox community. The Essenes, as the group was known, were more legend than fact for millennia. They are referred to by Philo and Josephus, but little was known about the group until 1947, when their library was discovered in adjacent caves and cliffs and their community center subsequently excavated. We now know more about the Essenes than we do about the Sadducees or the Pharisees before the civil war. The caves around Qumran contained biblical manuscripts, apocryphal religious texts, the handbook of the community known today as the *Manual of Discipline,* and an angry piece of apocalyptic literature known as the *War Scroll.* Much of their literature, hidden from the Romans around 70 C.E., bristles with rage not only at the heathen Romans but at other Jews deemed impure and faithless, especially the high priest and his cohorts in Jerusalem. In general, apocalyptic literature is produced in times of suffering, when endurance no longer seems possible. It is predicated on the assumption that the suffering of the present is a prelude to divine intervention in human affairs in which the righteous will be vindicated. God, through the agency of myriad angels and often a messianic leader, slays the wicked in their entirety and ushers in an age of blessedness. To quote Richard Horsley, " . . . The Essenes fantasized a final slaughter in which, joining with the heavenly hosts, they would massacre all the children of darkness."[12] Apocalyptic literature was fairly common in Jesus' day and entered into Christian consciousness especially through Paul's writing and the book of Revelation. Apocalyptic sectarians like the Essenes have and always will exist in most religious traditions. There are always a tiny few who will never compromise and are ferociously bent on achieving absolute religious purity. Of necessity, such people isolate themselves and attempt to cut off all contact with the outside world, counting the minutes before everything comes crashing down by virtue of divine intervention.

It is always tempting to dismiss sectarian religious believers as fanatics — ignorant, backward people who cannot bend or deal with reality. The Essenes, however, were far from ignorant. Theirs was a priestly and literate community. Its upper echelon was made up of celibate males from priestly families noted for their erudition and fidelity to Torah and ritual purity. Qumran had a large *mikvah,* or ritual immersion pool. As the *Manual of Discipline* makes clear, violations of Torah not only lead to impurity, but could be cause for expulsion from the community, a synonym for damnation. Entrance into the community, as is the case in any

---

12. Horsley, *The Sociology of the Jesus Movement,* 21.

sect, was a gradual and selective process. Novices were not housed with the community. They first had to learn Torah according to the theology of the Essenes and be ritually pure. Only in this way could they eventually share in the ritual meals and celebrations of the community which were understood as foreshadowings of the Reign of God.

The Essenes despised the Jerusalem priesthood because its members interacted with Romans and were willing, to varying degrees, to accept some of the cultural values of the Hellenistic and Greco-Roman world. Their judgment of the Temple's priestly managers is harsh and unrelenting. They are deemed arrogant, corrupt, and impure "sons of Belial," or Satan. The Essenes refused any contact with gentiles, especially the Greek and later Roman invaders who had destroyed the nation of Israel. Ordinary Jews, particularly the *'amme ha-arets,* do not fare much better in the Essene scheme of things. They, too, are contaminated and no longer really Jews. Nonpriests and ignorant, they can expect the same fate as the Romans and priests in Jerusalem — annihilation at the hand of God, with strategic assistance from the members of the Qumran community who will fight at the side of the angels. The theology of the Essenes is strikingly dualistic.[13] There are good people (very few) and bad people (everyone else). The terms "light" and "darkness" are found constantly in their literature. All other interpretations of Torah besides theirs are wrong and damnable. To paraphrase Cyprian of Carthage, a Christian bishop from third-century Carthage, "Outside of the church there is no salvation." Outside of Qumran with its ritual pools, collective dining room, and library, and the theology behind this antagonistic sect, there is no true belief or presence of God.

With the discovery of the Dead Sea Scrolls in 1947, scholars were quick to see a connection between what little we know of John the Baptist and certain aspects of Jesus' preaching about the Reign of God. If we can take Luke at face value, John's preaching has an Essene tone to it. "You brood of vipers! Who warned you to flee from the wrath to come? . . . Even now the axe is laid to the root of the trees; every tree therefore that does not bear good fruit is cut down and thrown into the fire" (Luke 3:7, 9).[14] Such an apocalyptic pronouncement fits perfectly with the message of *The War Scroll.* So too John's use of ritual purification in the Jordan, the precursor to Christian baptism, meshes well with the Essenes' stress on ritual purification. This sort of apocalyptic discourse and purification ritual were common phenomena in Second Temple Judaism, and John's theological

---

13. Dualism in Jewish theology came largely from Persian culture and religion. In the Greco-Roman world Platonism was the most dualistic of the prevailing philosophical systems.

14. Translation taken from the Revised Standard Version. All New Testament quotations are taken from this translation.

affinities are difficult to place in the first-century scheme of things. He could well have been a wandering Essene preaching to the masses. We have only Josephus and the Gospels to rely upon, and the Gospels' authors go to great lengths to craft, one might even say finesse, the connection between John and Jesus. Nonetheless, the fact that John baptized Jesus would seem to indicate Jesus' own sympathy with this type of religious mind-frame and behavior. The Essenes held solemn, eschatological banquets that they considered to be a foreshadowing of the Reign of God. So too did Jesus. But herein there is an obvious and major difference. For Jesus the Reign of God was an inclusive event. Everyone was capable of participating in its advent, not just priests or the ritually pure. In fact, the *'amme ha-arets* would be at the head table, a notion categorically rejected not only by the Essenes, but by the Sadducees and Pharisees as well. It is probable that Jesus shared the eschatological consciousness of the Essenes and certain Pharisees,[15] but he did not understand the Reign of God as being ushered in by massive slaughter. To the contrary, its advent was to be joyful. Turning the other cheek (Matt. 9:36) was hardly a virtue in Essene theology. Lashing out in murderous rage was deemed the best solution to Roman oppression. No doubt the thinking of the Qumran community fed the violence of political and social groups among the Jewish people such as the Zealots, some of whom were probably no more than thieves and murderers. Nonetheless, the anti-Roman diatribes of the Essenes legitimated the use of violence against the hated oppressors of the Jewish nation. Sophisticated and religiously pure, the Essenes were nonetheless a dangerous proposition. Like many sectarian groups, they were driven by anger and hatred. In the case of first-century Palestine, such emotions were certainly legitimate. But to act on them was the equivalent of collective madness.

Jesus Becomes the Christ

By the mid-second century the emerging Christian communities had essentially agreed on four canonical or authoritative narratives about the life and teaching of Jesus. Matthew, Mark, Luke, and John were accepted as definitive texts, excluding several other versions of Jesus' life, most of which were adhered to by Gnostic sects whose understanding of Jesus was different from that of mainline or catholic Christian groups.[16] It was obvious then and it is now that the four Gospels offered different portraits of Jesus and were produced in different places and times. Since Matthew and

---

15. Some contemporary scholars contest this point. The issue is complicated because the Gospels depict Jesus' awareness of the *eschaton* or end times in different ways.

16. Full Gnostic gospels like the Gospels of Thomas and Philip, among others, were discovered in Nag Hammadi, Egypt, in 1945. Prior to this date Gnostic literature was fragmentary. The materials were written in Greek and Coptic.

Luke replicate Mark nearly in its entirety, they clearly were written later. Yet there are sections of these two Gospels that rely on a source other than Mark, which scholars would come to refer to as Q. To complicate matters even more, Matthew and Luke do not coincide all of the time. Then, of course, the Gospel of John presents a story of Jesus that is quite distinct from the so-called Synoptic Gospels. So whose version is the most accurate? On which Gospel do we rely to draw the most accurate and historical portrait of the first-century Galilean Jew Christians proclaimed as the risen messiah? The answer, unfortunately, is none of the four texts that make up the bulk of the New Testament, at least without many reservations. The reason for such seeming skepticism is that the Gospels were not written as historical documents but rather as theological treatises whose purpose was to win converts to Christianity. The Gospels are Christological and ecclesiological documents. They set out a story whose purpose is to convince readers that Jesus is the Christ, the messiah who has been raised from the dead. In other words, they are Christological documents. Concomitantly, they describe models for how the Christian community should live out its beliefs. In other words, they lay out an ecclesiology or understanding of how believing Christians should function as a collective entity or body of believers. The Gospels do contain historical information, but it is always influenced by the Christological and ecclesiological agendas of its respective authors, all of whom wrote their texts in particular environments, about which we frankly know very little, despite some pious legends from the third and fourth centuries. So we can know something about Jesus' person and understanding of Judaism and his social environment on the basis of the Gospels, but hard and fast conclusions are elusive.

Of course, the amount of written material on the life of Jesus is enormous. Arguably, he is the most written about person in history. In the past few decades scholars like Borg, Crossan, Meyer, and Horsley, using archeological material and textual analysis, have made great strides in contextualizing Jesus' life and preaching. The search for the historical Jesus is often technical and enervating, but it has produced results that help us better understand Jesus' meaning and message in light of first-century Judaism. Christians have tended to overlook telling aspects of Jesus' life, his understanding of Judaism, and especially his social message. Crossan stresses the fact that Jesus made no distinction about those with whom he ate, and this is a telling social and religious gesture that deserves greater appreciation. For those of us who live in a pluralistic, twenty-first-century world, this may seem to be an insignificant detail. In antiquity, however, it was a shocking statement of nonconformity. One simply did not engage in table fellowship with social or religious inferiors, because eating was a socioreligious affair, not a prosaic activity. Yet all of the canonical Gospels are quite clear on this point. Jesus would eat with anyone, regardless of gender, social status, or compliance with the religious norms of his day. He paid no heed to what, for many, were nonnegotiable dictates of acceptable behavior. He surely knew that his actions were provocative, but his understanding of God led him to include those who were officially excluded from table fellowship — prostitutes, the economically destitute who could not pay their taxes, and the general riff-raff of first-century Palestine. By eating with such people Jesus was making an unequivocal statement about his understanding of God and Judaism. These people were not excluded but rather included in the Reign of God. Socioreligious distinctions were human constructs. They had nothing to do with the deepest meaning of Torah, which invited all to participate in a covenant based on mutual dignity and respect. The compulsive ritualism of the Temple, the stringent religiosity of the Pharisees, and the exclusive hostility of the Essenes were disregarded and refuted not by engaging in theological debate as much as by concrete action. Jesus placed no conditions on his invitation to participate in God's Reign other than willingness to examine and change one's life in light of an inclusive understanding of Torah.

Borg sees Jesus as the head of a peace party among the various Jewish factions,[17] and Crossan refers to Jesus' followers as making up a "kingdom of nobodies."[18] In many respects, we are dealing with a type of religious anarchy. The only authority in the community resides with God. The members of the community itself are all equal and called to serve each other without distinction. To quote Crossan again: "The kingdom of God is people under divine rule, and that, as ideal, transcends and judges all human rule."[19] Such a vision flies in the face of those who exercise political and religious power and often think of themselves as qualitatively better than those around them. They understand their power as a divinely merited gift. Their task is to control and even coerce their social and religious inferiors — the uneducated and unclean masses prone to resistance and rebellion. In the Gospel of Mark Jesus indicates that those who wish to participate in God's Reign must do so as children. "I tell you that whoever does not accept the kingdom of God like a child will never enter it" (Mark 10:15). There is a fair degree of irony in Jesus' assertion since children had no legal standing in antiquity. They were the literal property of their father, who could do whatever he wished with them as the *pater familias*. His authority was seen as God-given and nonnegotiable. Jesus, however, expressly requires that his followers treat each other with absolute equality. They are called to be unpretentious, much as little children can be.

17. Borg, *Jesus, a New Vision,* 137.
18. Crossan, *The Historical Jesus,* 266.
19. Ibid.

"If anyone wants to be first, he must make himself last of all and servant of all" (Mark 9:35). The only hierarchical aspect in Jesus' vision is
that between God and human beings. But even that relationship is one of
benevolence. The father depicted in the parable of the Prodigal Son (Luke
15:11–32) is forgiving and loving. Jesus' parable is meant to convey what
he thinks are the essential attributes of God's own self, especially forgiveness and love. His God does not require Temple rituals or proven religious
piety. He does not punish but rather rejoices.

The fifth chapter of the Gospel of Mark, the first of the canonical Gospels written, contains a vivid picture of Jesus' social and religious values.
Of course, some scholars debate the historicity of the three healing stories
found in this section of Mark. If nothing else, we at least have a packed
and powerful narrative that gives us insight into how early Christians
understood Jesus' approach to his social and religious world. The first of
the three stories concerns the so-called Gerasene demoniac. It is a classic
story of good and evil, God and demoniac powers, the latter cast out by
Jesus' god-like compassion. It takes places on the "other" side of the Sea
of Galilee, which had a heavy concentration of non-Jewish residents. For
most of us, the concept of diabolical possession is hard to believe. In the
first century, and up until a few centuries ago in the Western world, however, many people were convinced of the possibility of evil forces taking
over a person's body and mind. Rituals for exorcism still exist in most
branches of Christianity and are still employed on rare occasion. They
are the stuff of tabloids and, in the minds of some, proof positive of the
regressive nature of Christianity. Yet the behavior of the "demoniac" is not
so far-fetched. There is now a large body of psychological literature that
deals with the consequences of trauma. Although rare, victims of violence
can develop what psychologists call multiple personalities or dissociative
identity disorder. They jump from one self-understanding or personality
to another and are tormented by the many emotions and voices that roll
through their heads. In agony, they often harm themselves, engaging in
acts of self-mutilation, just as Mark reports in the first healing story of
this chapter. The self-inflicted violence is now understood as a coping or
soothing mechanism that momentarily jolts someone back into a more
normal state of mind. Unfortunately, it is not a cure, since the underlying
traumatic abuse is not adequately dealt with. Mark is almost coy in his
description of events. When asked their names by Jesus the "demons" in
the possessed man, namely, his traumatic memories and emotions, call
themselves Legion. There are over two thousand of them, and Jesus allows
them to enter into a herd of two thousand swine that fling themselves over
a cliff and into the Sea of Galilee (Mark 5:5–13). Could we not be dealing
with the victim of Roman oppression, a gentile victim of brutality living
on the fringes of society? Mark does not tell us, but the explanation has a

degree of plausibility to it. Although Jesus was nonviolent, he was surely aware of just how brutal Roman authorities could be. Everyone in the Jewish and Greco-Roman world was aware of the extraordinary savagery of the Romans and many had experienced it firsthand. The psychosis of the "demoniac" has its basis in the daily reality of a brutalized population. Jesus refutes the violence that has taken up residence in the "demoniac" by casting its many manifestations into unclean animals, whose evil leads to their own demise.

The next two stories are only slightly less dramatic. Jesus returns to the other side of the Sea of Galilee with its plethora of small Jewish communities. He is approached by a woman with some sort of physical disorder, perhaps gynecological in nature. She touches Jesus' cloak and is healed. There are two remarkable aspects to this story. The first is that Jesus does not claim to have healed the woman who touched him. It is, rather, her faith in Jesus' message and the God he proclaims (Mark 5:25–34) that has brought about this cure. Secondly, Jesus is delighted by her faith and desire for healing. In reality, he should have been incensed because by virtue of this woman's touch, he has been rendered ritually impure. Furthermore, since the event takes place in public, everyone else would have known as well. What Mark is saying obliquely is that Jesus paid no attention to the laws of ritual purity, what scholars now refer to as the Holiness Code.[20] Whether the author of Mark was Jewish or knew much about Judaism is open to debate. Still, women were not allowed to touch strangers and were stringently segregated from males outside of the home and marriage. This was as much the case in Jewish culture as it was in most of the Greco-Roman world. Finally, Mark tells the story of Jesus bringing an apparently dead girl back to life. Approached by her distraught parents, he enters the room where her supposed corpse is laid and simply tells her to get up. Mark has Jesus speak Aramaic in this instance, saying *talitha cumi* — "Child, get up" (Mark 5:42). The fact that Jesus touched the child means that we have another instance in which the norms of ritual purity have been broken. Only specific people could touch a corpse in Jesus' day. More important, however, is that what heals the child is the pain and compassion of Jesus and her parents. Collectively, they give her a new chance at life. The despair and derision of the mourners outside the house is negated by an act of concern and love that is life-giving. The social message woven into all three of these stories is powerful and revolutionary.

In recent years a great deal of archaeological, sociological, and textual work has gone on that sheds new light on Jesus' social vision and world. A sub-branch of scholars now focuses heavily of the Galilee region in Jesus'

---

20. The Holiness Code refers to the myriad rules and regulations, from diet to comportment, that pious Jews were expected to follow. It is drawn primarily from Leviticus.

day. Perhaps some of the most impressive work has come from the pen of Richard A. Horsley, who has written a number of excellent books on Second Temple Judaism, and specifically the Galilee region, from a socio-historical perspective.[21] In fact, we have cited him previously and his ideas inform much of this chapter's structure. Horsley's work, and that of other scholars coming from a historical and social vantage point, helps us better understand the Gospel and understand the theological agenda that informs them all.[22] To engage in something of a generalization, one can detect a process in the four canonical texts in which Jesus' concreteness as a person and the historical context play less and less of a role. In the Gospel of Mark, Jesus is a down-to-earth healer and prophet, who becomes the Son of God through a process of recognition, especially on the part of his disciples. In Mark 7:33–34 Jesus places his own saliva in the ears of a deaf man in order to heal him. He is almost frantic in his efforts to announce the Reign of God. In the prologue of the Gospel of John, Jesus is declared to be the preexistent Logos, or Word (1:15). In John's post-resurrection story, Jesus can pass through locked doors (John 20:26). In the Gnostic Christian tradition Jesus ceases to have a real body at all. His divinity is such that he can literally defy the laws of nature and fly. To use academic terminology, we are moving from a "low Christology" like that of Mark with Jesus' feet firmly on the ground to a "high Christology" like the Gospel of Thomas, which makes him a pure spirit whose body is not really real. But we are always dealing with Christological texts. Context and historicity were not the primary concern of early Christian writers. Conversion was, which makes perfect sense in light of the fact that Jesus' followers believed that he had been raised from the dead and was the son of God. To be a bit facetious, this is not information one keeps to one's self in dispassionate reserve.

To return to the Galilee region in the first century, however, we encounter a Jewish community threatened by rapacious taxes, Temple tithes, and haughty Roman authorities whose troops marched through the area with regularity. There was restiveness in the air, and it had sparked prior revolts with the predictable brutal response of Roman authorities. In 9 C.E. the Roman administrator P. Quintilicus Varus, crucified

---

21. Richard A. Horsley has published *Galilee: History, Politics, People*, and *Archaeology, History, and Society: The Social Context of Jesus and the Rabbis.* He has several other solidly researched works eminently worth reading.

22. Scholars like Horsley, Crossan, and Borg, members of the so-called Jesus Seminar, have their critics. Conservative Christians, especially evangelicals, see them as driven by skepticism so intense that it weakens Christianity itself. One might assert that just the opposite is true. To the extent that Jesus is rooted in history and the society of his times, his message is all the more credible. Centrist scholars like John P. Meier, N. T. Wright, and Luke Timothy Johnson question the methodology and results of the Jesus Seminar, feeling that it goes too far in stripping away sections of the Gospel that they feel are sayings of the early church, not Jesus.

two-thousand Jewish protestors and rebels.[23] Their pain-racked bodies stretched for miles. Whether residents or pilgrims, every Jew in Jerusalem was aware that a fortress adjacent to the Temple called the Antonia garrisoned Roman troops. Legionaries could see into the Temple courtyard and were known to make all manner of obscene gestures to the Jews below who had come to worship their God. In 63 B.C.E. the Roman general Pompey besieged Jerusalem and with its surrender defiled the Temple by entering the Holy of Holies, which only the high priest could do. In fact, gentiles were not even allowed within the Temple precincts. Pontius Pilate, known for his hostility to Jews and Judaism, constantly provoked the population, especially in Jerusalem, by bringing in statues of the emperor and military standards perceived as idols by believing Jews. In the Galilee region, Jewish peasants knew that their taxes were building pagan buildings that housed statues of the emperors. In their minds they were paying for blasphemy. Jewish peasants were not benighted bumpkins devoid of critical faculties. They knew what was going on and resented that they were paying the tab. Their ancient, ancestral way of life was being eroded by semibelievers or nonbelievers like Antipas, and the Romans treated them like chattel slaves. Smoldering class hatred had developed and the possibility of an uprising was always there. Semi-Jews like Antipas or the Greek-speaking pagans who lived nearby forever set upon down-to-earth and pious people, who only wanted to live in close-knit families and communities and practice their faith, as they understood it.[24] They knew full well that things were not supposed to be this way. In Temple and synagogue services they heard readings from the Torah that called for a covenant between God and the people of Israel predicated on justice and respect. They heard about the sabbatical and jubilee years called for by God and meant to redistribute land and wealth among Jews so disparity and injustice were avoided. They listened to prophetic readings from Amos, Hosea, and Isaiah, among others, which denounced injustice and false worship. As many scholars have pointed out, some of the strongest prophetic discourse came from the former northern kingdom, Israel, which encompassed the Galilee. Their Jewish heritage was the best available tool to critically assess what was going on. They had an alternative social theory, a different paradigm of what it meant to be human. It was Torah.

Today we generally make a distinction between the social, political, and religious dimensions of our lives. In antiquity, there was far greater cohesion. Jesus' preaching of Torah with its stress on compassion between God and humanity, and men and women among themselves, was as much a

---

23. Crossan, *The Historical Jesus*, 266.
24. Ibid.

social movement as it was a religious program. Christians have a tendency to decontextualize the central symbol of God's Reign, as if, to quote the Gospel of John, it were "not of this world" (John 18:36). Yet it was rooted in the social and religious crises of the day. As Horsley and others have pointed out, the Reign of God was a socioreligious movement whose purpose was to address the exploitation of so many people in first-century Palestine. It tried to directly remedy the injustices experienced by so many people due to exclusionary religious practices and Roman oppression. Although nonviolent, Jesus' movement was driven by protest and outrage at the day-to-day injustices experienced by his fellow Jews. Surely, people were attracted to him because he was doing something. He was forming an alternative social system based on an inclusive, egalitarian understanding of Judaism. Jesus did more than talk about the Reign of God. He invited people to join him in an effort to help make it real, to collaborate in God's plan for humanity. Precisely for this reason he was perceived as a destabilizing figure. He was crucified because he had followers intent on creating a new social and religious order.

There was ample room in first-century Judaism for theological debate, and Roman authorities paid little or no attention to the religious beliefs of those they conquered, so long as they presented no threat to Roman power. The Hellenistic world was a philosophical and religious supermarket with every imaginable commodity available. Religious movements with social consequences, however, were carefully monitored. Pontius Pilate and religious elites in Jerusalem were constantly on the watch for the slightest hint of socioreligious resistance. An event reported in all four of the Gospels, and one that scholars almost universally accept as having a historical foundation, is that Jesus protested or "cleansed" the Temple in Jerusalem. Jesus was not attacking the Temple per se, but the economic and religious system that had grown up around it. He was outraged by the manipulative use of religious rituals that placed one more burden on the consciences and pocketbooks of the poor. For Jesus the Reign of God was a gift. Entrance and the grace it offered were entirely free. The Temple, sacred in itself, was being used as an instrument of oppression, predicated on a false and abusive understanding of God. His protest went to the heart and soul of the socioreligious system that sustained the status quo. Jesus' actions were an intolerable affront and his rapid removal from the scene was deemed imperative. By "cleansing" the Temple he had signed his own death warrant.

Jesus, Paul, and after Paul

The development of the Jesus movement between 30 and roughly 50 C.E. remains a mystery. Paul will not begin to write his letters until the early

50s and the narrative called the Acts of the Apostles, written by the author of Luke at least thirty years after Paul had died, is driven by a theological agenda and portrays Jesus' followers and the community that they formed in an idealistic way. Paul is presented as a hero, a saint beyond question. He is at the forefront of reconciliation between various groups of Jesus' followers smoothing out tensions in such a way that leaves all happy. That scenario unfortunately does not mesh with Paul's own writings. There was acrimonious debate about the Law and how Jesus' followers should approach it. Were circumcision and dietary laws part and parcel of following Jesus or were they tangential, even unnecessary? The leadership of the Jesus movement remained in Jerusalem until its destruction by the Romans in the Great War of 66–70 C.E. And then it disappears in what is one of the great mysteries of Christian history. But by the time this catastrophe took place, missionaries like Paul had successfully re-created the Jesus movement in a Greek-speaking, Hellenistic environment. Some early missionaries used a well-established network of Hellenistic synagogues to present their message to Jews in the Diaspora. By and large this effort failed. But Paul's message, according to his letters, was directed at gentiles and had far more success. This, of course, does not mesh with Luke's presentation of Paul in Acts, which raises the question as to which version of events is the most accurate. Perhaps initially Jews formed a significant part of the Hellenistic Jesus movement, but there is no way of proving such an assertion. In his letters Paul refers to several women and men whose names are Jewish, and it is quite likely that they were Hellenistic Jews. But Paul did not focus on the Jewish community in the Diaspora. His energy was entirely directed toward non-Jews, despite Luke's version of Paul's missionary career, which invariably has him start his missionary campaigns in synagogues, something Paul never mentions.

The message about Jesus as the messiah and savior spread through the Greek-speaking parts of the empire. There were members of the Jesus movement in Rome by the late 40s. Our source for this information comes from the Roman historian Suetonius (d. 130), who reports that the emperor Claudius expelled the Jewish community from the city because of riots concerning a certain "Chrestus." Christians, of course, have asserted that Suetonius was a bad speller and actually meant Christus, the Latin word for Christ. Yet he was almost certainly right about problems within the Jewish community. Is it possible that its members were reacting to the Jesus movement because of its messianic content and unorthodox approach to the Law? We simply do not know, and since Suetonius knew almost nothing about Judaism or Christianity, the questions can never be answered. The one thing that can be said with certainty is that there was some type of Jesus movement or even proto-Christian community in Rome at an early date. When Paul wrote his letter to the Roman community in the late 50s, it seems to have been fairly well established, so much so that Paul wanted to curry its favor. But what may have been a form of Jewish Christianity did not survive much beyond the Great War. After the destruction of the Temple in 70 only the Pharisees survived as a strong force within the Jewish community, and cohesion was their paramount concern. Jews who asserted that Jesus was the messiah were expelled from the Jewish community as heretics. The tragedy that took place in Palestine gave a boost to the gentile-based Christianity that Paul had advocated. A few decades ago it was fashionable to say that Paul invented Christianity. He did not, but he definitely contributed to the birth of a messianic movement that became a Greco-Roman religion called Christianity.

Paul's letters, written over the course of at least a decade, generally address concrete community issues like worship, ethics, and day-to-day behavior. Galatians and especially Romans, however, are far more complex. In these two letters Paul tries to reconcile his Jewish beliefs with his understanding of Jesus as the messiah, often engaging in intense and convoluted theological discourse with Jewish-Christians whose ideas he vehemently rejected. Paul can be confusing at times. His emotions can be intense and his line of argument elusive. Nonetheless, we can extrapolate a number of Paul's principal theological and social values from his writings. The first thing that must be mentioned is that Paul, like his converts, was utterly convinced that Jesus was soon to return. Paul was a firm believer in the *eschaton,* or end of history, and Jesus' triumphal return, or *parousia.*[25] It was a matter of years at the very most. This belief shaped Paul's understanding of the social environment in profound ways. He was entirely focused on converting people, not changing a social system that was merely on borrowed time. We cannot understand Paul's approach to the larger world without taking this all-important factor into consideration. Paul is one of the most significant figures in the history of Christianity. He is also one of the most misinterpreted precisely because he is extracted from the context in which he lived. Some of Paul's most passionate disciples have failed to understand just how contextual his thinking and writing are, and the result has often been a distortion of what Paul meant to say.

Of the thirteen letters that bear Paul's name five or six may have been written by his followers in communities he founded or even by second-generation Christians in the late 90s who took up Paul's ideas as their

---

25. The Greek word *eschaton* refers to the final days; *parousia* refers to Jesus' Second Coming.

own well after their teacher's death, most likely in the early 60s, possibly in Rome during the reign of Nero. It was not uncommon in antiquity for a disciple or admirer of a person to write in his master's name. There is no question, however, about the authenticity of the letters we will analyze briefly to gain some insight into how Paul perceived and responded to the world around him. We will examine 1 Thessalonians, 1 Corinthians, and then Romans. Thessalonians is generally accepted as Paul's earliest work or the earliest that we have in the New Testament, while Romans is universally accepted as his last. The first two works are ad hoc responses to questions raised by members of the communities that Paul established in the eastern Mediterranean.

What should the community in Thessalonica do in light of the fact that some of its members had died before Jesus' Second Coming? In Corinth there were pragmatic questions. Was it licit to eat meat from animals sacrificed in temples? Should Christians and non-Christians remain married? There were problems in the community about the way the Eucharist was being celebrated. Some were getting drunk and pushing less wealthy members of the community around. Paul sends back an unequivocal response to this un-Christian behavior. Stop it immediately. So too in regard to the sexual mores of Christians' neighbors; there is to be no compromise with the immorality of nonbelievers. Everything is fairly clear.

Romans is another story. In all likelihood, Paul's long theological treatise was written to explain his beliefs to a small community of believers in Rome with whom he had no prior contact. In a passionate but not always coherent fashion he lays out his core beliefs about Jesus, Jewish Law, and God's plan for humanity. All of the Pauline letters we will examine have their limitations, but together they can help us appreciate something about Paul's beliefs. We constantly need to remind ourselves that there is no "Pauline System" per se. Furthermore, Paul was no different from any other religious figure. His ideas changed as he dealt with different issues and contexts. He constantly mulled over issues and even in a magisterial letter like Romans he clearly goes back and forth at times, laying out one argument and then another in ways that do not necessarily mesh. Like Augustine Paul was a theological genius and like any passionate religious believer often hard to understand. By the early second century Christians often remarked that Paul was hard to fathom — and they were almost his contemporaries!

Paul's belief in Jesus' return, or Second Coming, was the cornerstone of everything he preached. He insisted that when it occurred it would validate his interpretation of Jesus' message. Those who subscribed to Paul's message about Jesus and his return would be vindicated — the dead raised and the living ushered into heaven.

You brood of vipers! Who warned you to flee from the wrath to come? Bear fruits that befit repentance, and do not begin to say to yourselves, "We have Abraham as our father"; for I tell you God is able from these stones to raise up children to Abraham. Even now the axe is laid to the root of the trees; every tree therefore that does not bear good fruit is cut down and thrown into the fire. (Luke 3:7, 9)

This is the message Paul taught to the small community of believers he established in the city of Thessalonica situated in northern Greece. Paul was in a hurry to spread the word about Jesus' return and the end of history in the little time that was left. But in Thessalonica and most likely elsewhere, people had died before Jesus' return and were confused by how this could have happened. They obviously interpreted Paul's message about Jesus' return to be something that would happen almost immediately. Since most of them were poor and the victims of an oppressive imperial system, they were anxious to put an end to the misery they experienced day to day. Jesus' seeming delay and the fact that members of the community had died without experiencing the joys Paul had promised perplexed them. Paul tried to respond to their problems in the letter quoted above, which he wrote around 50 C.E. The same intense hope for the Second Coming existed in all of the communities that Paul founded, as well as in others that he had not. It is even an issue today among evangelical Christians and some Catholics who share a common animosity toward the world and await divine intervention.

The content of 1 Thessalonians can be summarized as follows: Jesus will return shortly but we cannot know exactly when; pay no attention to people who say otherwise and contradict what I taught you, and try to live your lives as normally as possible until Jesus does return. Other missionaries clearly had followed Paul and perhaps embellished or intensified his teachings about Jesus' return. The letter makes it clear that some members of the community had simply "unplugged" in terms of surrounding society. Convinced that a sinful world controlled by demonic forces was about to come to a screaming end, they refused to be involved with it. Aware of just how destructive this sort of exaggerated eschatological thinking can be, Paul wrote in an effort to temper it before the community in Thessalonica spun out of control. The fact that he had to write a second letter indicates that his fears were legitimate. The concept of the Second Coming is a two-edged sword. It can help believers appreciate the finite nature of history. It has a beginning and an end and human beings are merely part of a larger natural process, not its masters. At the same time, eschatological thinking can lead to bizarre, antisocial behavior. A once healthy community can devolve into a nasty, self-righteous sect that refuses to participate in the social order. It finds its meaning within itself rather than outside and bristles with hostility and self-righteousness. Paul believed the Second Coming was imminent, but he was still a realist. He wanted to save the world, not condemn it. Yet even today Christian extremists are the first to quote Paul. They refuse to recognize that Paul was wrong about the Second Coming. He was not wrong, however, about the need to address the pain and suffering in the world around us. As he makes clear in his letter to the Thessalonians, the date of the Second Coming is not important. What is important is creating communities based on love and justice that help make the Reign of God possible now.

Paul's first letter to the community he established in Corinth is one of the most useful for learning about the internal and external challenges the first generation of believers faced in the Greco-Roman world. Once Paul felt that the community he had set up in Corinth was capable of sustaining itself he moved on to his next destination. But he may have been excessively optimistic since problems soon emerged that threatened the survival of this small group of believers. They wrote to Paul in desperate need for advice and encouragement, not unlike anxious teenagers newly arrived at college. As New Testament scholars point out, Corinth was bound to be a challenging place for Paul and his message about Jesus. It was a port city that every itinerant philosopher and religious huckster traveled through in search of a new clientele. Filled with merchants and sailors who did not think of celibacy as a virtue, Corinth was home to a booming sex industry that left nothing to the imagination. Most people lived off the commercial traffic that went back and forth across the Isthmus of Corinth, a narrow stretch of land that travelers used as they moved between the eastern and western halves of the empire. We have little concrete information about the members of Paul's community, but in all likelihood most were poor and unrefined, perhaps a few comfortable and more sophisticated. In Corinth and elsewhere Paul insisted that his followers had assumed a new and common identity through baptism. All distinctions were to be set aside, including previous religious identity, ethnicity, and gender. The frequently quoted passage from Galatians 3:28 may well have been part of an early Christian baptismal creed: "There is neither Jew nor Greek, there is neither slave nor free, there is neither male nor female; for you are all one in Christ Jesus." It is impossible to imagine a more radical challenge to the Greco-Roman world or, for that matter, our own. All of the differences we put such stock in are simply set aside as meaningless.

The Corinthians found themselves hard pressed to live out such a demanding and counterintuitive vision. The community was divided along class lines and unable to come up with a cohesive way of responding to an oppressive, ruthless world with which they had to interact, like it or not. It appears that Paul's new converts were on the point of unraveling

as a community. In his response to their desperate questions he insists
that they maintain the tradition of radical equality that he taught them.
When they assemble as a community to share a meal or remember Jesus'
life, death, and resurrection, they must do so in complete unity. If they
do not their gathering is meaningless and their remembrance of Jesus
a mockery. To use contemporary language, Paul's message to the community in Corinth is blunt: Get your act together and do your job! Paul
will not allow any latitude when it comes to the ethical code he taught
his followers in Corinth. They must treat each other with the utmost
respect and so too everyone outside of the believing community. If you
call yourself a believer, you cannot think of yourself as superior to anyone because, in fact, you are not. And for Paul this is precisely why Jesus'
message is good news. We no longer need to lie about ourselves or to
each other. We can live our lives in peace without any need to impress
or impose on others. In response to questions of sexual behavior Paul
does not mince his words. If you objectify someone to the point of inflicting sexual violence on that person, you not only defile your victim, you
defile yourself. The victims of the Roman imperial system could be found
on every streetcorner selling their bodies — women, men, and children.
Paul has no tolerance for sexual misconduct among members of the community in Corinth for the simple reason that prostitution is a form of
violence that obliterates the humanity of its victims. The vast majority of
prostitutes in the Greco-Roman world were slaves beaten into submission
who had to choose between sexual degradation and death by starvation.
Paul's response to the questions about sexual ethics raised by members
of the community in Corinth is straightforward. You must treat everyone
as your sister or brother. If you objectify someone for the sake or physical
pleasure or to satisfy your lust for power you are not a believer; in fact,
you are a liar. Paul's message about social equality and ethical behavior
is the antithesis of the violently exploitative structure of Greco-Roman
culture, and perhaps this is why members of the Corinthian community
had such a difficult time grasping it. Paul tries to be a patient father but
ultimately is firm with his confused children. Love must reign supreme in
the community. There can be no distinctions among you. Furthermore,
you must not compromise with a dehumanizing, nonbelieving world. If
you remain firm in the faith you accepted when you were baptized, your
community will flourish and it will be a sign for those outside it who long
for the same dignity and freedom you now possess as members. By virtue
of your new identity as a follower of Jesus you are called to challenge a
distorted social order.

The last letter we will examine is Paul's indisputable masterpiece written around 60 C.E. to fellow believers in Rome. Paul wants to introduce
himself and clarify any misunderstanding that might exist about what he

believes and why he believes it. Romans, therefore, is different from any of his other letters. It is far more speculative and theological, which virtually guarantees that it is a hard letter to understand the first time through. Nearly every major theologian in the history of Christianity has grappled with Romans and all have come to slightly different conclusions about its meaning. The challenge with Romans is that its basic theme, the relationship between faith and salvation, is hardly an easy topic. These are abstract concepts that can only be discussed using metaphorical language with its inherent ambiguity. Paul is trying to do what is impossible, at least succinctly: explain a profound religious experience that he had in which Jesus appeared to him and changed the course of his life. As a Pharisee he had rejected all claims about Jesus' status as God's anointed one, the promised Christ. Yet somehow Paul's resistance broke down and his religious self-understanding unraveled. He came to the conclusion that what he had believed so fervently was actually wrong. Paul does not go into any details about his radical about-face, but he makes it clear time and again that suddenly he understood everything in a radically different light. The author of Acts, however, provides three stories about Paul's conversion each with slight differences. The conclusion is obvious: the author of Acts has his own agenda when it comes to Paul: his actions, speech, and even his journey are crafted to fit the author's theological project. He is not particularly interested in the "Historical Paul" any more than the authors of the Gospels were in the "Historical Jesus." Also, the fact that Acts was written about thirty years after Paul's death should give us pause in terms of its accuracy.

But what we can say with certainty is that Paul was a well-educated Hellenistic Jew. He lived in the Greco-Roman world with its particular culture-bound understanding of reality that conditions Paul's understanding of faith, salvation, Jesus, and Jewish Law. He was writing in response to specific issues and questions. He was not attempting to lay out an all-encompassing theological system valid for all people and all ages. Paul was writing to people who lived in an entirely prescientific culture that assumed that the world was a chaotic, often irrational, place. It was evident to everyone in the Hellenistic world that invisible but potent spiritual forces controlled every facet of the natural and social order. People were convinced that they were in the midst of a cosmic battle between the forces of good and the forces of evil that was drawing to an end. It was vitally important to understand what was going on in order to be saved. As a Pharisee Paul had done this through scrupulous observance of the Law, but his conversion experience stripped him of its comforts. He came to the conclusion that given the almost invincible power of evil, the only thing he could do was to fling himself on the mercy of God. And for Paul God's mercy was most visible in the person of Jesus, the messiah who had come to save humankind from annihilation at the hands of demonic powers. The challenge Paul presents to his readers in Romans is to recognize human powerlessness and, in faith, believe that God offered unconditional salvation in the person of Jesus, the Son of God who was raised from the dead. Paul's unrelenting theme in Romans is that salvation is finally possible. He is convinced that the cosmos itself is undergoing rapid change and that within his lifetime Jesus will return in glory. Everything that had happened in history actually was a prelude to this event — Adam and Eve's sin in the Garden of Eden, the Hebrews fleeing Egypt, Moses establishing the Law. As a Jew Paul followed Mosaic Law in its entirety, but because he now sees the meaning of history realized in Jesus he concludes that the Law, although good in itself, is no longer necessary. The only thing Jews and gentiles need to do in order to be saved is to believe in Jesus as God's definitive answer for humanity.

Paul was driven by a fierce sense of eschatological urgency that makes little sense to most of us today. He was convinced that he was involved in a lockstep process of salvation and that God was directing everything. This can create the impression that Paul did not care about the historical world or social order. To the contrary, he was passionate about its ultimate redemption, but because everything was at the point of being turned on its head, Paul saw no need for spending time and energy in transforming the here and now. He did not accept the status quo that he clearly saw as demonic, but he saw no real point in trying to change it.

This leads us to one of the most misinterpreted and misused parts of Romans, the thirteenth chapter. In Romans 13:1–7 Paul seems to assert that authority figures must be obeyed unequivocally. But he certainly is not suggesting that his readers acquiesce in the face of evil. Paul was writing to a community of Jews and gentiles that accepted Jesus as the messiah, but he was wary of people making disruptive eschatological claims that could lead to both internal and external problems. Paul wants to make it clear to his readers that his understanding of Jesus does not entail overthrowing the established order. As he had made clear in his letter to the Thessalonians, the Second Coming was indeed imminent, but "checking out" of the world at large was an over-reaction bound to provoke a hostile reaction from nonbelievers. Paul wants to make it clear to the Romans that he is a politically and socially prudent man. We have no trustworthy information as to where and when Paul died or how he dealt with the fact that the Second Coming did not happen in his lifetime. The temptation, naturally, is to dismiss Paul and his vision of history as the byproduct of wishful, delusional thinking, but there are real dangers in being so glib. A utopian symbol like Jesus' return and the transformation of history is not about dates or places; it is about how we approach history and the possibility of transforming it in ways that lead to a more humane and just social order. Every person of goodwill, believer or otherwise, has an indispensable role to play. The issue is whether we have enough faith to believe in a different future and actively work on its behalf. The tragedy of Romans 13 is that it has been used to legitimate fatalism and passivity by church and political leaders terrified by the prospect of religious equality within the church and a social order that is truly democratic.

Can We Square the Circle?

The precise ways in which the Palestinian Jesus movement evolved into a Greco-Roman religion known as Christianity will never be completely clear. The information we have is sketchy from a historical and sociological vantage point, but somehow a Jewish reform movement was successfully translated and transplanted in such a way that it was able to take root and grow on its own terms. Paul and others made this possible. They established Hellenistic "Jesus communities" that gave birth to early Christianity toward the end of the first century. To refer to this process of implementation and adaptation as universal or catholic is a stretch. If we use a lower case "c," however, the concept is not totally far-fetched. We are not referring to a single movement or anything approaching a unified church. That will not happen for nearly two centuries, and Catholic with an upper case "C" will not be a valid historical concept for half a millennium. One community's self-understanding and response to society was not that of another. This was both logical and helpful. No community saw itself as a paradigm. Even the system of leadership in these early communities varied. The tripartite leadership system of bishop, priest, and deacon or, far more accurately, supervisor, elder, and servant, began to emerge only in the second century, and there were several models early Christians decided on in their local communities depending on their needs.

To survive in a hostile environment the early Christian churches had to balance the eschatological fervor of Paul that proclaimed the imminent end of time and history with the obvious fact that the Second Coming had not happened and was not on the horizon. Some sort of middle ground between intensity and practicality had to be established. At one end of the spectrum was eschatological hostility and at the other acquiescing before a social order that was the opposite of Jesus' vision of the Reign of God. Each community worked out this tension as best it could, and certainly there were heated debates about how to handle such complex issues. The Roman social order, in its totality, was never accepted, but selective aspects of Greco-Roman culture eventually were. This allowed members of the early Christian movement to live in the day-to-day world without accepting all of the premises on which it was grounded. There was a bit of dialectic but not too much, rather like figuring out just how much salt and pepper it takes to make a good soup. It was only when Christians were confronted with a diametrical choice — Rome or the Gospel — that they had to take an unequivocal position. Those who refused to make any concessions paid with their lives, but surely many early Christians preferred to keep a low profile and go about their business in the day-to-day world. The Roman Empire was not about to go away, but it was possible to subvert some of its oppressive features in indirect and simple ways. Offering space and a meal in which people could feel like equals, rich and poor alike, was the antithesis of Roman hierarchy. Treating ordinary people as human beings when, in fact, nearly half of them were slaves or ex-slaves with no legal rights was a courageous thing to do. Roman authorities knew what was going on, although they generally preferred to do little about it. Christianity grew in small increments. It became a counterweight to some of the worse aspects of the Greco-Roman social order. At the same time, it was becoming part of it. An unavoidable question, however, remained: How much of a part? This question would not go away nor will it ever.

Chapter Two

The Slow March to an Imperial Church

Beating the Odds: The Emergence of Christianity

Religious movements, like human beings, are inherently contextual phenomena. We are born in a particular culture and historical moment that shape our self-understanding, creating lenses through which we see reality but also limiting what we see. Religions evolve and sometimes die. The Mediterranean basin gave birth to dozens if not hundreds of religions, yet few of them are around today. Perhaps their cultural matrix collapsed due to war, or their particular message simply ceased to make sense to people. On a purely sociological level, religions are human institutions that come and go; they are born and die. A small messianic Jewish movement that came to life in the mid-first century, however, continues to flourish. It could have disappeared like the Olympian deities or innumerable mystery religions that flourished in the Greco-Roman world, only to gradually disappear. Christianity, however, has proven to be a highly adaptive organism. It evolved from being a tiny Jewish sect and emerged as the dominant Greco-Roman religion by the end of the fourth century. It spread through the Greek-speaking half of the empire in a slow but steady way. Soon it started to grow as well in Latin-speaking North Africa, Rome, and Gaul. At first an illegal and persecuted sect, by 380 C.E. it was the official religion of the empire that had persecuted it; all other religions were officially outlawed with the exception of Judaism.

For weal or woe, Christianity fused with the late Roman Empire, producing a social arrangement that would come to be known as Christendom. Church and state began to function symbiotically, although not always harmoniously. Arguably, this alliance known as Christendom lasted until the modern era, and vestiges of it still remain. Almost all Europeans, and their colonial confreres who emigrated to North and South America, thought of themselves as Christian, although few acted as such. Culture, law, and morality were predicated on Christian values, at least in theory. The first three centuries of Christian existence are a remarkable historical era to study. In the pages that follow we will try to understand how Christianity became the faith of Roman emperors, who declared themselves the protectors of their new religion, while the clergy came to think of themselves as ultimate social and moral arbiters, guided by divine powers that surpassed those even of the senate and emperors.

Differentiation and Separation: The First Challenge

The movement that Jesus set in motion came to life in a Jewish, Semitic matrix that made up only a tiny fraction of the population of the empire. Not only were they a demographic minority, Jews were culturally and religiously different from their neighbors. Their insistence on strict monotheism was considered strange in a world with a plethora of religions and a god for every occasion. One can only speculate what would have happened to Jesus' movement had it not spread outside of the confines of Palestine. Would it have suffered the same fate as other Jewish groups such as the Sadducees and Essenes, who were annihilated by Rome? The question is moot, however, because Jesus' followers were avid missionaries, Paul being one of many, who spread their beliefs among Jews in the Diaspora and Greek-speaking gentiles. They did so with a special ardor in light of their conviction that Jesus would soon return. Jesus' message survived, albeit translated into Greek and reshaped to fit a Greco-Roman world with a radically different culture from that of first-century Palestine. Jews and Jesus' followers began to go their separate ways. The process was far from smooth. Paul, in his magisterial letter to the Romans, agonizes about the relationship between Judaism and his belief in Jesus. He is, of course, a messianic Jew, something of a "proto-Christian." He is pained by the general rejection of his message in the synagogues of the Diaspora, while he is energized by the reception he is given by Hellenistic gentiles. Among Jew and gentile alike, he would have used a common translation of the Hebrew Bible in Greek known as the Septuagint, which is usually designated by the Roman numerals LXX.[1] Just as the evangelists would later do, Paul cited the Septuagint to support his claim that Jesus was the messiah, a claim orthodox Jews just as adamantly rejected in most of thc synagogues he visited. In effect, an acrimonious squabble broke out about what the Septuagint said about the coming messiah and who was its "owner" — the Jewish community of the Diaspora or the members of a progressively more Greco-Roman religion soon to be called Christianity. The dispute was never settled because both parties soon were damning

---

1. According to pious legend, seventy Jewish scholars, whose individual renditions proved to be absolutely identical, translated the Septuagint in Egypt in the third century B.C.E.

each other to hell's fire. The rabbinic leadership of the Jews expelled Christians from the synagogue while Christians, following the ideas provided them by Paul, declared the Mosaic Law superseded by that of Jesus and the emerging church the New Israel. By the last quarter of the first century the breach was irreparable; leading to sporadic persecution of Christians by Jewish authorities, and the eventual persecution of Jews by Christians once they gained political and social power several centuries later.

The fight about the meaning of the scripture and Jesus' messianic identity was more than a theological squabble. If Christians were the heirs of the covenant and constituted a New Israel, they then had the right to demand recognition and even protection from the Roman Empire. Roman law distinguished between legal and illegal religions (*religio licita* versus *religio illicita*). Emperors and the senate carefully monitored religious movements, granting them the right to exist or persecuting them when deemed a threat. Roman authorities were more than mere administrators. They were responsible for maintaining a divinely established social order. The reigning emperor and Rome itself were sacred entities, placed in power to keep peace between heaven and earth, the immortal and mortal realms. Religions, especially new ones, and even philosophical movements, were carefully scrutinized because they could upset the natural order, inciting the ill will of Rome's gods. How else could famine, floods, and incessant plagues be understood in a prescientific world? Although Judaism was seen by most educated Romans as strange, if not unintelligible, it was a recognized religion of the empire due, in large measure, to its antiquity. Until its destruction in the Great War of 66–70 C.E., sacrifices were offered every day in the Temple in Jerusalem for the well-being of the emperor. Jews were generally tolerated in the empire and went out of their way to show themselves loyal citizens. Sporadic anti-Judaism in cities like Alexandria, where there was a large Jewish community, could be avoided by keeping a low profile and blending into the surrounding environment. The emergence in the synagogues of a disruptive splinter group making messianic claims about Jesus and calling itself the New Israel was surely seen by Jewish authorities as a dangerous internal threat that could lead to external persecution. With their official "excommunication" by the assembled rabbis at the so-called Council of Jamnia in 90 C.E., Christians lost any right to claim membership in the Jewish community. Christians were now outsiders rather than nettlesome insiders within the Jewish community. *Ipso facto*, Christianity became an illegal religion. Membership became punishable by death. A higher price was being demanded of those who dared called themselves Christian. For centuries, Rome would do its best to eradicate this band of anarchistic atheists with their claims about the inherent equality of all human beings and their outrageous insistence that Jesus was God incarnate come to save the world and replace Rome with the

Reign of God. Roman authorities were right. Christianity threatened the very foundations of the empire, predicated as it was on oppression, slavery, and violence. Furthermore, Christians were monotheists in a polytheistic world. They obstinately refused to worship the empire or reigning emperor whose image was everywhere, from courthouses to coins.

From Accommodation to Rejection: Cognitive Dissonance in the Early Church

Reading the New Testament in search of a coherent and consistent approach to the Greco-Roman social order in which Christianity was born can be a frustrating endeavor. In fact, each separate work in Christian scripture has its own perspective on its cultural and social environment. This plurality, which is ultimately something positive rather than negative, is due to the way in which the varied texts of the New Testament were produced. Each author had distinct ideas about Christianity, albeit within certain parameters. Each had a particular, context-based experience of the Christian community and its relationship to the surrounding world. In reality, the foundational texts of Christianity display passivity, acceptance, and overt hostility toward the non-Christian Greco-Roman world.

"Passivity" is not a word one would associate with Paul of Tarsus, an impassioned missionary whose life purpose was to spread the word about the Risen Jesus. Yet we find few critical or systematic references to the imperial Roman system in his relatively short and topical letters. Paul had experienced psychological and physical persecution at the hands of his fellow Jews and sometimes at the hands of followers of Jesus who disagreed with his theological points of view. It is doubtful that Roman authorities had any notion of Christianity other than as a splinter Jewish group until the Neronian persecution of the early 60s, which may have caught Paul in its wake. As we saw previously, Paul was steeped in an intense conviction that Jesus would return within his lifetime. He saw the social order around him as a fleeting phenomenon best ignored.[2] Like almost every citizen of the Roman world, Paul believed that God reigned over the social order and that authorities were to be duly obeyed. But eternal Rome would soon disappear, "in a moment, in the twinkling of an eye" (1 Cor. 15:52) with Jesus' return. Paul is no revolutionary in the modern sense of the word. In the letter to Philemon, he does not challenge one of the most egregious aspects of Roman society — slavery. Yet with Jesus' return a radically egalitarian social order would emerge, already foreshadowed in the nascent community of Jesus' followers. The communities that Paul founded in the eastern half of the empire were a blueprint for a radical

---

2. Meeks, *The First Urban Christians*, 164–92.

social order in which there would be neither "Jew nor Greek, slave nor free, male nor female" (Gal. 3:28) — notions that can only be described as utterly antithetical to the working assumptions of the Roman world. In certain ways, Paul can be characterized conservative about his immediate environment. However, in terms of the future, soon to be redeemed by the Risen Christ, Paul can be described as radically hopeful and revolutionary.

Eschatological consciousness — that is, the belief that the world is in its final phase and will soon be radically transformed — can prove to be problematic. Paul adamantly believed the *parousia*, or Second Coming, was near at hand, yet he had to caution early believers about a near paralyzing fixation with the precise day and hour in which this cosmic event would take place (1 Thess. 5:2). By the last quarter of the first century C.E. a degree of realism set in about the Second Coming. Although still a foundational element of Christian belief, then and now, it was increasingly obvious that Jesus' followers had to balance expectation with realism, hoping for cosmic transformation while simultaneously living in the day-to-day world. Luke, the author of both a Gospel and a narrative about the early church called the Acts of the Apostles, two works that were initially joined and meant to be read in tandem, tries to achieve this equilibrium. In the polished Greek of his Gospel and the Acts of the Apostles, whose principal protagonist is Paul himself, there is a subtle call to realism. Jesus *will* return, but in the interim, Christians are expected to live normal lives in the midst of their gentile neighbors. They are also called to spread Jesus' message to a needy world by dint of their behavior rather than a cult-like separation from others. In Luke's writings the Christian community is an inherently missionary endeavor. It is meant to exteriorize itself and gather new members, offering a saving transformation of both individuals and society at large.

In a somewhat quirky stylistic fashion, Luke ends the second volume of his narrative with Paul captive in Rome, awaiting trial according to the prerogatives of a Roman citizen. Yet the assumption is that Paul will continue his missionary activity, spreading Jesus' message as far as Spain. The tacit message is that the Greco-Roman world is being called to conversion. The small communities that Paul established are to be superseded by an inclusive, worldwide community of believers. The author of Luke-Acts, as the combined works are usually called, treats Romans and, by implication, imperial Rome, in a markedly benign way. In Luke 7:11 we encounter a God-fearing centurion who asks Jesus to heal his sick and beloved slave. In Acts 10 Peter converts another God-fearing centurion, preceded by a vision of an all-encompassing community made up of gentiles as well as Jews. Most telling of all, in Luke's passion narrative, Pontius Pilate, a notoriously brutal Roman official who had to be removed from office, finds Jesus innocent of the charges laid against him. He finally orders

Jesus' crucifixion, which he alone could do, succumbing to pressure from the "chief priests and crowd" (Luke 23:4).

There is no real note of confrontation between Jesus, the Christian community, and the surrounding Roman world. It can be converted, and two good centurions prove the point. Several centuries later Luke's assumption would prove to be true. In 337 Constantine would be baptized on his deathbed, becoming the first Christian emperor. At the end of the same century Theodosius would make Christianity the state religion of the empire. A crucified and risen Jesus, along with a once persecuted Christian community, was proclaimed the one and only savior and the sole religion of imperial Rome. Ironically, Christians would begin to persecute those responsible for internal dissent, that is "heretics," as well as anyone who resisted the authority of the Christian church.

Although the author of Luke-Acts may have felt fairly sanguine about the eventual conversion of the Roman Empire and the inevitable trajectory of Jesus' message to transform the world at large, others were less optimistic. Judging from his Greek, the author of Luke-Acts was a well-educated, gentile individual who mostly likely saw the Roman Empire and the *Pax Romana,* or "Roman Peace," as preludes to a Christian civilization, yet to be realized, of course, but part of an unfolding divine plan. For those less privileged, and certainly victimized by an imperial system based on slavery and violence, the notion of a Christianized Roman world, was far more remote.

Although the book of Revelation is notoriously difficult to understand, given its use of arcane symbolism and apocalyptic hyperbole, its author was hardly optimistic about the conversion of the empire. Perhaps writing during the reign of the emperor Domitian around 90 C.E., the author of this text and his community had experienced savage persecution. The choice had been unequivocal — fidelity to Jesus and the Reign of God or the idolatrous worship of Divine Rome and the emperor's divinity as the representative of the gods who supposedly sustained the Roman Empire. A simple gesture was required of Christians if they were loyal citizens: a bit of incense tossed on burning embers placed before the images of *Diva Roma* and *Divus Caesar,* "Divine Rome" and "Divine Caesar." To refuse this simple gesture was to be accused of capital crimes — sedition and atheism, notions that were inextricably fused in the minds of patriotic, pious Romans. Rome's gods and its empire worked in tandem. Those who challenged the logic of the empire were the most dangerous of subversives. Copious amounts of ink have been spilled over the thirteenth chapter of Revelation, but there can be little doubt that the horrid beast in question is that of an all-consuming, imperial state predicated on deception and self-worship. Rome certainly qualified on that score, as have so many imperial systems right up to the present. Throughout the history of Catholicism, and Christianity in general, the book of Revelation has called believers to a sober assessment of the blandishments of the social order that surrounds them, helping them to realize that we are prone to worship our own political creations, attributing a divine status to deficient and sinful social arrangements of our own making.

In many ways, Christians were on the horn of a dilemma brought about in no small measure by their foundational documents — the Gospels and the epistles of Paul. In the Gospels Jesus' relationship with his social and religious environment is presented in different ways. Jesus meant the Reign of God he proclaimed to have a concrete and transformative impact on the daily lives of the oppressed men and women who followed and listened to him. They thirsted for a modicum of justice and the recognition of their humanity, notions that went to the heart of Jewish belief. In Mark 6:34 Jesus "has compassion" on the crowd that follows him. They "have no shepherd." They are likewise hungry. Within a few more verses Jesus challenges his incredulous disciples to feed a multitude of hungry people. In the Gospel of Mark Jesus is always attuned to the spiritual and physical needs of those around him. The Reign of God is very much of this world. Yet in the Gospel of John a different picture emerges. Before Pilate Jesus declares that his "kingship is not of this world" (John 18:36). Early Christians were faced with a confusing set of options. Accept "the world" or reject it. With the Second Coming seemingly delayed, a choice had to be made — realism about the world or rejection.

This tension has been in place for nearly two millennia and like a pendulum, individual Christians and the church have gone back and forth. By the end of the third century something of a solution had been found. The majority of Christians came to grips with their surroundings, making a living and hoping to avoid the periodic persecution that Roman officials sporadically unleashed. Others took a "rejectionist" route and by the second half of the third century had headed to the deserts of Egypt and Syria to live out their lives as monks and nuns. Between 250 and 300 C.E. the church experienced a period of peace. Numbers in the Greek-speaking half of the empire were growing, perhaps 15 percent of the population. There were Christian communities in North Africa, Rome, and Gaul. Even a few members of the aristocracy asked for baptism. In the eyes of the fervent ascetics, however, the church was becoming soft and complacent about the benevolence of the Greco-Roman system. They preferred to wait out the Second Coming with the rigors of heat and self-imposed fasting that left many of them half skeletons. They would brook no compromise with a world they considered damned and fleeting. Even today, Catholic Christians deal with this unresolved tension with a majority being realists and a minority being "nonconformist," and both parties can draw on scriptural texts to validate their positions. The tension is perennial and, in many ways, necessary. When "the world" is accepted uncritically, Christianity becomes a chaplaincy service to the status quo. Rejected with disdain and hostility, it runs the danger of becoming an angry sectarian movement with little or no chance of making a positive contribution to the society that surrounds it.

The Hellenization of Early Christian Thought

The relationship between a given religion and its surrounding cultural environment is a balancing act. If it is to make sense to people it must, to some degree, resonate with prevailing values and cultural assumptions. Otherwise it ends up being esoteric if not actually incomprehensible to the majority of people. The term that scholars of religion use for this process of religious assimilation is "inculturation." But when religion is too contextualized, it can no longer exercise a critical social role. It begins to legitimate and "sacralize" the social order it is part of. The Roman Empire had such a state religion with an extensive network of priests and priestesses, temples and cultic centers, all of which proclaimed the divinity of the empire in multiple ways. The senate often posthumously proclaimed emperors to be gods, and a few, like Caligula, one of the most evil and psychotic emperors in the history of the Roman Empire, insisted on being proclaimed divine during his lifetime.

For both Jews and Christians, residing in the empire necessarily entailed uneasiness about the political and religious assumptions taken for granted by their fellow citizens. As monotheists they were an anomaly in a polytheistic world. Their neighbors perceived them as nonconformists who did not share their assumptions about the divine nature of their surroundings. To shield themselves from persecution and to be able to live their religious lives in a normal way, both Jews and Christians went to great lengths to explain themselves and their beliefs to their neighbors, particularly those who could be classified as members of the intellectual community, as well as to its governing authorities. The great example in terms of the Jews living in the Diaspora was Philo of Alexandria, who lived roughly around the same time as Jesus. In Christian terms, the author of the Gospel of Luke and the Acts of the Apostles might be characterized as the first Christian "apologist,"[3] who, as we have mentioned, suggests a basic compatibility of belief in Jesus and most of the structures of the Greco-Roman world. Even some of its religious assumptions seem acceptable to Luke. Despite being nonbelievers, emperors and Roman authorities

---

3. The term "apologist" has no connection with the colloquial notion of making an apology. Apologists set forth or explained their beliefs to nonbelievers.

were understood to be appointed by God, and Jews and Christians constantly asserted their loyalty to the empire, insisting that they prayed for the well-being of the emperor on a daily basis.

Both Jews and Christians went to great lengths to make their beliefs acceptable in the Greco-Roman world. Philo of Alexandria and Christians from the first to the fourth centuries attested to their loyalty to the empire and its emperors. More, however, was required. Writing around 30 C.E., Philo set out to explain Judaism to the educated citizens of Alexandria, drawing on the philosophical discourse of his time. Alexandria, which rivaled Athens in terms of its intellectual life, was home to a host of philosophical schools. None, however, was as dominant as Platonism, with Stoicism running in second place. In works like the *Timaeus* Plato asserts that the material world is a mere reflection of a more important mental world evident in immaterial ideas. Put another way, the material is a foreshadowing of a greater ideal reality that true philosophers, that is, seekers of wisdom, can infer and even fleetingly experience. Furthermore, in the Platonic system, God is totally immaterial, dispassionate, and self-contained reason. God is "mind" in its purest form. Today we think of philosophy as a largely secular endeavor, but in antiquity it often had a strong religious component. The Stoic tradition, like Platonism, also works with similar dualistic assumptions, putting particular stress on God's rational ordering of the natural world from which we can infer certain of God's qualities. God ordered nature in a hierarchical way, and so society must follow suit. Not all are equal because not all were meant to be equal.

Philo knew Plato as well as he knew Torah, and he fervently believed in the truth of both. He likewise resonated with the Stoic tradition with its stress on order and natural law. In works like *The Exposition of the Law,* he used Platonic discourse to point to the reasonableness of Judaism to both Jews and non-Jews alike. In his discussion of creation, he pointed to its rational and orderly nature. To circumvent the objections of non-Jews that the Genesis account was a crude and incredible narrative, he used a method of literary interpretation that was pervasive in Alexandria and central to Platonic hermeneutics — allegory.[4] A text like Genesis is not to be read and understood literally but rather figuratively or allegorically. God taking a refreshing stroll in the Garden of Eden, a concept that would repel either a Platonist or a Stoic, is actually a metaphor that points to a deeper truth beneath the surface of the text. Being immaterial, God could not have been strolling in the cool of the evening. The passage actually refers to God's reasonable concern for the created world, and Adam

---

4. "Hermeneutics," a word derived from the Greek, is simply a scholarly term for interpretation.

and Eve in particular. Philo created a sort of Platonic Judaism, with some Stoic underpinnings. Well versed in Philo's work, by the mid-second century Christians would take the same approach in trying to explain their beliefs in Jesus' incarnation and resurrection, concepts that non-Christian thinkers in the Greco-Roman world found ludicrous. What emerged, and still exists today, is a Christian theological system that has as much to do with Hellenistic philosophical assumptions as it has to do with the four Gospels.

By the second century early Christian thinkers attempted to systematize and explain their beliefs that heretofore had been only locally and loosely defined. Early Christianity was not an institution or organization in the modern sense of the terms as much as a diverse collection of local communities, each with its own style and varied understandings of Jesus and the Christian community. Only gradually did a shared or "catholic" theology emerge, and even today there is diversity and debate within the catholic community about its core beliefs and values.[5] The term "catholic" is derived from a Greek adjective that means commonly shared, that is, universal. The adjective, however, does not imply uniformity. Still, a pattern begins to emerge. In the early second century, Ignatius of Antioch, the bishop of that local community on his way to martyrdom in Rome, sent letters to various Christian communities exhorting them to follow the lead of a single bishop whose tasks entailed guiding his community and making sure that its beliefs were orthodox, in other words, true to the growing sense of what Christianity meant for the catholic community in its local manifestations. His exhortation to follow the lead of a single bishop, a concept scholars generally refer to as the "monarchical episcopacy," can lead to only one conclusion — that there were competing definitions of Christianity and models of the Christian community that Ignatius considered incorrect or heterodox. Of course, there was a certain logic to Ignatius's views. The Christian community was being persecuted, and cohesion and focused leadership were crucial for its survival.

Ignatius was not a theologian as much as a down-to-earth church leader. A few decades after his death, however, Christian theologians begin to emerge who shared his catholic understanding of Christianity. They began to write "apologies" or explanations of their beliefs with several purposes in mind. First, they wrote to the Christian community itself in an effort to fortify common assumptions about the core beliefs of its members. Second, they attempted to refute other versions of Christianity that they considered threats to their catholic interpretation of the Gospels and Pauline letters. Third, they tried to explain Christian beliefs

---

5. The use of a lower-case "c" is deliberate. It is far too early to speak of Catholicism, not to mention Roman Catholicism.

to educated non-Christians who found Christianity intellectually shallow if not bizarre and ridiculous. Few of these "apologists" were "cradle Christians." Most were converts who explored other philosophical and religious traditions before encountering Christianity. Many were students of Platonism prior to their conversions and carried over more than a few Platonic assumptions to their newfound faith. Although not the intellectual giants of Philo's caliber whose writings they surely were familiar with, they set out to do for Christianity what he had done for Judaism a century before. Without denying the specificity of what they believed, they nonetheless were intent on the inculturation of Christianity in the Greco-Roman world. Slowly but surely they would succeed in ways they could never have imagined.

It is interesting to compare and contrast the ideas of two of the most important Christian theologians of the late second and early third centuries. The Greek-speaking church, in which the majority of Christians resided, produced an undeniable genius in the person of Origen, a native of Alexandria who spent many years of his life in the Palestinian city of Caesarea, particularly when he was having difficulties with the presiding bishop of Alexandria — apparently a frequent occurrence. In the Latin-speaking West, specifically in the Roman city of Carthage, we encounter the sharp-tongued Tertullian, almost as prolific a writer as Origen, but a Christian whose understanding of his faith and the Roman world diverged in significant ways from that of his Alexandrian counterpart.[6] Tertullian clearly had difficulties with the nascent institutional church, which he came to see as tepid in its faith and too comfortably ensconced in the surrounding Roman world. We will first deal with Origen, the child-genius of the early Greek-speaking church.

Origen was unusual in many ways. He was a second-generation Christian steeped in Platonism as much as he was in Christianity. A brilliant systematic thinker and unparalleled biblical scholar, he used the allegorical method and the neo-Platonic method that it depended on to explain the Bible to both Christian and non-Christian readers in an intellectually convincing way.[7] He was also an extreme ascetic with contempt for all things bodily, including his physical condition. Origen was both brilliant and a fanatic of sorts, and many of his co-religionists found him difficult to understand and extreme in his body-mind dualism. His teacher was Clement of Alexandria, a few of whose writings on Christianity survive.

---

6. Evans, *The First Christian Theologians*. Evans offers a useful anthology of early Christian thought in contemporary English.

7. Platonism and neo-Platonism are variations on the same themes. In the third and fourth centuries, philosophers like Porphyry and Plotinus reworked the thoughts of Plato, attempting to make them more contemporary and adding a religious and mystical tone to Plato's original thought.

Although less dualistic than the works of Origen, they are nonetheless predicated on neo-Platonic assumptions — a philosophical tradition that was becoming a lynchpin of Christian intellectual discourse. Origen surpassed his teacher at an early age and became a renowned teacher in Alexandria, where he was the head of a Christian academy whose purpose was to explain Christianity to aspiring members, as well as to make it acceptable and rational in the eyes of its critics.

During his time in Caesarea Origen most likely produced his lengthy masterpiece, *First Principles*, which is a sophisticated but sometimes rambling treatise on the truth of Christianity and the nature of creation itself. It is a highly speculative work that most people today find quite difficult to read. For our purposes, however, another of Origen's works, *Contra Celsum*, or "Against Celsus," is of greater interest. Around 170 a Greek philosopher named Celsus wrote a savage critique of Christianity entitled *True Doctrine*, which does not survive but can be partially reconstructed from Origen's refutation, which cites it at length. Undoubtedly, Celsus had done his homework. He displays knowledge of both Judaism and Christianity that is impressive. He scoffs at Christians' claim to be the "New Israel," the definitive revelation of God in human history. He finds the belief in the incarnation and resurrection ludicrous impossibilities that defy reason and the laws of nature. In Celsus's mind, Jesus was a conman and magician who deserved to be crucified for perpetrating a massive fraud. He claimed to be the son of God for his own aggrandizement and duped gullible Jewish peasants, the dregs of society, into believing him. Christians themselves are portrayed as stupid and a threat to the well-being of the empire in light of their refusal to recognize its divine nature, accept civic responsibilities, or do military service. To use colloquial English, they are the "trailer trash" of the Greco-Roman world in Celsus's estimation.

Fifty years after Celsus wrote it, Origen refuted *True Doctrine* in his lengthy counterpoint, *Contra Celsum*. He accuses Celsus of using caricatures that misrepresent the real nature of Christianity. Celsus skimmed the surface of things but failed to see the rationality and wisdom of what Christians *truly* believe and why they live in the world as they do. Jesus was not a charlatan, but a manifestation of the Logos, a rational expression of God's creativity and love for humankind. His resurrection was not the preposterous resuscitation of a crucified corpse but his transcending the limitations of the bodily and material world as the son of God, the first of many who will do so. As for Christians being rebellious and unpatriotic, they are the best of citizens since they refuse to participate in the sham of political idolatry while praying for the health of the emperor and respecting his authority. They are in this world, but, like Jesus, not of it. Origen, who would eventually die from the consequences of Roman torture, both accepted the world around him and passionately expected to transcend it as a neo-Platonist and devout Christian. His impact on Greek-speaking Christianity, although complex, has been profound and lasting.

Moving westward across the Mediterranean, Latin would eventually replace Greek as the common language. Carthage was the capital of Roman North Africa, a city that took great pride in its *Latinitas*. This word is difficult to translate, but it refers essentially to the hard-nosed pragmatism of Roman culture. Carthage was a bustling port city filled with crass merchants and uncouth sailors who transported wheat, wine, and olive oil to Italy, especially Rome. North Africa was the breadbasket of the empire. In school the sons of the wealthy learned about Aeneas and the glories of Rome as they memorized Virgil's epic and propagandistic poem *The Aeneid*. Aeneas, the founder of Rome, was no mere mortal. His mother was the goddess Venus and his warrior father a valiant Trojan solider. Aeneas was fated by the gods to establish an empire that eventually would civilize the known world. The Roman Empire was not a secular proposition. It was a divine undertaking. Romans were meant to be militaristic and down-to-earth as opposed to the effete, bookish Greeks they had conquered. They held the world of speculative, philosophical discourse in little regard. Furthermore, the Greeks were *victi*, or conquered people, who quickly succumbed to Roman imperial power in the second century before Christ. In Carthage we would encounter Tertullian — a brilliant, complex, and sometimes cranky figure, often described as the first theologian of the Latin-speaking church.[8] He lived from roughly 160 to 220 C.E. and wrote thirty-one treatises that offer enormous insight into early North African Christianity. He describes the behavior and beliefs of early Carthaginian Christians as well as how they related to their non-Christian neighbors. Tertullian is hardly shy when it comes to sizing up the Roman world or the institutional church. His criteria for both were exceedingly high and inflexible. His oft quoted refrain, "What does Athens have to do with Jerusalem?" encapsulates his sentiments about the abstract theological discourse of Justin, Clement, and other Greek-speakers in a characteristically biting way.

Comparing Origen with Tertullian is a proverbial case of apples and oranges. Both were brilliant thinkers, but their approaches to Christianity and the world around them were quite different. Origen could engage in flights of speculative fantasy that most people would never grasp. Tertullian, on the other hand, shuns speculation and refuses to debate his operative presuppositions about how things work or how they should work. His treatises are generally short, lockstep, and logical discussions of aspects of Christian belief and practice written for Christians and

---

8. Dunn, *Tertullian*, Early Church Fathers, 39.

non-Christians alike. As a writer, Tertullian could exhort and scold. His writings are oratorical, with a splash of hyperbole thrown in for good measure. He was capable of caustic denunciations of those he disagreed with or had the audacity to disagree with him. He expected his fellow Christians to grasp and live out his perception of orthodoxy. He detested those he considered heterodox believers, especially Gnostics with their secret knowledge and special gospels they alone were privileged to have and understand. Tertullian did not hesitate to insult the Jews and their beliefs while he heaped burning coals on the heads of "pagan" thinkers. In his mind, they were either misguided, stupid, or both. For Tertullian, the truths of Christianity were self-evident and any intelligent person should understand and adhere to them. Any other approach was literally damned folly.

Like other early Christian writers, Tertullian saw himself as a loyal subject of the empire who prayed for the well-being of the emperor. He dismisses the accusations made against Christians of being seditious atheists. In reality, they are "super-patriots." The fact that Christians refuse to worship the pantheon of Roman gods is a result of their strict monotheism. Furthermore, they have no desire to overthrow the state, since, they believe that all authority is divinely established (Rom. 13:1–7). The problem lies in the ignorance and prejudice of Roman judges who know little about Christianity and even violate the due process Roman citizens are entitled to by law.[9] Furthermore, since the courts invoke the gods, they are based on idolatrous rituals that Christians are forbidden to participate in. It is important to realize that Tertullian believed in the existence of these deities, but for him they were demonic forces responsible for the evils of the empire. The same applies to the games put on in amphitheaters throughout the Roman world. They were riddled with idolatrous behaviors that Christians must abjure.[10] Furthermore, they were savage blood baths.

In one of his most sarcastic but insightful essays, entitled "On the Games" (*De Spectaculis*), he mocks Roman pretense. Using his inimitable rhetorical questions, he asks why a society that claims to be noble and just puts on sadistic gladiatorial combats, publicly tortures criminals and Christians in amphitheaters, and wallows in tales about the sexual escapades of its gods. For Tertullian Roman grandeur is a fabulous lie, the ultimate example of collective delusion. Even military service is forbidden since soldiers take an oath to the emperor and Roman gods and engage in

---

9. Ibid., 3.
10. Tertullian, "On the Games" (*De Spectaculis*), see Dunn, *Tertullian*, Early Church Fathers, 8.

violence that Christians cannot participate in because of their reverence for life.[11] For Tertullian the Roman world brims with sin that must be avoided at all costs. He is uncompromising, and there is an exclusivist note in his writing that borders on the sectarian. Still, he works with the assumption that once purified, the empire can be redeemed. Echoing the theme found in Acts, Christianity is part of God's plan for humanity and believers have an obligation to convert their neighbors. In the interim, however, Christians should willingly face martyrdom rather than compromise with the demonic forces that delude their neighbors. If they do so, even in the slightest way, they commit the most grievous of sins — apostasy. They cease to be Christian.

Tertullian's intransigence goes beyond the sins of the empire. He is no fan of married life, although he was married himself.[12] His views on marriage and sexuality are almost a paraphrase of Paul's first letter to the Corinthians (1 Cor. 7:1–11). Celibacy is the preferred state for Christians. It entails fewer compromises with the surrounding world, allows greater time for prayer, and makes one less hesitant to accept the pain of torture and horrors of martyrdom. In the event that he should die prematurely, Tertullian exhorts his wife not to marry but rather to be a widow who, as it were, regains her virginity. Although such ideas seem strange to most people in the twenty-first century, they were commonplace in the early church. They have their basis in Christian scripture, as well as Stoic and Platonic philosophy. Sexuality is seen as irrational and women as more prone to sexual misconduct than men because of their "weaker" and less rational nature. Anything to do with "the flesh" is ultimately defiling. Good, strong Christians should avoid it as an example to each other and as a way to edify nonbelievers. Tertullian's rigid morality even extends to clothing and cosmetics. Dress should always be modest. Hair should be kept plain and makeup is unworthy of a believing woman. Such behaviors border on the sinful since they are a concession to the false values of the world. It is no wonder that Tertullian is the bane of feminist believers and nonbelievers. He is perceived as misogynistic, although his ideas were hardly novel in the second and third centuries. Tertullian's asceticism is emblematic of a deeper hostility to anything that challenges a transcendent, Christian understanding of who we are as human beings who inhabit an ephemeral world. Sex, cosmetics, and pleasure in general are to be rejected because they distort our perception of reality. They throw us off a trajectory that should lead to the hereafter rather than the here and now. Only a Christian social system could possibly get things right, but Tertullian wonders if such a Christian polity, given human weakness,

---

11. Tertullian, "On the Crown" (*De Corona*), 7.
12. Tertullian, "To His Wife" (*Ad Uxorem*), 4.

can ever come to be. in the next chapter, when we look at the thinking and writing of Augustine, a fellow North African Christian, we will encounter the same underlying pessimism about the human condition.

One of the great mysteries of early Christianity is what happened to Tertullian. This prolific writer suddenly stops writing. One theory is that Tertullian broke with the catholic church in North Africa. There are indications in his writings of a growing displeasure with the institutional church, which he saw as making too many compromises for the sake of survival in a hostile world. Did this rigid man leave the church in disgust? Another hypothesis is that Tertullian joined the Montanist movement, a late second-century Christian splinter group that put much stock in prophecy and liturgical spontaneity.[13] Its stress on the apocalyptic dimension of Christianity may have appealed to Tertullian. The fact, however, that women played a role in Montanism should give us pause, but perhaps we are dealing with Tertullian's alter ego. Another hypothesis, and one that makes more sense than others, is that Tertullian died a victim of Roman persecution. Although sporadic and usually localized to particular cities with imperial administrators who were hostile to Christianity, an attack against the church could well have swept up Tertullian in its wake. Given his intransigence, he certainly would have died a martyr's death rather than compromise in any way. His fate is unknown and will always be.

Shifting Tides and Seeming Triumph

Throughout the fourth century the Roman Empire became progressively more Christian, despite ongoing debates about the nature and meaning of Christianity among Christian themselves.[14] Some theological disputes, which often reflected different political and social values as well, became intense to the point of violence. As the church became more powerful, defining beliefs and enforcing a particular version of orthodoxy began to have concrete implications. Theologians fought with theologians, bishops with bishops. Our principal but not sole sources for understanding events in the fourth century are provided by Lactantius, a Latin-speaking historian and theologian of the Western church, and his Greek-speaking counterpart Eusebius of Caesarea, likewise a historian, theologian, and influential bishop of the Eastern church. Both unequivocally assert that the emperor Constantine's victory over his rival Maxentius at the battle of the Milvian Bridge outside of Rome in 313, the Edict of Toleration in the same year that made the church a legal institution, along with Constantine's baptism in 337, were all part of a preordained plan that fulfilled

---

13. Ibid., 3.
14. MacMullen and Lane, *Paganism and Christianity*, 74–105, 164–72.

God's will for humankind. Any event that calls their thesis into question is recast or set aside. Despite their usefulness, our two Christian historians need to be approached with a certain degree of caution.

The fact that Lactantius's and Eusebius's versions of Constantine's actions and conversion during his long reign do not entirely mesh is problematic. Who was right and who was wrong? Or perhaps this very question is illegitimate since our two Christian authors were trying to legitimate a series of political, social, and religious decisions on Constantine's part that went in the church's favor, but could just as likely have gone the other way. After all, the catholic church experienced a savage persecution from roughly 303 to 305, decreed by the emperor Diocletian. A comfortable and increasingly conformist church was nearly brought to its knees. Had the church turned flaccid in its attempt to secure peace and quiet or was this final persecution part of God's plan meant to prepare it for ultimate triumph? Lactantius and Eusebius are convinced that the latter turn of events is what actually happened. Today we raise questions about what took place; our fervent historians, however, had absolutely no doubt about the deeper meaning of things. Did Constantine have a vision of Jesus and an auditory experience in which Jesus told him *In hoc signo vinces* — "By this sign you will conquer"? Did he have his legions paint crosses on their shields or did he have the Chi-Rho, the first two letters of the name of Christ in Greek, emblazoned on his standards? Was Maxentius's fatal decision to go to battle outside of the well-fortified city of Rome an accident or part of God's design for the Roman Empire? We need to keep in mind that Lactantius and Eusebius, both gifted and sincere men, were nonetheless propagandists, although they certainly would have taken offense at such an epithet. They sometimes give the impression that God waved a magic wand and the empire's conversion to Christianity was an ineluctable event. In fact, however, throughout most of the fourth century, the empire was a largely non-Christian society. Although scholars vary in their estimates, at the beginning of the fourth century probably no more than 15 percent of the Greco-Roman world was Christian.[15] There were far more Christians in the Greek-speaking East than in the Latin-speaking West, and rural areas, inhabited by *pagani*, or peasants, were almost entirely non-Christian and would remain so for centuries. When converted, often by coercion, they tended to weave their non-Christian beliefs into their new-found faith, resulting in contextualized versions of Christianity. (This inevitable and indispensable process still goes on today.)

In the minds of Lactantius and Eusebius, however, the conversion of the empire was an essentially linear process. There were, of course, a few

---

15. Estimates vary from 2 to 15 percent. As noted, the bulk of Christians resided in the Eastern half of the empire.

bumps along the way. Julian, emperor from 361 to 363, renounced his baptism and tried to reestablish the old religion of the empire. Julian, "The Apostate," naturally succumbed to God's wrath and the process of Christianization continued along its way. Anything that might call this theory into question was overlooked. In *On the Death of the Persecutors* Lactantius reveled in his gruesome description of non-Christian emperors who persecuted the church dying of horrible cancers and burst intestines. The godly Constantine, however, died in bed, comforted by guaranteed salvation. The fact that Constantine had his son Crispus executed, along with hundreds of other political opponents, and likely conspired in the grisly death of his wife, Fausta, who somehow could not open the door of her sauna and was scalded to death, are given short shrift. The catholic and orthodox emperor Theodosius slaughtered around seven thousand men, women, and children in Thessalonica around 390 because of a revolt and perceived insult to his imperial dignity. Confronted by the brave bishop of Milan, Ambrose, he was refused communion and threatened with excommunication, but ultimately repented and did the requisite penance. Although this flies in the face of modern sensibilities, in is important to keep in mind that in the minds of most ancient Christians, and even among some today, emperors, be they believers or nonbelievers, good or bad, were not to be questioned any more than God could be. Emperors, civic authorities, and church leaders were understood as God's regents. Questioning them was seen as both unpatriotic and sinful since the social order and its leaders were divinely appointed.

Constantine's conversion to Christianity, which was actually a long-term process, and his baptism just before his death in 337, forever changed the catholic community. From 303 to 305 the emperor Diocletian had unleashed one of the most savage and systematic attacks against the church. Now everything was calm. The age of martyrs was over. In 311 the emperor Galerius begrudgingly had legalized Christianity. In 313 Constantine welcomed Christians into the imperial scheme of things, full citizens like everyone else. In the Edict of Milan he had all of the church's property confiscated in the past returned to its leaders. The year 313 was miraculous and even magical. A heretofore powerless church was suddenly in possession of unanticipated support and resources. When and where should the winning ticket be cashed in and how should the prize money be used? A church that had been persecuted less than ten years before, and still was harassed in certain parts of the Eastern empire, was suddenly the recipient of imperial favor. Constantine began to funnel enormous amounts of money into the catholic church. Basilicas or "kingly" churches were built in the major cities of the empire with grateful bishops voicing their heartfelt gratitude for the emperor's generosity. Clergy were exempted from civil obligations, military service, and taxes.

Bishops began to function as civil magistrates, were granted senatorial status, and had unencumbered access to state resources. Christians were appointed to the most important positions in Constantine's administration. The power and prestige of the catholic church grew exponentially, and suddenly being a deacon, priest, or bishop was a heady and sometimes lucrative profession.

Nonetheless, this does not mean that the transition to favored status along with imperial financial support was smooth or unchallenged. Nor does it mean that the catholic church became the corrupt puppet of the imperial court. Reading Christian literature from the period quickly makes it obvious that there were different and sometimes antithetical reactions to the "Constantinian Shift." To employ an exaggerated polarity, there were those who saw Constantine as God's regent on earth while others questioned whether an emperor or empire could be truly Christian in light of the inherent nastiness and violence that are part and parcel of any political arrangement. Was Constantine's conversion the finger of God acting in history, almost as important as Jesus' incarnation, or was it a slippery slope that threatened the autonomy and integrity of the church? Reading the Church Fathers of the fourth century, one comes across various points of view. (There were Church Mothers as well, but their insights and writings were overlooked in what was a profoundly patriarchal and misogynistic culture.) Did Jesus not say in the Gospel of John, standing before Pontius Pilate, the epitome of Roman power and political cynicism, that his kingdom was "not of this world"? (John 18:36). What to do with the fact that baptized emperors routinely had their opponents tortured and murdered in order to maintain their stranglehold on power? Theologians of stature like Jerome, John Chrysostom, Basil of Caesarea, and members of the burgeoning monastic movement, among others, were leery of the growing proximity of church and state and near fusion in some instances. They knew the difference between the empire and the Reign of God, aware that human beings are prone to worship fleeting social and political arrangements. They feared political idolatry and the possibility that the church would become a pawn of the political system, bribed and manipulated by imperial favors and funds.

To return to our artificial polarity, we need to quickly analyze the viewpoints of those who expounded on the pros and cons of the church's new role in the fourth-century social order. The most outspoken advocate of the "pro" position was Eusebius of Caesarea, a highly respected biblical scholar, historian, and theologian. Eusebius's *Church History* and *Life of Constantine* are vitally important works without which we would know far less about early Christianity. Still, his enthusiasm for Constantine and the "Christianization" of the empire is a bit too intense and short on critical analysis for most of us today. A quote from the *Life of Constantine* proves the point:

> All rose at a signal, which announced the Emperor's entrance, like some heavenly angel of God, his bright mantle shedding luster like beams of light, shining with the fiery radiance of a purple robe, and decorated with the dazzling brilliance of gold and precious stones. Such was his physical appearance. As for his soul, he was clearly adorned with fear and reverence for God: this was shown by his eyes, which were cast down, the blush of his face, his gait, and the rest of his appearance, his height, which surpassed all of those around him.[16]

This saccharine description of the emperor's entry into the Council of Nicea, which he is reputed to have convoked in order to solve a raging controversy among the bishops and priests of the Greek-speaking church, gives us a sense of just how "wowed" Eusebius was by Constantine's person and power. Constantine's solicitude and theological genius supposedly solved the acrimonious debate about Jesus' relationship with God the Father that had bishops hurling insults and anathemas at each other across the splendid halls at Nicea that Constantine had made available to them. No mere mortal, Constantine was a source of divine intervention. Even his saintly mother, Helena, had special powers. On pilgrimage in Jerusalem, she discovered the true cross. Our awed and grateful bishop Eusebius, who is now on the imperial payroll, conveniently overlooks the fact that Constantine spoke little if any Greek and had no formal theological training.

To give Eusebius a bit of slack, we need to recognize that we are dealing with a classic panegyric, a florid piece of prose meant to flatter emperors and other court authorities. Reality is not the issue. Actually, Nicea failed to settle the theological controversies about Jesus and God, and they raged on for a century more. Eusebius, however, never alludes to these unpalatable events nor the fact that he himself was momentarily excommunicated in what turned out to be a nasty episcopal brawl. Fortunately or unfortunately, depending on one's viewpoint, Christianity is not a synthetic whole. There are four canonical or official Gospels with different approaches to Jesus, the Christian community, and the world outside its doors. When we add in the letters of Paul and other texts in the New Testament, honesty forces us to admit that there were, and are, many ways of understanding Christianity, even its catholic, orthodox form. Eusebius knew this, but being intent on writing a romantic and possibly imaginary description of events, he skirts the more complex and challenging aspects of his own religious tradition.

---

16. Eusebius of Caesarea, *The Life of Constantine*, book 3, para. 10, 125.

Eusebius helped legitimate a symbiotic relationship between church and state that presented a number of problems. To use a technical term, Eusebius lays the groundwork for a phenomenon known as "caesaro-papism" — a term that connotes a close, symbiotic relationship between church and state. A graphic example of how this arrangement worked is visible in the great Byzantine cathedral of Hagia Sophia, or Holy Wisdom, in Istanbul. The emperor Justinian built it in 537. In front of the altar there are two thrones. During the celebration of the liturgy the patriarch and emperor would sit across from each other. Furthermore, there was a passageway from the palace to the cathedral that allowed the patriarch and emperor to be in constant contact with each other. For more than ten centuries Byzantine emperors would manipulate patriarchs who in turn would try to outmaneuver emperors in what was often a ruthless cat-and-mouse game. In theory, however, both emperor and patriarch were indispensable authorities who were in harmonious concord.

The historical record hardly bears out this pious fiction. Toward the end of the fourth century, John Chrysostom, an eloquent and truly holy man recently named patriarch by the imperial court, had the audacity to criticize the emperor, empress, pervasive social injustice around him, and a corrupt clergy. He lasted two years as patriarch, was exiled, and died because of brutal treatment at the hands of ostensibly Christian soldiers. Church and state relationships in the western part of the empire, which would soon disappear as such, could be just as contentious. As we will see in chapter 4, the bishops of Rome won and lost political skirmishes just like their eastern confreres. The Holy Roman Empire that emerged in the West in 800 C.E. was rarely holy, and the papacy, involved in incessant political machinations, alternated between corruption and reformation, power and persecution. Although much later than the period we are examining, the example of Boniface VIII makes the point. In 1303 this power-hungry pope excommunicated an aristocratic Italian family and the king of France. He ended up being beaten, stripped nearly naked, and run out of the town of Agnani on a jackass. To be succinct, as a rule priests make poor politicians, just as politicians make poor priests — a lesson catholic history proves unequivocally.

Tertullian's critique of church and state would have been familiar to and likely read by fourth- and fifth-century Christian thinkers like Ambrose, the bishop of Milan; Augustine, the bishop of Hippo; Basil, the bishop of Caesarea; and Chrysostom, the short-lived patriarch of Constantinople. They resonated with Tertullian's ideas, although unlike him, they remained in the catholic church and participated in the social order of the empire. They felt that the Roman world could be Christianized, albeit imperfectly. Tertullian would have been far more skeptical. No doubt, had he lived in the fourth or fifth centuries, he would have scorched these great theologians with his often savage prose. criticizing them for conflating Caesar and God.

By the late third and early forth centuries monks and nuns who were intent on living the Gospel in an intense and unadulterated way began to appear in the deserts of Egypt and the mountains of Syria. They left their families, wealth, villages, and cities searching for an undiluted experience of God. Silence and solitude were indispensable ingredients of a successful search for the divine. In Egypt many lived in suffocating tombs built centuries before for aristocrats and gentry that served the ancient pharaohs. In Syria, some perched themselves on top of pillars, where they spent most of their lives, lowering baskets for food and dispensing spiritual advice to awe-struck admirers who were amazed at their obvious sanctity. Nuns generally lived in communities, and most monks would eventually do so as well, but regardless of how and where they lived, monastic women and men were seen as Christian "athletes" engaged in mortal combat with diabolical forces manifest in any form of human pleasure, especially food and sexuality.[17] They were the antithesis of the gluttonous, pornographic behavior of powerful Romans. They reluctantly ate to survive, but would eat only because starving themselves to death was suicidal and therefore a sin. If they managed to totally repress their sexual urges they felt they were on a fast track to salvation. Today we judge such behavior as bizarre and psychologically harmful. In late antiquity, however, skeletal and often fanatical monks and nuns were seen as heroes and saints who carried on the tradition of martyrdom in an age in which martyrdom was no longer possible, at least theoretically. How could one possibly deny that monastic overachievers were far more holy than ordinary Christians who married, raised children, and had to come to terms with the world around them with the many compromises this entailed? What emerges might be called "holiness stratification" — an assumption that cannot be reconciled with the Gospels but remains a central premise in most forms of Christianity to this day, especially Roman Catholicism. As if monks, nuns, priests, bishops, and popes, being untainted by virtue of holiness and their supposed separation from the world, had a direct telephone line to God!

There is no reason to doubt the sincerity of early monastic men and women. Still, they could not isolate themselves entirely from the world they had ostensibly rejected. Just as for any human being or religious group, contact with others and inevitable compromise were unavoidable. Famous for their body-denying asceticism, monks and nuns still had to eat *something* and this required bread, flour and leaven, olive oil, and the occasional glass of beer or wine to make liturgical feast days a bit more festive. The renowned Anthony of the Desert spent years in old Egyptian

---

17. Brown, *The Body and Society.*

tombs with their frightening wall paintings of the afterlife. Anthony lived on bread, water, and palm dates donated by strangers who would leave food outside of the latest tomb he inhabited. He hoped to achieve total isolation from the world. Nonetheless had to cope with lines of believers and non-believers who sought him out for guidance in their search for meaning and sanctity. In his best-selling *Life of Saint Anthony*, Athanasius, a contemporary of Anthony, the patriarch of Alexandria, and a ferocious theological "street-fighter" for the cause of catholic orthodoxy as spelled out by the Council of Nicea in 325, describes Anthony being harassed by visitors despite his efforts to hide. Anthony rejected the world, but the world managed to find him. When necessary, he would show up in Alexandria to offer his support to the beleaguered Athanasius, whose friendship he seems to have relished and whose theological position he fiercely defended. Monks often appeared in large numbers in the major cities of the empire and tragically became experts at demolishing temples, synagogues, and libraries that housed the priceless treasures of the classical world, which they deemed pagan and diabolical. Simon the Stylite lived several meters off the ground, but he nonetheless knew what was happening on it. From his famous pillar he delivered spiritual wisdom to believers and nonbelievers alike, becoming something of a tourist attraction and no doubt a boon to the local economy. Clearly seen as honest and unbiased, Simon also adjudicated the incessant legal squabbles over land, money, and titles that wealthy citizens of the empire loved to fret over and entertain themselves with. In turn, they filled Simon's basket with the necessities he required to survive on his dangerous perch.

A Tentative Synopsis

Christian monks and nuns had legitimate bones to pick with the institutional church, but it is important to point out that very few ever left it. They functioned as a sort of loyal opposition, convinced that the church was divinely established and to be obeyed in the final instance. They correctly perceived the underlying injustice and pathology of the Greco-Roman world and eschewed the lust for power and culture that caused so much dehumanizing violence. Yet, there was a shadow side to Christian monasticism. Male monastics were often consummate woman-haters. Few questioned the economic linchpin of the Roman Empire — slavery. There are more than a few contradictions involved here. Nonetheless, monks and nuns were right to worry about the commitment and mettle of new Christians who were being baptized in record numbers. Following Roman custom, it was common for people to convert to the reigning emperor's religion, or that of local authorities whose good favors had to be curried to provide a modicum of safety in an unpredictable world. As monks and nuns were wont to point out, once upon a time conversion was a dangerous decision that could lead to torture and death. Suddenly, being Christian was a smart career choice. Monks and nuns lived on the periphery of society, seemingly more pure than the neophytes knocking down church doors in a frantic effort to be baptized. Still, by virtue of their individual and collective lives, monks and nuns called into question the operating assumptions of a society based on material acquisition, class status, and an unquestioned belief in male superiority. They likewise called the institutional church to task.

Monastic communities were meant to foreshadow the Reign of God, thus abolishing the foundational distinctions that made the Greco-Roman world such a conservative and deadly proposition and the church more and more hierarchical. Many criticized the growing pomposity of the Christian clergy and refused ordination to the deaconate or priesthood, seeing clerical status as a trap. Unfortunately, monks who were experts at pointing out individual sin only went so far in their criticism of what was happening in society and the church they belonged to.[18] It was not in their best interests to do so. From the fourth to the seventh centuries, monasteries became more and more wealthy, exercising real economic power, in both the Eastern and Western halves of the empire. Monks, who had once woven baskets to survive, now could engage in uninterrupted prayer as peasants tilled the monastery's fields living and dying in squalid huts outside fortified walls.

One of the best pieces of recent scholarship on church-state issues in the fourth century is the magisterial analysis of H. A. Drake found in *Constantine and the Bishops: The Politics of Intolerance*. Drake provides a critical and incredibly detailed study of events in the Constantinian era. Because he is such an accomplished scholar, however, he avoids definitive statements about what is one of the most complex and sometimes mystifying centuries in Christian history. Drake works with the operative principle, which all of us need to take into consideration, that we are inhabitants of a science-oriented, Western culture driven by Enlightenment presuppositions about society and religion. Most of us subscribe to the separation of church and state. Well into the eighteenth century such a notion would have baffled most people, and in the fourth century it would have been seen as positively absurd. For nearly everyone in antiquity the fusion of politics and religion was good and necessary. Along with waging war and meting out justice, the emperors were expected to keep political and religious discord to a minimum. A certain degree of pluralism was

---

18. In terms of nuns, we have practically no written materials that indicate their take on things. Nonetheless, it is certain that many women entered monastic life to avoid arranged marriages, to gain a measure of self-determination, and to achieve holiness in their own way.

tolerable, but extreme positions were deemed threatening to public well-being. We no longer trust our politicians so blindly and, for most of us, diversity is an asset rather than a liability.

We will never know precisely why Constantine convened the Council of Nicea or decided to become a Christian. Certainly, he had channeled huge amounts of money into the church, hoping that it would function as a sort of glue helping to hold a fragile empire together. In all likelihood, he saw the catholic church as the most functional and homogenous institution in the empire, and he was looking for a solid ally. We can only speculate about the Milvian Bridge, Nicea, and the waters of baptism poured over the emperor's head as he approached death. A similar methodological humility is required when we try to understand what was happening to the institutional church in the fourth century. As we have seen, Lactantius and Eusebius were cheerleaders who went to great lengths to sweep contradictions under the proverbial rug. Although we may be wary of their assessment of historical events, they were not very different from most intellectuals in the fourth century. This was an age of belief and overarching explanations that assumed the guiding hand of God in human affairs. Agnostics hardly existed in antiquity and most people went to bed fairly certain of how the world worked. They were on it briefly and their principal task was to do everything possible to achieve salvation. Heaven and hell were not metaphors; they were real and eternal facts that any woman and man had best be contemplating or suffer the consequences.

What would come to be called Christendom is a very complex concept and did not "happen" in the fourth century. Rather, it began to take shape and would evolve over the course of decades and centuries. Arguably, it remained intact for at least a millennium and a half. Amazingly, some people today naïvely pine for its restoration. They suffer from a fallacious but apparently comforting assumption that Christendom was Christian, that moral ambiguity was nonexistent and virtue trumped vice. Would that things were so idyllic. In the fourth century crucifixion was banned, but torture was still an integral part of the judicial system. Compassion for the poor was preached from pulpits, but masses of indigent and sick women and men begged outside of church doors as they still do today in many developing countries. The fourth-century church is sometimes as enigmatic as its twenty-first-century counterpart. Still, a pattern has emerged. We can shift from a lower to an upper case c and talk about Catholicism. In the chapter that follows we will deal with one of its principal architects, Augustine of Hippo, the last and greatest spokesperson for the ancient Christian world.

Chapter Three

Augustine and the
Complexities of Genius

Asked to rank the most influential thinkers of the Catholic tradition, ancient, medieval, and modern, most scholars would place Augustine at the top of the list. This is not to deny the impact of Thomas of Aquinas, whose influence on Catholic thought has been profound and whose thinking we will explore in the next chapter. But Augustine was considered the preeminent theologian well into the medieval period, and for many remains so. The wise thing to do is to let people draw their own conclusions. Nonetheless, Augustine has the chronological edge over Aquinas — fifteen centuries as opposed to a mere seven. In the ebb and flow of Western Christian history, Augustine has played a central role. His thinking and theology have enjoyed something akin to canonical status in Christian theological literature. In the sixteenth century, Protestant and Catholic reformers drew on Augustine to give substance to their contentious arguments. Today Augustine is back full-force in what many scholars have referred to as a neo-Augustinian movement. Even before he died in 430 C.E. Augustine was variously analyzed, applauded, and attacked. The same applies today. There are those who see Augustine as the source of everything that is wrong with Western Christianity while others see him as an irrefutable genius whose analysis of human nature and society is unsurpassable. Certainly, we are dealing with an amazingly complicated and prodigious writer who generated at least five million words during an uncharacteristically long life.[1] Augustine outlived and outwrote nearly everyone in the late ancient world.

In his lifelong search for truth, Augustine turned over every stone within his reach and rivers of ink have been filled to overflowing by scholars trying to figure out his thinking. There is a bit of Tertullian and Origen in Augustine, a priest and bishop dealing with a down-to-earth flock and, at the same time, a speculative biblical and theological genius capable of the most abstract thinking. Like all of us, Augustine changed

---

1. O'Donnell, *Augustine: A New Biography.* As O'Donnell amusingly points out, Augustine never managed to crack a single real joke in all of his writings. He managed only occasional wry irony, invariably at the expense of one of his theological opponents.

with time. The early Augustine, a somewhat obnoxious twenty-year-old drawn to the dualistic cult of the Manicheans, is not the same as the mature Catholic bishop ruminating on his life and life's meaning as he approached death in 430 C.E. For all of his life Augustine inhabited the Western, Latin-speaking Roman Empire, never setting foot in its Greek-speaking other half. By the fifth century, if not earlier, the empire in the West was a tenuous proposition, with a host of internal and external problems. It was dysfunctional but still worked with fits and starts. But fate was not in Rome's favor, and in 410 C.E. the old capital of the empire was sacked. Twenty years later Augustine's adopted town of Hippo would be surrounded by the Vandals, whose name has become a synonym for wanton destruction. He died just before Hippo suffered the same trauma as Rome. In short order, the entire Roman province of North Africa would be under the control of non-Romans. The last Roman emperor in the West ruled in approximately 475–76 C.E., and he was nothing more than a puppet of foreign invaders.

The weight of Augustine's thinking, however, outlived the empire by a millennium and a half and continues to define our world, even if we have little or no explicit knowledge of Augustine's life and theology. In the paragraphs that follow we will try to summarize Augustine's approach to the social order and its impact on the Catholic tradition, past and present. At least two caveats are in order. What follows will be schematic. Any number of contemporary analyses go further into depth. They will be cited in the text and footnotes. Secondly, separating Augustine the social theorist from the Catholic theologian is somewhat artificial. He did not and could not separate his Catholic faith and the Roman culture and world around him. They formed an organic whole that he spent almost all of his life trying to understand and write about. In his unusually long life he never slacked off from this quest. This is not to say that Augustine did not differentiate faith from day-to-day existence, the former far greater than the latter, but he used the only optic available to him, the late antique world that was officially Christian but Christian in only a superficial way.

Where Augustine Started: Life in a Backwater

We face a predictable quandary. Can we understand Augustine's world, removed from us by more than fifteen centuries? The answer is an enervating yes and no. To a degree those born into Mediterranean or Latin cultures have a slight advantage since they experience many of the cultural, political, and social institutions that Augustine knew so well, with due mutations, of course. In Augustine's world race, class, and gender were all-important categories that determined a person's fate in life. This is still true in many cultures and societies. For Augustine, a person's place in the social order was God-given and essentially immutable. Born an aristocrat, you would most likely enjoy comfort and prestige throughout your life. Born a slave or serf, your daily fare would be drudgery, pain, and a death that would come earlier rather than later. Few women or men lived beyond forty. There were exceptions, but they were anomalies. In addition, who you knew determined your social fate. Augustine's world was thoroughly hierarchical, and what little social mobility there was resulted from the skillful manipulation of a patron/client system, from which most members of the lower classes, 95 percent plus of the population, were excluded. Advancement entailed finding someone who would help push you up the political and social ladder. As a client your obligation toward your patron was to display gratitude in public and private with obsequious gestures, dedications in books if you wrote them, and if you achieved office in the church or imperial bureaucracy, a hearty panegyric about your beneficent sponsor. Eusebius skirts around Constantine's murderous temper, and Augustine is duly discreet when it comes to Romanianus, litigious land and slave owner who was curried by Augustine's father Patricius. Romanianus defrayed Augustine's elite education and used his contacts in Rome and Milan to facilitate his young client's career. Those of us who live in Anglo-Saxon or Germanic cultures find this type of social arrangement baffling if not offensive. We like to think we live in a meritocracy despite so much evidence to the contrary. Few people in Augustine's world were naïve about how things really worked, but they kept their skepticism to themselves, just as we do today. To be somewhat crass, Augustine knew how to play the system and circumvent his conscience until his midlife conversion.

Augustine was born around 354 C.E. in a small provincial town in Roman North Africa called Thagaste.[2] This was the sort of provincial town talented young people would do their best to leave behind as soon as possible. Thagaste lived off exported olives, their oil, and revenues generated in Carthage and Rome. Latin-speaking squires who thought of themselves as socially superior to everyone else and more Roman than the Romans would hobnob in the baths to do business and discuss politics. They vied with each other for power but nonetheless agreed on their inherent right to rule. As long as they stayed in their reassuring environment, they were unchallenged and absolved of any self-criticism. In 146 B.C.E., after the third phase of a bloody imperialistic war, the Roman Republic finally conquered Carthage, its longstanding commercial rival for uncontested power in the Mediterranean. Latin replaced Punic, an Indo-European culture took the place of a Semitic culture, and Roman North Africa became the

---

2. Brown, *Augustine of Hippo.* Brown's work, first published in 1967, remains the classic, chronologically focused analysis of Augustine's life and theology.

breadbasket of the empire, renowned for its agricultural products. The Roman aristocracy in Italy, however, looked at its North African cousins as laughable green-grocers devoid of social graces. They were rustics who spoke Latin with an easily detected accent. There was a well-established pecking order in the late Roman world. Latin-speaking Italians held their noses in the company of their African counterparts who, in turn, despised their Punic-speaking workers, while both of them heaped contempt on the Berber-speaking "barbarians" who inhabited the surrounding hills. Augustine would take this social arrangement for granted until his dying days. He reveled in the company of intellectually polished and politically powerful friends. What little he knew of "ordinary" people was derived from his position as a priest and bishop. He certainly cared about the well-being of these people, but he definitely did not inhabit their day-to-day world.

What we know of Augustine's formative years comes from his magisterial exercise in self-revelation known as the *Confessions*. This lengthy and often convoluted autobiography has exerted enormous influence on Western culture to the present.[3] It is often referred to as the first psychoanalytical work of antiquity, and for the last fifteen centuries it has been seen by many as a paradigmatic exposition on human behavior and nature. The problem with such an assertion, however, is that Augustine was the exception rather than the rule in the late classical and Christian world. Intellectually brilliant and buffered from the ups and downs of daily existence because of economic and social privilege, he was hardly typical of his time and day. His family was not especially wealthy, but neither was it poor. His father was a landowner and a minor political figure. Recognizing his genius very early on, his doting parents, Patricius and Monica, made enormous sacrifices to provide Augustine with the best possible education. By his midteens Augustine was in the equivalent of an upper-class boarding school and subsequently a prestigious "university" in Carthage. By dint of class and education he never harvested wheat in the blazing African sun, picked and pressed olives, or cooked his own meals. Servants and slaves did all of this. This was the norm in Roman society, and gentlemen and intellectuals never had to dirty their hands unless they enjoyed gardening.

Augustine makes it abundantly clear that he despised his father just as he adored his mother. In *Confessions* II, 3, his contempt for Patricius is palpable. His father was guilty of "shameless ambition." He was "no

---

3. Augustine, *Confessions*, trans. Maria Boulding, preface by Patricia Hampl. Quotes from the *Confessions* utilizing the standard Roman numeral for book and Arabic numeral for chapter are from this translation (for example, II, 4); references using a three-digit Arabic numbering system are references to the system utilized by James O'Donnell in his critical edition of the *Confessions* (print ed., Oxford, 1992; available online at *www.stoa.org/hippo/frame_entry.html*).

more than a fairly obscure town councilor at Thagaste." Augustine found his father an embarrassment despite his efforts to provide his son with a sophisticated education. Spending a year off from his studies, back in Thagaste Augustine did what any Roman youth would do — he went to the local baths, where his father managed to thoroughly humiliate him.

> The thorn bushes of my lust shot up higher than my head, and there was no hand there to root them out. Least of all my father; for when at the baths one day he saw me with unquiet adolescence my only covering and noted my ripening sexuality, he began at once to look forward eagerly to grandchildren, and gleefully announced his discovery to my mother. (II, 3)

Patricius's glee at Augustine's manhood was mortifying. Throughout his life Augustine saw sexuality as a problem rather than a gift. As a young member of the dualistic sect of the Manichees, he marveled at the asceticism and celibacy of its members. Later, as a neo-Platonist and Christian, he saw the material as inferior to the spiritual realm. His dualistic psychology and religiosity presumed that mind should control body, and what today we would consider an involuntary process related to normal maturation was to him a volitional act and a manifestation of sin. Patricius's joyful announcement to his wife, Monica, of future grandchildren linked Augustine with the irrational and often sordid aspects of sexual intercourse. In all probability, Augustine presumed that chaste matrons like his mother knew little or nothing about sexuality in general or male sexuality in particular. If they did their "purity" was certainly questionable. Add to this fact that Patricius was verbally abusive and a philanderer and we have a recipe for smoldering hatred. Augustine's standards were far beyond those of his contemporaries who saw adultery as innocuous. Landowners sexually exploited their slaves and often had a host of illegitimate children. Despite his disdain for Patricius's behavior, Augustine too would take a mistress and have a child like most of his contemporaries.

Augustine's relationship with his mother was the polar opposite of that with his father. His love for Monica, as well as hers for him, was intense and unrelenting. (Naturally, long before psychotherapy had a name, Augustine was on the proverbial couch of a thousand psychotherapists.) Readers who want to explore this topic will find Brown and O'Donnell helpful. Monica was the most devout of Catholic Christians. Although there is no evidence that she had any biblical or theological training, as was the case for nearly every Christian woman in antiquity, certainly she knew what she believed in a most fervent way. Anything that smacked remotely of heterodoxy was tantamount to sin. North African Christianity, however, was not a synthetic affair. There were Catholics, Donatists, Gnostics, Manichees, and neo-Platonists with their sundry and often irreconcilable interpretations of the Gospels and explanations of how believers should relate to the surrounding world. (We will explore the main tenets of these theological and religious systems as they relate to Augustine in the paragraphs that follow.) For Monica, and later Augustine, there was a right and wrong way to be a Christian. There was no middle ground. As a child Augustine was exposed to his mother's unwavering Catholicism. As we will see, he would return to it in early adulthood. As an adolescent and young adult, however, he went through a predictable period of rebelliousness that made Monica both angry and sad, although she never doubted that her gifted son would eventually change his ways. She was right, and Augustine would be smitten with remorse.

> You stretched out your hand from on high and pulled my soul out of these murky depths because my mother, who was faithful to you, was weeping for me more bitterly than ever mothers wept for the bodily death of their children. In her faith and in the spiritual discernment she possessed by your gift she regarded me as dead; and you heard her, O Lord, you heard her and did not scorn those tears of hers which gushed forth and watered the ground beneath her eyes where she prayed. Yes, you did indeed hear her, and how else can I account for the dream by which you so comforted her that she agreed to live with me and share my table, under the same roof? (*Confessions* III, 11)

Ever the loving, patient mother, Monica lost some battles but won the war. She temporarily threw Augustine out of her house while he dabbled with Manichee theology. She grit her teeth when Augustine entered into a common law marriage while a student in Carthage but she knew how to bide her time. In 387 Augustine was baptized and Monica was there to celebrate this monumental event. The "concubine" would be packed up and sent back to Carthage. Monica would arrange a marriage with a "respectable" woman, a girl in fact, but Augustine would soon decide to embrace celibacy for the rest of his life. Monica apparently did not protest this decision since chastity was the fastest road to sainthood. She must have been ecstatic that her favorite son had finally renounced the desires of the flesh. A few years later Monica would die leaving Augustine so depressed that he could neither cry over his mother's death nor function for several months. She was his alter ego, and Augustine's loss changed his life. Once "intellectually promiscuous" the wayward son began to see the immutable truths that his mother had so subscribed to. He claims to never have had a serious temptation with matters of the flesh.

> For me, good things were no longer outside, no longer quested for by fleshly eyes in this world's sunlight. Those who want to find their

joy in externals all too easily grow empty themselves. They pour themselves out on things which, being seen, are but transient, and lick even the images of these things with their famished imagination. (*Confessions* IX, 10)

Augustine began a long search within himself, looking for immutable truth and a comforting vision of God. Life became a prelude to death, a notion that helped Augustine approach his own death with relative tranquility.

Why spend so much time on Augustine's relationship with his parents? After all, few of us manage to avoid the predictable "parent problem" that afflicts most human beings soon after being born. Having a bad father and good mother, or the reverse, is hardly novel, and Augustine is probably one of several billion women and men who have had to come to terms with the complexities of differentiation, self-definition, and the tantrums we start to throw by our second year. There are, however, several aspects of Augustine's parental experience that are important. He was the first person to go to such lengths to explain his own developmental processes. Not a few commentators have accused him of being something of an exhibitionist. More importantly, however, Augustine has functioned in the Western world as a paradigm of the human condition despite the fact that he is really an anomaly by virtue of intelligence and social status. Few of us can claim genius and most people do not inhabit the upper strata of society. More importantly, Augustine used his father and mother to fathom and classify reality in an unusually intense way. His father, Patricius, is a morally feckless clod. His airs of social superiority are utterly laughable given his lack of real status and residence in an insignificant provincial town. Monica has a few annoying character defects — she is a bit too possessive — but otherwise she is a paragon of sanctity. One can infer from Augustine's writing that Patricius went to hell while Monica went to heaven, both instantly.

Throughout his life, Augustine was prone to dualistic or polarized thinking. His greatest work, the *City of God*, is predicated on a fundamental division in human history.[4] This bifurcated thinking is particularly true of Augustine's early years. As he aged, he seems to have been more capable of nuance. The former Manichee and neo-Platonist could wax eloquent about the natural world, although he is a bit embarrassed when he does so. Still, the City of Man is inherently deficient, and we can free ourselves from its clutches only with death. This applies to the church as well. As priest and bishop, Augustine presided over a flawed institution, a "mixed bag" of Catholic believers. The pure and unblemished church, the City of God, lay in heaven, foreshadowed by its earthly analogue, but

---

4. Augustine, *City of God*, trans. Marcus Dos.

never coterminous with it. For Augustine there was a dialectical tension between realism and idealism, and this premise would become a central tenet of Western, Catholic thinking. For many it remains the case today.

The Personal and the Political

It is a cliché to link the personal with the political. Yet it is also valid. Augustine's reflections on his own life, pastoral practice, and approach to the Roman world were part of a continuous process. He understood life as a journey toward God that required rigorous personal honesty and a social system that allowed people to pursue this ultimate quest with as few impediments as possible. Augustine was realistic enough to discount the perfectibility of society, but he worked with the assumption that good citizens could create a modestly good society. He was an enthusiastic proponent of a "Christianized" empire, although he knew that any society would fall short of the mark. In his early years, however, Augustine displays marked confusion about himself, his role in society, and the goodness of the world around him. He alternately reveled in the world and wanted to leave it. The great symbol of this internal struggle is Augustine's understanding of sexuality and his oft-quoted aphorism, "Grant me chastity, but not too soon." He thoroughly enjoyed the pleasures and privileges of an upper-class Roman, yet he was always aware of the transitory nature of the world around him. With the help of Romanianus and others, he obtained teaching positions in Carthage, Rome, and Milan. He was admired at an early age and welcomed in elite circles. But success did not make him happy. He longed for solitude and the resolution of his inner conflicts. As his youthful self-assurance began to fray, Augustine started to come to terms with his mortality and the limitations of the Roman Empire whose culture and literature he so admired. As he puts it in the *Confessions* Augustine felt that he was "a mystery to myself."[5] The *City of God* concludes with the dour and dualistic assertion that human history, as opposed to God's history, is inherently flawed. We inhabit the world and work our salvation out within it, but it is ultimately deficient and incapable of answering our deepest questions about existence. The City of Man and the City of God are distinct realities, and confusing the two can only lead to tragedy. Eternal Rome fell because of the unrequited lust for glory that drove the Ciceros, Caesars, and Augustuses of history who were blinded by their relentless ambition. As Augustine points out time and again in the *City of God*, arguably the greatest and most influential of his works, great and noble Romans were often deluded.

---

5. *Confessions*, O'Donnell version, 4.4.0.

In the *Confessions* Augustine discusses his own personal delusions that would lead him to sin. Somewhat problematically, he would project his own failings on Roman society itself. He sees his lust and irrationality as emblematic of a deeper flaw or original sin that afflicts personal behavior and the course of human history. In the famous "Pear Tree Incident" Augustine and his rowdy, obnoxious friends strip a pear tree of its fruit and feed it to a herd of pigs.[6] A bit later on as a young student of rhetoric in Carthage Augustine is drawn to the theater with its artificial emotions and frequent erotic content. He sheds copious tears at the betrayals and misfortunes of classical heroes and heroines. His life is rudderless as he vainly attempts to find meaning in the here and now, missing the basic point about human existence whose meaning is found in God, not in the world. Yet history is the record of this deep-seated flaw wreaking havoc with individuals and the Roman world itself. In the *Confessions* his self-recrimination is relentless:

> At that time I was truly miserable, for I loved feelings and sought out whatever could cause me sadness. When the theme of a play dealt with other people's tragedies — false and theatrical tragedies — it would please and attract me more powerfully the more it moved me to tears. I was an unhappy beast astray from your flock and resentful of your shepherding, so what wonder was it that I became infected with foul mange?[7]

His irrepressible sexuality led to a marriage of convenience, more accurately, a type of socially acceptable "living together" that slaked his libido and produced his son, Adeodatus, who is described as "my son according to the flesh, born of my sin" (*Confessions*, O'Donnell version, 9.6.14). Augustine makes clear that he loved Adeodatus, but the sexual act that engendered him embarrassed and perplexed Augustine throughout his life. Fatherhood was an annoyance that only bogged Augustine down in his search for peace and ultimate meaning.

Augustine was asking questions posed centuries before by Paul, especially in his letter to the Romans. In essence, why do we sin in light of the fact that we really do not want to, and often know better? (This question, of course, is central to nearly every religious tradition and ethical system.) Augustine's angst about his behavior and humanity's in general was finally explained by innate depravity. Again, Augustine draws from Paul and particularly the letter to the Romans. Arguably, no theological construct has had a greater impact on Western culture and Christianity. Whether Augustine and his friends flinging pears at pigs are so perverse

---

6. Ibid., 2.7.15.
7. Ibid., 3.4.

is questionable. Augustine acted as a typical obnoxious adolescent. Likewise, his sexual behavior was normal, if not prosaic. Well-placed males were almost expected to fornicate. It was all a dry-run for a later marriage with a respectable young woman from one's own social class and the legitimate children she was expected to produce to maintain the family line. Augustine's self-revelation and semi-public flagellation are part of a heuristic pedagogy meant to help us come to grips with our sinfulness as we are forced to hear about his own. O'Donnell offers critical insight into Augustine's abominations:

> Then he discovers sex: book 2 is the book of the temptation of the flesh, and with it the primordial sin, the perplexing theft of fruit in the garden. A good biographer might worry about whether Augustine's adolescent sex life was much to speak of, and whether he and his friends really did steal those pears, but he would miss the point of the narrative. Augustine's strategy needs him to cave in to the hankerings of the flesh here, to lose the divine spirit and start down a bad slope.[8]

So the question for Augustine is how to reverse this downward slide before it destroys him and all of us. We need to make an obvious but crucial point. Augustine lived in a prescientific world. He knew nothing of biochemistry, hormones, and the psychology of human desire, and especially sexuality, as we understand these forces today. Hunger, sex, or any sort of craving was understood as a disorder of the will that could be suppressed with sufficient discipline, even in adolescence. Augustine is ashamed of his willfulness and his inability to control what he wills. His sinful behavior is both conscious and unconscious. As it were, he is hard-wired to do the wrong thing. The more Augustine sinned, the more desperate he became to control himself, failing miserably every time he did so. In the late fourth century, just as today, there was a vast array of philosophical and religious movements that claimed to have the answer to the human predicament and the means to eradicate the root cause of desire and our apparent compulsion to sin.

Augustine the Hearer

The student and soon to be teacher of rhetoric in Carthage first turned to the Manichees in order to better understand himself and control his seemingly uncontrollable emotions and physical drives. In their midst he found an explanation that soothed him for a number of years. The Manichees were a dualistic sect with certain Christian beliefs, although they were far from the

---

8. O'Donnell, *Augustine: A New Biography*, 67.

mainstream of Christian thought, particularly that of the Catholic community, where they were deemed a heretical aberration. Their founder was Mani (210–270 C.E.), a charismatic Mesopotamian religious thinker who borrowed from Zoroastrianism, Judaism, and Christianity, reinterpreting them while claiming to be a messenger of truth and divine revelation who surpassed them all. Along with Gnostic Christians, of whom there were many varieties in the Roman world, Mani believed there were two gods — one completely good and the other completely bad. The good god was immaterial and passive while the bad god had created the material world that he controlled with his malevolent will. Salvation was a question of becoming as otherworldly as possible. This entailed the most rigorous fasting and total abstinence from sex, at least for the "Elect" women and men capable of such rigors. The less strenuous were encouraged to emulate their betters to the extent possible. Fasts were less extreme and sex for the sake of procreation was accepted as a necessary evil, a concession to base desires and the need to replenish the human community. The Hearers like Augustine were expected to support the Elect financially so they could achieve perfection unencumbered with mundane considerations like money.

On some levels Augustine was not so different from the boorish, philandering father he held in such contempt. For many years Augustine lived in a common law marriage with a lower-class woman. He liked the community's intensity and marveled at the asceticism of the Elect. He felt comfortable in its midst and hoped its example would make it possible for him to renounce the pleasures, both emotional and physical, that he simultaneously relished and abhorred. Although loath to admit it, Augustine enjoyed domestic life and the warmth of a nameless woman who could never be his intellectual or social peer. Whoever she was, she did not interact with Augustine's male friends or participate in their heady intellectual discussions. She was certainly absent from any respectable social engagement. Furthermore, the Manichees helped Augustine deal with a major intellectual problem. Since his childhood in Thagaste, Augustine had been appalled by the apparent crudity of the Hebrew Bible. Did God really turn Lot's wife into a pillar of salt or sanction the Hebrews' slaughter of the Canaanites? As a rhetorician trained in classical literature and capable of refined public discourse, Augustine faced a problem even more acute. The Hebrew Bible struck him as incredulous and even repugnant. The explanation offered to Augustine by his Manichee hosts was attractive: the Hebrew Bible was to be rejected. It was nothing more than the workings of an evil god. Those who knew better could simply ignore the Hebrew Bible as so much rubbish. Brown is worth quoting at this point:

> Above all, as a serious and sensitive young man, Augustine could abandon the terrible father-figure of the Old Testament. The

Manichaean system studiously avoided the acute ambivalence that was later to be so important to the old Augustine's image of his God — Father, that is, who could be, at one and the same time, a source of tender generosity, and of punishment, vengeance and suffering. In Manichaeism, the stern Jehovah of the Jews was rejected as a malevolent demon; the Patriarchs, as dirty old men.[9]

Augustine's personal and intellectual problems appeared to be solved. Of course, the satisfaction was short-lived. Augustine the restless questioner began to detect inconsistencies in Manichee theology and would part company with his emaciated hosts.[10] The beginning of the end came with an encounter with a famous Manichee teacher called Faustus, who visited Carthage with much fanfare. Augustine eagerly awaited his arrival in order to clarify the vexing questions local Manichees could not answer. Faustus bobbed and weaved, much to Augustine's disappointment. "I must say, however, that when I raised these points for consideration and discussion he refused courteously enough, reluctant to risk taking on that burden; for he knew that he did not know these matters, and was not ashamed to admit it."[11] Had Faustus answered Augustine's questions to his satisfaction he may well have spent the rest of his life as a Manichee, joining the ranks of the Elect. But Faustus's failure and superficiality were unacceptable to a genius of Augustine's stature. His departure from this sect, which he excoriates in the *Confessions*, was inevitable although not immediate. He continued to have contact with the Manichee community in Rome after his departure from Carthage around 383 C.E. Whether Augustine totally excised Manichees thinking from his mind, however, is a topic of unending debate. He rejected their dualistic notion about good and bad gods, but he remained a practitioner of psychological and theological dualism that he never managed entirely to leave behind.

Augustine the Neo-Platonist

To continue with our artificial but hopefully useful chronological division of Augustine's quest for truth, we need to move from Carthage, to Rome, and ultimately to Milan, roughly from 370 to 385 C.E. In these fifteen years Augustine will become a recognized "scholar and gentleman," achieving recognition as an intellectual and success in the imperial bureaucracy and court. His own abilities made this possible without the ongoing support of Romanianus, who was frequently in Rome and Milan involved in incessant litigation. He spent considerable time and money in

9. Brown, *Augustine of Hippo*, 49–50.
10. Ibid., 44–46.
11. *Confessions*, O'Donnell version, 5.7.12.

the imperial courts fighting his opponents back in North Africa, appealing judicial decisions, and most likely greasing the palms of court officials and magistrates in what was a notoriously corrupt and slow legal system. Romanianus had connections and did not hesitate to mention the name of his grateful client Augustine, who soon left Rome for Milan, where he taught and enjoyed a high-level appointment as a rhetorician in the emperor's service. He was charged with writing and declaiming florid speeches about the glory of Rome and the wisdom of the emperor, even if he knew better. Although a professional success, Augustine was an existential mess. This was a period of great personal turmoil and pain. The teacher of rhetoric and recognized writer could not achieve inner peace. A passage from the *Confessions* is poignant:

> I recall how miserable I was, and how one day you brought me to a realization of my miserable state. I was preparing to deliver a eulogy upon the emperor in which I would tell plenty of lies with the object of winning favor with the well-informed by my lying; so my heart was panting with anxiety and seething with feverish, corrupt thoughts. As I passed through a certain district in Milan I noticed a poor beggar, drunk, as I believe, and making merry. I groaned and pointed out to the friends who were with me how many hardships our idiotic enterprises entailed. Goaded by greed, I was dragging my load of unhappiness along, and feeling it all the heavier for being dragged.[12]

The unhappy professional is frustrated on an intellectual and personal level. He feels corrupted by a propagandistic lie that he was paid to propagate. The Manichees had failed him, and in his desperation he looked for another solution. He found it in neo-Platonism, a philosophical movement that was all the rage among educated Romans in the fourth and fifth centuries. In this philosophical movement, with its roots in Plato along with an emphasis on a mystical encounter with the divine, Augustine found answers to his ongoing questions about human existence, good and evil, and the nature of God. Although Augustine ultimately rejected the non-Christian form of neo-Platonism, he eventually encountered Ambrose, the bishop of Milan, who had recast neo-Platonism, making it a foundational component of Christian thought and a central part of Augustine's self-understanding and theological system. The transition to Christian neo-Platonism, however, was not immediate, and Augustine was adrift and in agony for the better part of a decade. The journey from Carthage to Milan is more than a geographical phenomenon. It is also a metaphor for Augustine's existential and religious evolution. In the next

---

12. Ibid., 6.9.

paragraphs we will examine this school of thought that had a lifelong influence on Augustine.

Throughout this tumultuous period Monica played an enormous role in Augustine's life. In the *Confessions* Augustine flees Carthage in the middle of the night bound for Rome. He leaves behind his shocked mother, Monica. The wayward son "left by stealth; she did not, but remained behind weeping and praying."[13] A few years later Monica joyfully arrived in Milan. Assuming her role as mother and matriarch she would oversee Augustine's domestic life. He would chafe at Monica's dismissal of his female companion and question the wisdom of a contractual marriage to an upper-class young woman, but his mother won the day. Monica the matriarch monitored Augustine's journey from precocious childhood to licentious adolescence to confused early adulthood to midlife conversion to Catholicism. He admits to loving his common law wife but is embarrassed to admit it. He hopes eventually to fall in love with his promised wife, although he had never met her. To our sensibilities this is shocking, but it was a common arrangement among upper-class Romans for whom marriage was seen as more of a strategic alliance than a matter of romance. On a personal level Augustine longed for warmth, but it eluded him. As a neo-Platonist and eventually a Catholic bishop, he perceived women as ephemeral, irrational, and seductresses. The marriage, of course, would never happen. As we shortly will see, Augustine's "conversion experience" in Milan finally helped him control his libido and live a totally celibate life. In his thinking, none of this was accidental. It was part of God's plan. "In the light of that design of yours you laughed at our plans while preparing your own, for you meant to give us food in due time; you were to open your hand and fill our souls with blessing."[14] That blessing did not include women or the marriage bed. In fact, Augustine saw them as an impediment to a full intellectual life and true sanctity. In what can only be described as one of Augustine's more bizarre reflections, he suggests that Adam and Eve had sexual intercourse in the Garden of Eden, but did so without a trace of "foul lust."[15] Adam achieved an erection by willing it, not because of sexual desire.[16] Augustine was hardly alone in this strange, anti-sexual ideation. A virulent strain of misogyny had taken root in Christianity, fomented by the so-called Fathers of the early church almost all of whom were celibates, monks, or widowers. By the second century of the Christian era, women were second-class citizens in the church, a problem that lingers to this day.

---

13. Ibid., 5.9.15.
14. Ibid., 6.14.24.
15. Wills, *Saint Augustine*, xvii.
16. Augustine, *City of God*, 14:26.

After finishing his studies in Carthage Augustine, the new professor of rhetoric, began his teaching career. For roughly eleven years he instructed the sons of Rome's privileged families.[17] He did his utmost to help them appreciate the glories of Latin as Cicero and Virgil wrote it. He relished their refined prose and poetry, which struck him as the greatest literary achievement. Augustine also saw the Roman Empire as a great historical achievement, a message that he communicated to his spoiled and ungrateful students. All too often they let Augustine down, be it in Carthage, Rome, or Milan. Furthermore, he often had a difficult time making them pay his fees. The gap between the ideal and the real vexed Augustine the teacher just as it would later annoy him as a priest and bishop back in North Africa.

In his quest for perfection, and probably respite from his students, Augustine turned to the writings of the neo-Platonists. In very condensed terms, neo-Platonism was an attempt to bring Plato's thought up to date. Grounded in Plato's distinction between the real and ideal, it added a certain note of optimism about human beings' potential for experiencing something of the divine in this life. Presuming great discipline, study, and prayer, a few gifted men and an even smaller number of women would be fused with the divine after death. Its most noted spokespersons were Plotinus (d. 270 C.E.), and Porphyry (d. 305 C.E.) who reworked Plato's thought from five centuries before. Porphyry tried to explain Plotinus's convoluted thought in a dense but influential work known as *The Enneads*,[18] which was all the rage among fourth-century intellectuals. The text is full of complex intellectual allusions predicated on a psychology and even cosmology that only the most patient scholars understand today. Using Latin translations of Porphyry's writings, Augustine found the neo-Platonic explanation of good and evil convincing. It helped him solve one of the great dilemmas he had struggled with over the years. This required some mental gymnastics since Porphyry was an avowed anti-Christian. He had no problem with Jesus, but saw Christianity as a low-class religion for dupes manipulated by charlatans. His argument is not much different from that of Celsus two centuries before. But Augustine was wowed by Porphyry's intellect and managed to put this great philosopher's biases in perspective. Non-Christian neo-Platonists simply did not understand the real nature of Christianity, which was capable of even greater intellectual sophistication because it was informed by divine revelation.

Neo-Platonism was unabashedly elitist, which is why its audience was restricted to the Greek- and Latin-speaking intelligentsia in the major

---

17. O'Donnell, *Augustine: A New Biography*, xii.

18. Augustine never learned to read or speak Greek. Those who tried to teach him did so with such brutality that he rebelled and seems to have refused to have learned the language, although he was more than capable of doing so.

cities of the Roman Empire, a small circle of men among whom Augustine was soon numbered. Women, of course, were excluded except in the rarest of cases when a woman displayed masculine intellectual qualities. Porphyry and his devotees believed in an entirely immaterial and perfect god who was symbolized by the purest light. This majestic deity had no form or emotions. It was entirely "other," yet the foundation of everything, material and immaterial. This "god" was beyond human comprehension, an unfathomable mystery. Nonetheless, a privileged few gifted with extraordinary mental abilities and willing to lead the most ascetic and focused lives could at least achieve a limited sense of this utterly distinct deity through mystical ecstasy. Although hobbled by physical bodies and human emotions, the elite of the elite could extrapolate certain characteristics or qualities of this ineffable deity, provided that they recognized the limitations of their insights and conceded the futility of any definitive knowledge. Because the human mind is an emanation of the divine mind, it is possible to make inferences, but nothing more. What is evil in the neo-Platonic scheme of things? It is the negation of the good, a decision born of stupidity and sinful willfulness that causes us to reject primordial goodness. By our own choice we refuse to admit the real nature of reality. We wallow in our bodies and surrounding material world. We substitute the here and now for "eternal truths that transcend the visible, material world." We are the source of our own suffering and pain.

Augustine finally found his long-sought answers. He could leave behind the two gods of the Manichees once and for all. He stopped going to their meetings, which he attended when he was in Rome. He could now explain his own sinful behavior and unrelenting misery. He and he alone was the enemy. Augustine realized that he was ignorant, sinful, and living a sort of moral death. Recognizing his embarrassing, self-degrading choices in life was the required first step in the process of redemption and salvation.[19] When Augustine was still a smug brat throwing pears to pigs in Thagaste, Latin-speaking Christian scholars were recasting the writings of Porphyry in ways that made neo-Platonism a pillar of Christian theological discourse.

There is no greater figure in the reappropriation of neo-Platonism than Ambrose, the bishop of Milan who would baptize Augustine in 387 C.E. A highly educated aristocrat and powerful political figure, he went to great lengths to "Christianize" a philosophical and religious tradition that otherwise saw the incarnation and resurrection of Jesus as an impossible and even ludicrous assertion. God's materialization in Jesus, his bodily resurrection, and that of redeemed Christians was construed as too stupid for consideration. Without denying the ultimate immateriality of God,

---

19. See *Confessions*, O'Donnell version, 7.913–23.

Ambrose and his confreres nonetheless saw the body and material world as vehicles that help us grasp the ultimate, immaterial reality of God. There was no greater example than Jesus' incarnation that perfectly melded the immaterial with the material. As the Gospel of John bluntly states, Jesus is God's word made flesh, the very essence of divine rationality whose person and meaning are indispensable for salvation. Christian life, therefore, was seen as an *iter*, a journey from irrationality to true rationality, mortality to immortality in which we become what we really are meant to be, saints eternally worshiping an all-good and loving God. Ambrose, who used allegorical exegesis to read scripture "correctly," became Augustine's hero. The tactile Jesus of the Gospel of Mark, who uses saliva to heal and curses a fig tree, can be approached allegorically. Jesus' actions are not actual but metaphorical. The Gospel of John, however, requires few exegetical gymnastics since it is already dualistic and otherworldly. Christian neo-Platonism hit Augustine like a thunderbolt. It gave him hope and a reason to finally get his body under control, not to mention getting his body and mind ready for baptism as a Catholic.

Augustine the Believer

In Book VII of the *Confessions* Augustine provides a lengthy story of his conversion to Catholic Christianity. The text is a classic description of a sinner "seeing the light" or being "born again." It is analogous to Paul's conversion in Acts and his reflection on discovering Christian truth in Galatians and Romans. Augustine, like every Christian theologian of stature, was fascinated by Paul and knew his thinking from the inside out. Paul and Augustine's conversion experiences became paradigmatic. Francis of Assisi, Ignatius of Loyola, and countless other Christian saints went through analogous experiences leaving behind dissolute lives, suffering from anxiety and depression, and ultimately finding solace in the mystery of God. The concept of conversion, however, is often misunderstood as something precipitous and unanticipated. It never is. There are always predisposing factors, psychological and religious, that lead to the moment of insight and surrender. The lights are not turned on all of a sudden but gradually, achieving full luminescence that makes possible the great "ah ha" that brings to an end a convoluted journey. A century ago, another genius, William James, described conversion in the first lecture of *The Varieties of Religious Experience*. The language he uses is old-fashioned and stilted by today's standards, but his insights nevertheless apply perfectly to Augustine.

> There can be no doubt that as a matter of fact a religious life, exclusively pursued, does tend to make the person exceptional and

eccentric. I speak not now of your ordinary religious believer, who follows the conventional observances of his country. . . . We must make search rather for the religious experiences which were the pattern-setters to all this mass of suggested feeling and imitated conduct. These experiences we can only find in individuals for whom religion exists not as a dull habit, but as an acute fever rather. But such individuals are "geniuses" in the religious line; and like many other geniuses who have brought forth fruits effective enough for commemoration in the pages of biography, such religious geniuses have often shown symptoms of nervous instability.[20]

Augustine was certainly in the throes of "nervous instability" and had been for some time. By 387 C.E. he was at his wit's end. He had two choices: psychological dissolution or resolution.

> Within the house of my spirit the violent conflict raged on, the quarrel with my soul that I had so powerfully provoked in our secret dwelling, my heart, and at the height of it I rushed to Alypius (a close friend) with my mental anguish plain upon my face. "What is happening to us?" I exclaimed. "What does this mean? What did you make of it? The untaught are rising up and taking heaven by storm, while we with all our dreary teachings are still groveling in the world of flesh and blood!"[21]

The crisis will be resolved very shortly in a nearby garden while Augustine sits under a tree. The accomplished rhetorician and social climber will be taken aback by the voice of a child telling him to pick up a copy of the New Testament that he has brought with him. Is this a child's voice or some message from God joyfully and playfully exclaimed? Miraculously, he opens it to Paul's letter to the Romans, where he encounters a passage that will change his life: "Let us cast off the works of darkness and put on the armor of light; let us conduct ourselves becomingly as in the day, not in reveling and drunkenness, not in debauchery and licentiousness, not in quarrelling and jealousy. But put on the Lord Jesus Christ, and make no provision for the flesh, to gratify its desires" (Rom. 13:12–14).

Augustine describes the resolution of his existential pain with incredible flourish, as if he were blinded by a vision like Paul on his way to Damascus when he was knocked to the ground and confronted by the voice of Jesus. In reality, Augustine's "revelation" had been coalescing for some time. He had already come to accept the truths of Catholicism, but needed a definitive push to accept them, which is precisely what happened in the garden, the inverse of what happened in Eden. The rebellious

---

20. James, *The Varieties of Religious Experience*, 24–25.
21. *Confessions*, O'Donnell version, 8.8.9.

child who rejected his mother's Catholicism had come full circle, much to Monica's delight. "We went indoors and told my mother, who was over-joyed. When we related to her how it had happened she was filled with triumphant delight." Monica's joy was "far more abundant than she had desired, and much more tender and chaste than she could ever have looked to find in grandchildren from my flesh."[22] Augustine's human struggles were not over, but finally he knew *how* to struggle. Since his adolescence in Thagaste he had been like a cork in a stormy sea. Finally he had found his bearings and could start swimming to shore.

The Philosopher Priest

Augustine's conversion in 386 C.E. did not lead to immediate baptism. As was the practice in his day, he would wait until Easter, in the meanwhile ruminating on the profound neo-Platonic insights of Ambrose, the bishop of Milan whom both Monica and Augustine admired with great fervor. Ambrose's eloquence had won Augustine over to Catholicism, and his allegorical approach to scripture had relieved Augustine of a great intel-lectual burden. Having given up his common law wife and position in the imperial court, Augustine took refuge in the villa of a friend and patron located in Cassiciacum. He began to recover from the turmoil of his long search for meaning and truth, enjoying the leisure and intellectual indul-gence of *otium*, a word that Brown renders as a sort of cultured leisure reserved for upper-class intellectuals.[23] There was nothing particularly rig-orous or monastic about this short period in Augustine's life. All knew the asceticism of Anthony of the Desert, whose life as an Egyptian monk was made famous by his contemporary, Athanasius of Alexandria. Anthony was an extremist, a "Christian athlete" who longed to pray unceasingly and martyr himself with fasting since official martyrdom was no longer possible. Anthony was illiterate, intensely anti-intellectual, and from the lower strata of society. No doubt Augustine admired his sanctity, but he could not have been more removed from the scruffy life of a cave-dwelling hermit.

Augustine and his companions in Cassiciacum were abstemious, but abhorred any form of fanaticism since it was nearly a synonym for irrationality. Good conversation with a reasonable amount of wine did not offend their Christian sensibilities. Augustine spent half of his day studying and conversing with friends, and the other half instructing Adeo-datus and younger male students. Monica managed the household in a predictably controlling and possessive way. Her son was delighted with

22. Ibid., 30.
23. Brown, *Augustine of Hippo*, 115–17.

this comfortable arrangement. O'Donnell provides a wry description of life in Cassiciacum: "Very little changed, apart from Augustine's sleeping arrangements and the venue of his quite ordinary resuscitation."[24] Augustine read and reread classical texts, non-Christian and Christian alike. He thought about and lectured on topics as diverse as mathematics and music. He also mulled over the ideas of Ambrose, whose allegorical approach to scripture was enormously useful for Augustine's reappropriation of the Bible and acceptance of Catholic orthodoxy. The account in Genesis of God walking in the Garden of Eden seeking cool, fresh air was not a fact as much as a metaphor or symbol. Christian neo-Platonists knew that God did not have a body. The enlightened Christian knew how to read the text more deeply, which is the one and only way it was meant to be read.

Following his experience under the tree in Milan the thirty-two-year-old Augustine was relieved of the burdens of daily and courtly life. When his female companion of many years was sent back to Carthage and his pending marriage canceled, Augustine could finally pursue his search for truth unencumbered by the burdens of making a living or using his time and energy on a spouse and children. By contemporary standards his words are shocking. "How sordid, filthy, and horrible a woman's embraces seemed to you (himself), when we were discussing the desire for a wife. But that very night, when you lay awake, turning it over in your mind — it was different from what you supposed.... But do not cry! Take heart: you have already cried so much; it has only added to the illness in your chest."[25] These are the words of an elitist, sexist member of the Roman aristocracy. But it is important to keep in mind that they were commonplace in antiquity. The well-to-do longed to retire to their villas enjoying the glory of military triumphs and wealth accumulated by their vast landholdings and multitude of slaves. Augustine and his contemporaries worked with the notion that there was a God-given hierarchy responsible for the shape of human society. The bright and powerful were meant to rule; the rest of humankind was meant to be ruled. Any other arrangement was a recipe for anarchy and sin, a violation of God's design for the human race. Better a bad emperor than mob rule. Augustine saw the political and social world around him as riddled by sin, but it was to be endured rather than overthrown. Our modern concept of participatory democracy would have never occurred to Augustine. In fact, it was antithetical to everything he believed.

Baptized and now a new person, Augustine and his entourage set out for Carthage and eventually Thagaste. While preparing in Ostia for the

---

24. O'Donnell, *Augustine: A New Biography*, 61.
25. *Soliloquies* I, xii, 21. Quoted in Brown, *Augustine of Hippo*, 118.

grueling and always dangerous trip across the Mediterranean, Augustine had the most intense conversation of his life with Monica.

> But because the day when she was to quit this life was drawing near — a day known to you, though we were ignorant of it — she and I happened to be alone, through the mysterious workings of your will, as I believe. . . . Forgetting what lay in the past, and stretching out to what was ahead, we inquired between ourselves in the light of the present truth, the Truth which is yourself, what the eternal life of the saints would be like. . . . Our colloquy led us to the point where the pleasure of the body's senses, however intense and in however brilliant a material light enjoyed, seemed unworthy not merely of comparison but even of remembrance beside the joy of that life.[26]

Monica's death happened quickly; within slightly more than a week she had gone from health to the grave. Augustine was in intense pain and disoriented. For reasons that eluded him, he could not cry, even at his mother's burial. "No, not even during those prayers did I weep, but all day long I was secretly weighed down by sorrow, and in my mental turmoil I begged you as best I could to heal my hurt."[27] It will require time for Augustine to sweat out the "bitter sorrow" in his heart. He enters into a period of pitiless self-recrimination that leads to near paralysis and requires that he postpone his departure for North Africa for many months. Augustine would find a measure of consolation in the liturgical poetry of Ambrose that speaks of "the release from pain" symbolized in Christ's resurrection. In short order Adeodatus died. Augustine claims to have loved his son but likewise dismisses his death as one more burden he had to bear. Arriving back in Thagaste, Augustine enjoyed respite from the world when he returned to North Africa. He lived as a lay *Servus Dei* dedicated to prayer and meditation. His brother managed the family estate and the income allowed Augustine to set up a community very similar to that of Cassiciacum. This tranquil period of his life, however, was equally short-lived. Unlike the Jesus portrayed in the Gospel of John who is "not of this world" (18:36), Augustine would quickly find himself deeply enmeshed in it once again, like it or not.

Hippo

In 388 or 389 C.E. Augustine left Thagaste for Hippo, a Mediterranean port a few days away, where he intended to recruit an old friend as a member of his elite Christian community. This was one of the most

---

26. *Confessions*, O'Donnell version, 9.10.23–24.
27. Ibid., 9.32.

fateful decisions of his life. As a courtesy Augustine presented himself to Valerius, the good but somewhat wily bishop of the local Catholic community. The Greek-speaking Valerius with limited Latin met the Latin-speaking Augustine with limited Greek. Language aside, they soon ended up both liking each other and working together. The gifted rhetorician was named a priest by proclamation of the local Catholic community, much to Valerius's delight and Augustine's protests of inadequacy and unworthiness. Most likely, Valerius had planned things well in advance, anticipating Augustine's arrival with a sort of glee. Augustine was a commodity in the Catholic world. His intellectual reputation had been well established. His conversion was the talk of Roman drawing rooms. His writings circulated in North Africa and Italy, and even those who disliked him, and several prominent Christians and non-Christians did, nonetheless recognized his genius. The crafty Valerius could not read Augustine's treatises very well, but he definitely knew that a "prize" had come into town. When Augustine entered the church in Hippo Valerius was celebrating the Eucharist. He welcomed the newly arrived stranger with special warmth, and soon a cry arose from the assembled community. The congregation wanted Augustine to be its priest, like it or not. Valerius had set his trap perfectly. Augustine claims to have been taken totally off guard as well as intimidated by the enthusiasm of the people, yet felt that it would be sinful to resist the urging of the Holy Spirit. Within five years he would be the bishop of Hippo. Valerius undoubtedly went to his grave a happy man.

This sudden turn of events requires explanation. Since Augustine was not interested in being either a priest or a bishop, how did he become one? In the ancient church, Greek and Latin, members of the clergy were appointed by acclamation. When a vacancy arose, the community would assemble to discuss how it could be filled. Then a seeming miracle would occur. A candidate would be spontaneously proclaimed to the delight of all present. Often his name would be rhythmically repeated, and almost invariably he would accept. This had happened to Ambrose in Milan a few years before. A small child put his name into "nomination" and the congregation took it from there. Still a catechumen, he was baptized, ordained deacon, priest, and bishop in the course of a few days and then presided over the Catholic community of Milan for the rest of his eventful life. Although he was already baptized, Augustine's experience nonetheless paralleled that of his intellectual mentor and revered pastor. Why would Ambrose, Augustine, or others acquiesce to such an unanticipated and radical demand? The answer lies in a Latin maxim: *Vox Dei vox populi* — "The Voice of God is the Voice of the People." For most of us today, this is a tricky proposition, given the twists and turns of Christian history. We automatically think of hidden agendas and manipulation. In antiquity, however, there probably was less skepticism about such a seeming miracle. Ambrose and Augustine staunchly believed that the Holy Spirit was present in the Christian community and an active force that shaped the course of history. Responding to God's call was everyone's Christian duty, just as refusing it was a sin. If this required profound personal change and even coming down the social ladder a rung or two, so be it. Ambrose was a wealthy man from one of the most prestigious families in the empire. He had every possibility of becoming emperor and knew it. Augustine could easily have become a Roman governor if he played his political cards correctly. Certainly, Ambrose and Augustine were chosen because they were capable and presumably holy men. They also had connections not to be scoffed at. The Holy Spirit did not seem to have a problem with the patron/client system.

Another significant factor in the selection of clergy was the fragmentation of the church and who could best address internal tensions. Priests and bishops with theological skills and political savvy were expected to champion the causes of one form of Christianity as opposed to another. The divisions were serious and the stakes high. Winners could expect imperial support, which entailed money, prestige, and recognition in the court. By Augustine's time, emperors made a point of being surrounded by bishops and, of course, vice versa. Those who lost these ecclesiastical and theological games of hardball could anticipate exile, imprisonment, and even execution. Arians, Donatists (whose ideas we will examine shortly), some Gnostics, certain neo-Platonists, and even Manichees considered themselves Christian, and some felt they had a right to call themselves Catholic. "Catholicism" encompassed a spectrum of views and definitions of orthodoxy that were hotly contested. To use a slightly odd phrase, it might be more accurate to talk about "catholicisms." Or in more down-to-earth language, one person's orthodoxy is another person's heresy. But, obviously, the debate was as much about the church's power and social role as it was about theological niceties. Having an articulate, dedicated bishop willing to define and defend Catholic orthodoxy in terms of apostolic succession and the creed formulated at the Council of Nicea in 325 C.E. was crucial for winning in this high-stakes game of theological poker. Ambrose and Augustine definitely were staunch defenders of Nicean orthodoxy and would brook no dissent. The church's understanding of God, Jesus, and the Christian community set forth in 325 and 381/382 at Nicea and Constantinople were clear and nonnegotiable. Ambrose and Augustine were theological street fighters who would not hesitate to savage their opponents even if they claimed to be fellow Christians. Neither ever turned down a good theological brawl, especially Augustine.

Sin in Hippo

Augustine's ordination to the priesthood in 390 C.E. and the episcopacy in 395 C.E. meant the end of his life as a brilliant lay theologian from the leisured class of Roman society. The *otium liberale,* or cultured leisure, of Cassiciacum became a distant memory as the new priest and bishop was thrown into the thick of local squabbles, ecclesiastical and theological entanglements, and the frequent blank stares of his parishioners as he expounded on a passage of scripture, sometimes for hours. With the exception of periodic trips to Carthage and a few neighboring towns, he would have to content himself with life in Hippo. A port city on the Mediterranean, it had a few charms, as Brown points out:

> The town had been a *civitas romana,* a "city of Roman citizens," for two hundred years. Roman life had been established on a magnificent scale: There was a theatre to seat some five to six thousand, a great public bath, a classical temple crowning the hill on the site of an ancient sanctuary.... The values of a Roman pagan city, that Augustine would attack in his *City of God,* would have met his eye, frozen in stone, in hundreds of inscriptions.[28]

Hippo was no different than any ancient town or a modern one for that matter. It had more vice than virtue. Its economic elites were crass money-makers firmly ensconced in a society in which money and prestige were all-important considerations. Most people were ostensibly Christian, most Donatist and fewer Catholic. The Donatist movement had originated in the first quarter of the fourth century. Convinced that clergy who had succumbed to intimidation and torture during the persecution of Diocletian from 303 to 305 were apostates, they refused to have anything to do with them, especially any of the sacraments they performed. In fact, they felt that they had ceased to be deacons, priests, and bishops, and the rituals they performed were invalid and blasphemous. Rather than be defiled by any sort of compromise with lesser Christians, they set up their own parallel church. Augustine was one bishop and across the street was another with his own Donatist congregation. The Catholic and the Donatists literally were in shouting distance of each other, and they often were shouting. Both claimed to be Catholic, much like Catholics and Protestants today claim to be Christian. Both being fundamentalists, however, they refused to see even a glimmer of truth in their rival's position. In all likelihood, the local gentry were not particularly interested in abstract theological debates, just as many modern Christians are not particularly interested in or aware of what makes a Catholic different from a Lutheran.

---

28. Brown, *Augustine of Hippo,* 189.

They simply wanted their world left intact with their privileges respected. The church was supposed to be an institution that sanctified the status quo rather than challenge it. Priests and bishops were expected to distribute charity to the lower classes but not question why they existed. No doubt some of Augustine's flock saw him as a pushy priest and bishop who took himself too seriously. His polished Latin and upper-class mannerisms set him apart. The Donatists relished ridiculing Augustine as an opportunist and snob, and they were not entirely off the mark. Augustine matched them insult for insult. He soon concluded that the Donatists were thick-headed louts.

The Donatists were Augustine's nemesis throughout his tenure as a bishop in Hippo. No amount of argument, debate, or even threats could intimidate them. They were textbook moral dualists who lived in a world of obvious right and wrong blithely unaware of ambiguity. Augustine was something of a dualist himself, but he was far too sophisticated to deny that ambiguity was an inherent part of life and, in some ways, actually good. The Donatists insisted on a pure and perfect church and a black and white theology. Any equivocation was a sin and that made Augustine a sinner. Donatist bakers refused to sell bread to their Catholic neighbors.[29] Despite his awareness of sin that bordered on the obsessive, Augustine was aware of human fragility and the need for forgiveness. Had his tumultuous experience not borne this out? Which God was real — the thunderous judge or the compassionate father? Augustine came down on the side of the latter, although he certainly believed in a demanding God, merciful but likewise just. The dilemma revolved around a classic tension that besets every religious institution — where to draw the line between exclusion and inclusion. Augustine saw the catholic church as an *ecclesia permixta* — a hodgepodge of good and bad, bright and dim, committed and lackadaisical people. The Donatists believed more in the Jesus of Matthew 28: the judge of the living and the dead. Augustine did too, but he was also aware of Matthew 13, in which Jesus speaks of wheat and tares. Perfection was impossible in Hippo, and precisely for this reason Augustine refused to accept the Donatist notion of Catholicism. He would ultimately condemn these self-proclaimed saints as obdurate sinners. His invective is meant to sting. "The clouds above proclaim that the Church is rising everywhere in the world, while these frogs grunt from their little pond: 'Christians? None but us.' "[30]

This evolution in Augustine's thought would have an enormous impact on Catholicism and the social order that persists to this day. For Augustine and those who followed in his footsteps, refusing to conform to the truth of

---

29. Wills, *Saint Augustine,* 78.
30. Augustine, *Explaining the Psalms,* 95.11. Quoted in Wills, *Saint Augustine,* 78.

orthodoxy was nothing less than a disease that threatened the health of the church and civil society. Theological "deviancy" was rooted in arrogance and a powerful predisposition to sin. Augustine felt that the good had to be recognized and accepted as true, but he also felt that erroneous ideas were a cancer that had to be removed using all means available. This is obviously a slippery slope, and Augustine has often been used to legitimate the most un-Christians forms of violence.

Augustine is sometimes credited with the "invention" of original sin as a central theological notion in Western Christianity. In fact, the concept was set forth in the writings of Paul. In Romans 7 he speculates about the relationship between sin, law, and God's grace. How is it that Paul is at war with himself? He wants to resist temptation and sin, but is powerless. Only God's grace is able to free him from his own tormented self. Augustine surely resonated with Paul's thinking as early as his adolescence. He would expand on this notion of inherent or original sin in both an erudite and obsessive fashion as a philosopher, priest, and bishop, coming precariously close at times to denying free will. Augustine, like Paul, was a firm believer in human depravity and the sole remedy for its ravages — the grace of God. In lofty theological treatises, Sunday sermons, and personal introspection, Augustine was forever wrestling with questions of good and evil and, as it were, balancing them on a scale while hoping that God's grace would tip the balance and make the truth self-evident. Looking at his own struggles, Augustine was acutely aware of his inherent flaws and cognizant that only by the grace of God was he able to overcome them.

For centuries a debate has raged as to whether Augustine saw himself and all human beings as so depraved as to be incapable of affirming the good, and therefore God. Yet Augustine does not go so far as to deny human agency in terms of recognizing and responding to God's grace. Frankly, his thinking is sometimes confusing and murky. Pessimism and optimism seized him at various moments in his life. In old age, he simply pleaded for God's mercy, hoping in the possibility of salvation. The arrogant self-righteousness of the Donatists offended Augustine's most deep-seated ideas about the precariousness of human nature and the sovereignty of its creator. Donatists were convinced that their purity and rigid performance of rituals by faultless clergy guaranteed salvation. Augustine was not so sanguine. As he says in myriad ways, God is an utter mystery and only fools think they can force God's hand and smugly assume eternity in heaven. In the sixth chapter of the *Confessions* Augustine is explicit about his love of God but equally adamant that God is always elusive and unknowable. Claims to have definitive insight into God's being enraged him. In the final years of his life Augustine would lock horns with someone who thought that human beings were born sinless and could achieve salvation by their own merits. This upstart theologian vehemently denied Augustine's doctrine of original sin. His name was Pelagius. A Catholic Christian from Britain, Pelagius assumed that we were born in a state of innocence and need only respond to our innate goodness to be saved through asceticism and rigid adherence to his version of orthodoxy. Augustine was outraged, and perhaps rightly so. Did asceticism guarantee truthfulness? Could it not be a form of arrogant self-deception? What right did Pelagius have to create a church of elite Christians who were somehow superior to the rest of the Catholic community? Augustine would attack Pelagius with every ounce of his energy, his fury surpassing anything he ever directed at the Donatists. He turned Pelagius into the greatest heresiarch of fifth-century Christianity. Who the "real" Pelagius was is another question. We are forced to rely almost exclusively on Augustine's furious description.

Sin, the World, and History

Simply put, Augustine did not drift into a quiet and pleasant old age. In antiquity, the "Golden Years" did not exist. Augustine would have been baffled by such a modern concept and almost certainly would have rejected it as a childish evasion of adult behavior and inevitable death. Until he died in 430 C.E. he remained an active bishop watching his flock with a wary eye. Augustine was terrified about his own salvation and that of those he was charged with pasturing. As an old man he still hurled fire and brimstone at his flock; some listened while others fell asleep. Outside of church services his small flock was not terribly different from the other inhabitants of Hippo. Concerned with the here and now, they would occasionally cheat and lie. Much to Augustine's consternation, they practiced pre-Christian rituals. Every year they went to surrounding cemeteries with libations for the dead and became uproariously drunk. Even Monica had done so. His parishioners were not nearly as obsessed with sin and eternity as their pastor, and many had no compunction about participating in Donatist services. In all likelihood they were unaware of the theological differences between themselves and their neighbors. The Donatists were suppressed by imperial decree and Augustine had readily penned the letter to the imperial court. Antipathy had evolved into mutual disgust and hatred. Augustine made sure that his definition of orthodoxy prevailed. He alone was the rightful bishop, and he alone had the right to interpret scripture and define Catholic belief. Augustine believed in a sort of episcopal despotism that resembled his God, a blend of loving- kindness and unmitigated justice. The Donatists "converted" to Catholic orthodoxy in order to avoid fines, imprisonment, torture, and death. In reality the movement simply went underground, resurfacing with predictable regularity until Arab armies conquered North Africa two centuries later, wiping out all forms of Christianity. Augustine felt that church and state were obliged to impose right belief as well as good social order. He did not hesitate to use his many friends in the imperial service to influence the emperor and crush theological deviancy. No doubt Augustine thought he was doing the wayward a favor. He was certain that there was no salvation outside of the Catholic Church, and as a bishop he was entitled to define it. "Tough love" might result in violence, but in Augustine's mind it was far better than eternity in hell. Today we find such ideas abhorrent, as we should. Augustine, however, firmly believed that error had no rights, and tolerating it was one of the greatest errors.

In the same fateful year of 410 C.E., when Pelagius launched his first attack against the bishop of Hippo, Augustine and nearly everyone in the Roman Empire experienced a fearsome shock. Rome fell to Alaric and his semi-civilized Goths, who had served as mercenaries in the Roman legions. Following the ancient customs of war, they sacked the city for days, pillaging everything and raping women, especially those from the aristocracy. Such events were not supposed to happen to Eternal Rome. How could God allow such horrors? Jerome, one of Augustine's correspondents and a famous biblical scholar, put it this way: "I was so distressed that it was like the old proverb: I didn't even know my own name."[31] Many of the elite of Roman society fled to the closest safe province, Roman North Africa. Accustomed to the ways of "refined" society that he once so much admired in Carthage, Rome, and Milan, Augustine enjoyed their company and would recruit them in his campaigns against the Donatists and Pelagius while they waited for things to settle down in Rome. Together they ruminated on recent events, trying to make sense of why everything had gone so dreadfully wrong in August 410. Augustine was not so concerned about why Rome fell because in his thinking its demise was inevitable like that of every empire. Still, he wanted to respond to the cultured critics of Christianity whos felt that Rome fell because it had abandoned its old gods.

As part of a far more extensive explanation of history, Augustine attempted to answer their questions about Rome and go far beyond them. He wrote a massive book for them that has had a truly profound impact in the Western Christian world. Augustine's *City of God* is a masterpiece of political and religious thinking. Augustine referred to his largest and most difficult discussion about time, space, and the Christian's role in the world as a *magnum opus et arduum* — a great and arduous work.[32] Its twenty books are an astoundingly erudite commentary on history. It draws

---

31. *Epistles of Jerome* 126.2.2. Quote from O'Donnell, *Augustine: A New Biography*, 228.
32. Brown, *Augustine of Hippo*, 299–312.

from every facet of classical culture, literature, philosophy, and religion. It uses the Bible as its chronological point of reference, beginning with Adam and Eve and making Jesus the end point of history. Both Augustine's friends and foes were awed by the intellectual and literary prowess of this old but vital man. Augustine's motif is predictably polar — the city of man and the city of God. Yet they are not polar opposites as much as two ends of a historical spectrum. Properly understood through a Christian optic, the city of man is a prelude to the city of God. Rome rose and fell for a reason — to explain human self-delusion and our inherent sinfulness. What drove the "noble" Romans to conquer? Not greed, since they had limitless monetary resources. Not power, since they had it in abundance. What drove them was a lust for applause and glory, a sort of self-transcendence and immortality that made them different from the rest of humankind. Rome was their alter ego and a comforting idol that required innumerable victims guaranteed through conquest and subjugation. Augustine is unequivocal. The Romans loved their lies but God refuted them, as God always does. For Augustine, the fall of Rome was heuristic, an object lesson whose inevitability was part and parcel of its ingrown mendacity. Starting with Adam and Eve, sin had a purpose, even the arrogance of the Romans. Without it the incarnation would not have taken place and forever changed the nature of human existence and history. Augustine came to see sin, Adam and Eve's and every human sin, as a *felix culpa*, a necessary and ultimately redemptive failure that led to Jesus' birth, death, and resurrection. For Augustine, then, sin and salvation are intrinsically linked. Misery can lead to redemption — an insight Augustine began to grasp as a young man in Milan. An almost prosaic story of sin and redemption helped Augustine fathom the real meaning of existence, at least as he understood it.

The *City of God* is primarily meant to encourage Christians by giving them a larger vision of their existence in a transitory world. Augustine appreciated his contemporaries' shock at the fall of Rome, but he wanted them to look beyond it. In his last theological work, Augustine wanted Christians and non-Christians alike to put Rome in perspective, to relativize it as an epiphenomenon, a beautiful city and impressive but intrinsically unjust empire destined by God to fall. Then and now Augustine's thinking is counterintuitive. We desperately want to believe that empires last forever, Rome, Britain, or America. Augustine would quickly analyze the problem: a hard-wired penchant for collective self-delusion. Augustine is utterly clear. The city of man is necessarily transitory. We are called to live good and productive lives while we inhabit it, but we must keep in mind that we have to let it go. When we refuse to do so we inevitably inflict pain on others and ourselves by distorting the real nature of human existence and history. For Augustine only the city of God has real meaning and everything else is subsumed by its inevitability. Empires are unjust and violent by definition, and every Christian and intelligent person should know this. O'Donnell spells out the social and political consequences of Augustine's reasoning in a succinct passage:

> Augustine's view, elevated and devout, was deeply corrosive when it came to real secular societies, and his alternative to them was more potent than those dreamt by Plato and Cicero, because Augustine could claim that he was not dreaming but describing a spiritual reality. And so he could be punishingly dismissive: "What are kingdoms without Justice?" he asks sneeringly (meaning any kingdom not animated by and devoted to the spirit of Augustine's god). "They're just gangs of bandits."[33]

In his haste to criticize Augustine, however, O'Donnell misses a key point. In fact, most political arrangements are just that — "gangs of bandits" cloaked in an aura of civility. For millennia human beings have suffered from the illusion that they could create perfect societies, although a modicum of critical reflection makes such a sanguine assumption almost laughable. None of this self-serving deception escaped Augustine's searing eyes. The only way to escape this delusion, a manifestation of original sin, is to rely on an understanding of our humanness and history that transcends our own selves, our individual lives, and our collective existence. For Augustine, this can happen only if we rely on grace and mercy, and this requires that we come to terms with our built-in limitations, that we look beyond ourselves and affirm something greater. It is easy to dismiss Augustine as an anachronism, a product of a chaotic childhood and a world that no longer exists. All of this is true. But it is important not to dismiss the insights of a genius who spent his life searching for the truth. Difficult as he may be, Augustine still has the ability to provoke and make us think in our own chaotic world that he could never conceive. The Roman Empire died, but Augustine certainly lives on, which, somewhat ironically, may be one of our best examples of a *felix culpa.* To the dismay of some and the delight of others, Augustine will not go away. Until the thirteenth century he was the uncontested theologian and social philosopher in the Western Christian world. Aristotle and Aquinas diminished his centrality, but he never disappeared. Aquinas is steeped in Augustine and refines his thinking more than he moves beyond it. In Aquinas's system Plato cedes ground to Aristotle, but the same supposedly natural hierarchy of heaven and earth would have been completely familiar to Augustine despite seven hundred years of separation. When

---

33. O'Donnell, *Augustine: A New Biography,* 249–50; the words in quotation marks are from the *City of God,* 4:4.

the reformers disavowed Thomas and the scholastic intellectual universe he created in the sixteenth century, they filled the void with their new interpretation of the most catholic of catholics, Augustine.

In the 1970s and 1980s his influence in Catholic circles became obvious. John Paul II and Benedict XVI know Augustine by heart. They resonate with his definition of the true church as a tight, orthodox community set apart from a sinful society that must be listened to but never acceded to. The somewhat upbeat assessment of society and the social order that characterized the years immediately after Vatican II (1962–65) has been replaced by a more critical approach that some see as realism and others as pessimism. The twentieth century certainly gives one pause about human possibilities. The idolatrous pretensions of empires in the past hundred years have claimed millions of victims, and none of this bloody tragedy would perplex Augustine for a moment. He remains an invaluable interpreter. Yet his own genius has to be tempered by less diametrical filters. We live in a world in which truth is shaped by context, not by preconceived theories that require that reality fit its assumptions. Since the publication of *Rerum novarum* in 1891, Catholic social teaching has done an admirable job of taking context into serious consideration. It is precisely for this reason that the Catholic Church is still taken seriously even by those who reject what it stands for. Augustine lived his life and faith contextually, as a full participant in the political and social world around him. The lesson of our neo-Platonic bishop is clear. Like the incarnation, context is all-important and Christianity only makes sense when it exists in context.

Chapter Four

Different Lights

Thomas and Francis as Medieval Icons

The Great Luminaries

By the thirteenth century what we know today as Western Europe was as solidly Catholic as it would ever be. At least in theory, everyone subscribed to a divinely arranged social order, church and state closely allied, the former superior to the latter, each playing a crucial role in that most crucial of all endeavors — eternal salvation. The church channeled the grace of God and the state did everything in its power to help deliver it efficiently. Most accepted the status quo, while those who chafed at its assumptions and impositions generally kept a low profile and their mouths shut. Church and state were like an elaborate wedding cake, the pope, bishop, priest made up the *sacerdotium*, or priestly caste, while the emperor, aristocracy, and their appointed administrator made up the *principium*, or ruling caste. At the bottom of this arrangement was an enormous mass of women and men whose lives and labor made this social order possible. We know the names of popes and kings, a few bishops and aristocrats and, very rarely, that of a priest or a local authority. The names of everyone else, perhaps 99 percent of a given population, are lost. What they felt and thought is very hard to know since almost all were illiterate, and literate people paid little attention to them. Church and state kept a close eye on a social order that served their interests, producing a cavernous disparity between rich and poor, with few in between.

Ecclesiastical and social hierarchies were not an accident; they were an expression of divine will. Cardinals assumed the papal office because they were destined to do so. Emperors reigned because God wanted them to. Even bad popes and kings, and they were commonplace, were somehow part of a godly design whose purpose might not be evident but had to be accepted. People were not simply born; they were born *into* a particular social group as an aristocrat, serf, or beggar. Protesting fate was seen as futile and an affront to God's wisdom. The only way to ascend the social ladder was through the church, but even here the "higher" clergy were usually drawn from the nobility. Even for those lucky few who enjoyed relatively comfortable and secure lives, existence could be fleeting. What we consider common maladies like a cold or minor infection could be life-threatening. Large numbers of women died from the consequences of childbirth, and plague annihilated whole communities. We need to dispel fairytale images of knights in shining armor and damsels in beautiful dresses. Everyone had fleas, the church frowned on bathing, and the food was usually terrible, assuming there was something to eat.

Thomas Aquinas and Francis of Assisi are the indisputable giants of the thirteenth century; they symbolize genius and sanctity. Thomas was born around 1226, the same year that Francis died. We will examine these two figures in reverse chronological order in an attempt to move from theory to action. Thomas is a complex intellectual figure whose genius and writings remain compelling, although by anyone's standards a bit dry. Francis is an utterly charismatic saint whose life and legacy are nothing short of amazing. Of course, the thirteenth century abounded with scholars and saints, and anyone can pick their favorite: Dominic, Clare, or dozens of others. Most people, however, see Thomas and Francis as the great icons of medieval wisdom and sanctity. Thomas still has his philosophical and theological followers, and many Christians and non-Christians admire the holiness of Francis. Almost any academic library in the Western world has a copy of Thomas's greatest work, the *Summa theologiae,* or at least a few books on Thomas and his writings.[1] The *Summa* is still used in debates about the common good, the responsibilities of citizens and rulers, and the role of religion in society as a whole. Francis of Assisi is a symbol of a loving, God-filled human being who captures the imagination of believers and nonbelievers alike. Although most people are not familiar with the details of Francis's life, they think of him as a joyful and magnanimous man who embodies what is best in Christianity. Both men are famous but neither was in the least bit interested in fame. Their great joy was in fulfilling their appointed tasks, one elaborating an intellectual system that explained every facet of Catholic belief while the other tried to live out Christianity in its fullness in the highways and towns of the medieval world. But both were committed to making Christianity understandable in their world. They knew that truth must be understood in light of the context in which it is revealed. This requires constantly articulating it in words and deed.

---

1. The so-called *Summa* is Thomas's most important work. It is a six-tome collection of philosophical and theological reflection that attempts to exposit nearly every facet of Catholic belief. Thomas began to compose the *Summa* in 1266 and worked on it until a year before his death in 1274, never completing it. The standard English text for the *Summa* is *St. Thomas Aquinas, Summa Theologica,* trans. Fathers of the English Dominican Province (Notre Dame, Ind.: Christian Classics, 1948).

Thomas and Francis were simultaneously conservative and innovative. Both firmly believed that Catholic Christianity was the definitive revelation of God's truth, but each realized that truth was not a static proposition as much as an ongoing quest to find it in a particular culture and historical moment. There is a tendency among certain Christians, particularly Catholics, to look on the thirteenth century as the golden age of Christian life, a perfect model of human existence that only needs occasional fine-tuning to work to maximum effect. The thirteenth century nonetheless had its shadow side evident in intolerance for new ideas, not to mention brutal warfare and the slaughter of anyone who was different, non-Catholic Christians, Jews, and Muslims. Still, this was a century of exuberance marked by incredible accomplishments, the six volumes of the *Summa,* Francis's simple *Rule* and exquisite poetry, and the awesome beauty of Gothic cathedrals. Mind, matter, and imagination were given equal play. There is a paradox at play in the lives of these two men. Thomas the conservative moved the thinking of the Catholic Church in new directions, using but transcending the theology of Augustine. Plato gives way to Aristotle, an abstract world to a natural one. Sanctity leaves the confines of monasteries as Francis and his brothers preach on street corners, inviting lay people to imitate their lives of evangelical fervor as well. Almost by accident they turned the church and Western Europe on its head by unleashing something of a mass religious movement.

Thomas: The Angelic Doctor

Thomas was born in 1226 to an aristocratic family in Aquino, a village between Rome and Naples. Like other feudal aristocrats, Thomas's father, Landulph, lived off the produce of his fields harvested by serfs and tolls collected on roads that passed through his lands. In times of conflict he was required to offer refuge in his castle to everyone in the area and provide soldiers to his own feudal lord in times of war. Theoretically committed to the task of saving souls, albeit in different ways, the papacy and Holy Roman Empire were usually at each other's throats. Thomas's brothers were generally aligned with the papacy, but also served in the imperial bureaucracy, achieving significant influence at court. The social system was similar to that of Augustine's time in certain ways. Everyone forged a strategic alliance with someone else, and only the pope was beyond feudal obligations. The pope demanded and received fealty, a promise of loyalty, from emperors and kings, and if they reneged they could expect speedy excommunication. Aristocrats swore their allegiance to their monarchs, and serfs were required to serve the needs of the local lord with labor and produce. They were bound to the land and were severely punished if they tried to escape. No one could opt out of these complex obligations because their survival, in this world and the next, was at stake. Thomas lived a life of privilege and ate at a table replete with bread, cheese, and wine from his father's estates. Although a defender of justice, Thomas never questioned the feudal system per se. He was aware of its social injustice and the deficiencies of the medieval world, but he never experienced them personally.

There is an erroneous idea that church and state were essentially fused in the medieval era. Enlightenment figures like Voltaire, Rousseau, and Gibbons were relentless critics of the medieval world, and especially the Catholic Church, for which they had only contempt. They considered the cultural and intellectual life of the Middle Ages primitive, its politics barbaric and hypocritical. The church was supposed to guard people's souls through the sacraments but trafficked in indulgences and relics. Ecclesiastical posts were bought and sold at enormous prices. The state was no less corrupt and oppressive. It suppressed democracy and claimed a divine right to rule, even unjustly. Unfortunately, the critics of the Catholic Church were right, at least in some respects. Aristocrats routinely executed peasants for the infractions of feudal rules. Church and state were theoretically separate but constantly meddled in each others affairs, only compounding the contradictions and corruption. The church was the largest landowner in the medieval world and often spent more time defending its real estate than it did guiding its flock. So-called Christian princes were often no more than murderous thugs who were not in the least bit Christian in terms of their behavior.

The situation was profoundly unjust, but it lasted well into the sixteenth century, when church and state started to go their separate ways. In the medieval world flare-ups between ecclesiastical and secular leaders were unavoidable. Both were fighting over land and revenues. Perhaps the best example of the stormy relationship between church and state is the legendary enmity between the emperor Frederick II, arguably the greatest ruler of the Holy Roman Empire since Charlemagne, and Gregory IX, a wily politician in his own right. Frederick had grown up in the papal court of Innocent III, who most scholars consider the most powerful pope of the Middle Ages. After Innocent's death Frederick declared himself the sole power in his domains, rejecting the church's right to intervene in secular affairs. Gregory IX duly excommunicated him and labeled him Antichrist. But by 1231 Gregory needed to settle his dispute with Frederick because the people of Rome were in open revolt, and he had to flee to the nearby city of Agnani. The excommunicated Frederick was happy to oblige since once restored to the good graces of the church his vassals were required to obey him. These ongoing squabbles between the church empire and many

European monarchies, wore away at the fabric of Christendom, making the Reformation of the sixteenth century an inevitability.

When Thomas was born into this contentious mess, papal and imperial tensions were white hot. Yet despite so much wasted ecclesiastical and political energy, amazing things were going on in the surrounding world. Universities were emerging in major cities, and Gothic cathedrals were being built at a prodigious rate. Franciscans were preaching to peasants in their own languages rather than Latin. Intellectual life was being revitalized as the excessive focus on Plato gave way to a new interest in Aristotle, made available by Jewish and Muslim scholars. All brands of religious scholars were engaged in lively debates through analyses of their religious texts and personal encounters. Although it may sound like an odd term, the thirteenth century was a time of exuberance. Culture, economics, and politics were changing the surrounding world, sometimes subtly and sometimes forcefully. There is a common misperception that medieval Europe was intellectually monotone and theologically orthodox without exception. The papacy supposedly controlled every aspect of personal and religious life and the state every aspect of worldly existence. The picture, however, is more nuanced. So-called ordinary men and women knew how to nod at ecclesiastical and civil authorities and move on with their lives as if little had happened. It was a skill anyone in the feudal system with its stress on privilege and obedience learned at an early age. Deviancy was an art form and a survival skill. A few intrepid souls mocked popes, prelates, princes, and local authorities, seeing through their venality and insistence on orthodoxy as a self-serving charade. The best place to do it was the local tavern, where almost anything could be said and nearly everything said forgiven. The same dynamic existed in medieval universities. Students and scholars, even in theological faculties, raised serious questions about Christian beliefs, knowing that they were taking serious risks by not adhering to the strict theological norms imposed by the hierarchical church. As early as the eleventh century theologians were proposing new ideas that expanded Catholic religious discourse that essentially had been static for centuries. Anselm of Canterbury produced new insights into salvation, Peter Lombard systematized theological thinking, and the intrepid Abelard went so far as to say what doctrines had to be believed and what were tangential.

Although these thinkers pale in comparison to Thomas, they set the groundwork for him. As a student he wrote commentaries on their works, then a central aspect of theological education. Most specifically, Thomas benefited from his teacher and fellow Dominican Albert the Great, who tutored Thomas in Aristotle and took pride in a brilliant student who soon surpassed him. The pupil became the master of the Athenian's approach to biology, ethics, and political theory. By the end of his life Thomas had produced twelve line-by-line commentaries on Aristotle's philosophical works.[2] Despite his parents' insistence Thomas did not join the Benedictines in the nearby monastery of Monte Cassino, where he had begun to study around the age of five. He dashed their hopes of his becoming a child-abbot and eventually a high-ranking prelate who would fill the family coffers. The idealistic young nobleman joined a religious order known as the Dominicans. They were a new mendicant or "begging" order dedicated to learning and preaching with a focus of correcting those with wayward ideas and the religiously tepid. Founded in the early thirteenth century by Dominic de Guzmán, the Order of Preachers, the formal name of the Dominicans, played a central role in medieval universities, often to the consternation of older faculty members who felt that their power and prestige had been diminished. Dominicans were the epitome of orthodoxy and staunchly pro-papal. For those faculty members and students who were pro-imperial, the Dominicans were an unwelcome addition to the new centers of learning. Still, the intellectual accomplishment of these new friars was formidable. The greatest minds of the age were attracted to the Dominican "movement," especially Albert and then Thomas. The old feudal system predicated on land and small, fixed populations was coming to an end, and the church had to respond to new circumstances. New religious orders were replacing the static pastoral model of Benedictine monasticism as peasants moved from the country to cities and urban life was revitalized.

Although Augustine remained *the* theologian, it was clear that his neo-Platonic approach to Christianity with its negative approach to individual and social existence in a sin-riddled world was no longer the best fit. The sociopolitical and intellectual climate of the thirteenth century required a more open and positive approach to the world that Augustine simply could not provide. In the hands of Albert, Thomas and others, Plato's thought was balanced out by Aristotle's. The great advantage of Aristotle's writings was that they helped philosophers and theologians approach the natural world and human society in a less dualistic and more empirical way. Although not a scientist in our sense of the term, Aristotle was nonetheless committed to demonstrating truth in light of evidence and facts, rather than presuppositions about how things should work in theory. Thomas, therefore, approached the material world with an open eye, willing to learn from the way it actually worked. Like Aristotle, he could detect rationality in every facet of nature so nature itself was a source of knowledge.

Armed with Aristotle's reflections, along with scripture and tradition, Thomas now had the means to construct an all-encompassing explanation of the Christian life. Augustine's writings were generally topical; he

---

2. Finnis, *Aquinas: Moral, Political, and Legal Theory.*

dealt with one issue after another as need required. Thomas, on the other hand, was a systematic thinker. He attempted to produce a compendium of Christian wisdom, not so much as a definitive statement of truth, which he knew was impossible, but as the best possible statement of what Christians could and should believe in light of the world around them. With the help of several secretaries whose stamina he constantly tested, Thomas dictated his ideas on an array of topics that he considered central to a credible, substantive understanding of Christianity. His writings are more than philosophical and theological treatises. Although the terms and disciplines did not exist in his day, Thomas delves into areas as diverse as economics, ethics, human psychology, and political science. In the Angelic Doctor's mind, every aspect of human existence could be understood in the light of faith. This included a tentative understanding of God as revealed in nature, scripture, and Christian tradition. But Thomas was deeply aware that language, particularly when it attempts to say something about God, will always be deficient. There is a story that a few months before his death Thomas simply stopped dictating to his secretaries saying, "I can write no more." Was he simply too exhausted to continue thinking and writing, or did he realize that systematizing Christian thought was ultimately impossible?

Thomas's Political Thought

Thomas was attuned to the political and social order around him, although not on a grassroots level. He never mastered German or French despite many years in Cologne and Paris. Like all medieval scholars he communicated by speaking church Latin. But he kept in touch with his family. His brothers were deeply involved in imperial and papal politics, and as a professor Thomas dealt with highly politicized students. While in Paris, Thomas lived about two minutes away from the newly constructed cathedral of Notre Dame.[3] It was a beautiful house of worship as well as a statement about the power of the emerging French monarchy, which had become the "protector" of the papacy against the aggression of the Holy Roman Empire. France was also trying to outmaneuver the empire for its own political gain. Students and faculty were divided into three camps, and the university was a hotbed of political discussion so intense that it often led to brawls. For several weeks Thomas's kinsman, Louis VIII, had an armed guard posted outside of the Dominicans' residence because some professors resented the newfound prestige of the Dominicans. In 1256 "Thomas became one of the twelve masters of the Sorbonne," or University of Paris. At the age of thirty, five years below the minimum, he had

---

3. Ibid.

achieved one of the most prestigious academic positions in Christendom, working along with eleven other of Europe's top theologians.[4] Most likely this was a source of resentment for older teaching "masters." When disputed questions about belief and church/state affairs had to be resolved, the theological faculty of Paris along with Oxford frequently acted as a court of last appeal. Aquinas spent about fifteen years teaching in Paris in four phases and maintained a balanced approach to the ecclesiastical political currents around him. On occasion other scholars, who disagreed with certain of his analytical premises, attacked him, and especially his insistence that Aristotle, obviously a non-Christian, had much to say to Christians. He responded with equanimity and never showed impatience with honest criticism. He was a well-liked professor known for his commitment to rationality and a respectful interchange between teacher and student that he felt was the only way for anyone to learn anything effectively.[5] Also devoid of any ambition other than to know well and convincingly, he was a very rare commodity in the academic world.

For Thomas reason made humans distinct from other forms of life. Reason was God's greatest gift to us, the source of free will and thus basic to our ability to respond well or badly to the grace of God. Without reason we would be equivalent to irrational animals. Unlike the more aristocratic Aristotle, who felt that certain groups of human beings were so brutish as to be semirational and therefore semihuman, Thomas felt that all women and men, from an educated prince to an illiterate peasant, had the ability to reason and decide, in other words, to actively participate in the most crucial decision any of us can make in life, saying yes or no to God, being saved or being damned. Reason was intrinsically related to autonomy, and Thomas rejected any form of coercion. In other words, people could be helped to choose the best and most reasonable action by the church and state, but they could not be forced to accept and do it if it violated their conscience. Of course, the church was infallible and the state God's regent, and no reasonable person could reject these self-evident truths. Stubborn refusal to obey either the church or state was willful sin and, in extreme cases, punishable by death since such willfulness threatened the common good. It could be a poison that debilitated church and society. Heresy and political deviancy were the greatest threats in Thomas's mind. Therefore, church and state must always be on guard, correcting, coercing, and even executing those who refused to conform to God-given truths. In the twenty-first century, most people would disagree with Thomas and

---

4. Nichols, *Discovering Aquinas.*
5. Finnis, *Aquinas: Moral, Political and Legal Theory*, 11–12, quoting and translating a discussion held with students at the Sorbonne about reason, truth, and how academic inquiry should be conducted.

reject his ideas as a recipe for oppression. They are, and the contradictions in his thinking are self-evident. Theory does not mesh with practice because exercising one's freedom of conscience can lead to punishment and death. Yet these are enlightened ideas in comparison to Augustine's. Thomas, albeit timidly, believed in human rights. Augustine did, too, but he questioned whether they could be exercised effectively in a hopelessly sinful world. Thomas was more optimistic. Of course, Augustine's world was falling apart in front of him. Thomas's was reaching its high point.

Thomas's teaching and writing are deductive. For most of us today this type of argumentation is methodologically deficient. We work from the bottom up, not from the top down. Theories must be based on verifiable facts, not presuppositions based on preexisting philosophical norms. Most would, nonetheless, agree with or at least accept the validity of some of Thomas's assertions. Most people recognize that lessons can be drawn from nature, which has its own form of rationality. As Thomas pointed out, human beings have inherent dignity and rights. Even many nonreligious people would agree. But Thomas's top-down approach to truth no longer makes sense to modern thinkers. If students in modern universities read Thomas at all, they most likely read extracts from the *Summa* or a short passage from one of the commentaries on Aristotle. Perhaps a generation or two back, serious Christian scholars, generally Catholic, would have read large sections of the *Summa* and other of Thomas's texts that formed the core of Catholic education. There are few such scholars around today.

In a nutshell, many see Thomas's writing as so much wishful thinking, a projection of a medieval world that thought that truth existed with a capital T and the existence of God could be ascertained by the correct use of reason. Up until the 1960s Catholic theology was essentially "Thomistic." That is not the case today. It is no longer possible to understand the natural world or social order as Aquinas did eight centuries ago. Our understanding of nature is scientific and our approach to politics and society essentially pragmatic. As R. W. Dyson puts it, "The twenty-first century reader wonders why it ever occurred to anyone to be interested in some of the things to which St Thomas devotes pages of careful analysis. He is steeped in Aristotle, Roman law, the Bible, and the Fathers: we are not."[6] Thomas is hopelessly ponderous at times and working through his writings is laborious. Yet, he wrote some of the most beautiful hymns of the Middle Ages, which prior to the reforms of Vatican II (1962–65), were central to Catholic hymnody and devotion. For Aquinas everything was a revelation of God — nature, family relations, civic life, and participation in the rituals of the Catholic Church. He had a particular affection for one

---

6. Thomas Aquinas, *Political Writings.*

of his sisters and his nieces. He visited them as often as he could, happily making detours on his many trips to spend time with them. The common purpose of these varied sources of grace was obvious to him, to help us achieve our final destiny, the beatific vision in which we contemplate God face to face.

Thomas provides a transcendent dimension to something as nasty as politics. It is not a "dirty word" for Aquinas. Drawing on Aristotle's famous maxim about humans as political animals,[7] Thomas sees politics as that dimension of collective existence in which we maximize good and minimize evil in order to achieve our common destiny as children of God. Thomas, however, was hardly a romantic when it came to power politics. His brothers had experienced both success and failure in the political games of their times. For a while one was on the run from the wrath of Frederick II, whose temper was legendary. But this is an aberration, not the essence of politics. Again, taking his lead from the man he constantly refers to as "The Philosopher," Thomas sees politics as a sort of applied exercise in ethics in which ruler and ruled conform themselves to divine revelation in its varied forms — nature, human law, scripture, and church tradition. Thomas is a democrat in the sense that he insists that everyone must participate in the political life of his or her community. Men *and* women are called to involve themselves and shape the social order even if it is just their humble village. He does not, however, understand democracy in the way we do — one person one vote in which everyone enjoys the franchise. As a Christian Thomas believed in the fundamental equality of all people; as a philosopher steeped in Aristotle, however, he believed that some are meant to teach and rule while others are meant to learn and obey, although always with consideration and respect. For Aquinas any attempt to circumvent these necessary distinctions among people was a violation of God's laws and a fast track to chaos and tyranny at the hands of an ignorant mob. Thomas did not see achieving a measure of happiness in this life to be a form of delusion as Augustine did, but he thought that what happiness we can achieve can be brought about only through the guidance of the church and the beneficent rule of a wise monarch.

As we have seen, Aquinas's approach to social issues is conservative, and the only thing that separates it from Aristotle's is the Christian concept of the Reign of God, an idea that Aristotle would have considered unintelligible. Aristotle's beliefs, if any, are hard to discern. But "the Philosopher's" assumptions about politics and society are crystal clear. He is quoted throughout the *Summa* as well as in the one work that Aquinas

---

7. Aristotle, *The Politics and the Constitution of Athens,* 1:2 (1253a2).

devoted to the political and social spheres exclusively, *De regime princip-ium*, "On the Rule of Princes."[8] *De regime principium* follows Aristotle's *Politics* topic by topic, and Thomas accepts its premises unequivocally, only adding Christian refinements as need requires.[9] For Aristotle monarchy is simply a reflection of nature. Royal workers who in turn are served by wingless drones who are at the bottom of a hive's social system serve what he calls the "King Bee." Of course, Aristotle has the gender of the bees backward but how could he ever imagine a female insect being in charge of anything? Aristotle projects what he thinks nature should be with no knowledge of what it actually is, and Thomas falls into the same trap. For him hierarchy was indeed natural, but it was also a revelation of God's will clearly laid out in the Hebrew Bible and the Pauline sections of the New Testament, especially Romans and the Pastoral Epistles.[10] The social task of the Christian monarch is weighty, and his power should be uncontested. His nobles reinforce his power with wise counsel and obey his commands without hesitation. Violating this chain of command is a recipe for disaster, in other words, the constant warfare among Christians that caused so much suffering in the medieval world. Thomas abhorred war and violence, as any Christian should, and although he says little about the violent clashes between popes and emperors, it is doubtful that he would have deemed them legitimate since they too threatened the common good. Saintly popes and godly princes, therefore, are indispensable to minimizing the danger of useless conflict. They are, therefore, to be obeyed instantly. Thomas is unequivocal: "Again, those things are best which are most natural for in every case nature operates for the best; and in nature government is always one" (*De regime principium* 1.3).

Thomas is well aware that any form of government can go awry. Original sin is an individual and collective affliction that taints everything we do. Individual popes and monarchs could and did fall victim to the blandishments of sin. In the tenth and eleventh centuries some popes had been literally psychotic and did not hesitate to murder their rivals. Not a few emperors had been incompetent, megalomaniac, or both. Even Frederick II, about whom Thomas knew a great deal, had fallen victim to sin. Frederick was raised in the household of Pope Innocent III, a man of intelligence and integrity, but his upbringing seems to have had little impact on Frederick's willingness to reject the primacy of priests over princes in the civil realm. Centuries before Frederick's predecessor Otto II (955–982 C.E.) had gone so far as to appoint his own pope, and several of

---

8. Thomas Aquinas, *Political Writings*, xxiii–xli.

9. Aristotle, *The Politics and the Constitution of Athens.*

10. No New Testament scholar who subscribes to the historical-critical method of biblical analysis considers the Pastoral Epistles to be genuinely Pauline. They were written after Paul's death and are the products of a different social environment than the one Paul lived in.

his successors did the same. Frederick saw no theological justification for bowing to the pope in secular matters, especially when they went against the interests of the empire. He was excommunicated and denounced as Antichrist by Gregory IX in 1227. Frederick apparently was not intimidated although he was condemned to hell and his vassals no longer owed him allegiance since he was a public sinner. He sacked the Benedictine monastery of Monte Cassino and papal cities throughout Italy. Gregory soon had to backpedal. He rescinded his ban of excommunication in 1232 when he needed Frederick's help to suppress a revolt by the people of Rome, who clearly hated their bishop even if he was the Successor of Peter and Vicar of Christ. It is hard not to be cynical about this cat and mouse game, and the irreverent songs of medieval students about popes and princes make perfect sense.

Thomas in the Twenty-First Century

Given Thomas's profound influence on the Catholic Church and his ongoing centrality to its social teaching, unavoidable questions arise. Is Thomas's understanding of human behavior and the sociopolitical world merely an anachronism? There are still ardent Thomists in the world. Likewise, there are Christians and non-Christians who vehemently reject Thomas and the Thomists who followed him. Opposition to Thomas was a central aspect of the Reformers' effort to recast Christianity in the sixteenth century. They condemned Thomas's ideas because they melded a pagan philosopher with Christian theology with no justification in scripture for doing this. Enlightenment figures were even fiercer in their rejection of Thomas given his conservatism, distrust of democracy, and centrality to the Catholic Church's ongoing support of monarchical and oppressive governments. With the emergence of secular societies in the nineteenth century, Thomas's philosophical and theological writings were relegated to bookshelves except in Catholic institutions. It was completely obvious that Thomas's understanding of nature was totally unreasonable and unscientific. Thomas proved what he wanted to prove — from hierarchical social structures to the existence of God in order to legitimate the medieval world.

With the publication of *The Origin of Species* in 1851 Thomas's assumption that the natural world was rational and created by an all-knowing deity became difficult to reconcile with hard scientific evidence. The central notion in Aristotle's and Thomas's understanding of natural phenomena as having an innate purpose or finality did not square with the theory of evolution. Increasingly religion and science were working with different assumptions about the makeup and purpose of the material world. The church, following Thomas's reasoning, continued to insist that there is a God-given purpose and revelation in nature from which it is possible to determine right from wrong. For most scientists, however, this Aristotelian and Thomistic premise had increasingly less to do with their efforts to decipher the complexities of the natural world. Scientific work became more value-neutral with God no longer a part of the equation. Perhaps an anecdote will drive home the point. Napoleon Bonaparte began his military career as an artillery officer; his field of specialization required knowledge of mathematics if one were to hit the target with accuracy. Intrigued by the writings of the most famous mathematician of the time, Napoleon invited Pierre-Simon Laplace to discuss his work about mathematics with him in Paris. When Napoleon asked Laplace about the role of God in his books his answer was simple — "I have no need for that particular hypothesis." The separation between faith and reason was becoming complete.

This bifurcation is most obvious in contemporary debates about human reproduction and sexuality. The church remains committed to a Thomistic understanding of natural law. Admittedly, great progress has been made in the church during the last fifty years. Sexuality is no longer seen as a concession to human weakness, something required for the continuance of humankind but nonetheless messy, irrational, and best left behind as soon as possible. Since the foundation of the early church, celibates have been perceived as more saintly people, less encumbered by the desires of "the flesh." Now, however, sexuality is seen as intrinsically linked with intimacy and mutual support, a God-given source of grace. That said, its primary purpose is still understood to be reproduction, and all sexual behavior must be open to this possibility in order to fulfill its natural purpose. Otherwise, it is a violation of its innate purpose, in short, a sin. When Pope Paul VI published *Humanae vitae* in 1968, a sharp division was created in the church between those who approach natural law in traditional ways and those who are willing to expand its scope in light of modern psychological and sociological information. A narrow understanding of natural law that forbids the use of contraception remains the institutional norm in the church. It is a non-negotiable litmus test of orthodoxy in the minds of the Magisterium, the teaching authorities of the church from pope to diocesan bishop. That said many Catholics are less inclined to subscribe to what the Magisterium of the church says about ethics and sexuality. Of course, morality is not a question of public opinion, but there is a yawning gap between what the church proclaims and what many Catholics actually consider acceptable ethical and sexual behavior. The overwhelming majority of Catholics have no problem with birth control. Nor are most Catholics inclined to stand in judgment in terms of homosexuality. One can argue that there is both beauty and wisdom in Thomas's understanding of natural law. But in the twenty-first century we know far more about nature than Aristotle or Thomas could have imagined. If the "disconnect" between the pulpit and the pews is ever to be remedied, new information and insights about nature and sexuality must be included in the way the church approaches natural law and moral issues.

So what are we to do with our medieval genius, the pride of the Dominican Order? Does Thomas still make sense today? On many levels, the answer is an unequivocal yes. Thomas has a message that needs to be heard and reiterated. He speaks about the glory of the natural world and the inherent dignity of human beings. *We* are the apex of God's love and the reason behind the Incarnation. Unlike the often dour Augustine with his obsession with original sin and its near paralyzing power over human will, Thomas speaks about our freedom and right to exercise our conscience to its fullest, as long as we do so in light of scripture, tradition, and the well-being of other people to whom we are accountable. At the same time, we need to recognize the limitations of Thomas's worldview. He was a thoroughly medieval man and a member of a clerical system that was far removed from the challenges of daily life. His family was part of an oppressive aristocracy and therefore distant from the trials and tribulations of the vast majority of people in the medieval world who lived from meal to meal and often suffered the consequences of aristocratic injustices. Like Aristotle, Thomas had no use for democracy. In fact he considered it a recipe for disaster. His envisioned a Christian world in which church and state acted in tandem, one plotting society's moral course and the other making sure the citizenry would follow it obediently. For most people in today's world such a clerical/aristocratic arrangement is simply unacceptable. Furthermore, we have learned that democracy is not such a bad idea. It does require enormous amounts of energy if it is to work properly, but it is far better than the medieval alternative of a static social order in which those who wielded power were generally opposed to any form of sociopolitical change.

Francis of Assisi: A Different Light

Thomas Aquinas was born in the same year that Francis of Assisi died — 1226.[11] Thomas's impact on Western Christianity has been enormous, Francis's immeasurable. For this reason we will end our analysis of Catholicism and the medieval social order focusing on its most beloved figure, the iconic Francis, proclaimed during his lifetime as "The Second Christ." A few people visit the convent in the southern French city of

---

11. House, *Francis of Assisi*. This very readably book presents Francis's life in a cogent way, mixing historical fact with good analysis.

Toulouse where Thomas's bones eventually came to rest. Francis's bones are a different matter. Since his death millions upon millions have visited the Romanesque basilica in Assisi that holds his remains in an enormous stone sarcophagus. As well as Francis, it houses some of the most beautiful art of the medieval period. Francis was canonized two years after his death, but even before 1228 people had been flocking to Assisi to find comfort in his final resting place, driven by stories about the saint's miraculous powers. Despite the enervating throngs that descend on Assisi today, there is an air of reverence inside the two-storied church. Regardless of their beliefs, most people seem to fall into a reverential silence once they pass through the portals of the church. Francis would not have appreciated the fuss that is lavished on him in a dark, cool crypt. He would have suggested that people go outside to enjoy "Sister Earth who sustains us with her fruits, colors, flowers, and herbs."[12] He would have preferred a potter's grave somewhere in Assisi, surrounded by the anonymous poor that he loved and served. He would not have wanted his life depicted by the greatest of medieval artists, Cimabue and the students of Giotto. He only wanted people to live the Gospel as well as possible. When he was dying in extreme pain he asked his brother Franciscans to strip him naked and lay him on the ground, which they did. It is hard to imagine a deeper gesture of humility toward the natural world he loved so much. He saw life as a cycle and "Sister Death from whom no one living can escape" as a blessing to be welcomed.

Francis was born and baptized in 1182 in Assisi, a walled medieval town in an area of central Italy known as Umbria, not far from the Apennines. At the time Italy was a mosaic of towns and cities divided by their allegiance to either the papacy or the Holy Roman Empire. A tiny number managed to remain independent. Assisi was an imperial town. To this day one can see the remains of a castle that housed German-speaking soldiers and nobility. Although Florence to the north and Rome to the south could be reached by foot in a few days of dusty travel, few people left their local environment. Travel was tedious and the roads frequented by robbers. You either traveled with an armed escort or with a larger group that offered a measure of protection. Merchants and pilgrims often banded together for mutual protection. Francis's parents were from peasant stock, but his father, Pietro Bernadone, had become a wealthy man. Somehow he managed to ascend the social ladder by becoming a cloth merchant and landowner. He made enormous amounts of money selling luxury cloth to the aristocracy and was able to purchase extensive amounts of land,

---

12. *Canticle of Brother Sun and Sister Moon.* Most scholars believe that Francis wrote this exquisitely beautiful canticle in the last year of his life. He had it sung to him by his Franciscan brothers as he lay dying. Various translations are available on the Internet.

heretofore a right reserved to feudal aristocrats. Little is known about Francis's mother, Pica, other than the fact that she was an overly indulgent parent with a remarkable ability to put up with her son's pranks. In his youth Francis was the proverbial "party animal" famous for his extravagance and moral laxity. He frequently accompanied his father to fairs in southern France where merchants bought and sold expensive cloth. Francis was so enamored of Provence that he learned a bit of the local language and memorized the songs of troubadours who specialized in the tradition of courtly love.[13] Their story line of this poetic tradition is classic: the young knight is stricken by a burning love for a beautiful lady who, unfortunately, is already married. He has no choice other than to break into doleful song, sung as close as possible to her balcony. Although flattered, she is a paragon of matrimonial virtue. Meanwhile her husband is out of the castle, most likely fighting a battle somewhere and wooing his own lover. When Francis returned to Assisi he loved to impress his friends with his repertoire of romantic songs as they partied and caroused. Baptized with the name of John, his friends gave him the nickname of Francis, or the "French Man," a moniker that stayed with him for the rest of his life.

Thomas lived in a rarified academic and clerical world with a predictable schedule of prayer, study, and writing. Francis lived in a more fluid environment and his behavior was unpredictable and worldly. His father was emblematic of an emerging social class made up of nonaristocrat businessmen who were as wealthy as many aristocrats. They exercised near total control of the political system of their towns with an internal pecking order based on wealth rather than birth. Families contended with families to gain the upper hand in local politics. The members of the merchant class knew each other quite well. When Conrad, count of Assisi and duke of Spoleto, descended from his castle, the inhabitants of the lower town did not break into applause. They assumed he wanted to levy new taxes and they knew they were paying for the incessant warfare between the papacy and Holy Roman Empire. These wars were of no benefit to them. They disrupted trade and destabilized the economy.

As a political institution the papacy was seen in a similar light. As the Vicar of Christ the pope was acknowledged as the supreme head of the church. As a medieval prince, however, he was no different than his imperial opponents. In order to maintain the Papal States, the popes imposed heavy taxes on dioceses, parishes, and municipalities. Both the empire and papacy used the myths of chivalry and the crusades. Godly princes and holy popes were crucial for the maintenance of Christian values. They were also responsible for the conversion of non-Christians. By the end of

---

13. At this time French and Italian as we know them today were only beginning to emerge. People spoke dialects of a root language.

the eleventh century a series of generally failed crusades was launched to subdue the Muslim world. As a narcissistic braggart Francis was caught up in this fantasy world of Christian chivalry. Pietro paid a significant amount of money so Francis could pretend to be a knight in shining armor riding a gallant steed. Francis lusted for knighthood, but in his first battle against the neighboring town of Perugia he fell off his horse in the first charge and spent a year rotting in a prison. His father and other well-to-do citizens of Assisi paid an enormous ransom to rescue their sons and save them from torture and death. Francis never recovered from the experience of hearing men scream as their bodies were ripped apart. Slowly his self-understanding changed and the libertine began to question his assumptions and values, or lack thereof. When the failed knight-to-be returned to Assisi, his friends noticed that he had changed. He was no longer quite as much fun to be around. He was less enthusiastic about parties; he drank and sang less; and he showed little interest in "after-party" excursions. Francis's happy-go-lucky life as a brat was coming to an end.

Aristocrats and merchants lived relatively comfortable lives by medieval standards. Castles were notoriously damp and windy, and merchants' homes had none of the amenities we consider necessities today — bathrooms, heating, and running water — but there was food and servants to help with domestic tasks. The poor lived much more modestly, sometimes with nothing more than a roof over their heads. A bad crop or social turmoil could spell hunger. The truly impoverished survived by begging on the street or outside the churches. They pleaded with high-pitched voices often surrounded by their children to dramatize their plight. If they failed to jostle the conscience of a few of their social superiors they faced starvation. The only safety net was the church, which did provide some social services in the form of shelter, handouts, and hospitals. Much depended on the goodwill of the bishop. What worked in the beggars' favor was the Christian notion that charity was pleasing to God and a way of diminishing time in purgatory.[14] The utterly destitute were the lepers, people who suffered from an array of disfiguring skin diseases, from real leprosy or Hanson's disease to psoriasis or eczema so severe that they were covered with festering, stinking sores. They were ostracized from society and forced out of towns. They had to literally stay downwind of travelers and announce their presence with a bell. They generally lived in "lazar houses" named after Lazarus, the leper in the Gospel of Luke whose ravaged body

---

14. In Catholicism purgatory is seen as a transition place where the souls of the dead prepare themselves for admission to heaven by remitting the punishment due to venial sin. Those who have died with mortal sin on their souls are consigned to hell for eternity. Catholicism is the only branch of Christianity that holds to belief in purgatory. It looms large in Dante's *Divine Comedy*.

was licked by dogs (Luke 16:19–31). In his youth Francis was repelled by the sight and smell of lepers, and he was not alone in his revulsion. All worked with the assumption that lepers must have committed a terrible sin to deserve such a horrible affliction. Although the church was allied with the upper class, it showed concern for the poor, even lepers.

Guido, the bishop of Assisi who would befriend and protect Francis, was conscious of the poverty around him and cajoled the wealthy to be more mindful and generous toward their social inferiors. He funded lazar houses in the Assisi area. Yet he never questioned the social order that produced such misery. He had a vested interest in keeping things as stable as possible. It was an intrinsic part of his job. As a bishop he controlled vast estates that had been bequeathed to the church over centuries. He administered sacraments and at the same time managed large amounts of revenue. When he was not in church Guido was often acting as a magistrate in Assisi as well as litigating on behalf of the church, frequently in the papal court in Rome. But he was a devoted and ethical bishop and when rumors reached him that Francis was acting in odd ways he had a feeling that the merchant's son might be doing more than being a fool. He wondered if Francis had become a committed Christian unlike his peers.

What was happening to Francis? A young man with everything going for him throws it all away. Everyone in Assisi thought he had gone insane. Even Francis questioned his own lucidity, yet he felt compelled to move forward although he had no idea about where he was going. He began to burn his bridges with his family and friends in response to deep subconscious urges he did not understand. Two events are symbolic of the complex process of redefinition he had embarked on. He knew that he had to come to terms with his revulsion for lepers, and the only way to do so was to approach and embrace those people he feared the most.

> One day he met a leper when he was riding near Assisi. Despite his overpowering horror he dismounted, gave the man a coin and kissed his hand. The leper gave him the kiss of peace in return. Francis then knew that to win a complete victory he must follow this first attack on his phobia with a second.[15]

His next impulsive move was to steal and sell a bolt of luxurious cloth from his father's business and go to a nearby lepers' hospital where he distributed the funds, kissing everyone's hand in the process. Francis would look back at this event as one of the most grace-filled of his life. Pietro Bernadino, however, saw only an irresponsible and thieving son. He confronted Francis and demanded that he return his property. By this time Francis seems to have drawn the conclusion that his father was an arrogant

---

15. House, *Francis of Assisi*, 57–58.

and greedy man and that he would neither follow in his steps nor obey him. This was almost sacrilege in the medieval world. Francis's behavior made a fierce confrontation unavoidable. In the upper basilica in Assisi there is a striking fresco most likely painted by students of Giotto. Pietro stands with the respectable citizens of Assisi behind him as he accuses Francis of disobedience and theft. His face is contorted with rage. Francis points his arm heavenward. Then the utterly unimaginable takes place as Francis strips himself naked. Francis renounces his father, Pietro, while Bishop Guido, who was acting as a magistrate hoping to end this bitter quarrel, looks completely embarrassed as he wraps his episcopal robe around Francis.[16] Pietro returned to his comfortable home while the naked Francis went to the nearby forest to begin life as a beggar.

Francis was at the first phase of what psychologists call a conversion experience.[17] This concept requires a brief explanation since it is often misunderstood. It has little to do with a flash of light or thunder from heaven. In the Acts of the Apostles Paul, on his way to Damascus, is startled by an intense light and hears the voice of Jesus. He falls to the ground blinded. As a committed Pharisee he was on his way to round up and prosecute Jesus' followers. Ananias, a member of the earliest Christian community, cures Paul of his blindness in Damascus. When Ananias approaches Paul and lays his hands on his head, scales fall from Paul's eyes (Acts 9). Paul, however, says nothing about these events in his own letters and his silence is telling. The author of Acts is trying to tell us about the significance of Paul's conversion. In reality, we are dealing with symbols rather than facts. Paul then retreats to the desert for a long period of time. As William James pointed out a century ago in his classic book *The Varieties of Religious Experience*, conversion is the result of a process, the culmination of an inner journey in which a person plumbs his or her depths. Eventually, the person's self-understanding begins to change as a truer self-understanding begins to emerge.[18] The person's former self does not entirely disappear but it is transformed significantly. It has taken a quantum leap forward, but often does not know exactly where to go. The destiny emerges with time. Francis's growing but still unconscious resentment toward his father was generating inner heat that would lead to explosive hostility. He had experienced his father's avarice when he accompanied him to trade fairs. He saw his contempt for the beggars who came to his door hoping for scraps of food. Certainly the disaster outside of Perugia was another experience that caused Francis to question who he really was. His fantasies about being a chivalrous knight wooing a fair

---

16. As found in Thomas of Celano, *The First Life (Vita primia)*.
17. James, *The Varieties of Religious Experience*.
18. Ibid.

lady now seemed stupid. Like so many profligate young people of his time Francis hoped to go on a crusade and so redeem his soul from damnation, but only after he had had his fun. He had begun to see the folly of his ways. He was nearly paralyzed by a sense of sinfulness, what today we call shame. He felt, perhaps correctly, that everything he had done with his life was a sham. He was both an idiot and a liar.

The good citizens of Assisi agreed entirely with Pietro, and after the great confrontation they tossed his lunatic son out of Assisi. People began to insult him and throw rocks to make sure he stayed away from their town. He entered into a state of discomfort and confusion. Thomas of Celano, one of Francis's first followers, describes this period as one in which "nothing satisfied him."[19] Francis was numb and quite likely depressed. He had nothing to rely on and no idea about what to do or where to go. Things changed profoundly and rapidly when Francis went to pray in the church of San Damiano, a small chapel on the outskirts of town. There his ability to feel and enjoy life returned. While in deep and painful prayer about the future of his life, Francis heard a voice that emanated from the crucifix in San Damiano. He had a mystical experience in which the crucified Jesus asked him a question and then gave him a command. "Francis, don't you see that my house has collapsed? Go and repair it for me." "Yes, Lord, I will most willingly."[20] Francis took the request at face value and bought bricks and mortar to repair the neglected church. The priest assigned to San Damiano was perplexed and worried about what was going on but tolerated the busy self-taught mason. Francis would eventually realize that rebuilding a "collapsed" church meant the institutional Catholic Church. It was at the height of its political and social power but losing contact with ordinary people, many of whom were put off by the church's lust for supremacy in every facet of their lives and its insatiable demands for money. Prelates would pass by with their luxurious retinues, and the parish priest who lived up to his vows was becoming an endangered species. Scandal bred resentment.

Francis would emerge from the forest every day and work on the walls and roof of San Damiano with donated bricks and mortar. The priest provided him with enough food for survival. This was the "desert phase" of Francis's life. He had left behind a dissolute youth but was still searching for an identity as a committed Christian. The parallels with Jesus' life are obvious. In the Gospels of Mark, Matthew, and Luke Jesus goes through a period of temptation and trial in which he has to affirm his identity as a prophet proclaiming the Reign of God. Francis had to make himself

---

19. Thomas began his biography in 1228 at the request of Gregory IX, a friend and supporter of Francis. The book is known as *The First Life* (*Vita primia*). The common abbreviation used to designate the work is C or Cel. The section in question is 1 Cel. 3.1.

20. As quoted in House, *Francis of Assisi*, 64.

vulnerable as a true disciple, something he had never done before. His indulgent parents had provided him with prodigious amounts of money that he immediately squandered with rarely more than a scolding from his father or mother. Francis now had no resources. His only asset was the tunic on his back. He walked barefoot in the snow and on the sizzling roads during the height of the Umbrian summer. He fasted constantly and his body became thin from his many penitential practices. The only robust part of him was his odor. But Francis was content. He was in love with Lady Poverty and the Christ who had spoken to him in the church of San Damiano.

After a while he aroused the curiosity of some of his former friends in Assisi. They visited him, and his happiness was contagious. Although well to do themselves with bright careers ahead of them as merchants or local authorities, a group of followers grew up around Francis. The number is predictable — twelve. Their conversion was similar to Francis's. They decided to "opt out" of the status quo and be nonconformists. Their families must have reacted with the same bewilderment and anger as Pietro Bernadone had a few years before. It is unlikely that Francis foresaw what was happening, but he welcomed his new companions with unrestrained joy. This first group, not yet known as Franciscans but rather the "lesser brothers" slept in a lean-to packed like sardines on the ground.[21] They shared whatever food they had with anyone who asked for it, and soon there were many people waiting outside the door of their flea-infested hovel. They went hungry rather than refuse what little food they had to those in need. The same literally applied to the clothes on their backs. Francis gave away his tunic whenever he saw someone who needed it more than he — walking away in his underwear. His brothers did the same. The group was informal and democratic in all that it did. Their one and only criterion as a small community was replicating the complete poverty that Jesus had lived in the Gospels; nothing else mattered. They used the model of the first Christian community found in the Acts of the Apostles as a paradigm for their community life. Francis was not an abbot or bishop but a brother among brothers. His confreres respected his commitment and wisdom but everyone had equal voice and vote. He encouraged and chastised others and they did the same with Francis, always out of a spirit of mutual love.

To some in the church, however, this insignificant group of semi-fanatics presented a problem. Francis's vision seemed wildly improbable. It was also an affront, not only to plump members of the hierarchy but to monastic communities whose wealth sometimes was greater than that of

---

21. The official title for Francis's followers is the Order of Friars Minor, abbreviated as O.F.M.

kings. The Benedictines owned enormous estates worked by serfs. For the most part monks had ceased to do manual labor. At least in theory this allowed them more time for prayer as well as an opportunity to say masses for the abbey's feudal benefactors. The poverty and simplicity of life laid out in Benedict's sixth-century *Rule* had become quaint memories. Abbots had become power-brokers and, as we saw in the case of Thomas Aquinas, noble families vied for the chance to have a son become an abbot or a daughter an abbess. Diocese were bought and sold while powerful families bought the votes of cardinals when they convened to elect a new pope. Francis never criticized members of the hierarchy or the nearby Benedictines, who frequently were kind do him and his "lesser brothers." The reaction of some members of the papal court, however, was not so charitable. Most of all they feared a challenge to their authority and anyone who had the nerve to do so was quickly branded as a radical and heretic.

In the late twelfth and early thirteenth centuries a number of movements like that of Francis had emerged, often in reaction to the privileges of the higher clergy who were also secular lords and even prince-electors in imperial conclaves. Others were prince-archbishops or ennobled abbots with all the prerogatives of high-ranking civil authorities. They had coats of arms and often their own armies. When Francis was a boy tagging along with his father in the south of France he must have heard about Peter Waldo, "a rich merchant who had paid for the translation of the gospels into French and given away his wealth to the poor."[22] Waldo started a movement of lay men and women who preached in the streets of medieval towns and cities living as closely to the spirit of the Gospels as they could. They formed their own communities. This may seem innocuous but Peter Waldo and his followers were violating church law. Lay people were forbidden to preach. Only the clergy could do so and they had to be deacons or higher up in the clerical system. They alone were allowed to interpret the Bible. Allowing "uneducated" men and women to do so was seen as a recipe for heretical misinterpretation.

All religious communities had to be recognized and approved by the pope. They were carefully monitored by local bishops once they were. In 1184 Waldo was excommunicated. His followers were persecuted and many burned at the stake for heresy. Few people missed the point. Living the Gospel could be a dangerous thing and challenging the church almost suicidal. The church, of course, did provide assistance to the poor, but it was paternalistic and controlling. Peter Waldo tried to create an egalitarian Christian community in which all had voice and vote. The church worked from the opposite angle. It was the patron and the poor its clients. They were expected to be docile and grateful. Francis and his companions

---

22. House, *Francis of Assisi*, 87.

avoided Waldo's fate by walking to Rome, perhaps motivated by a blend of humility, fear, and strategic wisdom. Their principal reason was to ask permission from the pope to continue to live as they had chosen to, not outside of the church but within it, as loyal sons rather than rebels. As the group of twelve walked to Rome they had no idea what the outcome would be. Other groups had tried and failed to receive papal approval. The bedraggled Francis pleaded for an audience with the pope and was granted it. Francis was allowed to speak to Innocent III, the most powerful man in Christendom. The son of a merchant came face to face with an aristocrat who had been elected to the papacy at the age of thirty-seven. The stuff of legends, the meeting would change the course of history.

One of the most intriguing frescos in the Basilica of St. Francis depicts Innocent III asleep and dreaming, in full papal regalia nonetheless. In his dream Innocent sees Francis carrying the church of St. John Lateran on his back as he walks away from the pope. The basilica was the official papal cathedral and the papal residence was attached to it. Innocent held court there surrounded by his advisors, most of whom were high-ranking prelates, especially cardinals. Whether the frescos depict precise historical events is difficult to say. What is important about the painting is its message. Innocent's power over the church was absolute, and he insisted on his right to intervene in all civil affairs. He excommunicated a record number of emperors and kings who resisted his will. He lusted for power but he sincerely wanted to reform the church. He denounced the corruption of certain prelates and tried to loosen the bonds that linked the church and state together, often to the church's detriment. Precisely for this reason he insisted on the superiority of the church over the state and believed that popes, as the Vicars of Christ, were the ultimate secular authority.

For all his claims about the absolute authority of the church, Innocent lost more than one battle to emperors and kings who outfoxed him. He also knew that the church's influence over the social order was in peril because of its corruption and lack of effective pastoral presence in so many parts of Europe. He knew something had to be done: new people had to be found to revitalize the church, but he was wary of new groups. The lesson of Peter Waldo was still fresh, and Innocent had called for a crusade against the Albigensians in southern France and northern Italy who entirely rejected the claims of the institutional church. His crusade quickly turned into a bloodbath with Christian killing Christian. Innocent was taken aback by the violence of the forces he unleashed, just as he would be by the savagery of the Fourth Crusade, which he sanctioned in the hope of regaining the Holy Land for Christians. The crusaders made it only as far as Constantinople, where they sacked and seized the city, creating animosity among Orthodox Christians that persists to this day.

When Francis and his companions arrived in Rome they had the good luck to encounter Bishop Guido, who was there to defend his interests in the papal court, a frequent occurrence for this litigious prelate. But he had only affection for this young man who had once embarrassed him in front of the notables of Assisi. Guido introduced Francis to Cardinal Giovanni di San Paolo, a former Benedictine and a powerful figure in the papal court. San Paolo was taken by Francis's enthusiasm and loyalty to the church. He questioned him for several days as he tried to discern what Francis was all about. Was he just one more madman or was he a sincere Christian? He most likely thought that Francis's commitment to absolute poverty was unrealistic, but he knew that the short and dirty man in front of him was truly holy. Soon thereafter di San Paolo made a statement in the papal court that made it possible for Innocent to meet Francis the next day.[23] "I have found a really excellent man who wants to live according to the gospel, preserving precisely its evangelical spirit. I am convinced our Lord wishes to renew the faith of the holy church, all over the world, through him."[24] Innocent talked with Francis the next morning in a kindly, pastoral exchange, but he could not make up his mind about approving Francis's simple rule and told him and his companions to wait until he could decide. Then he had his famous dream. The next day he gave provisional approval to Francis, who was subsequently ordained a deacon so he could preach officially. Francis was never ordained to the priesthood although he had the most profound respect for priests, even notoriously bad ones. In the spring of 1209 charisma and power met amicably and both won the day.

Francis's successful journey to Rome and legendary interaction with Innocent III led to a series of events that he could never have anticipated. A band of brothers became a religious movement that forever changed institutional Catholicism and its relationship to the social order. Because the amazing expansion of Francis's movement has been described well by many scholars, suffice it to say that twelve became a hundred and then thousands within Francis's lifetime. It was no longer limited to Italy and quickly became an international phenomenon. As Francis and his followers traveled the highways and byways of Christendom to preach, they attracted new followers in what can be described as a snowball effect. The problem was that Francis never intended to create one of the largest religious orders in the history of Catholicism. The *Rule* that he had written in the first stages of the group's life was short and simple but definitely not suited for a large order that required housing for its members as well as formation and education for those who entered it. Francis had forbidden the ownership of property or money but was now beset with pragmatic

---

23. Ibid.
24. Ibid., 93. House is quoting from *1 Leg. 3. Comp.* 48.

issues that often overwhelmed him. It was clear that the *Rule* had to be emended. It was Francis's last chance to insist on absolute poverty as the foundation of the Franciscans. He succeeded before his death as his companions accepted his pleas to never relent on their absolute commitment to evangelical poverty, but soon after Francis wrote the final version of the *Rule* it was overridden by papal decree. Perhaps he had a sense that this would happen, that evangelical idealism would give place to institutional realism. He wanted nothing to do with it.

Francis was a troubadour, and his love for Lady Poverty was all-consuming, his fidelity to her absolute. Francis would have been counter-cultural in any day or age. Yet this truly countercultural man was happy rather than a gloomy ascetic. He loved all people, especially the poor, and the natural world nourished his expression of divine love. He slept on the ground for ascetic reasons but also because he reverenced the earth. Like any human being Francis needed intimate human contact. He relished the company of his followers, but the most important person in his personal life was Clare of Assisi. When Francis was dying in 1226, she left the confines of her convent to bid farewell to her closest friend. He had played a central role in her personal and religious development, not as an authority figure but as a beloved companion. Francis's reliance on her was equally deep. When he was at his wit's end with institutional problems, she was the person he would consult, for the sake of comfort and clarity. They were spiritual advisors to each other. Clare was born into an aristocratic family in 1194. Clare, or Chiara in Italian, was the first daughter of Count Favorino Scifi. She resided within the confines of her wealthy parents' home with brief walks through town and attendance at religious services in the nearby cathedral. Members of her family or a family servant always accompanied her since girls of the aristocracy were never allowed to be on their own.

One day she encountered Francis preaching on the streets and was captivated by his exaggerated mannerisms and obvious zeal about Christianity. The year was 1210, and Clare's life was about to change radically. Her parents had arranged a marriage for her with the son of another aristocratic family. In the medieval world daughters were used to forge alliances between members of the same social strata. Marriage was not about romance; it was about power and maintaining the family line by entering into a contract with one's social equals. In all likelihood Clare had never met her husband to be and seems to have rebelled against the prospect of an arranged marriage or any marriage at all. She did the nearly inconceivable: in the dead of night she left her highly fortified home and fled to Francis who was living with his companions on the outskirts of Assisi. Immediately on finding Francis she professed her desire to be admitted to his movement. He received her with tremendous joy.

As was the custom in the monastic traditional, Francis cut Clare's hair and received her vows of poverty, chastity, and obedience. He then conducted her to a nearby Benedictine convent. Friars and nuns, obviously, lived apart despite their common vows and shared loyalty to the charism of their particular religious order. Clare's younger sister, Agnes, followed her within days, although she did not profess her vows immediately. Francis then led Agnes to the same convent. Francis and Clare, in different ways, had reneged on the expectations of their families and their social peers. Clare's relatives tried to remove her forcibly from her convent, but because she had pronounced her vows, they had to relent. Her new status as a nun provided her with the protection of the church. Taking vows was considered a second baptism in which the church redefined a person's identity, and any violation of religious vows was considered a serious sin. When they tried to abduct Agnes a few days later she literally kicked and screamed until they gave up. In light of the fact that they were knights accustomed to battle, she must have put up a spectacular fight.

By 1224 it was clear that Francis was approaching death. He was in excruciating pain and nearly blind. He never complained even when physicians cauterized his head with hot irons, purposefully scarring his temples in an attempt to alleviate his growing blindness and pain. He neither cried out nor flinched and thanked Brother Fire for his help. It is quite possible that Francis was suffering from malaria and trachoma, an intensely painful eye disease caused by parasites. Given his depleted state from fasting and travel, he had spent all his energy and resistance to disease. On foot and occasionally with the help of a mule, Francis left Assisi for his last forty-day retreat in a part of Tuscany called La Verna. It was a remote, wooded area that Francis often visited because of its rugged beauty and quiet forests. He stayed entirely by himself with food brought to him by his companion Leo, who left small portions that Francis occasionally ate. Leo, one of the few priests in the Franciscan movement and a member of the original group of twelve, knew Francis intimately. He respected Francis's request that he be left alone, although he was deeply concerned about Francis's physical weakness.

At La Verna Francis once again experienced a profound transformation. While in deep prayer he saw a blazing seraph, a type of angel. Completely transfixed, Francis's body assumed the wounds of Christ's crucifixion on his hands, feet, and side. In his account of what happened Leo mentions that he saw a flash of brilliant light, but Francis alone heard the voice of the seraph. He experienced pure ecstasy when he did. Exactly what happened on September 24, 1224, will never be known exactly, but there is no doubt that Francis was emotionally and physiologically transformed. Others, including Clare, saw the stigmata when Francis was on his deathbed two years later, although he had done everything possible to conceal it despite the bleeding and pain that made him hobble. It is hard to imagine that the wounds were self-inflicted. Because this was the first case in Christianity of someone experiencing the stigmata, Francis could not have had any preexisting idea of what it was or any predisposition to experience it. Francis was certainly under enormous stress when he went to La Verna. Once again he was revising the *Rule,* trying to maintain its total commitment to poverty. The stigmata that appeared on Francis's body have been a source of endless debate, and there is no definitive explanation. Perhaps the question should be approached symbolically rather than psychologically and physiologically. Francis always wanted to be one with Christ and experience the agony of his crucifixion. He also wanted to experience Christ's joy as the resurrected son of God. At La Verna he achieved his goal. He was ready to meet God face to face. He now added a new sentence to his famous *Canticle of the Sun* that he requested be carved on his coffin: "Praised be Sister Death." In the final hours of his life he asked his companions to remove his clothes and place him on bare ground so he could touch the soil of Umbria and Assisi that he loved so much.

Matching Bookends

It is difficult to juxtapose Thomas and Francis. They are different people, a proverbial case of apples and oranges. How do you reconcile a dispassionate intellectual with a passionate street preacher, a rationalist with someone who almost reveled in irrationality? These two icons of thirteenth-century Catholicism, however, are not so much polar opposites as two ends of a spectrum. They shared a common faith, and their approach to the institutional church was one of total loyalty. Both knew, however, that institutions and the ideals behind them can never be synchronized perfectly. There is always disparity. This insight drove Thomas to systematize Christian theology so it could be understood more readily, and Francis to hit the streets preaching to people so it could be lived more fully. Both tried to reform medieval Christianity, conscious that Christendom was a far cry from Jesus' vision. They were fully aware that the medieval world was unjust and violent. They knew that Christianity was used as a façade to legitimate non-Christian behavior. Religion was being used as an ideological weapon in the service of domination just as it is today. They certainly accepted the idea that God ruled over human affairs, but were not so naïve that they thought social constructs were an expression of divine will. Emperors and kings may have thought that, just as politicians do today, but Thomas and Francis would never have succumbed to such self-serving logic. Still, they lived in a world in which church and state were far too close to each other. In their own ways they wanted to make a clearer distinction, one by creating an elaborate social theory that carved out distinct realms for the spiritual and the secular, the other by living in such a way that indirectly he called the social order into question. They were reformers and like all who try to push things forward, they met with mixed results. In both cases those who followed them were lesser lights who could never match their genius as thinkers and actors. Who could? Thomas's great intellectual achievements were soon institutionalized by Thomists with their disparate interpretations of the master they claimed to follow. As Francis was dying his fellow Franciscans were beginning a great squabble about who could own what. Within a few years the movement would split and go in several directions.

Thomas seems stodgy by today's standards. He comes across as terrified by change. He certainly distrusted it, but he was not a political or social reactionary. The Middle Ages were not static but rather unstable and violent. Alliances were made and broken, and one of the few constants was war. Thomas, like any legitimate conservative, was wary of politics and social change that were driven by self-interest. As we know too well today, most revolutions are quickly betrayed by revolutionaries who are frequently self-deluded messiahs. Thomas wanted to avoid social turmoil because of the inevitable victimization it entailed. Yet his conservatism was not well served by his subservience to Aristotle, whose affinity for elite, top-down government is often a recipe for oppression. Because Thomas parrots Aristotle, his approach to the social order is easily manipulated in such a way that it contradicts Thomas's own principles. This critique first coalesced in the early phase of the Reformation and has been a major source of anti-Catholicism ever since, particularly since the eighteenth-century Enlightenment. No one can deny the intellectual power of the *Summa,* but it simply does not mesh with the political and social assumptions associated with the modern world — which is not to say that modernity is an unambiguous step forward. Thomas would have been outraged by many events that mark our contemporary world, from the genocidal conquest of the Americas by the Spanish and Portuguese to the systematic genocide of the twentieth century. Thomas was a true believer in justice and the innate rights of every woman and man as the image of God. Theory and practice, however, are always distinct phenomena, and one of the sadder aspects of Catholic history is the church's inability to live up to the ideals that Thomas himself sets forth. It is impossible to deny that institutional Catholicism often sides with top-down social structures, hoping to "Christianize" those with power and create a more Christian society. The Middle Ages make it utterly clear that this never works. As Thomas makes clear, you can never make people do the right thing.

Francis's legacy is easier to assess because it has a timeless quality to it. He was the subject of biographies soon after his death, and the number of books about him produced over the centuries would fill a small library. Thomas of Celano was commissioned to write Francis's biography two years after his death. And Bonaventure, the third master general of the Franciscans, combined various accounts of Francis's life in his official and perhaps most detailed biography around 1263.[25] Although sometimes Francis's biographers buffer their description of him, it is clear that Francis was a social critic, although he never would have used that terminology. But he did try to turn conventional wisdom on its head. Several of his earliest followers were from the merchant or aristocratic strata of Assisi, and Clare's Order of Poor Ladies freed women from the constraints of a patriarchal society. It also provided them with an education and self-worth that women otherwise could never have experienced. To refer to Max Weber, one of the great social analysts of the early twentieth century, there often is a connection between religion and critical social action.[26] There has always been a tension in Christianity between the real and ideal, and this is true of almost all religions as well. At their best, religions challenge distorted notions of God. People who live up to the ideals of their religious tradition are always countercultural and generally resented. Soon after Thomas's death the bishop of Paris condemned his theology. During his lifetime Francis was called a crackpot, and many of his own brothers refused to follow his vision. Yet "The Dumb Ox" and "God's Fool" forever changed the nature of Catholicism and its role in the world.

---

25. There is no doubt that both Thomas and Bonaventure attempted to write accurate stories of Francis's life. A constant problem with hagiography, or pious stories, is that they often contain exaggerated accounts that distort a saint's life. Thus, Francis tames wolves, and birds listen to him as he preaches near a tree.

26. Max Weber, *The Protestant Ethic and the Spirit of Capitalism* (New York: Penguin Books, 2002).

Chapter Five

Reforms and Revitalizations

Storm Clouds

As the previous chapter hopefully made clear, the Catholic Church was at the height of its power in the thirteenth century. Innocent III had created a highly centralized and efficient papacy-oriented church that also exerted control over most facets of secular society. The church was an all-pervasive watchdog, although there were still nooks and crannies in which a few nonconformists could hide. By mid-century Thomas Aquinas had elaborated an all-embracing theory that set out church/state relations in a detailed way. The church was the ultimate authority to be obeyed unequivocally, but Thomas respected the autonomy of the secular sphere in matters of government, as long as they conformed to church teaching. Until the beginning of the fourteenth century the church continued to have the upper hand despite ongoing conflicts with both the Holy Roman Empire and the French crown. The tables, however, turned from 1302 onward as the power of the church began a precipitous decline. The institutional church lurched from one crisis to another. It was like a child's top, a toy one hardly finds anymore, but the analogy is useful. The church had been spinning on a fixed axis for a century, but it suddenly began to slow down and spin erratically. Although it did not entirely stop, it came close to doing so. We need to trace its trajectory and the many forces that sent it bobbing around from the early fourteenth century until the mid-sixteenth — a long period of significant internal and external crises. The first crisis came in 1302 when Boniface VIII's attempt to extend the power of the church in an unprecedented way backfired, making the papacy a puppet of Charles IV, king of France. This led to the catastrophe known as the Babylonian Captivity. In 1307 Clement V moved from Rome to Avignon, a pleasant Mediterranean town close to the French border. There would be no resident pope in Rome for more than seventy years. Resolving the first debacle led to the second. Pope Gregory XI returned to Rome in 1377. When he died in 1378 the cardinals first elected Urban VI, but when he showed obvious signs of mental instability, they elected Clement VII. There were now two popes. By 1409 there were three popes claiming to be the legitimate successors of Peter. This second crisis was resolved in 1415, but by the mid-fifteenth century the church was bogged down once again as one corrupt pope followed another in what is generally referred to as the Renaissance papacy. There were, of course, reformers during this period, but none really succeeded until the sixteenth century when Luther's call for reformation took root and spread through northern Europe like a wild fire. We begin with the first crisis in the first few years of the fourteenth century.

The church possessed enormous wealth in the form of land and revenues generated by indulgences, the performance of rituals, and the scourge of simony. As centralized, money-hungry monarchies emerged, kings cast an envious eye on such vast wealth. Holding court, fielding armies, and establishing strategic alliances were expensive propositions. At the end of the thirteenth century, Philip IV, the young king of France, imposed taxes on the national clergy. The reaction of the Italian pope Boniface VIII was immediate and hostile. In 1292 he issued a papal document known as *Clericis laicos*. It had an arrogant tone that reflects Boniface's understanding of the papacy and church as extensions of God on earth. He defined the clergy as a profession qualitatively different from any other. It could not be taxed nor could derelict clergy be tried in civil court. The church was not bound to obey any civil statues, and wayward clergy could be tried only by ecclesiastical tribunals. Any prince who so much as suggested "revenue sharing" with the church could expect excommunication.[1]

In 1302, as his fight with the French king Philip IV intensified, Boniface issued another papal decree known as *Unam sanctam*, in which he asserted specifically that popes enjoy supremacy over kings even in terms of the internal policies of their nations. Boniface's understanding of papal authority went far beyond anything Thomas had proposed or would have considered prudent. Philip, now excommunicated, was not about to be intimidated by a pope who claimed to have the right to interfere in the internal affairs of his kingdom. On a personal level Philip detested Boniface and made no secret of his scorn for a man he saw as nothing more than a rapacious tyrant in priestly robes. Under pressure from the king, theologians at the University of Paris condemned Boniface on trumped-up charges of heresy and therefore no longer pope. In late 1302 Philip's henchman attacked Boniface in his hometown of Anagni. Attacking an old man is repugnant, but doing so to the bishop of Rome, the Vicar of Christ, was seen as a sacrilege. The traumatized pope fled to Rome, where he died a month later, perhaps due to the treatment he had been subjected

---

1. Boniface was not the first bishop of Rome to insist on the supremacy of the pope vis-à-vis the social order. The concept went back centuries, but Boniface's claim was especially strident.

to in Anagni. Philip ultimately apologized for the excesses of his retainers, but the goal had been accomplished. The papacy had been weakened, and the church in France was now under the thumb of the crown.

After Boniface died the papacy went into a tailspin. For the next two centuries there were a few good popes but many bad ones, who often were elected to advance the dynastic interests of powerful Italian families. The mentally unstable Benedict XI, who reigned for only a few months before he was likely poisoned, succeeded Boniface. The cardinals then elected one of their French confreres, who took the name of Clement V. After a sumptuous coronation attended by Philip IV in the southern French city of Lyon, Clement moved the papal court to Avignon. In order to appease Philip Clement tried to tone down Boniface's hyperbole with regard to the papal office. Clement was more than willing to rubber-stamp Philip's policies, even those that had a negative impact on the institutional church. A spectacular papal residence was built in Avignon to house the pope, cardinals, and ambassadors to the papal court from all over Europe. An enormous banquet hall was used for luxurious meals planned and executed by the best chefs in Europe. Fish were brought in from the British Isles and the finest silks and spices were on sale for ecclesiastical potentates and ambassadors who exchanged gifts and busied themselves with a thousand political intrigues. Avignon became a brokerage house that bought and sold ecclesiastical and political favors. Popes ruthlessly taxed dioceses throughout Europe that were required to pay yearly tithes or *annates* that represented 10 percent of diocesan revenues. Papal representatives functioned as aggressive tax agents who zeroed in on every source of available revenue. Running Avignon was a very expensive proposition. The popes and cardinals were hopelessly enmeshed in the nasty but lucrative power politics of France, the Holy Roman Empire, and other European monarchies. In its day-to-day activity the papacy was hard to distinguish from any other monarchy with its courtiers and army of hangers-on. The Catholic Church had entered into one of its most scandalous periods, rightly known as the Babylonian Captivity. Although some of the Avignon popes were men of integrity and even tried to temper some of the obvious abuses, attempts to clean up the church were generally blocked by members of the papal court who saw reform as a threat to their vested interests. The upper strata of the institutional church had become hopelessly corrupt and incapable of seeing its own behavior in an honest light.

Medieval Christians revered the bishop of Rome as the Successor of Peter and Vicar of Christ on earth, but what was going on in Avignon was a farce and sin in the eyes of many people, particularly educated men and women who were serious Christians. How could the pope be a pastor if he lived like a prince and an absentee landlord? In the *Canterbury Tales*

Geoffrey Chaucer laments the lack of integrity among many members of the clergy. The pope and priests became the butt of graphic jokes sung in inns and taverns. With the "top" of the church in disarray a near miracle happened at the "bottom." In 1376 a woman from Siena associated with the Dominican Order walked from her hometown in Tuscany to Avignon accompanied by a group of women who were as outraged as she was about the dismal state of the papacy and the church in general. Catherine of Siena was a devout and tenacious woman with uncanny strategic skills. When others had given up on the church, her love for it compelled her to walk several hundred miles and challenge the pope to do what he was called to do — be the bishop of Rome in Rome. In an age in which women had little overt power, Catherine convinced Gregory XI to return to his diocese despite his reluctance to leave the orange groves and sea breezes of the Riviera. As Catherine and Gregory's entourage traveled through Italy, crowds cheered them on.

Catherine died in 1380 only to have seen her efforts at reform undone by cardinals and other members of the papal court who had no intention of staying in a city that was in an advanced state of decay. Pilgrims still traveled to Rome to visit the tomb of St. Peter and other holy sites, but the city itself had lost its luster once the popes departed. It was rife with malaria and plague as well. When Clement died in 1378, the cardinals elected Urban VI, who soon proved to be another mentally unbalanced tyrant. With Urban VI still alive, they elected another pope, Clement VII, declaring that they had been coerced into electing Urban. Clement and his cardinal electors promptly returned to Avignon, much to the delight of the French. A crisis of legitimacy ensued that threatened the foundations of the papacy as never before. There had been rival popes in the past but usually the squabbles were short-lived with one party outmaneuvering the other in short order. This time there were powerful geopolitical forces behind each of the two popes. Not surprisingly, the French crown recognized Clement while the English monarchy, along with the Holy Roman Empire, sided with Urban. Spain and other European monarchies shifted their allegiance to fit their political agendas. Theologians in Paris recognized the pope in Avignon while their English counterparts in Oxford recognized the pope in Rome. Faculties of theology were dancing to the tune of their respective monarchs and realized that their interests were those of the king they were expected to serve, not the church.

The Western Schism was a continent-wide scandal that called into question the very nature of the papacy. How could a divinely established institution have become so overtly corrupt and church leaders so cynical? As always, there were popes and theologians of integrity who worked furiously to address the scandal of the Western Schism, but chaos reigned until 1417 with various claimants to the papal throne engaging in every possible form of dirty politics. A church council was called in 1410 and met in the Italian city of Pisa in a good-faith effort to clean up the scandalous mess that was eating away at the core of Catholic Europe. There was hope in the air since both the pope in Rome and his counterpart in Avignon had agreed to resign for the good of the church. When a new pope was elected at Pisa in 1415, both of the reigning popes immediately reneged on their promises, creating even greater chaos with three papal claimants denouncing each other as "antipopes." Who was the real pope — Gregory, Benedict, or Martin?[2] Eventually the Roman pope Martin V was recognized as the sole leader of the church, but the reputation of the papacy had been severely tarnished by an ecclesiastical debacle that blended the pathos of a Greek tragedy with the tawdriness of soap opera.

Between the Babylonian Captivity and the Western Schism the church was depleted and discredited in the eyes of many people, but secular society was hardly in better shape. One crisis and war followed another with the Ottoman Turks advancing on eastern Europe almost unopposed. From 1337 until 1453 an intermittent conflict between France and England known as the Hundred Years' War raged on. There was no real outcome other than ravaging French cities and slaughtering large numbers of peasants. Both countries nearly went bankrupt. Joan of Arc, betrayed by the French crown, was handed over to the English and the bishop of Beauvais and burned at the stake as a witch. From 1347 to 1351 bubonic plague ravaged Western Europe. Nearly 75 percent of the inhabitants of Florence died, and in other areas 30 to 50 percent of the population perished. Bubonic plague killed quickly but horribly. Chaos and death were everywhere, and desperate men and women looked for some form of respite for their suffering, not to mention an explanation for what they felt was the wrath of God. All sorts of bizarre and grossly magical religious behaviors emerged. Relics multiplied, and selling them became a major business. Popes and bishops sold indulgences to remit a person's time in purgatory. Jews were sometimes blamed for the plague and ruthlessly persecuted throughout Europe, often killed by the thousands. Some blamed the corruption of the papacy for their suffering. If only a saintly pope had resided in Rome perhaps the anger of God could have been averted. In 1978 the great historian Barbara Tuchman wrote a book entitled *A Distant Mirror.* The subtitle captures her thesis perfectly: *The Calamitous 14th Century.* The fifteenth century was not a great deal better.

Yet the calamity was not total, and despite the odds new Christian intellectual life was emerging. The fall of Constantinople in 1453 to the Turks

---

2. The Roman Catholic Church asserts that the Roman line of popes is valid; all others invalid. This is a reasonable assertion, but it is not at all clear at times who was who and whether he was duly elected.

created a flood of Byzantine scholars with Greek manuscripts in hand. They tutored theologians and secular intellectuals who now could read the New Testament in its original language and patristic documents from the Eastern church in Greek. It soon became obvious that Jerome had made mistakes translating the New Testament from Greek to Latin. For a millennium the Vulgate had been the only Latin translation of the Bible Catholics could read and now scholars questioned its accuracy. Many also learned Hebrew with the assistance of rabbis, and it became obvious that the same translation problems applied to the Hebrew Bible, or Old Testament. By 1440 it was clear that the "Donation of Constantine," reputedly a document in which Constantine gave Pope Sylvester control of the entire church, East and West, as well political control of the Western empire, was a poorly written forgery from the eighth century. The administrative, moral, and theological crises of the papacy and institutional church raised a host of serious questions. Why obey a pope who claimed to be a prince as well as a priest on the basis of a bogus document? Why watch papal taxes cross the Alps bound for Rome? No one was rejecting the spiritual authority of the church, but many questioned whether it had the right to veto the coronation of a prince as the king of England. The concept of a national church united with Rome symbolically but in charge of its own affairs internally began to make sense in ways that were previously unimaginable.

Early Reformations

In his superb book *The Reformation: A History* Diarmaid MacCulloch asserts that the Reformation in the sixteenth century is the byproduct of many antecedent "reformations" that were taking took place before Luther tacked his ninety-five theses to the castle church door in Wittenberg.[3] He, along with Calvin, Ignatius of Loyola, and the Catholic bishops who initiated the Council of Trent in 1545 were the end-products of a convoluted process of religious and sociopolitical change that had been taking place for a century. In order to address the crisis of credibility provoked by the Babylonian Captivity and the Western Schism, as well as the instability caused by never-ending wars, reform-oriented theologians, princes, and humanist intellectuals began to think about new models for the church and society that could better respond to changing times. It was clear that the old feudal order was breaking down and the church along with the state had to adapt to a new set of challenges. Five centuries removed from what was happening in the fifteenth and sixteenth centuries we use terminology like "late

---

3. MacCulloch, *The Reformation*, xvii. Most of the material about the "reformations" of the fifteenth and sixteenth centuries is drawn from MacCulloch's book.

medieval" and "early modern" that would have made little sense to intel-
lectuals in those times, but many clearly detected a shift taking in place
in the world around them. As a result of the Babylonian Captivity and the
Western Schism many people in the church called for frequent councils
that would oversee the papacy and set the tone for the church as a whole.
The so-called conciliarists wanted a pope and church that resembled the
Christian community that existed before the conversion of Constantine.
They wanted to re-create a community of equals with bishops and priests
serving the larger community rather than exploiting it. But councils are
notoriously inefficient when it comes to running a complex institution,
and even popes who recognized them in principle often resisted them in
practice. The conciliarists themselves were not united. They proposed several competing models for the church and often engaged in small-minded
squabbles with Oxford pitted against Paris, one theologian denouncing
another like boys fighting in a schoolyard.

But there were theologians of stature with coherent visions of a reformed
church. One of the most significant in the fourteenth century was Jan Hus.
Hus was outraged by the sale of papal indulgences and denounced them as
irreconcilable with the Bible a century before Luther would do the same.
He likewise condemned the insensitivity of a German-speaking church
hierarchy that held the Czech people in contempt. Hus gave voice to an
intense desire for church reform as well as the recognition of his people's
right to self-government as sovereign citizens of the Holy Roman Empire.
He demanded free access to the Bible translated into Czech and the right of
the laity to receive both consecrated bread and wine during the celebration
of the Eucharist so they could participate more fully in this all-important
sacrament.[4] In 1415 Hus was summoned to appear at the Council of
Constance, which had been convoked to resolve the Western Schism, and
actually did so. Hus asked the emperor Sigismund for safe passage to the
Council, where he was willing to discuss his theological positions. The
emperor agreed to protect him, and Hus took him at his word. He had
the presence of mind, however, to make out his will before he left Prague.
Hus still hoped that reform was possible and assumed that if he were
given a chance to explain his ideas they would be deemed acceptable. He
was wrong. The hierarchy of the church along with the German-speaking
princes was not about to debate someone who threatened their power. When
Hus arrived in Constance Sigismund retracted his promise of protection.
John XXII, a pope from the Pisa line, had Hus arrested. He was tried without
the right to defend himself and condemned to death as a heretic because he

---

4. Cook and Herzman, *The Medieval World View*, 205. The Fourth Lateran Council held
in 1215 prohibited the laity from receiving consecrated wine during the celebration of the
Mass. The right was reserved for the clergy.

refused to recant. He was burned at the stake on July 6, 1415, and his ashes were thrown into the Rhine with the hope that his memory likewise would be washed away. Legend has it that Hus's followers gathered up handfuls of ash at the base of the stake and secretly brought them back to Bohemia. To this day statues of Hus dot Czech cities, where he is revered as a patriot who died resisting the tyranny of the church and empire. As MacCulloch points out with great insight: "The pope's continuing problems with authority sprang not so much from the Church's enemies as from its friends."[5]

Religious Change and Social Conflict

October 31, 1517, is a day of mythic proportions for Protestant Christians, who refer to it as Reformation Day. Despite Hus's failure and treacherous execution, there had been small but successful reforms of the church going on in the late fifteenth and early sixteenth centuries. In Spain Queen Isabel and her advisor Cardinal Cisneros addressed the many forms of corruption that had afflicted the Spanish church for decades. Teresa of Avila and John of the Cross reformed the Carmelite Order, endured interrogations by the Inquisition, and wrote some of the greatest literature in the Spanish language. In 1516 Erasmus of Rotterdam produced a new translation of the Greek New Testament and became an international spokesperson for church reform. His theological and humanistic writings were prodigious. He was a committed member of the church but capable of ridiculing its contradictions and corruption. His most famous work, *In Praise of Folly*, mocks the pomposity of popes, the venality of prelates, and the scams of priests selling everything from fake relics to bogus indulgences. But Luther went far beyond Erasmus; sarcasm was replaced by rage. Luther had none of the social grace Erasmus was known for. Luther loved a good fight while Erasmus avoided conflict at all cost. An Augustinian monk, Luther had become progressively more skeptical about many of the church's claims, particularly papal power and the sale of indulgences based on what Diarmaid MacCulloch sarcastically calls the "purgatory industry."[6] Luther's criticism was based on the fact that none of these classic Catholic beliefs had any foundation in scripture. Luther knew the Bible by heart and was particularly knowledgeable about Paul's letter to the Romans. This long and enormously important letter had convinced Luther that Christians are saved by the grace of God alone, not by the ministrations of popes or sacraments performed by priests, albeit sincere ones.

---

5. MacCulloch, *The Reformation*, 37.
6. Ibid., 15.

Luther was finally pushed to his limits when the Dominican friar John Tetzel appeared in Wittenberg selling indulgences. A professor of scripture at the local university, Luther insisted on debating the whole issue of purgatory and the church's right to sell people "time off" from purgatory. Initially Luther was dismissed as one more backwater crank from a small German university, but the ferocity of Luther's attack forced officials in the church to deal with him. In a series of pamphlets and an eventual face-to-face debate between Luther and John Eck, a respected theologian allied with the papacy, the two theologians locked horns in a formal debate attended by many observers. Luther forcefully argued that there was no scriptural basis for the papacy, the doctrine of purgatory, and therefore the sale of indulgences. The debate took place in 1519 and lasted several days. Luther stated his views with characteristic intensity and was not about to be convinced otherwise by Eck who, like Tetzel, was a member of the Dominican order. Luther and Eck were skillful debaters well-versed in the Thomistic theological tradition that put stress on logical, sequential discourse. Something of a tennis match took place with the ball bouncing between two accomplished theologians, both of whom were convinced that their position was the correct one. The audience was equally divided between those who advocated reform and those who sided with traditional doctrine and practice. Almost all of Luther's colleagues at Wittenberg, both scholars and fellow Augustinian monks, supported their colleague, who risked his life by engaging in public debate. Everyone was aware of what had happened to Jan Hus a century before. Even before the controversy exploded they had listened to Luther and judged his position true. They sincerely wanted to reform the church in a way that reflected the simplicity of the first Christian community found in the Acts of the Apostles. They wanted a church with real moral authority, unlike the one that had emerged after the conversion of Constantine and the official recognition of Christianity as the religion of the Roman Empire. To their way of thinking, power-hungry popes who fielded armies in defense of papal territories and claimed to be accountable only to God were monstrous aberrations that had distorted the core message of the Gospel.

The tensions between Luther and the church were becoming more intense, and the possibility of resolving them amicably was evaporating. Luther wanted to reform the Catholic Church, to make it more biblical and democratic, but he was treated much as Hus had been a century before. His ideas were condemned, and he was finally excommunicated in 1520 by the Medici pope Leo X, who, like his papal predecessors, was too busy putting the final touches on St. Peter's to bother with one more nettlesome monk. He simply issued a papal bull that referred to Luther as a "roaring boar." Luther did not tremble as the prospect of eternity in hell because by 1520 he was convinced that the pope had no authority to send him there. He burned Leo's bull of excommunication in public, heaping scorn on the very idea of a corrupt pope condemning a sincere Christian. Luther was not a lone voice. His personal anger was especially intense, but he represented the discontent of many other Christians who were tired of the abuses inflicted on them by the institutional church and the aristocracy of the Holy Roman Empire. As a German Luther took particular offense at the ways in which poor people were duped and manipulated by unscrupulous church officials who pocketed a portion of the revenues they generated and sent the rest over the Alps to help rebuild churches in Rome, particularly the new and massive St. Peter's. Many also resented the exorbitant imperial taxes imposed by princes to maintain their castles and lavish lifestyles. Neither local merchants nor overworked peasants saw any benefit come from the money they were forced to hand over to bishops and princes. Peasants were especially resentful. Their lives were precarious at best, yet they were required to hand over a share of their crops and provide free labor on their masters' estates.

As Luther would soon realize, traditional deference to one's ecclesiastical and social superiors was beginning to unravel. From 1517 on Luther's proposed reforms happened with incredible speed. Towns that were Catholic became Protestant within a matter of months. Monks and nuns left their monasteries and convents in prodigious numbers and married. The Catholic Mass was suppressed in Wittenberg and other cities by municipal decree. In some places the anger against the established church was so intense that church buildings were attacked and the iconography so central to Catholic worship was defaced or destroyed. Luther had not foreseen what was happening and tried to restore order. He was a reformer, not a revolutionary and felt that events were unfolding in a chaotic way. On a social level there was another development that Luther had not foreseen. A sense of apocalyptic expectation was in the air and exploded in 1524 in a massive grassroots uprising against the feudal order, led by the ex-priest Thomas Müntzer, which ended up being a bloodbath. About three hundred thousand peasants took up arms and one hundred thousand died in one of the most violent uprisings in German history. Luther and other reformers were aghast at the level of rage that had been unleashed. Initially disposed positively to the peasants' grievances, when violence erupted Luther panicked and in 1525 wrote an infamous pamphlet entitled *Against the Murderous, Thieving Hordes of Peasants*. He did not hesitate to suggest to the German princes that they "smite, strangle, and stab" peasants who opposed their power and the divine rights of the Holy Roman Empire.

For many Luther had betrayed the Reformation not because of his theology but because of his social conservatism. Luther is sometimes portrayed as an "early modern" figure but more accurately he was a "late medieval" man. His commitment to church reform was courageous, but on a social level he was far less radical. Nonetheless, Luther and other reformers like Zwingli and Calvin had a rallying cry with tremendous social consequences: Faith Alone, Christ Alone, Scripture Alone. As the only means of salvation, the implications for the institutional church of such a theological position were monumental. But just as monumental was the impact of such a declaration for the church's role in people's day-to-day lives. Believers no longer needed the mediation of the pope or his priests to achieve salvation. If they could read scripture they could respond on their own to divine revelation. As Luther put it with characteristic bluntness when he was debating with John Eck about indulgences, a peasant with scripture was just as powerful as a pope presiding at Mass in St. Peter's. Therefore, every member of the Christian community was on an equal footing and capable of responding to God's grace through faith.

Trent and the Beginning of Tridentine Catholicism

When it became apparent that a third of Christendom had been "lost" to Protestantism, Paul III finally convoked a general council of the church in 1542. In 1545 it began to meet in the imperial city of Trent to the north of Rome and sat in various sessions until 1563. Its purpose was to refute the Protestant movement by making an unequivocal statement of Catholic belief and reforming facets of the institutional church that were in obvious need of repair. It succeeded on both scores, producing a systematic explanation of Catholic theology as well as reinvigorating the battered structures of the institutional church. The so-called Tridentine reforms remained normative for the Catholic Church until the Second Vatican Council, held from 1962 to 1965. Trent was theologically and socially conservative. Ecclesiastical and social hierarchy were strenuously defended. Although it took several decades to implement the decrees issued by the Council, Trent produced a clear statement of Catholic belief as well as a particular approach to the social order. Both were profoundly hierarchical. The reformers had rejected the pillars of medieval Catholicism — the papacy, the Mass as the efficacious and literal reenactment of Jesus' death, the existence of purgatory, and the superiority of scripture over tradition. Trent restated these central Catholic beliefs, condemning every assertion of the Protestant movement.

The tensions were not about theological differences alone; they were also about the geographical and political power blocs that the Reformation had helped create. Western Europe was being divided up increasingly between the Catholic Church and different strains of Protestantism, particularly those associated with Martin Luther and John Calvin. About two-thirds of present-day Germany sided with Luther, and parts of Switzerland and most of the Netherlands followed the lead of Calvin and the Reformed Church he had established in Geneva. In 1534 England would also side with the Protestant cause as Henry VIII broke with Rome. Rome's refusal to annul his marriage with his first wife, Catherine of Aragon, as well as his desire to appropriate church property to fill state coffers, led to the creation of the Church of England. In the Holy Roman Empire prince-electors chose sides according to their theological preferences as well as their economic and political interests. Since there were only seven of them, the way they voted for a new emperor was a major consideration. The nobility of the empire soon formed leagues to defend their respective territories. Catholic and Protestant aristocrats began to eye each other warily. In the sixteenth century armed conflict between hostile theological and political camps was sporadic, but in the seventeenth century it became truly bloody. From 1618 until 1648 the Thirty Years' War engulfed central Europe with devastating consequences for the future of Christianity. After the ardor of the early Reformation burned off, fewer and fewer people knew exactly why they were Catholic or Protestant other than the fact that they had been born in Bavaria and were therefore Catholic or were raised in Hamburg and were therefore Protestant. The Thirty Years' War led to a general fatigue with theological squabbles and skepticism about whether the church had a positive role to play in society. For many, particularly educated Europeans, religion became a personal affair, and by the end of the eighteenth century, an increasingly irrelevant one.

Trent saved the Catholic Church from total disaster. It put together a solid statement of its beliefs contained in a catechism issued in 1566. The Catholic position was spelled out in black and white, along with a condemnation of anyone who dared challenge it. Trent was not theologically innovative in the least, but it did clean up facets of the institutional church in dire need of repair, particularly the episcopacy and priesthood. The episcopacy was in particularly bad shape because of the twin evils of pluralism and absenteeism. Since dioceses could be lucrative business propositions, savvy bishops often bought another whenever possible. Avignon had been infamous. Nearly any ecclesiastical position could be purchased as church law was overlooked for a price. The so-called Renaissance papacy of the late fifteenth century had produced a new wave of simony. Pope Alexander VI, a member of the Medici family, made enormous amounts of money by appointing people to church offices, including his bastard sons. Many bishops never set foot in their dioceses. Many had revenues transferred to them through medieval banking concerns, which made physical presence in their diocese unnecessary. Bishops' retainers acted like financial officers whose job it was to make sure that diocesan parishes paid their tithes on time. Obviously, few bishops were pastors even in a nominal way. Prior to Trent bishops were not accountable in any real sense of the term. If they were astute enough as ecclesiastical politicians, they had little to fear, and many were willing to call on secular authorities to defend their power. These abuses diminished after Trent, and increasing numbers of bishops were men of integrity. When Charles Borromeo, an ecclesiastical reformer and fierce advocate of the Council of Trent, arrived in Milan to lead the diocese in 1560, he was the first resident bishop in eighty years. He encountered a predictable array of problems. Many priests were living scandalous lives and were the butt of jokes. Most people were religiously illiterate. Catholicism was a sort of identity card but not a real part of their lives.

Borromeo set about cleaning and reforming the church with unparalleled intensity. He literally cleaned out the cathedral by removing ornate shrines and family tombs that had become more prominent than the cathedral altar itself. He did not even spare the tombs of his fellow Medicis. When plague struck Milan, he opened up every available church building to help its victims. He did not hesitate to spend time on the streets directing efforts to help people in every way possible. He was almost fanatical in his zeal. He expected 100 percent compliance with the decrees of Trent and tried to micro-manage every facet of daily life for the citizens of Milan. He had a strange proclivity to try to supervise people's family and sexual lives, but on this score he met with little success. Nearly everyone ignored him. But Borromeo set the tone for episcopal leadership — a hard-nosed, no-nonsense bishop but one who cared for the people of his diocese. Despite initial resistance Borromeo became a respected bishop. Priests and laity obeyed him. Clerical celibacy was reestablished and men and women formed confraternities that strengthened their Catholic identity. Borromeo won the hearts and minds of many people in Milan. Because of Borromeo and bishops like him, Trent worked when other councils had failed. Few people had the time or ability to read its decrees, but the reform of the church was becoming more evident, and people began to feel optimistic about its future. Naturally there were still problems. Institutions generate them by their very nature, but the Council of Trent pushed the church forward. Pluralism and absenteeism disappeared. Bishops could no longer leave their diocese without explicit papal permission to do so. They were being held accountable, judged for the administration of their dioceses as well as the fervor of the faithful they now ministered too. Of course, the hierarchical structure of the church remained intact. Bishops remained monarchs who ruled with an iron fist. Priests were seen as soldiers under episcopal command. Orders were to be obeyed without the slightest hesitation. Just as priests obeyed bishops, laymen and women obeyed their priests. Parishes were also monarchies. The pastor was the supreme authority who was also to be obeyed with complete docility. Trent was clear about the hierarchy of the church. It had been established by Christ, and its power therefore was sacrosanct.

Even a hands-on bishop like Borromeo remained a distant figure for most people, with the exception of the clergy. Few Catholics knew much about their bishop other than his name, and for some even that was a stretch. Then and now, a bishop is usually seen as an aloof authority figure who might appear in a parish on a rare occasion such as a confirmation ceremony, but otherwise has little to do with ordinary people's religious lives. Catholicism is no different from any other religious tradition: hierarchical leadership is an unfamiliar and distant abstraction. Belief is local and contextual. The priest, however, is another story. He interacts with ordinary men and women all the time. A good parish priest knows his people, and this requires more than the perfunctory celebration of baptism, Mass, marriage, and funerals. If he is a good priest he rubs elbows with the people around him. He knows the joys and sorrows of people's lives. He may well know many of his parishioners' names and those of their children. The priest is the person who explains and presumably lives out the meaning of Catholicism in relationship to those he is called to serve. He is the crucial link between the church and the social order, in many ways far more important than a pope, cardinal, or bishop. Prior to the Council of Trent the education of priests was a haphazard affair. Religious orders like the Augustinians, Dominicans, and Franciscans did have a system in which candidates went through a novitiate, an initial phase of discernment and intense observation, followed by studies and ordination if a candidate was deemed worthy. The expected result of this training was a committed member of the order and a virtuous priest. Luther is a good example.

The road to ordination for diocesan clergy, however, was not as structured or strenuous. A few priests were educated formally but many were barely literate. They memorized the Latin text of the Mass, sometimes cranking out as many Masses as they could for the sake of the stipends they needed to live on. Some, of course, were exemplary pastors, but too many were not. The majority of priests probably fell in between, neither saints nor sinners. Since the episcopacy was in such terrible shape prior to Trent, few priests received guidance from their bishops. Simony was also rife in the priesthood. Parishes could be bought and sold from a bishop, and not infrequently an "owner" was not even a priest. Actual priests often were hired on a contractual basis and expected to perform rituals and sacraments for the local population. In one of the ironic twists of history, John Calvin, the reformer of Geneva, received an annual stipend from a parish his father had obtained for him from the bishop of Noyon in northern France. It paid for his education at the University of Paris, where he left the Catholic Church and became one of its most articulate critics. But Calvin had never been ordained to the priesthood — not such a rare situation in the early sixteenth century. For Calvin, who gave up his ecclesiastical appointment before he left the Catholic Church, such an appointment was indicative of the deep-seated corruption that had eaten the church from the inside out. Calvin was an intellectual who was capable of seeing the larger picture. Like Luther, he insisted that most aspects of the institutional church were illegitimate trappings, mere accretions from the past that needed to be cast off.

Most ordinary priests, however, did not spend time worrying about the institutional church, nor did they have the theological training to do so. Many lived in remote villages ministering to a largely illiterate population, providing sacraments and doing their best to maintain Christian "micro-societies." In *The Voices of Morebath* Eamon Duffy presents the observations of Christopher Trychay, Morebath's chatty pastor. "Sir Christopher," as he was known, was an honest and sincere priest.[7] There is no indication of any impropriety on his part, and he served his flock of thirty-three families as well as he could. A humble population of peasants and artisans, most of whom were poor and almost none of whom had ever traveled more than a few miles from their self-contained village, generally appreciated him. Yet Sir Christopher hardly refers to the diocesan bishop, who would have been unlikely to set foot in a remote sheep-raising village anyway. It is not really clear how Sir Christopher prepared for the priesthood or how he ended up spending the rest of his life in Morebath — with apparent satisfaction. The informality of priestly training, however, was about to change. Trent established a system of education and formation that would last until the mid-1960s, shaping innumerable generations of priests and bishops.

After Trent seminary education became a highly structured, cookie cutter process. Whether candidates for the priesthood studied in Italy or Hungary made no difference. Every class was taught in Latin, and philosophical and theological studies were based exclusively on the writings of Thomas Aquinas and later Thomistic commentaries. Church history was taught with the premise that every facet of Christian history legitimated the claims of a highly centralized papacy. Jesus had set everything in motion when he named Peter the first pope. Of course, there had been bad popes, but the papal office and almost every aspect of the institutional church were divinely mandated. Insiders in a state of grace were saved, but even good outsiders were presumably damned. The Catholic Church was the all-important and only conduit of God's grace. Eastern Orthodox Christians were schismatics, but Protestant reformers were heretics. The former might squeak into heaven, but the latter were consigned to

---

7. The title of "Sir" was an honorific title given to priests. It is the equivalent of the term "Father" used for most priests today. It does not denote any sort of knightly or aristocratic status.

hell. Candidates for holy orders were trained rigidly as future defenders of the Catholic Church, told over and over again that they were called to do battle with the likes of "nonbelievers" like Luther and his ilk.

Seminarians were expected to know the decrees of Trent inside out and backward. Unqualified loyalty to the church and papacy was a given. Seminary training was analogous to basic training in the military. Daily life consisted of unending time in chapel along with a "yes Father" mentality. Students who could not make the cut were unceremoniously shown the door. As future priests they were expected to refute the lies of anyone who refused to accept the self-evident truth of Catholicism. Protestants willfully refused to accept real orthodoxy and Jews and Muslims were willfully ignorant. Neither could be saved. Seminaries were hermetically sealed environments just like modern boot camps. They had to be purified of any sort of intellectual or moral temptation. Wayward ideas or personal behavior that did not conform to rigid intellectual and moral norms, particularly around sexual issues, meant immediate expulsion from the seminary. A generalized atmosphere of repression prevailed, which was considered necessary and wholesome for troops preparing for life-or-death combat. Women were expressly feared as temptresses, intent on seducing wholesome seminarians and priests. Mothers and sisters were only rarely allowed to visit seminarians, and even after ordination, priests were expected to maintain a prudent distant from almost every female. But the shadow side of this sort of formation is obvious. Future priests might ask for clarifications of theological issues but were not allowed to raise critical questions about anything else. Any expression of personal need was considered a dangerous sign of sinful weakness. Personal issues could be addressed only in the secrecy of the confessional, and even there a confessor might demand that a student leave the seminary forthwith. Ordinary Catholics saw priests as strange creatures with little experience of day-to-day life — marital sexuality, raising children, and putting food on the table. The clergy was put on a pedestal but also was perceived to be a rather odd species different from everyone else.

There are two phenomena that symbolize the oppression and repression that became the cornerstones of priestly formation after Trent. One is the Index of Forbidden Books, established in 1542, and the other the Roman Inquisition begun in 1559. The purpose of the Index, as it is commonly known, was to make sure that Catholics, lay and clergy, did not read any written works that the institutional church considered heretical. Willfully doing so was considered a mortal sin. Seminaries had so-called Index Rooms in which the works of the reformers and even secular writers were kept under lock and key. Students could read them for the sake of research, but only to the extent that doing so provided greater insight into the very errors the works contained. And they could do so only with the explicit permission of the seminary rector. Asking to read a book in the Index Room naturally was the kiss of death. Why would anyone want to read bad ideas to begin with? When the Index was abolished in 1967 it had grown to include the works of Victor Hugo and Jean-Paul Sartre. The Index was akin to the Inquisition — the former rooted out heresy while the latter made sure no one had a chance to be exposed to it. Seminary students studied texts but rarely questioned their meaning or recognized their deeper significance. Conditioned to conform at all costs, they often ended up being agents of intolerance, confusing blind obedience and social conformity with virtue. The premise of the rigidity that set in with and after Trent is an old one that goes back to Augustine, namely, error has no rights. Thinking and behaving that deviated from the norm were seen as a cancer that threatened the welfare of the church and the common good. It had to be eradicated as quickly and unequivocally as possible to make sure it did not spread.

Just as there was one true theological system, there was one true social behavior — one supervised by the church and conformed to its definition of a Catholic society. Belief was supposed to mesh with a personal and social order, thus maximizing the possibility of eternal salvation. Priests and bishops were supposed to do everything in their power to help make this possible, confessing sin and encouraging action that maximized the possibility of salvation. There was no middle ground, no gray territory in the struggle with eternity. Trent was based on certainty and therefore there was zero tolerance for doubt or ambiguity. The church alone knew what was best for the individual and the social order because, guided by the hand of God, it alone could speak infallibly. For precisely such reasons the Catholic Church was adamantly opposed to any separation of church and state well into the twentieth century. Personal liberty was possible but only so long as its exercise conformed with established church teaching. On ethical, social, and theological levels priests and bishops were trained to look backward toward a supposedly Christian era in which church and state co-existed, an idyllic but ultimately imaginary moment in which individuals and the social world they inhabited were more virtuous than the present. This Golden Age harkened back to Innocent III, Francis of Assisi, and Thomas Aquinas — the idyllic thirteenth century that actually was far less Christian than it was imagined to be. In many ways the Council of Trent looked backward rather than forward. It succumbed to nostalgia for the past and had great difficulty with the present. Theological and social conservatism became the stock and trade of the Catholic clergy, wearing vestments that harkened back to imperial Rome rather than the early modern era. Even today, despite a gap of five hundred years, there are those who think Trent should still be the norm, with its rigid theology and its connection with the medieval world — an unsurpassed glory that somehow can be replicated in the twenty-first century. Protestantism has been surpassed by a new enemy — a complex and pluralistic modern world that knows little or nothing about what Catholics believe and therefore fails to see the truth.

Ignatius of Loyola: Trent's Great Warrior

In 1492 one of the most momentous events in Spanish history took place, one that rivals Columbus's "discovery" of the Americas. The last Muslim city in the Iberian Peninsula fell to Spanish forces, ending a long struggle of "reconquest," known in Spanish as the *Reconquista.* Since the eighth century Christian kings had chipped away at the territory under the control of the Moors. When Isabel and Ferdinand, *los reyes católicos,* or the Catholic kings, took possession of Granada they finally had the opportunity to create a homogenous Catholic country. Isabel headed up the campaign with unparalleled intensity. She was a woman of unusual talent — highly intelligent, theologically versed, and politically astute. Isabel was also an intensely devout queen who wanted to reform the Spanish church, which was as corrupt and dysfunctional as the rest of its counterparts in Europe. She succeeded where others had failed, creating a political and religious culture that was almost synthetic. Although Spain had been culturally and religiously diverse prior to the reconquest, with Jews, Muslims, and Christians living and working together in relative harmony, that all changed in 1492. Pluralism became a vice and cultural homogeneity a requirement for living in the kingdom. Within months of the fall of Granada Jews and Muslims faced an agonizing choice, conversion or exile. Some accepted Catholicism but most left Spain. A once flourishing intercultural and religious experiment came to a tragic end. The Inquisition in Spain helped create a Catholic "monoculture" searching for the slightest sign of political or religious deviance. Everyone was subject to scrutiny because of a vast network of domestic espionage. Jewish and Muslim converts to Christianity were subject to particular scrutiny. Even the slightest hint that they continued to practice their former faiths in secret led to interrogation, possible torture and trial, and sometimes execution. Non-conformity had become a crime.

Ignatius of Loyola was born in the Basque country of northern Spain in 1491 to an aristocratic family that prided itself on military service to the crown and an unwavering loyalty to the Catholic Church. Northern Spain had been Catholic for centuries. Ignatius's family took enormous pride in its warrior pedigree and had been well rewarded by grateful Spanish kings. Once Ignatius managed to stand he could look over his family's feudal lands and the serfs who worked them every day. Church steeples and roadside chapels that attested to a deep-seated, medieval Catholic faith marked the landscape. Ignatius knew from early childhood that he was destined for great things. He was, but in ways he never could have anticipated. As soon as Ignatius was ready his father had him sent to court, where he was expected to learn proper manners, the art of political intrigue, and how to be a soldier, like every other male member of the Loyola clan. He took his lessons seriously and did well on every count. Ostensibly a devout Catholic, Ignatius nonetheless had more than his share of vices. He reveled in flattery, particularly from young aristocratic women. His vanity was boundless and likewise his self-righteousness. The slightest perceived affront to his sense of honor could produce a murderous reaction. He was a narcissistic, dangerous nobleman addicted to tales of chivalry and convinced that he soon would be invincible on the field of battle.[8] Ignatius was the sort of person most people secretly detest, understandably fear, and do their best to stay away from. Ignatius says so himself.[9] Few Catholics saints, with the exception of Augustine, have left so much autobiographical information, and the amount of subsequent historical study about Ignatius and the Society of Jesus he founded in 1540 is enormous. Ignatius and the Jesuits would soon be propelled to the forefront of the Counter-Reformation set in motion by the Council of Trent.[10] In 1521, however, Ignatius was still a pompous dreamer with visions of worldly glory. His plans, however, came to an abrupt end. Defending an indefensible castle against French troops he stood alone against an unstoppable assault. Although his fellow soldiers had the good sense to retreat, Ignatius was not about to cede an inch of Spanish territory. But he was not able to stand his ground very long because his leg was shattered by a French cannon ball that nearly killed him, both physically and psychologically.

The Battle of Pamplona saved Ignatius from historical oblivion. If he had been remembered at all, it would have been as one more minor aristocrat who survived the horrors of war and retired to his country estate to enjoy the pleasures of a feudal lord. Ignatius escaped such a prosaic fate because after his encounter with defeat in battle, he discovered an inner and heretofore unknown spirit and power that changed the course of his life. He would become one of the great figures of Western Christianity, arguably as significant as Augustine or Aquinas. After Pamplona, Ignatius was carried back on a stretcher to the family castle in Loyola to recuperate from his wounds. Nearly unbearable physical and psychological pain awaited him, bringing him close to the brink of self-destruction.

---

8. Meissner, *Ignatius of Loyola.*

9. Ignatius of Loyola, *Personal Writings*, 13.1.

10. There is a growing consensus among historians that the term "Counter-Reformation" may not be the most adequate term for Catholicism after the Council of Trent. Some now refer to this period as the "Catholic Reformation."

He had to engage in a mighty battle to save his body and soul, both of which had been smashed. Perhaps naïve or self-deluded, Ignatius thought initially that he would be able to return to his former life in court and on the battlefield. Pleasure and glory still awaited him. He put his faith in the ability of surgeons to put him back together again, enduring excruciating surgery in the process. When their effort failed and he still walked with a limp, he insisted that they operate again. Without the anesthesia we take for granted today, it is hard to imagine the pain Ignatius went through. But once again surgery failed, and it gradually dawned on Ignatius that there would be no more flirtations with beautiful women or displays of swordsmanship for admiring onlookers. When it became obvious that all of the additional pain had come to nothing Ignatius went into what we know today as a major depression. His symptoms were classic: a sense of utter worthlessness and a near total disregard for his own well-being. He ate only because he was ordered to do so. Ignatius clearly preferred to die rather than relinquish his dreams and endure the humiliation of having a flawed body. He could not bear the thought of scorn as a semi-invalid.

Due to the devoted nursing of his beloved sister-in-law Magdalena, one of the few people Ignatius would listen to, his body did begin to heal.[11] His spirit did as well, thanks to one of the most important books of medieval Christian spirituality, *The Imitation of Christ*, written by the fifteenth-century mystic Thomas à Kempis. Thanks to Kempis and long periods of prayer that he would come to relish, Ignatius found a new purpose in life. Although he would never be in physical combat again, he came to see that he had a future as a pilgrim/warrior fighting for salvation, his own and that of others. As Ignatius went through the painful process of redefining himself, he had an intense spiritual experience of comfort and love like none other in his life. He mentions in his autobiographical writing that Mary appeared to him holding the child Jesus. He suddenly felt loved in ways that he had not experienced before. His mother had died when he was an infant and Ignatius's father rarely had anything to do with him, a typical pattern among aristocratic fathers and sons. Whatever happened, and there certainly are purely psychological explanations for what occurred, Ignatius finally felt accepted and affirmed. He was overwhelmed by a wave of maternal love. He was no longer a slave to his narcissism and *macho* vanity. He replaced his self-absorption with an all-absorbing desire to achieve a victory for God. The glory of Spain had been replaced by the glory of God. *Ad majorem Dei Gloriam* (For the greater glory of God) is a motto that became the principal metaphor for the rest of Ignatius's life and the central purpose of the Society of Jesus that was soon to be born.

---

11. Meissner, *Ignatius of Loyola*, 44–65.

The details of Ignatius's life between his conversion experience in 1523 and the foundation of the Society of Jesus in 1540 are well documented. During this phase of his journey Ignatius developed a profound method for examining who he was, discovering the will of God for his life, and following through with a plan of action. Although we will never know what happened exactly during Ignatius's convalescence, perhaps he was unconsciously putting together a strategy that would provide him with the self-knowledge and strength he needed to find a new purpose in life. His feelings, thinking, and writing coalesced into one of the great classics of Western Christian spirituality — *The Spiritual Exercises,* — a series of reflections that he began to write after he left Loyola on his way to the famous shrine of Mary in Montserrat near Barcelona to pray in thanksgiving for his physical survival and spiritual regeneration. *The Exercises,* as they are generally known, are based on a month-long process of intense inner scrutiny in which everything is set aside in order to ascertain who a person really is and what God is asking him or her to do. There are no distractions or prior assumptions. The slate is wiped clean during the first days of the retreat. The person on retreat speaks to no one accept a spiritual director and only then for a few moments each day. A simple passage from scripture is read, and the text is plumbed for its meaning for the next twenty-four hours. The spiritual director helps the person interpret the passage, but its application to daily life is something the person making the retreat decides and carries out. In Ignatius's case he saw himself called to proclaim the word of God as a fearless missionary preaching and defending Catholic truth. It is hardly surprising, given his Spanish background, that he saw himself trying to covert Muslims to Christianity. Although there are many twists and turns in the story, Ignatius came to realize that his destiny did not involve instant martyrdom in a Muslim country, but rather in more mundane ways that were still to be revealed by God. Ignatius's *Exercises* put great stress on "discerning spirits," and he had no doubt that God would eventually tell him what to do.

In the meantime, however, he realized that he was woefully inadequate on an intellectual level. He knew about chivalry but virtually nothing about philosophy and theology. Ignatius the pilgrim became Ignatius the student as he studied in a series of Spanish universities, finally ending up at the University of Paris. Because of his age and limp he stood out from his fellow students. He was an odd commodity, but he still possessed his courtly charm and unusual courage. At first a bit at a loss in an academic environment, he eventually began to find his voice as he acquired the knowledge and skills he felt he needed to preach and defend the truth of Catholicism. A few of his fellow students were attracted to this strange, middle-aged man trying to create an intellectual framework for his still to be defined purpose in life. Just as Francis had done three centuries before, Ignatius quickly became the father and brother, fellow pilgrim and spiritual director, of a small band of devoted followers. Once again Ignatius was commanding troops, and he knew what to do instinctively. He created a tight formation and waited for orders from his superior officer. He went to Rome and met with Paul III, a reforming pope who was trying to convoke a council to counteract that challenge of reformers like Luther and Calvin.

Ignatius and his young followers proved to be the best troops available in what was shaping up to be an out-and-out religious war. Paul III was an intellectually gifted pope, and he could sense the fervor and talents of the men before him. They were articulate, urbane, and unequivocally committed to the institutional church. They were likewise committed to lives of poverty, chastity, and obedience. Ecclesiastical bureaucrats who — despite the revolt against the church going on in Germany and other parts of Europe — still hesitated to engage in the hard and embarrassing work of reform were holding up Paul's plans for a general church council. A new and dedicated group of men could only work in Paul's favor. Two decades of condemnations and defensive maneuvers had failed to stem the tide of Protestantism. A serious counteroffensive was required. Like medieval knights, Ignatius and his followers had taken a public and special oath of loyalty to the pope. Between the newly recognized Society of Jesus and the clarity achieved by the Council of Trent, the Catholic Church could finally stand its ground.

Ignatius's initial missionary impulse to convert Muslims evolved into a commitment to save non-Catholics as well as non-Christians. Ignatius and his companions held the age-old belief that outside of the church there is no salvation and the only true church is Roman Catholic. For Ignatius this was an absolute truth whose defense was worthy of martyrdom. It impelled him, therefore, to convert and save as many people as possible, not out of a desire to conquer them but out of concern for their eternal salvation. Whatever the cost, Ignatius was willing to pay the price. Protestants were not the only people in danger of damnation. There was also a newly discovered world of countless souls who knew absolutely nothing about Jesus and his church. In the minds of sixteenth-century Catholics, and Protestants as well, these unfortunate beings lived in total darkness and needed the light of Christ to avoid eternity in hell. There was a tremendous urgency to move as quickly as possible, but the "reconversion" of Protestants and the Christianization of "heathens" required a solid intellectual formation and nerves of steel. After his conversion experience Ignatius had devised the perfect training program based on years of spiritual and intellectual formation and a total willingness to fight to the death, defending and preaching the Catholic faith. The newly founded Society of Jesus had been put together in such a way that it was unencumbered by the restraints of medieval monastic life. Ignatius and his companions were not interested in monks' regalia or deferential treatment as members of the clergy. There were no monastic estates to maintain or endless Masses to be celebrated for benefactors. Ignatius had created small, agile companies of soldiers capable of moving quickly and adapting new strategies on the fly. Within a few years of its foundation Jesuits like Peter Canisius was "winning back" German Protestants and Francis Xavier was training Japanese noblemen for the Catholic priesthood.

One of the reasons for the early success of the Jesuits was their recognized ability to teach well nearly anywhere. Ignatius insisted that his followers be as adept as teachers as they were committed as pastors. Like any good teacher they used cutting-edge pedagogy kept up to date with the latest scholarly insights. Much of the Jesuits' energy was directed at training young men from well-placed families with the hope that their solidly Catholic spiritual formation and orthodox education would not only define who they were but shape their future careers as political and social leaders. There is no doubt that this top-down education system worked, and even after their formal educations ended, well-placed Catholics relied on the advice of their old Jesuit teachers and spiritual directors. It is not an exaggeration to say that the Jesuits were often a "power behind the throne," which gained them the hostility of certain of their fellow Catholics, most notably the eminent French mathematician and philosopher Blaise Pascal, who considered them sophists who confused means with ends. Protestants had a particular loathing for the Jesuits. They were stereotyped as the quintessence of everything evil connected to the papacy and Roman Catholicism. They were nothing more than highly educated liars who presented a clear and present danger to everything accomplished by the Reformation. As the great Puritan John Milton put it in seventeenth-century English, they were "a grim wolf with privy paw" — consummate schemers disguised as men of virtue. The stereotype of the arrogant and socially connected Jesuit, however, is something of a useful fiction. Many Jesuits worked with people at the bottom of the social ladder. Ignatius tirelessly ministered to prostitutes in Rome, trying to provide them with a way to escape early death as "fallen women." Members of the hierarchy and Rome's social oligarchy were scandalized, but he continued his work with women whose existence was considered an embarrassment and sinful. It is clear, nonetheless, that the Jesuits were politically and socially cautious despite the glaring inequalities of the world around them. They were reasonable conservatives who saw the social order as a fairly static proposition that could be improved only in small, multigenerational increments. They were intensely committed to a hierarchical church. Yet their religious vision was fresh and invigorating. They helped breathe new life into the institutional church after Trent. But on a social level, the Jesuits were hardly gripped by revolutionary fervor.

As foreign missionaries the Jesus had far more success than they did in Europe, which was now hopelessly polarized as Catholics and Protestants damned each other as heretics. They traveled in the wake of Portuguese and Spanish ships, but generally did not make the mistake of other missionary groups that turned a blind eye to the brutality of *conquistadores* like Cortés and Pizarro, whose cynicism was matched by their savagery. Most worked with the assumption that conquest was a necessary prelude to conversion, a necessary violence ultimately worth the toll it exacted on savages who had to be saved. The Jesuits were more astute politically and culturally more sensitive. They had to admit that the Asian people they encountered in India, China, and Japan were highly sophisticated. The same was true of the highly developed civilizations of Mexico and Peru. In terms of religion the Jesuits were hardly relativists, but they were capable of appreciating the variability of culture. They were not about to put the truth of Catholicism on the table where it could be analyzed and picked over. But they realized that there was a difference between culture and Christianity: the first was a medium, the second the message. Imposed Christianity could never be real Christianity. Belief had to be understood and affirmed as true, not forced on people trying to mollify their conquerors for the sake of survival. In India Robert de Nobili became a skilled linguist with a vast knowledge of Sanskrit and Indian religious beliefs. In China Matteo Ricci gained admission to the imperial court, where he was a respected astronomer and mathematician.[12] De Nobili and Ricci met with some success because they were willing to look beyond their own world. They were gifted men who knew that truth and God were ultimately a mystery that no culture, intellectual tradition, or theological system could explain. They were light years ahead of most of the Catholic hierarchy, who tended to think that the only way to perceive the truth of Christianity was through a European lens — that of European civilization and Latin Christianity. As long as a cultural or religious belief did not blatantly contradict church teaching many Jesuits were willing to at least consider its usefulness if it were somehow analogous to Christian beliefs. Many recognized that there was truth in the Hindu Vedas and the teachings of Confucius. Given the rigid dogmatism of sixteenth-century Catholicism, this was a remarkable type of openness. Tragically, the larger church was not able to move beyond its "Eurocentrism." In the early eighteenth century all efforts to incorporate the cultural and religious world of non-European peoples came to an end. A papal decree condemned the efforts of men like de Nobili and Ricci as examples of

---

12. Spence, *The Memory Palace of Matteo Ricci.*

misguided relativism. Future missionaries were required to take an oath swearing that they would not repeat the errors of these innovative Jesuits. Catholicism and Western civilization were one and the same. Without any reference to the culture and historical context behind the Council of Trent, it became the only way to understand and explain the Catholic tradition to non-Christian people. A unique opportunity for intercultural and interreligious dialogue was squandered because of an obsession with conformity and an unwillingness to appreciate the power of different human beings' imaginations.

Murdering the Common Good

The greed of colonial authorities combined with the myopia of church officials led to unparalleled violence as Europeans thrust themselves on Africans, Asians, and Latin Americans. Given the sophistication of some cultures, particularly in Asia, it was possible for them to resist colonial power and forced Christianization. Other people did not fare as well. Without a highly developed and long-established defense system, the weakest victims of colonialism paid the highest price. In Latin America the Spanish were able to defeat militarily almost every group they encountered. Given their experience in the fifteenth century, they were masters at setting one group against another, creating strategic alliances and then abandoning their allies when their support was no longer useful. They had no compunction about wreaking havoc on other people's lives, just as had been the case in 1492. They used a timeworn and almost universal device to legitimate what they were doing: lofty religious language. Catholicism was the motor behind the *Reconquista,* and it became the ostensive reason for the *Conquista* that Spain unleashed in its newly acquired territories. The leaders of the Catholic Church in Spain were being used, but they were also willing to be used because of the social benefits a close relationship with the monarchy provided. The church was a powerful, state-subsidized institution that provided cover for the crown by agreeing to a lie that legitimated Spanish aggression. What was happening was a civilizing and Christianizing mission. As a result of the conquest of Mexico and Peru prodigious amounts of money were remitted to Spain while enormous churches with gold-leaf interiors were built throughout Spanish America.

Although it is hardly an excuse for its unwillingness to challenge what was happening in the Americas, it is important to keep in mind that the Catholic Church in Spain was not an autonomous or independent institution. Because of a papal privilege granted to Isabel and Ferdinand, the crown exercised what is known in Spanish as the *real patronato,* which allowed it veto power over every appointment and decision that the church made, from the naming of bishops to the assignment of parish priests. Naturally, only the most loyal and unquestioning members of the clergy could expect promotion. There were, however, a few courageous exceptions to the rule, bishops and priests gifted with honesty and prophetic courage. Fifteen years after Columbus stumbled across the Americas, the Dominican friar Antonio de Montesinos had the integrity and guts to preach the truth to a Spanish congregation that included Columbus's son Diego, the recently appointed governor of the island of Hispaniola in what is today the Dominican Republic.[13] He told the Spanish the very opposite of what they expected to hear. There was no boring homily to sleep through as they probably expected. They were told that they were liars and murderers who "were born in mortal sin and would die in mortal sin" because of the crimes they had committed. Montesinos was accusing the Spanish assembled before him in December 1511 of offending God and committing crimes against humanity. He was immediately denounced for preaching a "strange religion" and forced to return to Spain. But his sermon has never been forgotten. In the harbor of Santo Domingo there is a statue of Montesinos. His arm is stretched toward his face and his hand cups his mouth. The words carved into the monument repeat the chilling question he raised in his sermon — *¿Acaso no son seres humanos?* "Are these people not human beings?"

In their typically cautious and nuanced way, some of the Jesuits did their best to mitigate the violence of their fellow Europeans. In areas that today make up Peru and Paraguay, the Jesuits did everything in their power to learn about the cultures and languages of the people they were sent to Christianize. Their motives were not simply utilitarian. Some came to respect the cultures of the native people they met, going so far as to admit that their cultures and religious traditions contained elements of truth that complemented the truths of Catholicism, albeit deficiently. In other words, there were legitimate pre-Christian cultures and social systems that were worthy of respect. Today such an assertion is self-evident, but in the sixteenth century it was almost unimaginable. The Jesuits agreed with Montesinos. The native peoples of the Americas had human rights. They were not expendable beasts of burden, a subhuman species that could be exploited to death. The Jesuits petitioned the Spanish crown for a rare privilege — the right to established autonomous, "Spanish-free" zones where indigenous peoples could live in relative peace and hopefully consent to what the Jesuits saw as perfectly obvious — the truth of Catholic Christianity. The *reducciones,* the autonomous areas under the supervision of the Jesuits, were designed to be economically self-sufficient communities in which men and women could continue to speak their

---

13. Gutiérrez, *Las Casas: In Search of the Poor of Jesus Christ.*

languages and live according to their cultural traditions — with the exception of pre-Christian religious practices that they were expected to quickly abandon once they realized how erroneous they were. The task of the Jesuit was to be a loving father guiding his wobbly child to truth and eventual salvation.

The reductions had their shadow side. Converting to Catholicism was mandatory, although most Jesuits realized that forced conversion was a contradiction in terms. Church attendance and religious indoctrination were obligatory and those who missed prescribed rituals or classes were fined and punished. The Jesuits could be harsh disciplinarians. But the very fact that the humanity of indigenous peoples was recognized was a type of subversive statement. Beyond their success in mitigating Spanish violence, the reductions called into question the religiously sanctioned violence of the conquest. They proved that indigenous people were ethical, organized, and capable of running their own affairs in an industrious and productive way. They really had no need for the Spanish or the supposedly superior civilization they brought with them. But such assertions, mostly oblique, had their consequences. The Portuguese and Spanish were enraged by the effrontery of the Jesuits and indigenous people living in the *reducciones* because they refused to accept brutal servitude as their lot in life, to roll over and die as a people. There can be no doubt that many of the Jesuits, and other members of the church as well, were remarkable people. Nonetheless, their insistence on European culture and Western Christianity as "more true" than the beliefs and worldview of indigenous women and men was paternalistic at best and imperialistic at worst. Beyond the inflated and self-serving myths about the conquest, there is little evidence that the "civilizing" and "Christianizing" that followed in the wake of Columbus did much good, and the harm it unleashed is irrefutable. Advanced cultures were destroyed and millions of human beings died as Western Europeans unleashed nothing less than a genocidal invasion of the Western hemisphere. The greatest fallacy about the European conquest of the Americas is that it had anything to do with Christianity at all. As Montesinos had pointed out, the non-Christians in need of conversion were the Portuguese and Spanish, not the victims of their aggression and greed. The fatal flaw in the efforts of missionaries like the Jesuits was obvious: their European compatriots refused to act like human beings endowed with souls. They were completely incapable of feeling the pain they were inflicting on others, which violates a central tenet of Christian belief and behavior. If the possibility of a Christian culture and social order ever existed in the Americas it arrived in the New World stillborn.

Trent: Truth in a Straightjacket?

It is difficult to enter a Baroque Catholic church in Bavaria and not be taken aback by the fusion of gold leaf and a pervasive creamy white color, the paintings and statues of Jesus, Mary, and an array of saints. The visual images create a psychological impression of almost sensual exuberance and religious self-confidence. With the addition of a Mass by Mozart, a person can approach sensory overload. There is a message that comes with the building and its aesthetics: this particular church is part of a larger whole, the Catholic Church. It reflects the glory of God in the world right now but it calls us to think about something infinitely greater — eternity in heaven. Here you have a piece of bliss, but there is infinitely more that awaits you. This type of experience would not be possible without the Council of Trent. After the trauma of the Reformation it provided the church with newfound confidence sometimes bordering on the smug. Despite the dry Thomistic orthodoxy Catholic theologians used as their weapon of choice against Protestants, there was a vital fermentation taking place that was more life-giving. Roughly two-thirds of Europe remained Catholic and in southern Germany, Spain, France, and Italy, staunchly so. But the beauty and harmony of the Catholic Baroque world created by Trent had a less attractive side as well. Fixated on the thirteenth century as if it were the high point of Catholic history, the church looked askance at anything that did not fit its past. The Council of Trent had called the institutional church a *societas perfecta* — a perfect society — so why change a church that worked perfectly well?

In so-called mission countries the church was thoroughly "Eurocentric" while in what remained of Catholic Europe it became a fortress defending the faithful from the assaults of the faithless — Protestants, growing number of religiously indifferent intellectuals, and eventually proponents of a secular social order in which the church would play no role other than that of an anachronism. The church's unwillingness to concede a modicum of legitimacy to the call for change and the challenge of its critics exacted a terrible price. Well into the eighteenth century the church had served as the willing chaplain of divine-right monarchies, and there is no better example than France. Surrounded by the splendors of Versailles, French kings knew that they could count on the church to legitimize their claims to absolute authority as a part of a divine plan for humanity's well-being. When the cry for social justice led to the French Revolution in 1789 the church was caught off guard. Disconnected from most ordinary people, the hierarchical church reacted defensively to the turmoil that erupted in French society. When extremists hijacked the revolution, the church became the target of their almost psychotic rage. Thousands of bishops, priests, and religious women were forced to leave France and a significant number ended up victims of the guillotine. Baroque churches were still places of beauty, but their religious and social relevance had begun to wane. Among intellectuals agnosticism became all the rage and antipathy to Catholicism and institutional Christianity in general a fad. There were, of course, educated Catholics who remained loyal to the church and committed to its social vision, just as there were nonreligious thinkers who were willing to have a respectful conversation with their religious counterparts. But a new polarity had begun to emerge — the Catholic Church versus modernity, the religious world with its secular counterpart, neither well disposed to listen to the other. The infallible decrees of the Council of Trent may have provided the comfort of an unfailing compass for two hundred years, but after the French Revolution the magnetic poles of the world had changed. The church, too, would change but true to form would do so very slowly.

Chapter Six

The Ambiguity and Challenge
of Modernity

The Foundations Shift

As we saw in the previous chapter, the Council of Trent gave the Catholic Church a new lease on life. With its theology made crystal clear and its religious practices set in stone, the Tridentine church seemed unassailable. The Jesuits and members of several other new religious orders not only warded off attack; they went out to the field of battle to preempt any challenge to the church's theology and social power. Thomas's philosophy and theology were seen as the final word and therefore uncontestable. His notion of social hierarchy as the best form of government — a hierarchical and oligarchic arrangement that precluded democratic government beyond the local village — became the paradigm for church/state relations. There was no middle ground in the eyes of stalwart Catholics. Orthodoxy meant unflinching loyalty to the church, especially papal leadership. Like the church, society and government were understood as innately hierarchical and their structure an expression of God's will for humanity. Both the church and social order were divinely constructed pyramids and questioning the way they were structured was an affront to God's wisdom, a sin that entailed heresy as well as sedition. As an institution, the Catholic Church continued to work closely with those who wielded political power based on the assumption that rulers who were Catholic would exercise power in ways that benefited the common good most directly.

Trent reinforced the pomp of Catholic rituals that reveled in the power of popes and priests who presided *over* the faithful celebrating the sacraments *from* altars that were physically separated from the congregants, who were not allowed access to the sacred precincts reserved for clergy. The tone of the rituals and the very architecture of Catholic churches spoke of top-down power rather than an inclusive community of equals. Protestants tried generally to democratize their rituals by simplifying them and stressing the common bond between the pastor and his congregation. There was still a certain hierarchical dimension to Protestant worship, of course, but Luther and other reformers insisted on the "priesthood of the

145

faithful," which made every member of the believing community a full-fledged member. They also felt that ordinary Christians working within the church rather than a hierarchy exercising power over it best served the social order. There were now competing Christian theologies, Catholic versus Protestant, and two approaches to the social order, one more hierarchical and the other more participatory. Catholics tended to look to the Middle Ages as paradigmatic, while Protestants rejected most facets of the medieval world as anachronistic, if not anti-evangelical. Tradition guided the Catholic Church as much as scripture, correctly interpreted only by the pope and those he appointed to positions of authority, the so-called *Magisterium,* or teaching body of the church. Among Protestants power was diffuse and local. Leadership was seen as functional rather than an expression of God's will for the church. The word of God found in scripture alone was infallible, and its interpretation was understood to be the right of any members of the believing community, although not in isolation from the other members of the church.

Intense polarization set in after Trent with frequent acts of violence as Catholics and Protestants attacked each other with increasing ferocity. The fight was as much about who controlled town hall as it was about theological differences. A new religious map was being drawn up that created economic and political fault lines that threatened the cohesion of a once-unified Christendom. Christians had killed each other before over theological differences, but the level of hostility and intolerance was unprecedented in the sixteenth century.[1] Realists on both sides of the fence recognized that inter-Christian violence had to be brought under control, in large part because neither side could really win. This was especially true in the Holy Roman Empire, which had been something of a tenuous proposition ever since it was created by Charlemagne in the ninth century. Because the emperor was elected by a small number of princes rather than being chosen along hereditary lines, the threat to the survival of the imperial system was obvious to anyone who exercised power, regardless of theological inclinations.

In 1555 the Peace of Augsburg, essentially a treaty between the Catholic and Protestant princes, laid out a map that separated their territories along theological lines. More than half of the German-speaking parts of the empire were aligned with the Protestant cause. Scandinavia, the Low Countries, and England would soon separate themselves from the Roman church as well. About a third of Europe, almost entirely the northern

---

1. The formal, state-sponsored persecution of Christians went back to the time of Constantine, when he banned Arians and other deemed heretics from the empire. A century later Augustine would ask the emperor to send troops to suppress the Donatist movement in North Africa. Crusaders killed Orthodox Christians as "heretics" as well as former Catholics in Western Europe, for example, the Albigensians.

part of the continent, was now Protestant, with Lutherans, Calvinists, and Anglicans controlling their spheres of influence. Protestants put up with their fairly minor theological differences to fight a common enemy — the Catholic Church. The entire Iberian Peninsula, France, the territories controlled by the Hapsburgs, and Italy remained Catholic, both religiously and politically hostile to the parts of Europe that were now Protestant. There were pockets of Calvinists in France, and Switzerland was a crazy quilt of Catholics and Protestants, but most people knew what their specific Christian identity was by virtue of where they were born — Leipzig Lutheran, Geneva Calvinist, London Anglican, and Madrid Catholic. Whether someone from Leipzig knew exactly what it meant to be a Lutheran or someone from Madrid what it meant to be a Catholic was another question. Few people sat down and read the Luther's *Commentary on Romans* or *The Catechism of the Council of Trent*. In the rare event that a Protestant was theologically literate and decided that she or he should return to the Catholic Church or a Catholic decide that Luther presented a better vision of the Christian life and wanted to be a Protestant, there was an easy solution to their dilemma. Pack up and move. The Peace of Augsburg was predicated on an assumption that today seems absurd: the religious affiliation of a prince determines the religious identity of his subjects. There was simply no such thing as religious freedom in sixteenth-century Europe. Intolerance was seen as a virtue rather than a vice.

Despite the tensions created by a new religious map, however, Christendom remained intact in some ways, albeit shaken and less cohesive than it was in the medieval period. Europeans retained a sense of themselves as Christian. Monarchs still relied on the church for legitimation, and day-to-day life was conducted on the basis of a Christian value system and worldview. Catholics followed the old liturgical traditions; priests performed the seven sacraments; Christmas, Easter, and the feasts of saints were celebrated with collective exuberance. Protestants tended to be considerably more restrained, less "pagan" than their Roman counterparts, although their sense of time and space was religious as well. Catholics tended to be more collective, Protestants more individualistic in their approaches to Christianity and the social order. Differences aside, however, everyone was convinced that Christianity was the one true faith. The churches remained powerful institutions that princes and peasants alike looked to for guidance and support in the short space between the here and now and eternity. Nonetheless, in different ways and at different chronological moments, the Catholic Church and its Protestant counterpart began to lose ground as the arbiters of religious and sociocultural values.

For well over a millennium, the Catholic Church had been the most powerful institution in Europe. It dictated the terms of religious belief and behavior and, as we saw previously, intervened in secular affairs with impunity, sometimes winning the battle to control the secular world, sometimes losing, but always a force to be reckoned with. The Protestant churches were likewise powerful institutions, although their influence on the social order was less direct than that of the Catholic Church. Protestants differed among themselves and there was obviously no form of centralized leadership. But it is now clear that by the mid-seventeenth century the churches' power as a whole had begun to decline. A complex combination of events like the Thirty Years' War, the French Revolution, a series of revolutionary movements in the nineteenth century, the emergence of fascist and Marxist dictatorships at the beginning of the twentieth century, along with two unbelievably violent world wars forever changed the self-identity of the Western world. Little by little, the notion of a "Christian Europe" became a thing of the past, a nostalgic concept for some, an anachronism for many. The Catholic Church and Christianity, of course, did not disappear, but the social order that the church had shaped for a thousand years was altered radically and the role and nature of the church as a social institution forever changed. In the paragraphs that follow we will try to grapple with some of the ways in which Europe and much of the Western world was "de-Christianized" and "de-churched" from the mid-seventeenth century to the present.

The Great Collision: Catholicism and Modernity

Historians who focus on the evolution of Western civilization use conventions to block off one time period from another. This otherwise useful device does have its limitations, however. In some ways it is arbitrary, and inevitably there is an array of definitions about when a particular block of time begins. What, in fact, makes one time period ancient, medieval, or modern other than the perspective of a particular historian or a particular school of historical studies? Whose culture and historical experience are we talking about anyway, that of princes or prelates, artisans or peasants, women or men? Those methodological problems aside, there is some agreement that modernity is a useful concept that helps us to understand events that began to take place in the post-Reformation period when the dust raised by the first theological controversies between Catholics and Protestants began to settle. We will look at the geopolitical events that ushered in the modern period and then try to understand the impact they had on the Catholic universe. A small but growing fissure began to separate intellectuals, writers, and political leaders from their Catholic heritage soon after the Thirty Years' War, and by the mid-eighteenth century religious relativism and even overt skepticism were commonplace among the upper strata of society. Among the poor there was growing resentment toward the church due to its unflinching support of an oppressive social system that was still predicated on the feudal privileges of the aristocracy. On an intellectual and social level the church was "behind the curve," and it would soon pay a high price. There were committed Catholics who were aware of a looming crisis, but they had to fight the enormous forces of inertia that held the church firmly in place. They insisted that the Catholic Church had a powerful and relevant message that the emerging modern world could benefit from, but their ideas were either ignored or condemned by an institutional church bogged down in the past. The medieval church and the feudal social order were in their death throes, but few church leaders were able to see things correctly. Their response was slow and usually awkward, not unlike what happened at the beginning of the Reformation when Luther caught the late medieval church off guard. What is clear about the convoluted and tortured three centuries in which the modern world emerged is that the church was entering a radically new phase in which it would soon resemble the church that existed before Constantine issued the Edict of Milan in 313. Bit by bit, the church lost its religious authority and social prerogatives. It would often find itself on the defensive, attacked culturally, intellectually, and politically in ways it could never have anticipated prior to the Reformation. The Catholic Church was no longer an impregnable fortress, and those inside it often were fearful of what was becoming an increasingly secular and essentially nonreligious world. Serious questions arose as to what the best course of action could be. Should the church come to terms with certain aspects of the modern worldview? Should it resist to the death? There were varied opinions within the church just as there are today.

The First Crisis: The Thirty Years' War

In 1555 the political authorities of the Holy Roman Empire, regardless of what side of the Christian fence they stood on, attempted to control the internecine violence that had enveloped large parts of central Europe by signing the Peace of Augsburg. It was doomed to fail from the outset. It was simply a truce between warring factions that detested each other and had no intention of living amicably together. For a few decades it helped control the violent tensions that had erupted in the 1520s, but it simply could not resolve a religious dispute predicated on irreconcilable definitions of Christian orthodoxy. Each side's truth claims also had a geographic dimension. Europe, particularly the Holy Roman Empire, had become a chessboard with princes advancing their pieces across the board in the hope of gaining advantage in a game that was as political as it was religious. One prince played against another, and sometimes Catholics aligned themselves with Protestants and vice versa if their respective agendas could be advanced. Neither the Reformation nor Trent had any impact on the tawdry business of day-to-day politics, which was driven more by self-interest than religious principles. A volatile mix of political interest and religious fanaticism threatened to blow the empire to pieces, and the Peace of Augsburg only slowed down a burning fuse. Ordinary people were caught between forces they could not control and rarely understood. They were pawns in a convoluted game. Honestly living out one's religious beliefs and following the dictates of conscience were often dangerous things to do. The Inquisition was a terrifying force that used spies to pry into every facet of people's lives. John Calvin stood by while Michael Servetus, a Spanish physician and theologian, was burned at the stake for questioning the Christian doctrine of the Trinity. Having escaped from the clutches of the Inquisition, Servetus had fled to Geneva, expecting that the Protestant community would offer him refuge. He was arrested almost immediately after he arrived.

Although it was unlikely that anyone would win, Catholics and Protestants redoubled their efforts, convinced that it was possible to inflict a death blow. In London clergy who refused to recognize Henry VIII as the head of the church in England were hanged and eviscerated. In Holland and parts of modern-day Germany monasteries were sacked, nuns and priests turned out on the streets. In 1572 the French monarchy, controlled by Catherine de Medici, ordered the slaughter of Protestants in France, known as Huguenots. Over a hundred thousand died. The fabric of the Holy Roman Empire had been frayed since 1517, and in 1618 it finally ripped apart in a catastrophic way. Offended by their Catholic governors, the civil authorities of the largely Protestant city of Prague threw them out of the windows of the castle they were meeting in. According to legend, the Catholics landed on a pile of garbage that broke their fall, but their "defenestration" marks the beginning of a war that cost at least ten million lives, including at least two-thirds of the population of Bohemia.[2] Central Europe was savaged by Catholic and Protestant armies, or simply by groups of mercenaries who fought for whatever side paid the best wages. As always, the overwhelming majority of the dead were innocent civilians who died because they were Catholic or Protestant, in the wrong town at the wrong time. The violence was not entirely along denominational lines. Cardinal Richelieu, the prime minister of France, willingly subsidized Protestant armies in the hope that the Empire, France's traditional rival, would be shattered, leaving France the greatest power on the continent. He was right. Describing the Thirty Years' War as a purely religious conflict

---

2. González, *The Story of Christianity.*

is an exaggeration, largely a byproduct of eighteenth-century antireligious rationalism. It many respects it was the first of Europe's world wars. Every major European monarchy participated in the struggle to one degree or another. The suffering it caused was incalculable, but the damage done to the credibility of Christianity in all its forms was just as severe. It sounded the death knoll for Christendom and the fragmentation of the culture and social system that had held it together for nearly a millennium.

In 1648 the exhausted parties signed the Treaty of Westphalia. It allowed people to practice their chosen form of Christianity, but church and state were still fused and remained so in most countries until the early twentieth century. The questions raised by the Thirty Years' War were quick to surface, especially among intellectuals. Whose god and what god could have unleashed three decades of bloodletting? These rhetorical questions, however, skirted the real cause of the conflict: the use of religion to legitimate the geopolitical agenda of political entities. God, essentially, was an excuse for the Thirty Years' War, a useful word that allowed political cynics to tap and manipulate religious tribalism. The credibility of both the Catholic and Protestant churches was severely damaged and would never be restored entirely to its pre-seventeenth-century stature. In the minds of many, Christian orthodoxy of whatever stripe had become a synonym for intolerance. For many people the age of unconditional faith was over. The modern world that emerged after the Treaty of Westphalia finally made religious freedom possible. It also made disbelief a perfectly acceptable alternative, something that would have been unimaginable a century before.[3] Public agnosticism remained a liability throughout the seventeenth century but by the eighteenth century some leading thinkers and political authorities no longer felt compelled to cover over doubts about the validity of Christian truth claims or the usefulness of religion on a social level. Even an ostensibly believing Catholic like René Descartes advocated a philosophical system predicated on systematic doubt. The fact that he felt the need to demonstrate the existence of God speaks to the growing skepticism of his fellow European intellectuals. In England Isaac Newton, a fervent Christian, nonetheless concluded that the central Christian doctrine of the Trinity was erroneous and the divinity of Christ overstated. John Locke tried to create a type of generic Christianity, eliminating dogma in an effort to make religion reasonable. His Scottish intellectual successor, David Hume, questioned whether truth itself could be ascertained because of the subjective nature of all human knowledge. The Catholic Church remained relatively strong because it was the cultural foundation of France and southern European nations. Because of its ongoing relationship with traditional monarchies, it retained public visibility as a national

---

3. Cooke, *The Distancing of God.*

religion and was ostensibly supported by those who wielded political power, but it was losing its grip over both intellectuals and many people in urban environments whose lives were no longer influenced as directly by religious values. The fist glimmerings of a secular culture had begun to emerge.

The Train Wreck of 1789

Beyond a doubt Versailles is the preeminent symbol of the French monarchy. Built in phases during the seventeenth century by Louis XIV, the "Sun King," it was constructed purposefully to display his absolute, almost godlike power. He had his palace built away from the twisting, dirty streets of Paris to emphasize the qualitative difference between the king, his court, and the ordinary citizens of the kingdom he rarely saw. Louis's architects created an environment that exuded opulence, a parallel universe in which a king could indulge his fantasies while carrying on the affairs of state. There were tranquil gardens and luxurious apartments for the king and his entourage, perfect places for trysts with courtesans. The court was packed with the king's admirers, attendants, and an army of schemers, all intent on playing whatever game was necessary to advance their position in life. But Louis did not pay the bill for Versailles; the people of France did. Despite the lofty ideals of the Enlightenment that stressed the equality and inherent right of every person to be recognized and respected, France remained an oppressive state. Ordinary people lived precarious lives, and they were aware that their leaders had little sense of what they had to endure or, for that matter, much interest. They were heavily taxed, and even goods moving within the kingdom were subject to high tariffs that filled the royal coffers. There was a growing sense of desperation and anger as the price of food and staples increased with predictable regularity throughout the late eighteenth century, while members of the court enjoyed every imaginable luxury. When Louis XVI left Versailles in 1775 to be crowned king of France in the cathedral of Rheims, there was concern about the nineteen-year-old king's safety. There had been food riots in Paris and surrounding towns because of a sharp rise in the price of bread, and troops had to secure the roads for the royal entourage.[4] Although there was still a measure of respect for the monarchy, people were beginning to ask questions about a social system that made most of their lives short and miserable. As the king of France, Louis was supposed to be the father of his country, but he seemed unable to understand the lot of those he governed. Everything he knew about his subjects was filtered through his advisors, most of whom saw ordinary people as riff-raff. He was a malleable adolescent fascinated by springs,

---

4. Doyle, *Oxford History of the French Revolution.*

locks, hunting parties, and parlor games. His assistants ran the nation; he signed the decrees.

The young Louis had inherited a country that would soon be caught up in an economic and social crisis that neither he nor his advisors could ever have imagined. Less than twenty years after his coronation Louis would be dead, as would be most of his inner circle. Aristocrats would be sent to the guillotine in prodigious numbers. Everyone in France would be enveloped in an eruption of fury unlike any before it. Even the French Catholic Church, the "First Daughter of the Church," would be the target of collective rage. Most of the prelates who had walked through the halls of Versailles resplendent in scarlet robes would be dead or in exile. Part of an enormous patronage system, they dispensed appointments and favors just as Louis did. Bishops were wealthy men who wielded power on every level of French society, and the episcopacy itself was controlled by noble families who had sons and nephews appointed to ecclesiastical positions even if they had neither the desire nor the ability to serve as bishops.[5] As central players in the Ancien Régime they did the court's bidding as the sole religious authorities of the kingdom, constantly emphasizing that God, not mere mortals, had made Louis king of France. These same prelates invariably turned a blind eye to the excesses and immorality of Louis's court. The church in France owned 10 percent of the country with extensive estates farmed by peasants who were little more than serfs.[6] There were over three hundred bishops, far more than were necessary for the administration of the French church.[7] Parish priests, however, inhabited a different world. Their incomes were modest if not meager. They were appointed by their bishops and were hardly more than employees. They were "the Church's undervalued, underprivileged workhorses" with neither voice nor vote when it came to the affairs of their dioceses, although they were required to remit a sizeable percentage of their parish's income to the bishop.[8] Many chafed at the indifference of bishops who spent more time in court than in their dioceses. This split-level ecclesiastical arrangement was a vestige of a feudal order that no longer worked or made any sense because of the economic and social changes that were altering the core identity of France and other European nations in the eighteenth century.

To understand what happened to the church during the French Revolution, we need to appreciate the influence and power of two of its principal opponents — the French intellectuals associated with the Enlightenment

---

5. Ibid., 34. According to Doyle, archbishops and many bishops and abbots were millionaires by today's standards.

6. Ibid., 33.

7. Ibid., 34.

8. Ibid., 35.

and the intensely anticlerical politicians who attacked the French church with nearly pathological fury throughout the 1790s. The French Enlightenment, of course, is a complex cultural and intellectual phenomenon. Some of its proponents remained Christian while others drifted toward a type of generic, nature-based religiosity known as deism.[9] The most renowned French deist was Jean-Jacques Rousseau. Rousseau was critical of religious institutions and dogma and saw nature and its wonders as signs of a divine presence that everyone could perceive and respond to given the freedom to do so. Churches and dogmas were primitive and senseless anachronisms. For Rousseau the Catholic Church was the principal obstacle to enlightenment and progress, a medieval relic that intelligent people should simply ignore. The sometimes petulant God of the Hebrew Bible disgusted him. Jesus' miracles in the New Testament struck him as impossible violations of nature's laws.

Rousseau's idealistic philosophizing and intellectual disdain for Catholicism paled in comparison to the intense anticlericalism of his contemporary Voltaire. Voltaire was a literary genius known for his biting sarcasm, and his writings were the equivalent of best sellers in prerevolutionary France despite the efforts of both the crown and church to suppress them. Voltaire detested the institutional church's blind loyalty to the monarchy and willingness to act as its agent by purveying superstition and imposing a code of political and religious orthodoxy that equated criticisms of the established order with heresy. Voltaire's hostility toward the institutional church is captured by a remark that peppered his letters and writings — *Écrassez l'enfâme* — "Crush the damned thing." By the end of the eighteenth century many people in France agreed with Voltaire's assessment. When political demagogues hijacked the Revolution and began to attack the church shortly after Louis's execution, many saw what was happening as comeuppance for centuries of ecclesiastical complicity with an oppressive regime. Certain revolutionary leaders and factions created a false but politically useful dichotomy — the monarchy and the church, or the Revolution and the Republic, the decrepit and oppressive, or the new and democratic. The choices were not an abstraction; they were a matter of life and death.

The Revolution caught most members of the French clergy off guard. The intense pace of change that swept through the country produced varied and often contradictory responses. Bishops responded to the Revolution differently than priests did because they came from different social strata, the former desperate to maintain the status quo, the latter willing to change it. "Upper" and "lower" clergy in France were often pitted against each other. Although institutional unity was never completely

---

9. Hampson et al., *Enlightenment and Revolution.*

shattered, the Catholic Church in France experienced severe internal tension as it tried to understand and respond to convoluted political events and unprecedented levels of hostility that went beyond anything it had known since the age of Roman persecution.

The French Revolution made sense to a considerable number of priests who were familiar with the shadow side of the old order. They served its victims and sometimes lived on the edge of hunger themselves. They saw the Revolution as a way to revitalize the church by sloughing off medieval appendages that limited its flexibility to respond to new pastoral demands. Many were also passionate about social reform, part of a movement known as the Catholic Enlightenment, which resonated with a vision of social equality without the deistic and anticlerical tendencies of some French thinkers. They were convinced that the Catholic Church could make a contribution to the emerging modern paradigm. They recognized that many criticisms of the institutional church were legitimate and should be addressed. Many priests thought of themselves as loyal members of the church as well as committed patriots. In the first few years of the Revolution they were well received, and some played a key role in the short-lived Estates General and after 1789 in the national Assembly and Convention that replaced it as the governing bodies of France for the next decade.[10] But priests' commitment to the Revolution soon became a more difficult proposition as revolutionary governments became more involved in the internal affairs of the church. The Assembly's first efforts at reforming the structure of the church made sense and were accepted without much opposition. The number of dioceses and parishes was reduced drastically. Monasteries and convents that did not have an obvious social role were closed down. In fact, many of them had been half empty for decades. But the Assembly went too far in the minds of many clerics as well as the laity when it required bishops and priests to take an oath of allegiance to the state. As Doyle points out, legislation known as the Civil Constitution of the Clergy that required a formal, public oath "was certainly the . . . Assembly's most serious mistake. For the first time the revolutionaries forced fellow citizens to choose; to declare themselves publicly for or against the new order."[11] Pope Pius VI wrote to Louis, who was still king of France, although now accountable to the Assembly, asking him not to promulgate the Civil Constitution. Louis signed it, in all likelihood because he had no choice. In short order, the Catholic Church in France was split down the middle, as was the country as a whole. The oath became the dividing line between those who accepted the Revolution and those who

---

10. Cooke, *The Distancing of God*, 132–52.
11. Doyle, *Oxford History of the French Revolution*, 144.

rejected it.[12] In many ways, the church was now a hapless victim caught in the crossfire of two warring armies.

The Civil Constitution of the Clergy made the church an agency of the state, subject to its supervision and therefore incapable of criticizing the state in any effective way. Under the monarchy the church worked with the monarchy but not for it. There was a certain dialectical tension, albeit small. Suddenly bishops were to be elected by regional assemblies, priests by local councils, and everyone had a right to vote simply by dint of citizenship alone. A series of questions arose immediately. Was the Catholic Church in France still Roman Catholic? The pope continued to be recognized as the spiritual head of the church, but since he no longer had a right to participate in the internal affairs of the church, was it now schismatic? "The First Daughter of the Church" had always been a bit headstrong. Since the Middle Ages the French church had enjoyed a high degree of autonomy in terms of Rome, and the crown had certainly felt it had a right to intervene in the internal affairs of the church if doing so was deemed in the best interests of the nation. More than one king had defied papal authority and told his bishops what to do. But the situation in 1790 went far beyond the state meddling in ecclesiastical affairs. The situation became even more difficult for clergy and practicing Catholics as the Revolution became anticlerical and even anti-Christian. Due to the fact that almost every bishop and nearly half of the priests in France refused to take the oath, when monarchist opponents of the Revolution attempted to overthrow it, the church was construed as the focal point of resistance to revolutionary change. The bishops and half of the priests in the country were denounced as traitors. Political demagogues stirred up hostility toward the church, often invoking the Enlightenment's call for reason and the suppression of superstition in order to disguise their attempts to achieve absolute power and impose their particular interpretation of the Revolution. If a democratic society based on reason and toleration was to be created, the church had to be destroyed because it was the main source of irrationality and intolerance. The Christian calendar was abolished, Notre Dame was turned into a Temple of Reason, and clergy that refused to swear allegiance to the new republic were declared enemies of the state and could be executed on the spot. Doyle provides poignant insight as he discusses revolutionary anticlericalism:

> Once launched it was eminently democratic. Anybody could join in smashing images, vandalizing churches . . . and theft of vestments to wear in blasphemous mock ceremonies. . . . Other contributions took more organization, but Jacobin clubs and popular societies, not to

---

12. Bokenkotter, *Church and Revolution*, 14.

mention local authorities, were quite happy to orchestrate festivals of reason, harmony, wisdom, and other such worthy attributes in former churches.[13]

Many members of the clergy left the ministry. A few were caught up in the wave of hostility toward the church, happy to renounce their vows in public and blend into the angry mob. Most, however, either took a low profile or left the country altogether, becoming ecclesiastical vagabonds.

It is a challenge not to think of what was going on in France vis-à-vis the church as a sort of collective madness. But part of the explanation is prosaic. The vast wealth of the church offered an easy target for politicians looking for funds to field armies that France soon would send to neighboring countries in an attempt to bring them into the sphere of French interests. They too were to be transformed into revolutionary societies, converted into modern societies like France, the paradigm of a new social order. Furthermore, if the Revolution were to succeed, its leaders had to break the power of the last institution in French society that could challenge its authority and vision — the institutional church. Despite its deficiencies it had always been more credible than the monarchy. French Catholics may have resented the wealth and privileges of their bishops, but most appreciated the pastoral care of their parish priests. Radical politicians, however, had no intention of allowing any competition. The Revolution offered its own sort of spiritual vision, a type of political transcendence on an epochal scale, and the state alone would provide social services. Everything had to be nationalized and secularized, that is, under the watchful eye of revolutionary elite. They created a polarity between the church and the Revolution, and when anyone vacillated between these artificial extremes, the reaction was immediate and savage. During the Terror of 1793–94 over forty thousand people were sent to the guillotine. Radical politicians, who felt that they alone knew the meaning of *liberté, égalité,* and *fraternité,* turned France into a living hell that made some long for the Ancien Régime that had once oppressed them. After a decade of political and social chaos the French reached a point of exhaustion and welcomed the soon-to-be dictator Napoleon as a solution to the excesses of the past decade. Although hardly a pious Catholic, Napoleon reestablished ties between church and state. He recognized that the institutional church still had credibility and power despite what had happened to it before his rise to power. He was willing to grant the church a degree of freedom as long as it served his political interests. But the church hardly had a free hand in French society or in those parts of Europe that Napoleon conquered. In 1804 Pope Pius VII was "invited" to

---

13. Doyle, *Oxford History of the French Revolution,* 260.

attend Napoleon's coronation as emperor in the cathedral of Notre Dame. In the portrait commissioned to commemorate the event, Pius is clearly uncomfortable — reasonable enough given the fact that essentially he was Napoleon's prisoner.

The Dangers of Nostalgia

France was the dominant political power in eighteenth-century Europe, and its status as the continent's intellectual capital was indisputable. It had become a synonym of the Enlightenment and progressive social thought. Despite moments of chaos and violence, the Revolution had created a new political model of participatory government in Western Europe. It had tapped the energy and imagination of ordinary men and women who were capable of governing themselves without the paternalistic guidance of the aristocracy. For conservatives, however, the Revolution was a plague that had to be contained before it destroyed the ordered, hierarchical world they inhabited. Louis's execution sent shock waves through the Western world. If the king of France could be executed and the French aristocracy decimated, could this not occur elsewhere? Everything depended on a person's social location. You were terrified that your head would end up in a basket or you waited for the day in which you would become a full citizen of a new, egalitarian society. Throughout the nineteenth century Europeans experienced something akin to geological plate tectonics — two massive subterranean forces grating against each other causing regular eruptions — reactionary conservatism and revolutionary radicalism. The Napoleonic Wars temporarily halted the revolutionary movement in France, and after Waterloo the Congress of Vienna restored the old order. Louis XVIII became king of France, restoring the Bourbon monarchy to the throne. Great Britain was now an uncontested power and kept a watchful eye on the French because of their seeming addiction to political experimentation. But the spirit of the Revolution was not extinct nor had the Ancien Régime been restored in all its former glory. Western Europe had undergone irreversible change, and the impulse to create a more democratic social order could not be kept at bay forever. There were "revolutionary years," the most notable in 1848 and 1871, that swept through France, Italy, and other countries.

The exclusive rights and privileges of the aristocracy were a thing of the past. The new power brokers were the bourgeoisie — the urbane, educated merchants and industrialists who had achieved considerable economic and political success since the Revolution. In many cases, they were wealthier than the aristocracy whose "old money" was no longer so abundant. The nature of the state itself had changed. Economic and political power now had to be shared between the upper and middle social strata in ways that would have been unimaginable prior to 1789. But the nation-states that emerged after the Congress of Vienna were hardly democratic entities. They were economically and politically stratified. Urbanization and the beginnings of industrialization were creating an enormous population of disenfranchised workers, many of whom had moved from rural poverty to urban misery. Once again tensions began to arise between a slightly more inclusive but still small minority of "haves" and a vast sea of "have-nots," whose living conditions were often dehumanizing. Many of the "haves" identified with economic liberalism and scientific rationalism, but they were not egalitarian in their approach to the political order. They were true believers in laissez-faire capitalism and a type of heightened individualism that limited their commitment to the common good. They equated their class interests with the welfare of their nation and tried to keep a firm hand on the political system that they now controlled. Even the nobility had to broker deals with the triumphant bourgeoisie. The contempt of bourgeois liberals for the "have-nots" was often equal to that of any eighteenth-century aristocrat. New and inevitable animosities were starting to fester under the skin of Europe that would lead to uprisings that would be violently suppressed. A new wave of radical political discourse was born. It pushed the message of the Revolution to new lengths by calling for the abolition of private property and the eventual eradication of all forms of social hierarchy. Marx and Engels were the most famous and doctrinaire spokespersons for radical social thought, becoming near synonyms for socialism despite the fact that they represented only a minor fraction of the socialist political movement.[14]

Once again, the Catholic Church would be caught in a political and social struggle it failed to understand adequately, often making serious mistakes that weakened its credibility and increased its marginalization. Like someone who has lived through an earthquake, the Catholic Church jumped every time it sensed a revolutionary aftershock, often reacting in a disproportionate way. The antipathy of liberals toward the Catholic Church, however, was real and the hostility of socialists palpable. Bourgeois liberals realized that religion still enjoyed a degree of credibility and the institutional church was a force to be reckoned with, but they tried to marginalize it at every turn. Radicals, however, were another story. They relished the day in which religion in all its forms would disappear and felt no need to engage in conversation with an institution they hoped to obliterate once they gained political power. In the nineteenth century the Catholic Church had two enemies — one subtle, the other blunt. Because bourgeois liberals monopolized the economic and political systems of most

---

14. Bokenkotter, *Church and Revolution*, 133–72.

countries, the church was often at political loggerheads with the proponents of laissez-faire capitalism and the new bureaucratic state. Catholic
politicians, to the extent that they were allowed to function as such, often
formed strategic alliances with conservative political groups, and even liberal parties if they were not overtly anticlerical, in an effort to defend the
church's role as a social institution. In what were often convoluted and
almost Machiavellian skirmishes, Catholics and non-Catholics sparred
with each other trying to gain the upper hand.

The Papal States were dissolved during the Napoleonic Wars but were
restored by the Congress of Vienna. The pope was once again a political ruler as well as the head of the Roman Catholic Church, controlling
a sizeable portion of central Italy. He was the nominal head of a civil
bureaucracy that included a police force. Although the pope delegated the
day-to-day business of the Papal States to his assistants, he was an absolute monarch with the right to impose his will if necessary. His territories
were officially Catholic, although small numbers of Protestants and Jews
were tolerated. The Inquisition was still an official institution with the
power to arrest and detain those accused of moral or theological deviance.
In the eyes of political liberals, particularly Italians, the Papal States were
an irritating throwback to a medieval world that should never have been
re-created. Had it not been for the church's willingness to come to the
aid of the old political order by denouncing the Revolution from its pulpits, and perhaps a sense of pity for the brutality it had been subjected
to during the French Revolution, it is unlikely that the British, Austrians,
and Russians would have acceded to the re-creation of the Papal States.
The English and Russians were not Catholic and the Austrians had a long
history of locking horns with the institutional church. One of their reasons for restoring the temporal authority of the papacy in Italy was the
hope that the Papal States would impede the unification of the Italian
peninsula, thus avoiding a challenge to the balance of power laid out by
the Congress of Vienna. The Papal States were utterly inconsequential on
a geopolitical level, but the symbolic power of the papacy was still significant. In the minds of most liberals in Europe, however, the Catholic
Church was a hopelessly reactionary institution, the antithesis of everything they associated with modernity and a progressive social order. As a
whole, the liberal bourgeoisie had little use for religion other than for rites
of passage. Most were simply cultural Christians who looked askance at
any sort of serious religious behavior as irrational and embarrassing. Outside of baptisms, marriages, and burials, few were likely to step foot in
a church. With the implementation of civil birth and marriage registers,
as well as the legalization of divorce in some countries, even a cursory
visit to a church was no longer necessary. For the hierarchy of the church,

however, religion had an explicit and indispensable role to play in society. The church had to be recognized and established as the only valid religious institution in Catholic countries with the right to participate on an official level in discussions of belief and behavior, private and public. Only the church had the means to guide people's lives in a meaningful way, to educate their children and take care of the sick and those in need. In effect, the Catholic Church should be the state's principal social agency, working in tandem with those in positions of political power just as Thomas had suggested in the thirteenth century. This was the only formula to maximize the common good and avoid repeating the antireligious, immoral anarchy of the Revolution. Given the rapid pace of secularization among the nineteenth century, bourgeoisie and the "de-churching" of the working class throughout Europe, the church became progressively more antagonistic toward anything associated with modernity and a secular worldview. There were some political and social liberals who were willing to cede some ground to the Catholic Church and provide a public space for religion, albeit with conditions. Likewise, there were Catholics who were willing to accept certain aspects of the modern world and secular state, convinced that a respectful conversation was possible. But for most of the nineteenth century hyperbole trumped reason. As it were, both sides had excommunicated each other.

False Starts and Painful Reactions: The Church Responds to Modernity

After the debacle of the French Revolution the institutional church in most European countries moved toward the conservative side of the theological and political spectrum. A minority to begin with, progressive members of the clergy were almost completely marginalized. On nearly every level, the church "tended to be defensive and unimaginative," hoping that the worst was over and that it could regain some of its former influence on a social level.[15] Especially in France, there was an urgent need to patch up the battered remains of the postrevolutionary church. Traumatized bishops returned from exile and battle-weary priests tried to restart pastoral ministry in areas that had not had a resident pastor for years. The challenge was acute since there were twenty thousand fewer priests than before the Revolution. But there were deeper questions beyond numbers and parish appointments. Although some conservative members of the church thought the clock could be turned back, a profound sociocultural shift had taken place that required a different approach to a world that was no longer as religious or deferential when it came to institutional religion.

---

15. Cooke, *The Distancing of God,* 242.

Being a Catholic now was entirely volitional. There were no particular advantages to being a believer and, in some circles, being a committed Catholic implied being a monarchist and an enemy of political and scientific progress. Still, the leaders of the church banked on the conservative dynamics of the post-Napoleonic era hoping they could forge a strategic alliance with right-wing political forces and find a niche for the Catholic Church once again. Others felt that restoration was nothing more than a nostalgic dream that would eventually backfire. Out of loyalty to the church rather than hostility to its leaders, some Catholics questioned the wisdom of the hierarchy's conservative agenda. They would be referred to as Catholic liberals, a term that requires clarification since the word "liberal" has so many connotations.

Three Who Failed

The Catholic liberals who achieved such notoriety in the first part of the nineteenth century were theologically open-minded men. Their beliefs were orthodox and their respect for church tradition deep-seated, but they insisted that Catholic belief had to be explained in ways that made sense to people in a given historical context. Catechesis, the pedagogical process in which the Gospel message is communicated, therefore had to be revised and re-presented on an ongoing basis. Truth existed, but those who proclaimed it had to reformulate their message constantly if people were to grasp and affirm it consciously and correctly. In terms of economic and sociopolitical issues, Catholic liberals rejected most aspects of the status quo. They denounced laissez-faire capitalism as oppressive and the political horse swapping of the bourgeoisie as a threat to the common good. They were mavericks and innovators on almost every level. They argued for freedom of religion when the institutional church still opposed it. They saw the separation of church and state, as well as secular education, as steps in the right direction when the hierarchy decried such a position as the equivalent of heresy. They pointed to the empty rhetoric of politicians who talked about democracy but subverted it by disenfranchising the working class. The three giants of Catholic liberalism in France were Robert Lamennais, Jean-Baptiste Lacordaire, and Charles de Montalembert. They were convinced that Catholicism could offer a value system that would allow people to "reach agreement on the basic principles needed to form a just society,"[16] thus creating a social order that was focused on the common good rather than the myopic economic and

---

16. Bokenkotter, *Church and Revolution*, 53. The author provides an excellent synopsis of the lives and contribution of these three French Catholics.

political interests of the well-to-do. They poked and prodded an institutional church that said little about the grotesque social injustice caused by industrialization and savage capitalism. They annoyed politicians because they refused to compromise when it came to their Christian values. Ultimately, they alienated the ecclesiastic right and the political left. They would be censured by the church and dismissed by politicians as hopeless idealists.

The liberal Catholic movement originated in the seminal writing of Robert Lamennais. He came from a middle-class family that had experienced the shadow side of the Revolution but nonetheless resonated with many of its ideals. He had questions about the truth claims of the Catholic Church as a young man, but eventually recognized their validity. He was ordained a priest in 1816, although he became progressively more disenchanted with the institutional church. From the outset of his ministry, he was convinced that the church's brittle conservatism was holding it back from its rightful place in French society as an institution with a liberating message. Its sole task was to proclaim the Gospel and so revitalize the world around it. By trying to regain its status as an officially recognized religious monopoly, the church was ultimately contradicting its real reason for existence. When Lacordaire and Montalembert read Lamennais's writing they were overwhelmed by the cogency of his arguments. They met, became close friends, and soon would spearhead a multifaceted campaign to help people, Catholic and otherwise, understand their message about an open-minded type of Catholicism. Lamennais did most of the writing, Lacordaire, who was also a priest, did most of the preaching, and Montalembert, an aristocrat who nonetheless resonated with the democratic ideals of the Revolution, did effective work as an elected official in national government. They produced bestsellers, packed churches, and won the respect of secular politicians. They were far ahead of their time on every level. They insisted on complete religious liberty, freedom of education and the press, the right of free association, and the decentralization of both the church and state in order to allow everyone real voice and vote in their religious and civil communities.[17]

From the vantage point of Catholic liberals the church had to win over people's hearts and minds by virtue of the reasonableness of the Christian message and their recognition and acceptance of the rich spiritual resources the Catholic Church could offer them. There was no doubt in the minds of these three enthusiastic Catholics that this would happen if the church presented the Gospel unencumbered by the political entanglements that had hobbled it in the past. Almost unwittingly, they were making a point that conservative members of the hierarchy reacted to with

---

17. Ibid., 52.

consternation — that the anticlericalism of the 1790s could be explained by the policies and social values of the church itself. Its vast wealth and willingness to sanction the abuses of the monarchy virtually guaranteed that certain people would attack it. The church had contributed ipso facto to the violent de-Christianization of the Revolution by being a part of a non-Christian social system. Because it was chained to the monarchy the church was incapable of being a prophetic voice at the precise moment when one was desperately needed. Filling a vacuum, radicals managed to kidnap the Revolution and pushed it in such extreme ways that the vision behind it was betrayed. In short, the church had been blinded by self-interest, deaf to the cries of the poor and oppressed and mute when it was so important to articulate a Christian social vision. Catholic liberals were branded as disloyal and dangerous almost immediately, and the Vatican was soon informed that it had a problem on its hands. Ironically, the secular bourgeoisie was often more responsive to the message of liberal Catholics than their co-religionists.

Liberal Catholic thought caught the imagination of the French public almost immediately. Lamennais's thinking was a refreshing change from the constant denunciations of the Revolution and modernity voiced by church leaders. The all-important vehicle for his ideas was a newspaper he published called *L'Avenir* — The Future. It was a highly regarded publication that many non-Catholics read even if they disagreed with its position on the role of religion in society. Lamennais proposed a free market of ideas in which people could choose the values that made the most sense to them. The only role of the state when it came to these ideas was to make sure that all of them could be expressed freely. He was confident that the French would see the value of their Catholic heritage and once again assent to the truths it contained, not because the church told them to but because they had come to agree, as adult members of society, that Catholicism made sense and could make France a better country. *L'Avenir* turned Lacordaire and Montalembert into instant believers in its message about the future of Catholicism as a rejuvenated social force. They were soon members of its editorial board, working in close collaboration with Lamennais. Their ideas became more focused and their strategy for promoting liberal Catholic thought more systematic. They were intent on both winning the hearts and minds of their fellow Catholics and convincing nonbelievers that religious belief was reasonable and compatible with democratic freedoms. Catholic conservatives were naturally appalled by what they were reading and hearing. Almost every aspect of Catholic liberal thought infuriated them. They felt that trying to meet the modern world half way was a profound error because modernity itself was an error. What *L'Avenir* proposed was tantamount to brokering a deal with the devil. They were convinced that the only way the Catholic Church could maintain an effective social presence in France was through legal recognition as the national religion with a guaranteed role in education and other forms of social service just as had been the case before the Revolution. Liberal Catholicism was seen as the worst sort of enemy, a Trojan horse that would destroy the church from the inside. Hardly naïve about church politics Lamennais, Lacordaire, and Montalembert traveled to Rome in 1831, hoping to plead their cause with the pope. Surely Gregory XVI would recognize that they were loyal sons of the church concerned about spreading its message in the modern world in the most effective way. They were unduly optimistic.

After waiting in Rome for months for a papal audience, the three weary pilgrims headed back to France, still hoping to find some middle ground with their conservative Catholic opponents. Not everyone in the Vatican, in fact, was hostile to their cause, and they were convinced that what they espoused was completely orthodox and politically reasonable. In their minds, liberal Catholicism was not a question of theology. It was about the best strategy for promoting the future of the church in modern society. Gregory, however, was simply waiting for them to leave town before hurling his thunderbolt — a papal encyclical called *Mirari Vos.* "The document . . . condemned liberal Catholicism. The Church, the encyclical declared, did not need regeneration; granting freedom of conscience would be sheer madness, separation of church and state a bad idea, liberty of the press an abomination."[18] Gregory was not about to have a conversation with three "renegades" who had been denounced by French bishops as threats to the church's well-being. Furthermore, what they proposed threatened the foundation of the Papal States themselves, in which there was no real freedom of religion, association, or the press.

Gregory was saying in no uncertain terms that Catholics had to follow the position of the institutional church on social issues just as much as they had to when it came to core doctrinal beliefs. The social and theological dimensions of the church were thus conflated, leaving virtually no room for Catholics to maneuver in their social environment in an autonomous, flexible way. Everyone connected with the Catholic liberal movement was told to cease and desist or face excommunication. Lacordaire and Montalembert agreed to do so immediately. Lamennais agonized and waited but eventually signed the required oath in the hope of saving what was left of the movement he had set in motion. Perhaps he felt it was better to suffer inside the church and quietly continue his efforts to change it than to be stripped of his membership and left powerless on the outside. His resentment, however, was intense and he eventually ceased to function as a priest or a practicing Catholic. He felt betrayed and

18. Ibid., 56.

humiliated by an institution he loved but could no longer live with. For all intents and purposes liberal Catholicism seemed dead by 1850. The chance of finding common ground with secular nonbelievers on social issues seemed nonexistent. Certainly many non-Catholics nodded their heads in a sort of "Told you so" reaction. The last glimmer of hope seemed to be extinguished with the publication of the *Syllabus of Errors* in 1864 by Pope Pius IX and the decree on papal infallibility promulgated by the First Vatican Council in 1870. Yet there was still a faint heartbeat. Catholic liberal thought was not totally dead despite the best efforts of the hierarchy to bury it. It was an idea whose time was yet to come but would come eventually. Although defeated in their lifetimes, Catholic liberals opened up new possibilities, and their thinking would lay the groundwork for a productive conversation between the modern world and the Catholic Church. It would be another century, however, before that possibility could be realized.

Pius IX: The Definitive No

Predicting how long a pope will live has proven to be a risky proposition. When Pius IX was elected pope in 1846, however, it is unlikely that anyone expected him to be the bishop of Rome for the next thirty-two years. When the cardinals assembled to elect a successor to the intensely conservative Gregory XVI, they were looking for a compromise candidate, someone who was moderate and predictable, capable of keeping the church on an even keel in stormy weather. Pius IX, however, would soon push the church in unanticipated ways, creating storms inside and outside the church that were as intense as those of the sixteenth century. Pius IX is nearly synonymous with two of the most important and controversial church documents of the nineteenth century, mentioned just above: The *Syllabus of Errors* and the decree on papal infallibility, which was made a nonnegotiable doctrine of the Catholic Church in 1870. These texts and the theology behind them defined his papacy and set the tone of the Catholic Church's stance toward the modern world that lasted to the papacy of John XXIII in 1958 and the Second Vatican Council in the early 1960s. Although somewhat different in terms of their content and the reasons behind their publication, the two documents share a common theme: the rejection of most of the values that inform the modern, secular world as antithetical to the beliefs and values of members of the Roman Catholic Church. Both documents are polarizing "with us" or "against us" propositions, making it crystal clear that modernity and Catholicism are essentially irreconcilable propositions. It is crucial, however, to appreciate the context in which the *Syllabus* and the dogma of papal infallibility emerged. They are complicated, nuanced statements that were written in response to specific challenges the church faced in the mid-nineteenth century. To understand them properly we have to ask a number of questions. What was going on in the larger sociopolitical scene that the Catholic Church was part of in the mid-nineteenth century that gave these documents their particular content and tone? Who was Pius IX as a person and what aspects of his personality shaped the content of the documents. After all, popes are human beings and are therefore a bit idiosyncratic. One might argue that Pius IX was a bit more idiosyncratic than most.

It is unlikely that either the *Syllabus of Errors* would have been published in 1864 or the decree on papal infallibility promulgated by the First Vatican Council in 1870 had it not been for his fateful election to the papacy. A century and a half after his death, the legacy of Pius IX is still in dispute. Some conservative Catholics are convinced that he got it right and said it the way it had to be said — no middle ground, no surrender. For many liberal Catholics, however, Pius IX is emblematic of conservative extremism. His rejection of the modern world has only made it harder for them to participate in pluralistic societies in which some non-Catholics perceive the church, erroneously of course, as a threat to their democratic liberties.

Within a matter of months after his election in 1846 as the bishop of Rome Pius was confronted with a revolt against papal rule. The citizens of his diocese and the surrounding provinces, particularly the bourgeoisie who were influenced by French republican ideas, wanted to create a secular state free from the grip of a medieval church that seemed to thwart their aspirations in the emerging industrial world. They were also Italian nationalists and saw the church as the last obstacle to the unification of their country, a project that popes had frustrated for centuries. Since most were at least culturally Catholic, few were opposed to the papacy itself, but the Papal States were another matter. Either the pope had to relinquish temporal power voluntarily or it had to be taken away from him by political force. Almost immediately after his election, Pius had to flee from Rome in disguise as an angry mob seized his palace and proclaimed a secular republic. Eventually he was able to return to the city, but only with the support of French troops sent by Louis Napoleon, the cynical and despotic nephew of the church's old nemesis. In order to maintain his hold on papal territory Pius had further alienated political liberals who were fighting reactionary monarchies in many parts of Europe and gave more ammunition to socialists who saw the Catholic Church as a symbol of reactionary, antimodern oppression. Like his predecessors, Pius equated the defense of the Papal States with the defense of the Catholic Church. For Pius the only thing that was more damnable than political liberalism was Catholic liberalism. As the chosen successor of Gregory XVI he

rejected everything connected with Lamennais and his attempt to initiate
a conversation between Catholics and secular members of French society
after the fall of Napoleon. An equation was being made by Pius and his
advisors that conflated the approach of the institutional church to a given
social situation — which is essentially a question of strategy and therefore
open to discussion — with assent to the teaching of the church on doctrinal issues, which is a different matter altogether. Perhaps because he
felt beset on every side, Pius displayed something akin to paranoia when
it came to even the slightest challenge to his authority and would lash
out at nearly anyone who questioned his point of view, including bishops
and ambassadors to the papal court, some of whom questioned his mental stability. Pius IX demanded that Catholics choose sides immediately:
either obedience to the papacy and salvation or complicity with an evil
world and damnation. In many ways, the white-hot polarization of the
post-Reformation era was back in full force. More temperate Catholics,
however, knew that such extremism was uncalled for and insisted, albeit
in whispers, that there were more prudent alternatives.

The *Syllabus of Errors* contains eighty "mistakes" about Catholicism
and the social order that members of the church must recognize and reject
immediately. Few have applicability to the world today, reflecting rather
the cultural and sociopolitical tensions of mid-nineteenth-century Europe.
Others, however, are more significant and require some analysis because
they run in the face of commonly held assumptions about what constitutes a free and democratic society. For Pius and those who wrote the
Syllabus for him, the modern world they were contending with was the
end product of a tragic sequence of events that began in the sixteenth century with the first successful attacks against the hegemony of the medieval
church.[19] The Reformation, the Thirty Years' War, and the French Revolution were all part of a piece. The stress on individuality and the primacy
of conscience so central to the Reformation, religious indifference that set
in after the Treaty of Westphalia, and the attack against ecclesiastical and
civil authority that kept the guillotine running full-force in the 1790s were
manifestations of a diabolic process of de-Christianization that seemed
nearly unstoppable. Pius was convinced that the sins of modernity had
to be attacked head on. Educated in a closed Tridentine seminary system based on a rigid, post-Reformation interpretation of Thomas, Pius
had no use for intellectual niceties. As a divinely established institution
the church was in sole possession of the truth and, as the Vicar of Jesus
Christ, Pius had a precise job to do — lay out the truth and make sure
people accepted it even if that entailed being offensive. When the *Syllabus*
was issued in 1864 Pius clearly thought that he was mounting a barricade

---

19. Wills, *Papal Sin.*

to defend the church in hand-to-hand combat. In fact, there was a literal dimension to his defiance. Italian nationalists already had unified most of the peninsula and had their eyes set on the city of Rome as their new capital. They would soon be lobbing cannon balls at the Vatican.

For Pius, the Catholic Church was right and those who opposed it were wrong. There was only one true religion and valid form of Christianity, the Roman Catholic Church. This meant, therefore, that the church should be a legally recognized institution in Catholic countries with the exclusive right to define Christian beliefs, oversee education, monitor behavior, and celebrate religious rituals in public. For Pius real freedom meant willingly following the teaching of the Catholic Church. The freedoms associated with the modern world — the right to believe or not, to follow one's conscience even when doing so was a challenge to religious authorities, as well as freedom of association and the press — were actually delusions caused by willful disobedience to the will of God. What the *Syllabus* proposes, therefore, is nothing short of a restoration of a medieval world more closed than any proposed by either Augustine or Aquinas, who were social realists and nuanced theological thinkers. To preclude the possibility that someone might think otherwise, the eightieth and final error laid out by Pius condemns those who believe that "the Roman Pontiff can, and ought to, reconcile himself and come to terms with progress, Liberalism and modern civilization." The *Syllabus* provoked intense reactions just as Pius wanted it to do. Many political leaders were appalled by its belligerent tone and blanket condemnation of modernity. It was a formula for a new wave of division and tension that threatened the social order. In non-Catholic countries like Germany and the United States, the political loyalty of Catholics was now more suspect than ever. In an effort to save face, some Catholic moderates tried to explain the excesses of the *Syllabus* as the theatrical ploys of an overly zealous professor trying to make an otherwise reasonable point.

The *Syllabus of Errors* has been consigned to the footnotes of Western history for a long time, an obscure document that only scholars and those who are well-versed in Catholic history know about. The concept of papal infallibility, however, fares better. Although the origins and content of the doctrine are rarely understood, there is a sense among people familiar with Christianity that is it a special belief that sets Catholics apart from Eastern Orthodox and Protestant Christians. Sometimes the dogma is described in ways that are hardly more than a caricature. The pope, as the head of the Catholic Church, always "gets it right" when it comes to moral and theological issues. He enters into a trance-like state and utters irrefutable truths that Catholics accept at face value. Even when it comes to nondoctrinal issues, from the style of liturgy to the best way for Catholics to participate in the social order, the pope's wishes are obeyed without question. In fact, the doctrine of papal infallibility has nothing to do with blind obedience. It is about the reliability of what the church believes as an embodiment of Jesus who continues to guide it toward the truth as it negotiates the complexities of historical existence. Its beliefs are laid out in ancient creeds and explained by its leaders as need requires, particularly by the bishop of Rome and those charged with episcopal leadership. Their task as pastors is to teach and help the Catholic community understand and respond to the truthfulness of what they believe in the particular historical moment. They do not impose the truth; they lay it out and help people affirm it.

We are talking, therefore, about a type of "collective truth," rather than the imposition of a truth-claim by leaders exercising absolute authority without regard for the experience and insights of their fellow Catholics. The decree issued by the First Vatican Council in 1870 is remarkably terse in the way it lays out the criteria for a binding definition of moral and theological truth by the institutional church. The pope can make an infallible statement _only_ after having consulted his fellow bishops about the moral or theological issue that requires definitive clarification. They must come to the same conclusion and be in agreement about what they are going to say. The bishops play a vital role in helping the pope formulate church teaching on a given issue because of their proximity to the lay members of the Catholic community who are affected by church teaching in the most direct way. An infallible papal pronouncement is meant to be rare by definition. One can speculate whether the formal decree on papal infallibility would even have been issued were it not for the events already mentioned — the defensive position of the Catholic Church in nineteenth-century Europe and the aggressive "papal persona" of Pius IX. It provided nineteenth-century Catholics with the security of knowing that the pope and institutional church were right when it came to moral and theological matters, but this sense of certainty was purchased at a price. The internal and external life of the church was altered. Theological creativity was curtailed as pro-papal conservatives cracked down on more open-minded members of the hierarchy and theologians who questioned the rigid Thomism behind Pius's theology and approach to the social order. For non-Catholic political leaders the doctrine of papal infallibility and the "Romanization" of national Catholic churches presented problems that were even more acute than those caused by the _Syllabus._ In the event of a conflict between church and state over political or social issues, how could Catholics possibly be loyal to their own countries?

The bishops who gathered in Rome in 1869 knew that Pius expected them to vote in favor of the dogma of papal infallibility with a minimum of theological debate. Different versions of the decree itself were worked through committees with sections added or deleted to achieve as much consensus as possible. With the Papal States surrounded by hostile Italian troops, Pius wanted a display of almost defiant unanimity from his fellow bishops. Because almost all of them subscribed to an intensely hierarchical, Vatican-centered approach to the church, there was never any doubt that Pius would have his way. Many bishops were dealing with anticlerical governments just like Pius was and resonated with his call for a rigid chain of command based on an unflinching commitment to Tridentine Catholicism. Most felt that the official promulgation of the doctrine of papal infallibility was the culmination of a long process of historical and theological evolution that they were being asked to bear witness to as members of the hierarchy.[20]

Still, there were a few bishops who raised objections to the ideas behind the doctrine because there seemed to be little focus on the role of episcopacy in the church. The bishops were being subordinated to the papacy in an unprecedented way. They accepted the principles behind papal infallibility but insisted that there had to be checks and balances to make sure that the doctrine was not abused. Certainly, the excesses of medieval popes like Boniface VIII were in the back of their minds. In addition, there was an ancient tradition in certain European cities of clergy meeting and selecting their own bishop rather than waiting for authorities in Rome to make an appointment. Experience had proven that a bishop chosen by the local clergy often had a better sense of the cultural and social environment of the Catholic community he had been asked to serve as an episcopal leader. There was also concern that the antimodern tone of the decree with its strident refusal to recognize the limitations of doctrinal language gave the impression that Catholicism was frozen in time. The bishops who raised these objections were hardly relativistic in their approach to the truth, but they recognized that culture and context necessarily limit our ability to grasp and express what it is we actually believe. Truth must be appropriated on an ongoing basis because it is a living reality that words can never capture completely. Conversation with nonbelievers, therefore, can actually be helpful. Pius IX, however, saw the truth as something that is timeless and immutable. With only a modest theological education and a visceral dislike for anything that smacked of ambiguity, Pius IX saw the church as the antidote to the intellectual challenges presented by Enlightenment thinkers and attacks against the church as a social institution. Those who questioned Pius' position feared that he was putting the church into an intellectually absurd position of Catholic *fideism,* in other words, you believe something because the pope tells you to even if you think it makes no sense. If necessary, you sacrifice your own intellectual integrity for the sake of church unity even if that requires suppressing

---

20. Küng, *Infallible? An Inquiry.*

your own ideas about what you believe. The overwhelming majority of the eight hundred bishops assembled in Rome signed the decree on papal infallibility. Some conveniently left the city before the end of the Council. A few refused to sign and eventually left the Catholic Church.

One of the nineteenth century's best Catholic historians and theologians, John Henry Newman, felt uncomfortable with the looming issue of papal infallibility. A former Anglican priest and convert to the Roman church who would become a cardinal, he feared that a formal decree would only anger Protestants all the more after the debacle of the *Syllabus*. They resented the adamant refusal of Pius and other Catholic conservatives to see anything legitimate about the Reformation as well as the explicit denunciation of freedom of conscience and religious liberty that were the cornerstone of nineteenth-century European liberalism. Although they too were contending with an increasingly irreligious and secular world, they were not about to condemn modern civil liberties as errors. Less centralized organizationally and more tolerant doctrinally, Protestants were less threatened by the Enlightenment and the emergence of the modern social paradigm than Catholics. Well placed socially, Newman was also concerned that an explicit decree on papal infallibility would only fan the flames of anti-Catholic political sentiment in his native England, where Catholics had only recently gained full civil liberties. His reservations were typically well thought out and motivated by intense loyalty to the branch of the Christian church he had come — after a painful process of self- and scholarly examination — to consider authentic and true. Newman was an Oxford-trained theologian who could sight-read the early Church Fathers in Latin and Greek. He knew the background of their theology as well as he did that of the post-Reformation Anglican Church he was baptized into and served as a priest before his conversion to Catholicism. Newman recognized that the papal office had played a central role in the Western church from at least the fourth century on. The bishop of Rome was afforded special respect and his opinion on jurisdictional and theological issues given particular weight at an early stage in church history. Newman saw the church as a community of believers infallibly guided by God's spirit in its midst yet he approached most facets of the institutional church as a means to an end — living out Christian truth in the most effective way possible. Newman pointed out frequently that the truth the church proclaims and the way its bishops express it can sometimes lead to something of a disjuncture or "misfit," given the limitations of language. Doctrine, therefore, has to be reinterpreted and retranslated on an ongoing basis.

For Newman we approximate the truth but we never "achieve" it. The task of the pope and church councils, therefore, is to proclaim and reproclaim the truthfulness of what Christians believe. As opposed to Pius's static and essentialist understanding of dogma Newman was proposing an evolutionary approach that meshed with his years of study of church history and the development of dogma that it pointed to. After he signed the decree on papal infallibility Newman's former Protestant colleagues accused him of theological dishonesty. His prior conversion to Catholicism in 1843 was bad enough, but his willingness seemingly to sign away his intellectual autonomy was intolerable. Newman responded to their criticism with a typically Catholic rebuttal — the co-equal status of scripture and tradition. For the Anglican convert who had become a Catholic bishop God was as present in the ups and down of Catholic history as in the pages of the Bible. Both were trustworthy resources that explained how to live a fully Christian life. Despite its aberrations, the papacy had proven to be a trustworthy institution that had provided sound doctrinal guidance over the centuries. Newman had little success in winning over Protestants to the Catholic position on papal infallibility, of course, but he presented his arguments in an intellectually respectable way in a series of articles that he wrote after the Council. By pointing to the historical and theological complexity behind the doctrine of infallibility itself, Newman also helped blunt the force of ultra-conservatives in the church who wasted no time in using the decree to attack Catholics they considered less stalwart than themselves, particularly those who were still willing to engage in a conversation with people outside of a now hermetically sealed Catholic world.

A Tentative Yes

By the mid-nineteenth century the idea that something could be changeless or immutable no longer made sense to most people. To the contrary, there was an obsession with change and a general assumption that it was the same as progress. Darwin had proven that the biological world is driven by change. It was clear that mutability is at the core of nature itself, a sine qua non for its development and success. Political and social structures were likewise seen as evolving and mutable rather than fixed. In the minds of many people there was no celestial helmsman guiding the course of history. For weal or woe we determine its shape. The processes behind biological evolution were conveniently adapted to the economic order by the proponents of laissez-faire capitalism who advocated an entirely amoral approach to economic and material life. Just as nature found the right course of action over time, so too would the "invisible hand" of capitalism that Adam Smith had postulated as the guiding force of economic self-interest in *The Wealth of Nations*. For nineteenth-century capitalists it was the equivalent of a sacred text whose insights were to be accepted on blind faith exactly like a dogmatic decree based on papal infallibility. The acquisition of wealth became the crucial measure of progress with little reflection on the consequences for the body politic or common good. In the medieval world there was at least a shared Christian ethical system that, in theory, limited the excesses of the rich and powerful. In the minds of many economic liberals, however, the acquisition of wealth was really not an ethical issue at all. Those who possessed wealth were at the apex of the evolutionary pyramid because of their superior abilities in what was now an amoral, Darwinian world. For those who still considered themselves Christians, morality was a private affair that had little connection with what took place on the floor of a stock exchange.

Caught up in a futile attempt to preserve its cultural and political prerogatives, the Catholic Church had said little about the increasingly desperate plight of the working class in industrial countries.[21] In most urban areas churches were empty. The dynamics had changed since 1789 when the church had been attacked because of its connection with the aristocratic order. With the exception of socialists like Marx, few people were anticlerical or as antireligious as they had been fifty years before. They were now essentially de-churched and irreligious rather than explicitly agnostic. As they tried to survive on miserable wages if they were lucky enough to have jobs, the "eternal truths" of the church were of little interest to them. By the end of the nineteenth century, however, the church had regained some of its former influence as a social institution. This was due in large part to the election of Leo XIII in 1878. A scholar trained in civil and church law who had traveled and worked widely in Europe, Leo XIII had a more ample sense of the church than his predecessor. He had lived in Belgium, where a type of progressive Catholicism had flourished, and had also experienced life in Protestant Great Britain with its newfound political might and intellectual preeminence.[22] As a priest and member of the papal diplomatic corps, the future Pope Leo had come into contact with clergy and laity in France and Germany concerned about the plight of working women and men in their countries who were subjected to the worst excesses of uncontrolled capitalism.[23] Committed to a Thomistic understanding of the common good, these doctrinally conservative but socially progressive Catholics felt that the church was morally obligated to say something about the degrading living and working conditions of workers that stripped them of their humanity.

---

21. In the 1850s Lacordaire was one of the few exceptions to ecclesiastical silence on social injustice. Charmed by his eloquence, the bourgeois Parisians who crammed Notre Dame to hear his Lenten sermons were nonetheless angered by his denunciation of economic injustice in France.

22. Shannon, "Rerum novarum."

23. Mich, *Catholic Social Teaching and Movements.*

In addition, Leo XIII was the first pope to pay any real attention to the American Catholic Church, which was now standing on its own two feet and grappling with questions of its own identity in the world's most aggressively capitalist nation. Made up almost entirely of immigrants whose economic lives were precarious and who were politically marginalized in a Protestant country, American Catholics looked to Rome for guidance. Unlike their European counterparts, many were still intensely committed to the Roman Catholic Church.[24] Socially and theologically conservative on most levels, Leo XIII was the first pope nonetheless to address the social order as a concerned teacher open to the possibility of Catholics playing a positive role in society. In 1891 he published a papal encyclical entitled *Rerum novarum*. He reflected on the "new things" or concerns that affected the Catholic Church and its members in the late nineteenth century. It was a watershed document that laid the foundation for a new presence of the Catholic Church in the social order. A century and a quarter later some of its language is archaic and the issues it addresses are no longer pertinent, but many of the values it lays out for a good and just social order remain foundational aspects of Catholic social teaching.

As an ardent disciple of Thomas Aquinas, Leo XIII felt that God had put the natural and social world together in a hierarchical way. Human society was meant to be stratified with different groups dedicated to specific tasks, from manual labor to the art of government. The church was meant to oversee and guide everyone involved. Each job, humble or important, was a calling or vocation, and each group was to act synergistically in a common effort to sustain life in this world and, depending on the quality of one's efforts, enjoy it in the next. A bit of a romantic from an aristocratic Italian family, Leo looked back nostalgically at the Middle Ages and guild system in which a shared Christian vision supposedly protected artisans and laborers from the worst forms of exploitation. Certainly there had been structural injustices in the medieval period, but there was a stress on charity as a moral obligation, and church-sponsored charities mitigated the worst excesses of the medieval world. Influenced by the monastic ideal of poverty and worldly renunciation, medieval Christians saw wealth as a blessing but not an end in itself. Those lucky enough to be affluent were expected to return what they did not need to the poor. There was a "social mortgage" attached to material possessions, and a person's right to private property was conditional rather than absolute in the ethical system laid out by Thomas Aquinas.

The Darwinian capitalism of the nineteenth century, however, was not predicated on Christian charity or values. The useful conceit of

---

24. Ibid., 17–18.

natural selection allowed many capitalists to think that their affluence was the result of their own intellectual superiority and innate skill as entrepreneurs. Some were quite generous with their wealth, but few questioned how they came about their riches in the first place. In a winner-takes-all economic system, the poor were seen as their own worst enemies, the hapless victims of poor education or, as was often implied, lack of moral fiber. Leo recognized that industrial capitalism had led to "marvelous discoveries" in the field of technology and science but had also created "elements of conflict" because of "the enormous fortunes of some few individuals, and the utter poverty of the masses."[25] The future pope had spent extensive time in some of Europe's most industrialized countries, and knew just how appalling the conditions of the working class were. At the beginning of *Rerum novarum* he insists that "some opportune remedy must be found quickly for the misery and wretchedness pressing so unjustly on the majority of the working class."[26] For Leo the very notion of the common good was being threatened by a materialistic "economism" that denied the transcendent dimension of human existence. The members of the bourgeoisie were as materialistic as hard-lined socialists: the former offered salvation in the form of vast fortunes that allowed them to live in splendid isolation from the poor while the latter preached a utopian communism that would put an end to every form of injustice by smashing the capitalist system once and for all.

Leo makes it clear from the onset of *Rerum novarum* that the suffering of the working class is the result of greed. The accumulation of wealth had become an obsession, the acquisition of capital an easy rationalization used to justify the most egregious forms of exploitation. Workers had been turned into "revenue vectors," readily replaced at the first sign of wear and tear. Their suffering was not the result of mysterious market forces or a consequence of their lack of willingness to live productive lives. The poor were being exploited by a small segment of society that has gained a stranglehold over every facet of economic production. In addition, the wealthy had a monopoly over social resources in the form of education, health care, and public safety. Due to an exponential increase in the population of Europe in the nineteenth century, workers were entirely at the mercy of employers who could pay the lowest wages and fire laborers for the slightest provocation. Leo knew that laborers were caught in a vicious circle. Regardless of how hard they worked it was nearly impossible for them to escape from the clutches of poverty, in large part because they could no longer negotiate the value of their own labor. Given their economic vulnerability and the risk of being labeled as social agitators,

---

25. Shannon, "Rerum novarum," paragraphs 1, 2.
26. Ibid., 3.

workers found it difficult to fight abuses in the workplace. Still, some workers had begun to form unions and agitate for better working conditions by the mid-nineteenth century. Remarkably, a few intrepid priests in Europe and North America had encouraged workers to press for their rights, as well. They promoted Catholic workers' associations and unions, making it clear that workers' rights were basic human rights, that those who worked in factories were no less important than those who owned them.

Rather than discouraging this type of commitment on the part of the clergy, Leo encouraged it. He listened carefully to the thoughts of so-called "labor priests" and socially engaged laity.[27] Following their lead, Leo insists in *Rerum novarum* that workers be paid a wage that reflects the real value of their labor rather than the lowest possible price dictated by market forces. Leo wanted to create an organic economic structure in which workers and industrialists would be part of a common effort to better the social order using their respective skills rather than competing with each other in unrelenting class warfare. Workers are to be afforded time to rest with their families, study if they so desire, and worship on Sunday without any pressure to work. These are their natural, God-given rights *as* workers. They have the right to organize and when necessary strike for better working conditions.

In light of prior papal teaching with its resistance to most forms of participatory democracy and frank emphasis on "pie in the sky" compensation for earthly injustice, Leo started to move the church in an innovative direction with the publication of *Rerum novarum*. Although Leo seems to tiptoe around the sensibilities of the wealthy at times, he also poses serious questions about the morality of an economic system predicated on the acquisition of wealth for its own sake. Leo wanted to find middle ground and avoid another volcanic eruption of social tension. In the late nineteenth century Europe and North America were being torn apart by labor unrest that had created a vicious circle of repression and retaliation. For Leo the best way to avoid social strife and suffering was to reaffirm the dignity of every person in the productive process without radically altering the hierarchical nature of the economic and social system itself. Except for scholars and historians, few people today read *Rerum novarum*. Its archaic language, especially the papal "We" Leo uses to refer to himself, seems antiquated and haughty. Most of the abusive working conditions he denounces seem like scenes from a novel by Dickens and unimaginable in Europe or North America. But we are a bit naïve, perhaps conveniently so. Most of the conditions Leo condemns as an affront to human dignity are part and parcel of the global economy today. The same

27. Mich, *Catholic Social Teaching and Movements.*

abuses persist — miserable wages and working conditions, child labor and debt bondage, and the systematic repression of workers' organizations. Globalization has brought many benefits, but it has created a type of savage, multinational capitalism that has actually increased the poverty and vulnerability of workers throughout the world. Despite the odd pronouns and out of date economic terminology, *Rerum novarum* still makes sense. It is about distributive justice, the dignity of workers, the responsibility of the state to protect those at risk, in other words, the basic economic and human rights that should be the foundation of a humane social order.

Beyond the Train Wreck

We began this chapter by alluding to the difficulty involved in defining the meaning of modernity, and in all likelihood the concept is as nebulous now as it was many pages ago. Historians are not especially helpful since they revel in fighting over when a particular historical moment begins and ends, what makes it what it is, and whether the concept even makes sense at all! But there can be no doubt that the ground began to shift under the medieval paradigm in the sixteenth century, and a new framework began to emerge predicated on different values — religious first and foremost, but economic, political, and social as well. The reformers attacked the pillars of the medieval Catholic system: the centrality of the papacy and the co-equal status of scripture and tradition that had provided legitimation for the church's claim to authority over nearly every aspect of medieval life. In their efforts to update and revitalize Christianity the reformers re-created it in many ways, forcing individual believers to stand on their own feet supported by the grace of God alone. The support of the humble parish priest and mighty pope was no longer necessary. With the rituals of the church cut to the bone and the Bible proclaimed as the only compass necessary for the Christian community, the church became a far more democratic polity, although not all branches of Protestant Christianity were equally egalitarian. Once the fog of religious hierarchy was lifted, it was not long before the same process of deflation was applied to the sociopolitical world as well. Popes and princes were brought down to ground level just like everyone else. Protestantism was as much a sociopolitical phenomenon as a theological one. The Council of Trent, of course, was a fierce counterattack against everything the reformers had proposed and thanks to the commitment and genius of Counter-Reformation figures like Ignatius it was a success. The hierarchical nature of the church was reaffirmed and because of strategic alliances with various monarchies the Catholic Church continued to play a central role in various European countries. Nonetheless, there was a shadow side to the victory. Tridentine Catholicism stressed tradition to the detriment of scripture, and the emphasis on the hierarchical nature of the church was so extreme at times that any notion of the church as a community of disciples was nearly lost. To use Thomistic categories, the "accidental" aspects of the church, nonessential and negotiable facets of governance for example, were nearly conflated with the church's "essential" mission, proclaiming the Gospel. Pius IX and Vatican I created a church that was so "papal" and centralized that much of the agility and vitality of local Catholicism was compromised. Although it survived the challenges of the modern world, the institutional Catholic Church did so in an almost entirely *reactive* way. It chastised and condemned rather than exhorted and encouraged, and in the minds of many people it became the principal symbol of antimodern conservatism. *Rerum novarum* was the first church document since the Council of Trent to say anything positive about the modern world, and even then Leo was sparing in his praise.

The Catholic Church does not exist for its own sake. It has only one purpose: to proclaim the Reign of God as best it can. But even gifted and sincere members of the church have fallen into the trap of "ecclesiocentrism" — conflating the institutional church with the message it is meant to proclaim. Under ceaseless attack, the leaders of the church put all the more stress on the importance of the institution itself. In an age in which monarchies were beginning to disappear, the papacy became more autocratic. At a moment in the political history of the Western world when democracy was taking root the church became more hierarchical. There was an almost paralyzing nostalgia in the Vatican for the Middle Ages in which the church was at the center of people's personal lives and a key player in the social order, overseeing behavior and trying to shape a world that Augustine and Aquinas would feel comfortable in. That world, however, began to disappear in increments beginning in 1517, when Luther tacked his theses to the Castle Church door in Wittenberg, and probably had come to an end by the time Louis XVI's head was shown to a howling mob in a Paris square in 1793. Religious authority, along with absolute monarchy, was a thing of the past. Used to imposing its will, the Catholic Church had a difficult time understanding and responding to modern freedoms. Church leaders assumed that they needed the recognition and support of the state to do their job and consequently blundered into a series of alliances with reactionary political groups that only alienated those committed to modern liberties all the more.

From the late eighteenth century to the mid-twentieth, the Catholic Church became a synonym for knee-jerk conservatism, both religious and political. Nothing symbolizes this "disconnect" between the Catholic Church and the modern world more than the decree on papal infallibility on the one hand and *The Origin of Species* on the other. For Catholics truth could be found unequivocally and infallibly in the Catholic Church.

For Darwin truth was far more elusive and complicated. If it existed at all it was in the chaotic muck of natural and historical processes whose outcome was impossible to predict. The same assumptions were applied to the political and social order. Paul's claim in Romans 13 to the contrary, God had little to do with appointing those who exercised power. They could be voted in and out of office and when deemed expedient sent to the guillotine. Revolutions did not provoke outbursts of divine wrath, and despite the foibles of day-to-day politics it seemed possible to create just societies through democratic and secular processes. Neither God nor the church was necessary to define the common good. Society had become a secular proposition. To survive in the modern world the church finally realized that it had to go about its job of presenting the Gospel in a different way, winning people over rather than imposing its point of view as it had for more than a millennium. It had to demonstrate the truth and logic of the Gospel in cultures and countries in which belief was now entirely optional. It took up that task at the Second Vatican Council in 1962 and continues to fine-tune its strategy in what is now a multicultural, global world. Prior to the Second Vatican Council the church would often be referred to with the Latin phrase *societas perfecta* — the perfect society. After the Council a humbler metaphor came into use — the People of God. No longer consumed with defending the past, the church could now focus its energies on the present and future.

Chapter Seven

Reassessment and Regeneration
The Second Vatican Council

Church and Context:
Between a Nightmare and a Dream

By the end of the nineteenth century the Catholic Church was on the defensive in the majority of European countries that were still identified by the Tridentine Catholic world. Church and state had been separated or soon would be in Belgium, France, Italy, and elsewhere in Europe, where an ethos of secular indifference was considered the norm among "sophisticated" people. The triumph of modernity and bourgeois liberalism seemed complete, especially in countries where intellectuals and political elites identified with the Enlightenment and the French Revolution. The situation in the United States and Canada, however, was more upbeat. Immigrants from Catholic countries in Europe were intensely loyal to the church, particularly the Irish, Germans, and Poles. Many saw the church as an ally that helped defend them against the bigotry of certain Americans and Canadians who defined them as outsiders. Church schools, financial institutions, and labor organizations provided protection, and to the consternation of papal advisors some members of the episcopal hierarchy in the United States and Canada were committed to real dialogue with a largely Protestant population. Without negating the specificity of Catholic belief, they tried to stress the fact that Catholics shared common Christian beliefs with Protestants, following the well-established tradition of denominationalism. French-speaking Canadians were fervent believers by and large, and the church exercised considerable social influence in Québec, a stalwart defender of the "Other Canada."

Leo XIII's openness to labor issues and social justice, so obvious in *Rerum novarum*, helped the church's fortunes, but he was no liberal when it came to ethical and theological issues. Leo was a hard-line Thomist and firm believer in Christendom, just as his predecessors had been. He considered the separation of church and state to be one of the fundamental errors of modernity and the principal explanation for its "godlessness." He could wax nostalgic about the disappearance of medieval guilds, hardly admitting they were long gone and actually quite selective in terms of membership and privileges. Until the election of John XXIII in 1958 every pope was socially and theologically conservative to one degree or another, and even John was a cautious centrist. The church was the last absolute monarchy in Europe with all the pomp and circumstances of an imperial Roman court. From at least the third century, the bishop of Rome had been deferred to by his fellow bishops as the most important member of the episcopacy in the Western church, but Vatican I had made the pope a synonym for Catholicism and absolute obedience to the pope's will a badge of orthodoxy. Bishops were carefully chosen for their unquestioned loyalty and were expected to follow the Vatican's lead when it came to social and theological issues. Serious matters were referred to the Vatican, and bishops would often wait months and years for a decision to be handed down. As an institution the church had become a highly centralized, top-heavy operation. The old maxim "Rome has spoken; the issue is resolved" was truer than it had been since the papacy of Innocent III in the thirteenth century.

There is no doubt that centralization helped the institutional church respond to many of the challenges it faced in the nineteenth and twentieth centuries, but there was an inevitable tension involved in the process. Catholicism is the sum of its parts. It is a collection of communities that understands itself as Catholic. These communities have their own cultures, languages, and sociopolitical traditions that are constantly changing and require assessment and response by those Catholics who are part of them. On a purely sociological level, the Catholic Church is no different from any other institution. Good management requires a willingness to let local leaders and believers mediate their own solutions to the inevitable challenges and crises their environments produce. Although people in the Vatican were concerned about the best interests of the church as a whole, they sometimes lacked the contextual knowledge they needed to make the right decisions. When they were confronted with diverse points of view about challenges local Catholic communities faced, they invariably gave priority to those groups that seemed to display unquestioned loyalty to Rome. The Vatican's decisions were slow in the making and were invariably conservative on both a theological and sociopolitical level.

The dogma of papal infallibility proclaimed in 1870 was no guarantee that the institutional church's mundane decisions would be right. Infallibility was about ethical and theological truths alone. On that level, the Holy Spirit guided the church. The day-to-day affairs of the church, however, were another matter. Steering the church is really an art form. Channels change and sandbars seem to move of their own accord, testing everyone's skills. An overly rigid hierarchy can sometimes be a liability. Vatican I was a response to the first phase of the modern period and the chaos that ensued during and after the French Revolution. But subterranean change was taking place that would require a new response from the Catholic community in what was becoming a post-Christian world, particularly in Europe. At the turn of the twentieth century everything seemed to be going nicely, at least on a secular level. Bourgeois culture with its stress on consumption and comfort seemed to have triumphed. The great German social scientists Max Weber and Ernst Troeltsch predicted social orders that would be more efficient and bureaucratic with private issues, such as religious belief, relegated to the sidelines. Progress and secularization were nearly synonyms in the minds of many people, and neither force could be stopped. Many Catholics had come to grips with the fact that Christendom was a thing of the past and they would have to live amicably with people who did not share their religious values. The majority of Protestants subscribed to a liberal version of Christianity that fit snugly into the socioeconomic and political status quo despite the fact that there was still tremendous economic and social injustice in most countries.

European powers had carved up large chunks of Africa and Asia creating the equivalent of geopolitical vacuum cleaners that extracted natural resources with ruthless efficiency. The United States exercised blatant imperialistic control of most of Latin America. Colonial imperialism often was justified in the name of "civilizing" and "Christianizing" benighted non-Europeans. Missionaries frequently followed in the wake of colonial armies, often relying on them for protection as they tried to spread the Gospel. American Protestant missionaries began to arrive in Latin America, working from the rather amusing assumption that Roman Catholics are really not Christians and unlike Protestants need to be evangelized the "right" way. This smugness, however, would be short-lived with the façade of Christian morality and cultural superiority shattered to pieces. Rationality gave way to an orgy of irrationality and unbridled violence: two world wars and the symbol of utter evil the Western world still grapples with — the Holocaust. The crisis began in August 1914 when European powers, for no substantive reason, began a bloody war that bled them dry and shattered any pretense about Europe as the bastion of civility and reason. Corpses rotted in trenches that moved forward a short distance and then fell back the next day. At the Battle of Verdun in 1916 a quarter-million soldiers died and a million more were wounded. Nothing was accomplished. Science was put to murderous use to produce ever more lethal weapons that blinded and maimed everyone without distinction. For some the answer to the madness of the First World War was nihilism. More insidious still was the temptation of secular messianism embodied in bloody dictators like Lenin, Stalin, Mussolini, and Hitler, who exactly twenty-one years after the first war ended began a second conflict that killed seventy million more human beings, many because of their race, religion, or political views.

The task of the church in the twentieth century would be profoundly different from what it had been in previous centuries. The respect for human life that was so central *both* to Catholic thought and the Enlightenment project was put to an unbelievably severe test in the 1930s and 1940s as human decency and reason nearly vanished in an orgy of hyper-violent inhumanity. The transcendent vision of life so central to Christianity, along with the stress on reason and optimism behind the Enlightenment were overshadowed by blood-drenched political ideologies that immolated people with ruthless precision. The old theological squabbles of the Reformation and eighteenth-century spats about the truth claims and social prerogatives of the church were no longer relevant. Believers and nonbelievers alike were faced with the challenge of keeping hope alive after the near triumph of evil.

Almost miraculously, a remarkable generation of Catholic thinkers would emerge from the ashes of World War II, producing innovative theology that gave new strength and hope to weary believers. One of the most important and innovative was Karl Rahner, a German Jesuit who despite his first-hand experience of Nazi evil spoke about God's ongoing offer of grace and freedom that was everyone's birthright as a human being. He began his theological career in the rubble of bombed out cities in Austria and Germany. Throughout his long and illustrious career as a teacher and theologian Rahner constantly spoke about freedom and grace as divine gifts available to everyone without exception. By having the courage to say yes to the word of God we move from fragmentation to wholeness, even after the horrors of the Second World War and the specter of the death camps. And although it was not much more than a ray of light on the horizon, a few keen observers were aware that new forms of Catholicism and Christianity were beginning to appear in Asia, Africa, and Latin America.

The postcolonial era was dawning with a whole new set of vital challenges. The church was becoming more "catholic," or universal, at a rapid pace. The postcolonial era was about to begin, raising questions about the very meaning of the adjective "Roman" for people whose experience of Catholicism was almost entirely local and rooted in non-Western cultures. Although some missionaries had used the coattails of colonial powers to preach the Gospel, others let go of them quickly, investing their energy in creating local churches that would outlast their temporary presence. Certainly, the agony of the postwar world had to be addressed, but at the same time the growing self-confidence of the church outside of Europe and the so-called developed world had to be recognized and encouraged. A significant change was taking place that was altering the inner core of

Catholicism, what Karl Rahner and other theologians would refer to as a Second Pentecost. It was clear in the minds of a few prescient and courageous leaders of the church that it was time for the church to meet as a whole, in an ecumenical council that could move beyond the problems of the past and encourage innovative responses to the growing energy and hopefulness of an emerging, non-Western church. The response to these challenges was the Second Vatican Council, commonly known as Vatican II. Unlike Vatican I with its defensive and sometimes hostile tone toward the larger world, the Second Vatican Council was about listening and responding to a world in need of hope. Its focus was on the future rather than the past. Rather than closing doors it opened them, sometimes with unexpected consequences. As we begin the twenty-first century the meaning and implications of its texts and teachings are still debated, sometimes hotly. Before we actually examine some of the documents and consequences of Vatican II, however, we need to gain a better insight into two phenomena that lay behind it — the crisis of Western modernity that caused so much suffering in the first half of the century and the rise of new forms of non-Western Catholic Christianity that began to offer new hope from the 1960s to the present.

The Crisis of Modernity: From Certainty to Fear

A year after the guns fell silent in 1918 the Irish poet W. B. Yeats wrote a poem entitled *The Second Coming*, which captures perfectly the sense of desolation that had set in after four years of senseless bloodletting in Europe. He describes a social order without a purpose, twisting as it falls downward yet desperately trying to grasp onto something that might prevent its crash:

> Turning and turning the widening gyre
> The falcon cannot hear the falconer;
> Things fall apart; the centre cannot hold;
> Mere anarchy is loosed upon the world,
> The blood-dimmed tide is loosed, and everywhere
> The ceremony of innocence is drowned;
> The best lack all conviction while the worst
> Are full of passionate intensity.

For four years Europeans had killed each other at a prodigious rate for the sake of ridiculous nationalistic agendas. In 1917 the United States had entered the conflict hoping to secure a niche in the postwar scheme of things, securing more economic and geopolitical power in the wake of a global catastrophe. Yeats and his educated colleagues from Trinity College, Oxford, and Cambridge had lost their sense of certainty about the meaning of life. They found a measure of comfort in literature and the arts in which they could explore their inner anxiety and express their dismay at the barbarism unleashed by the First World War. The majority of people, however, looked for a more palpable solution to their needs. The Great Depression that set in after 1929 nearly brought the supposedly rational capitalist system to its knees. Germans dealt with hyperinflation that made their currency useless. Throughout Europe and North America millions lost their jobs, with unemployment often reaching 20 percent or more. Desperate for a way out, many sought a solution in the "religionless" religions of Marxism and fascism. There was a deep longing for order and a transcendent vision of life, and many felt that organized religion had failed miserably in providing them with the sense of purpose they needed to live a meaningful existence. The church was stuck in the past, obsessed with defending its arcane dogmas, social prerogatives, and medieval buildings. Some nuns and religious orders of men might provide useful social services, but who needed Latin-speaking men running around in ecclesiastical robes hobnobbing with what was left of the aristocracy?

In the Soviet Union Lenin and his soon-to-be-heir Joseph Stalin imposed a ruthless version of Marxism that promised to create a secular paradise for the masses. In Italy and Germany Mussolini and Hitler provided equally messianic solutions for people desperate to believe in something and someone who could lead them out of the dead-end street they were trapped in. Germans felt especially humiliated by the Treaty of Versailles, which seemed to place all of the blame for the war on their shoulders and saddled them with impossible payments to the victorious Allies. Hitler concocted an ultra-nationalist ideology predicated on an all-consuming anti-Semitism. A readily available enemy and explanation had been found: the "other" whose ethnicity and religion were different. Communism and fascism were eschatological dreams that promised redemption for true believers.[1] They were delusions created and manipulated by megalomaniacal tyrants who were nonetheless cunning politicians. They were all convinced atheists, but all of them appreciated the psychological appeal of rituals and made sure they were portrayed in ways that mimicked the divine. They were men of kindness but firmness; they exuded an aura of confidence and wisdom with their right arms sweeping heavenward toward a workers' paradise, a new Roman Empire, or a Third Reich for those worthy enough to gain entry. Christians were face to face with a new set of challenges. In the nineteenth century the churches had tried to maintain a place for themselves in increasingly secular social systems. The challenge now was to survive the hostility of atheistic regimes intent

---

1. Lilla, *The Stillborn God.*

on destroying them sooner or later. How could they best respond to such all-encompassing, idolatrous value systems? What role should they play in the social order? Should they fight and face persecution or should they keep a low profile and find a niche for themselves, content with exerting an oblique role in society, hoping that the worst would eventually subside? There was debate and tension within all of the churches. Catholics faced the special challenge of being transnational by definition. Church teaching was crystal clear when it came to theological issues, but mediating the murky waters of a given political context was another question. The institutional church often seemed to offer confusing advice, in no small measure because the men who ran it were themselves confused about what to do. Some were diehard conservatives still wed to a traditional hierarchical relationship with those in political power, even if they found them distasteful. Others felt a more liberal approach was necessary, even if this entailed dealing with secular political leaders and movements that had no explicitly Christian values but shared a commitment to the common good.

Between a Rock and a Hard Place

The rise of fascism in Italy and Germany in the 1920s presented the church with special challenges. These were countries with deep Christian roots. Although many Italians were more cultural Catholics than practicing ones, the church was still a powerful institution with a vast network of schools, hospitals, and parishes. Since the early sixteenth century popes had been drawn entirely from the Italian hierarchy — a tradition that would not change until 1978 with the election of John Paul II. They were culturally and intellectually conservative men who felt that they were in a life-or-death struggle to preserve the rights of the institutional church and Catholic culture in Italy and the Western world. The dissolution of the Papal States in 1870 was still a bitter memory, and Mussolini and his fascist thugs who gained power in the 1920s made no secret about their hope of marginalizing the church even more. Germany was about a third Catholic, with heavy concentrations of Catholics in Bavaria, Westphalia, and the Rhineland. Like everyone else in the country, German Catholics had been profoundly affected by the hyperinflation and political turmoil that set in after the First World War because of the enormous indemnity imposed by the Treaty of Versailles. They were frightened by the communist-led revolts that swept across the country after the collapse of the monarchy in 1918. Most were conservative, middle-class people who put great stock in public order and social conformity. In the 1870s German Catholics had endured repression at the hands of the Protestant chancellor Otto von Bismarck, who questioned Catholic loyalty to the nascent German state, and the prospect of a new wave of persecution at the hands of Marxists pushed many Catholics toward the political center and even the right. Germans as a whole were desperate for political and social stability, and, of course, Hitler had put together a perfect explanation for their suffering along with a facile solution. It was all because of the victorious Allies and their Jewish bankers. He had the program to restore Germany to its former glory by rearming the country and expelling the Jews. Caught up in his message of salvation, few Germans questioned what was happening, and Hitler's Gestapo soon had near total control of the country. Christian resistance to Nazism became extremely dangerous, but there were Catholics and Protestants who resisted, sharing a prophetic understanding of Christianity that transcended the divisions of the Reformation.

Since the Christianization of the Roman Empire in the fourth century, members of the church hierarchy had worked in tandem with kings and emperors. As Augustine and Aquinas made clear, the church's sphere of influence was spiritual, while that of political leaders, temporal. But in classic Catholic social thought these two forms of power worked synergistically rather than separately. The church was the more important of the two institutions since it was a divinely established medium of grace, but the sociopolitical world also had a role to play in the God's plan. For the church this arrangement might entail putting up with a less than competent or saintly king, but the price was worth it. It had a guaranteed place in the social order as the arbiter of right and wrong and the ultimate source of the king's legitimacy. Kings, who were crowned in cathedrals, could be outmaneuvered or excommunicated if necessary and, of course, eventually they had to die. But communist and fascist dictators were not losing sleep over the prospect of damnation, and when they interacted with the church it was for the sake of their own political advantage.

Mussolini recognized that there were still committed Catholics in Italy who wielded political and social power. He had to tolerate the church, although he enjoyed mocking it in his bombastic, hours-long speeches. Nazi ideology drew heavily on the anti-Christian philosophy of Nietzsche and the racial mythology of Wagner's operas for an aesthetic prop. The Teutonic warrior crushed his foes without a trace of mercy. Compassion was for fools. Catholic Bavaria and the Rhineland were the industrial powerhouses of the country. And with his appetite already set on annexing Austria, which was predominantly Catholic, Hitler simultaneously courted and intimidated members of the church. In 1929 and 1933 respectively, concordats of mutual recognition were drawn up between the Vatican and the Italian and German governments.[2] Long and careful negotiations had gone on under the direct supervision of Pius XI and Cardinal Eugenio Pacelli, who would become pope in 1939, taking the

---

2. Carroll, *Constantine's Sword.*

name of Pius XII, an obvious sign that he intended to follow the cautious principles of his mentor. In both instances the church was granted status as a recognized religious institution with the right to maintain schools, hospitals, and parishes without interference on the part of the state. At the same time, the church agreed to stay out of the political life of both countries by refraining from any comment about government policies.[3] Sermons by bishops and priests were to be totally apolitical. Presumably, church leaders felt that they had struck the best possible deal under the circumstances and that the continued existence of the institutional church would allow the Christian message to exert an influence over the Italian and German people. Nonetheless, they ended up with the lesser half of the bargain, especially in Germany. Hitler immediately capitalized on the concordat, and most Catholics either acquiesced or supported his rise to supreme power in 1933. Pius XI and Pius XII were capable popes but also deeply conservative men whose fear of communism was so intense that it seems to have limited their ability to appreciate that fascism, particularly Nazism, was predicated on assumptions that were just as malevolent. The antireligious rhetoric of Marxists was overwhelming, and Christians were being persecuted overtly in the Soviet Union. Fascists tended to be less forthcoming in terms of their animosity toward Christianity, mostly for the sake of political expediency. Perhaps this generated a false hope that some sort of middle ground was possible.

Nightmares

We now have to deal with the most complicated issues connected with the Catholic Church in the twentieth century: its response to the most palpable evil associated with fascism, namely, the systematic extermination of human beings, mostly Jews but also anyone else deemed a "deviant" or "defective." Many argue vehemently about whether the institutional church did the right or wrong thing in response to fascist and especially Nazi policy toward the innocent millions that were slaughtered from 1939 to 1945. Pius XII is defended and condemned unequivocally. In the minds of many he helped save Jews by intervening on their behalf whenever possible. In the minds of others he was an accomplice after the fact who knew about the Holocaust almost from the outset but chose to protect the institutional church, thereby condemning innocent victims to hellish deaths.[4] In fact, there is much that we simply do not know about Pius XII. He had very few confidants other than his confessor and a few members of the Vatican hierarchy. He came from Italian nobility and came across as

3. Bokenkotter, *Church and Revolution*, 265–97.
4. Cornwell, *Hitler's Pope*.

aloof, although he was actually painfully shy. Yet he was hardly immune to the suffering that surrounded him. He knew the Nazis were slaughtering Catholic clergy and intellectuals as well as members of the Jewish community, and he agonized over their fate. Yet Pius had to live with the church's checkered relation with Jews, not just during the Middle Ages but as recently as the early twentieth century. The church had been less than enthusiastic about the political emancipation of Jews made possible by the Enlightenment and French Revolution. Many in the church continued to see Jews as a threat to Christian Europe, the proverbial enemy within the walls, responsible, in their minds, for some of the worst aspects of modernity: hostility to the church and the emergence of a secular state. During the Good Friday service Catholics prayed for the conversion of Jews who lived "in darkness," not just in error, like Orthodox Christians and Protestant Christians.

In 1858 Pius IX had papal police remove Edgardo Mortara from his Jewish parents' home in Bologna, a city under papal jurisdiction. The family maid, a devout Catholic, claimed that she had baptized the boy during a medical emergency in order to save him from damnation. By law Jews could not raise Christians, and the boy was taken from his home by church officials and later sent to the Vatican. There was an international outcry at what had happened. Loyal and well-placed Catholics pleaded with Pius to return the six-year-old boy to his frantic parents, but he refused because they would not agree to convert to Catholicism. The boy grew up in the Vatican and was ordained a priest by Pius himself. He was never reconciled with his family. In France ultra-conservative Catholics were part of a plot to frame an innocent Jewish army officer, Alfred Dreyfus, who was convicted of treason and condemned to life on the penal colony of Devil's Island. Looking for a scapegoat for the disastrous Franco-Prussian War of 1870, reactionary Catholics and right-wing nationalists insinuated that French Jews were responsible for nearly everything that was wrong with modern France.[5] Dreyfus was eventually retried and acquitted, but the revelation of what had actually gone on only fueled anticlerical sentiment among the secular French population. When the political climate changed in 1905 all connections between the church and state were severed. This track record of de facto anti-Semitism made it hard for the institutional church to mount a credible defense of the Jewish community in Europe with the rise of fascist racial ideology. Toward the end of the 1930s Pius XI and Pius XII denounced racism as incompatible with Christian values, but they did so in oblique language, presumably to avoid jeopardizing the safety of Italian and German Catholics. Certainly, fascists were violent

---

5. Carroll, *Constantine's Sword.*

and antireligious, but the possibility of genocide was impossible to imagine. Perhaps Pius XI and Pius XII thought there was still enough of a Christian substratum in European society to ward off the worst aspects of fascism, a sort of Catholic counterweight that would somehow stop the scale from tipping toward the side of evil.

In the midst of this ambiguity and complexity, however, it is important to remember that Christian principles were lived out in the most courageous ways. Jews and others marked for death found refuge in convents, monasteries, and the houses of Christian families. To be caught harboring Jews meant death. You would be sent on the same train to Auschwitz. Committed German Catholics were inspired by the example of Clemens von Galen, the bishop of Münster, who denounced Nazi racial and so-called eugenic laws from the pulpit as Germans with physical or mental limitations were given lethal injections in state-run institutions. Von Galen was too popular and visible to arrest, but the Gestapo nonetheless harassed him mercilessly and Hitler made it clear that von Galen would be one of the first to die after the "final victory." Dietrich Bonhoeffer, a brilliant young Protestant theologian who was teaching at Union Theological Seminary in New York City, voluntarily returned to Germany after Hitler came to power. He felt he had to dedicate his energy and intellect to fighting Nazism. The Gestapo executed Bonhoeffer in 1945, days before the Allies liberated the prison he was held in. Despite the timidity of the institutional churches, small groups of Catholics and Protestants did their best to fight back in the face of a vast system of domestic espionage that made any form of opposition extraordinarily dangerous. For committed Christians, however, it was simply impossible to look the other way. The heart and soul of the Gospel was at stake and the challenge was as poignant as it had been for Christians persecuted by Nero and Diocletian to stand by their beliefs and values. In April 1944 Hitler was nearly killed by a bomb placed in a bunker where he was meeting with his general staff. A Catholic member of the German army, Klaus von Stauffenberg, placed the bomb as close to Hitler as possible. He had served on the eastern front and had witnessed the systematic slaughter of Jews and civilians by the Nazi SS. Along with his fellow conspirators he had come to the conclusion that it was imperative to kill Hitler, and end the suffering of so many innocent people. Although the bomb went off as planned, it failed to kill Hitler who emerged only slightly wounded. The same day the Gestapo began the hunt. One after another the conspirators were captured and executed, some on meat hooks. Their courage was based on faith that good ultimately triumphs over evil, a proposition that seemed naïve given the nightmare that enveloped the postwar world.

Light in the Darkness

The relief produced by the defeat of fascism in Europe and the imperialistic pretensions of the Japanese Empire in Asia was short-lived. The struggle against totalitarianism was soon followed by the Cold War, the battle between capitalism and Marxism as all-encompassing propositions. Now there was the possibility of nuclear annihilation as well. Hiroshima and Nagasaki became symbols of a new and even more frightening mutation of human self-destructiveness, this time total. The Soviet Union soon had the same destructive capacity as the United States. The slightest geopolitical miscalculation could lead to a catastrophe that would make the Second World War pale in comparison. But the young Catholic theologians we mentioned were already at work trying to stop the seemingly unstoppable madness of human beings. They began to craft a "new theology" with a more balanced outlook toward contemporary society rather than the traditional one predicated on mistrust and social conservatism. They recognized the reality and even legitimacy of disbelief among many people, but felt the Gospel contained a social vision that still made sense. The war and the genocide that came with it were the result of whole societies having lost consciousness of God's presence in history and, more specifically, the transcendent dimension of every human being. Their "new" theology actually was based on old Christian beliefs and behaviors — fellowship in a community of equals, simple but moving liturgy rooted in the Bible, and a political and social ethic predicated on the sacredness of life. At first their scholarship was not well received in the Vatican, but eventually it would have an enormous impact on every level of the church.

There were also monumental changes taking place in the so-called developing world. A postcolonial Christianity, Catholic and Protestant, was beginning to emerge.[6] The church was becoming less European and North American and more Asian, African, and Latin American. Although an exact date is impossible to determine, sometime in the early 1960s there were more Catholic and Protestants in developing nations than in advanced, affluent ones. A whole new set of issues had popped up overnight, catching the institutional church almost asleep at the wheel.[7] At the same time, many of the "emerging churches" were part of the postcolonial economic and political system. There were deep-seated injustices that needed to be grappled with in order to create sustainable societies. The challenge Christians faced in the developing world had little to do with the modern, capitalist world's crisis of meaning. It was about the raw suffering experienced by millions of people whose lives were becoming progressively more difficult. What were Christians going to do? How

---

6. Jenkins, *The Next Christendom*.
7. Bühlmann, *The Church of the Future*.

could they best articulate and work for a social order that would lead to greater justice? By the 1950s it was clear that new navigational charts had to be drawn up because the currents had changed. The church as a whole needed to set a new course.

The pope who finally moved the heavy rudder of tradition was elected in 1958. John XXIII replaced Pius XII, who had been bishop of Rome for nineteen arduous years. The cardinals chose Giuseppe Roncalli, the patriarch of Venice, assuming that he was a safe candidate who would follow in the conservative footsteps of his predecessor. He was already in his late seventies, and there was little chance that he would rock the boat. The cardinals seem to have misunderstood or underestimated him. He was no carbon copy of the reserved and upper-class Pius XII. John XXIII came from a farming family from the north of Italy that was often on the brink of destitution. He understood powerlessness and marginalization firsthand. Born to devout parents, he entered the seminary at an early age. During the First World War he was drafted into the Italian army and served as a stretcher-bearer and chaplain. Affable and intellectually gifted, he became secretary to a bishop and eventually a member of the papal diplomatic corps. Because of his talents rather than ambition the peasant's son ascended the ecclesiastical ladder quickly. As the papal nuncio or ambassador in Greece and Turkey during World War II, he issued as many Vatican passports to Jews as he possibly could. In 1944 he was named the papal ambassador to France, one of the most prestigious and important positions in the church's foreign service. In 1953 he was named a cardinal, and the president of France insisted that he be given the red hat of a cardinal in the presidential palace — an enormous gesture of esteem given France's thoroughgoing commitment to secularism or *laïcité*. A man of profound faith, he was aware of and pained by the "disconnect" between Catholicism and the modern world.

The Second Vatican Council that took place from 1962 to 1965 is sometimes described as his brainchild entirely — a flash of sheer inspiration — but there is far more behind the call for a council he issued in 1959, less than three months after his election to the papacy. It is clear that John had felt for some time that the church had a great deal of business to deal with that could be handled properly only if it did so as a truly catholic, international body represented by its leaders. The Vatican itself was not up to the task. It could manage certain aspects of the church well enough, but the issues the Catholic community faced after the Second World War and the end of the colonial era were far more complicated. The crisis of disbelief in the West and the rapid growth of Catholicism in the developing world clearly required an unprecedented level of collective reflection and response. Many Vatican bureaucrats were intensely conservative and resistant to any change in the church's theology or social teaching. In effect, they were fighting the old nineteenth-century battle with modernity, unable to read what John referred to many times as the "signs of the times." Humble but wily, John knew how to wear down conservative members of the church's bureaucracy and, when necessary, use the papal "trump card."[8] He was, after all, the bishop of Rome. John intended to draw on the "new theology" and emerging forms of contextualized Catholicism to help the church chart a course for the future, counterbalancing the excessive centralization that was holding the church captive to the past. Vatican I had been about the papacy and the threat of modernity. Vatican II would be about the church as a community of believers grappling with the future.

Pope John made sure that the agenda for the Council was as open-ended as possible, precluding an end-run by conservatives who wanted to determine the Council's outcome before the actual event. A complex process was set in motion in which bishops throughout the world were consulted regarding what issues they thought the church should be addressing on an internal and external level. How should the church be reformed so its own self-understanding could be strengthened? How could it better respond to the world at large with its mix of hopes and sorrows? Thousands of questions and answers went back and forth from Rome, where they were duly studied, compiled, and made available to every member of the hierarchy. The process was democratic, and any and every point of view was accepted. Of course, the quality of questions and observations varied enormously. Some were superficial, others profound. Varied issues were addressed: a better knowledge and use of the Bible by Catholics who were far less versed in it than their Protestant counterparts, reforming the liturgical life of the church so that it would be more intelligible and life-giving, and updating theological discourse in order to make the church's faith more understandable both to its members and those outside of it. It was also clear from the outset that Pope John was intensely concerned about the church's relationship with the world at large. He wanted to strengthen the church internally so that it could participate in the larger world more vigorously. John often used the metaphor of opening up the church's windows and letting in fresh air. He wanted the church to participate in the world in a positive way. It was not a fortress of self-righteous saints hurling epithets at the unredeemed but rather a community of committed Christians passionate about their faith and the well-being of their neighbors. John XXIII was convinced that the church could be a source of hope for everyone, Catholic and non-Catholic alike. There was, naturally, a legitimate political dimension to the Council. Although the terms should be used with caution, conservatives and liberals in the hierarchy

---

8. Alberigo and Komonchak, *History of Vatican II*, 1:1–9.

tried to shape the discussions and final documents of the Council in light of their theological and social visions. Ultimately, more open-minded bishops formed a working majority in the Council as it evolved during the four working sessions that took place from 1962 to 1965. Giuseppe Alberigo, a highly respected historian of Vatican II, has referred to their shared mindframe as a "conciliar consciousness."[9] There was a shared optimism about the church's prospects. Most of the bishops in attendance were convinced that a whole new array of possibilities was beginning to emerge for the church on a global level. The old tensions began to disappear and many began to speak about dialogue with the modern world. Vatican II was an experience of spirit-filled optimism. And there was another amazing aspect of the Council. Bishops were speaking Mandarin, Hindi, Swahili, and Arabic. There were Protestant observers. There was even a small number of women invited as official observers, although they could only sit and watch. Nonetheless, half the human race had now gained observer status despite being relegated to a balcony!

Seismic Events

Church councils have always been complex events with a host of subterranean cultural and theological currents pushing factions in one direction or another. Confronted with an acute crisis or challenge, bishops who are usually pastors rather than "full-time" theologians try to achieve consensus on complex issues, often nostalgic for the more familiar problems of their home dioceses. Even when councils seem to end they may well go on for quite some time, and Vatican II was, and is, no different. When the bishops concluded the Council of Nicea in 325, for example, nearly all signed the creedal statement that ended the Council. Once they were home and their bags unpacked, however, a fierce debate ensued about what it was that they had actually agreed to. It took more than a century to settle the debate. In the contemporary Catholic Church a council is a monumental undertaking, and the speed at which preparations for Vatican II took place borders on the miraculous. Rome may have an enormous tourist industry, but finding housing for several thousand bishops, abbots, and other church officials from all over the world is an incredible challenge. Getting them back and forth to St. Peter's? Dealing with the quirks of men used to calling their own shots nearly all of the time? Vatican I was relatively easy to arrange since the overwhelming majority of the bishops were from Europe. Almost all spoke fluent Latin. Vatican II was a multicultural and multilingual meeting. Many of the bishops were unable to communicate in Latin and had to rely on a small army of interpreters.

---

9. Alberigo, *A Brief History of Vatican II*, 93–130.

Some were church insiders with Vatican connections; others were the bishops and administrators of small dioceses with minimal daily contact with the institutional church and a small social profile in their countries of origin, especially if the country in question was non-Christian. Being the archbishop of Paris is quite different from being the archbishop of Karachi. Theoretically, all were well versed in theology, but many were relying on textbooks they had read in their seminary days. The questions were diverse and daunting. What was the church going to say to the Western world that had just gone through the worst experience in its history? With the Cold War raging in the early 1960s how could the church play a positive role in the international community, helping newly independent countries avoid the traps set by both the United States and the Soviet Union?[10]

The mechanics of the Council were handled by a highly skilled group of theologians, bishops, and church officials who formed committees and did the nearly impossible job of pulling everything together and writing up reports and schema for the participants in the Council so they could know what discussions were going on and what decisions would have to be made when they were called upon as a group to vote on finished documents. In what was something of a palace coup, the assembled bishops decided from the very outset of the Council in October 1962 that they would avoid the old language of condemnation that had pervaded so much of church discourse for the last century. The Council's documents would be inspirational rather than dogmatic and infallible. The tone of the Council would be upbeat and encouraging. From the outset John XXIII and the bishops decided that despite some of the past mistakes of the church and the shadowy side of modernity that had led to such palpable evil in the 1930s and 1940s, there was reason for hope that believers and nonbelievers alike could celebrate a common future. John XXIII was a hard-wired optimist who resisted those he called "the prophets of doom" in the church who seemed to remain traumatized by the intellectual and social upheavals of prior centuries, convinced that the medieval world, not the modern one, remained the best model for the church and Western society. John knew that the church was trapped in its own past. It also refused to admit its own failures, thus provoking legitimate criticism from non-Catholics and nonbelievers. But as a member of the papal diplomatic service, John had come to appreciate and accept that the church was now part of a pluralistic, secular world that it had to come to grips with, even when it disagreed on some of the presuppositions behind modernity itself. Convinced of the

---

10. Just before his death in 1963 John XXIII addressed this issue in one of his most important encyclical letters, *Pacem in terris* (Peace on Earth). He pointed to the dangerous polarization that had set in after the Second World War, as well as the right of developing countries to independence and self-determination.

truth of Catholicism, John nonetheless recognized that if the church were to engage in an honest conversation with those it differed with, it might be possible to end the "dialogue of the deaf" that had been going on since the Enlightenment and French Revolution. He called for *aggiornamento*, or updating, of the church, letting go of the meaningless trappings of the church that no longer had anything to do with its core mission — proclaiming the Gospel. Although he was hardly an iconoclast, John made it clear that he found the elaborate rituals that had evolved around papal ceremonies to be outdated if not downright silly. He admitted to being both embarrassed and terrified as he was carried on a mobile throne through St. Peter's. Meeting a group of Italian rabbis he introduced himself by saying, "I am your brother, Joseph" and sat among them to have a conversation. He beamed as he visited jails and orphanages in Rome, something popes had not done for decades.

The purpose of the Council was to strengthen the church's inner life so it could make a more significant contribution to the world at large. It had to find new ways to proclaim the Gospel in an increasingly post-Christian Europe and in developing countries in which Christianity was assuming a non-Western form. The tone of John XXIII's letters and sermons before and during the Council was marked by respect for those within and outside of the church. He realized that his call for a council would provoke anxiety among church conservatives and made sure they had a central role to play in conciliar processes. Orthodox Christians, Protestants, and members of other religious traditions, not to mention nonbelievers, wondered if the Catholic Church was really capable of being sincere in its attempt to engage in dialogue after centuries of hostility to their beliefs and values. As a papal nuncio John XXIII had read Jean-Paul Sartre and Albert Camus. He had met with archrivals Kennedy and Khrushchev, both of whom considered the pope a mutual friend. By allowing progressive theologians — many of whom had been harassed during the reign of Pius XII — to help formulate the agenda for the Council, John made it clear that he was drawing on scholars who were thoroughly versed in the philosophical and social presuppositions behind the modern world. Theologians like Rahner, Congar, and De Lubac knew as much about Kant and Heidegger as they did about Augustine and Aquinas. Many bishops from developing countries feared that a "Eurocentric" council would overlook their cultures and the sociopolitical challenges they faced back home. Heretofore the Vatican had invested a great deal of energy in "Romanizing" emerging churches, often complicating the challenge of creating truly indigenous forms of Catholicism. These fears were quickly assuaged. The liturgies celebrated during the Council were deliberately multicultural, showing beyond a doubt that the church was a vast community of people united but not constrained by a common faith. Bishops of different theological persuasions from an array of countries all reported experiencing a powerful infusion of energy and grace, much like that reported in Paul's letters and the Acts of the Apostles.

The Documents: Consequences Inside and Out

Over the course of four sessions the Council produced sixteen documents that were approved by the overwhelming majority of the bishops. Decades later, some seem anachronistic, others timeless.[11] Debates still go on as to what some of the texts mean, particularly those that deal with theology of the church, a branch of theological analysis known as ecclesiology, and those documents that treat the church's relationship to other religions and the contemporary social order. Was the Council contiguous with the church's past or did it actually break with some of its long-held theological assumptions? Does the recognition in Council documents that certain theological points raised by the reformers in the sixteenth century were valid contradict the Council of Trent and Vatican I or merely go beyond them? Is the recognition in *Gaudium et Spes,* one of the most important documents of Vatican II, that the behavior of the institutional church itself led many people to reject the truths of Christianity mean that the church now accepts at least some of the premises behind the Enlightenment and modernity or are they still at odds? The theologians and bishops who made up the various committees charged with writing conciliar documents had a formidable task on their hands, not the least of which was the challenge of trying to achieve as much of a consensus as possible among themselves. None of the documents they produced were intended to change Catholic doctrine, but they were meant to update the way the church's core beliefs were articulated and practiced in the daily life of believers. Intense debates about some documents were held up to the last few days of the Council in order to achieve as much support as possible. This was particularly true of *Gaudium et Spes* and *Dignitatis Humanae,* the Declaration on Religious Freedom. The documents were written in a deliberately didactic, upbeat style devoid of "power words."[12] They encourage and cajole as need requires and even exude positive energy at times, something few people would expect from a hierarchical church used to making ponderous statements. The documents of Vatican II are meant to be teaching documents for the Catholic community, as well as texts that those outside of it can read to gain a better insight into the church's beliefs and position on contemporary social issues. This entailed helping Catholics achieve an adult, informed understanding of their faith that would allow them to move

11. O'Malley et al., *Vatican II.*
12. Ibid.

beyond the rote, catechism-based learning of the past, which discouraged critical reflection and serious questions. It also required acknowledging that truth cannot be contained in a tidy Catholic package. It transcended the church and Christianity itself. When the bishops returned home in 1965, most of them threw themselves enthusiastically into explaining what had occurred during the Council. Tremendous energy was channeled into implementing the reforms made possible by Vatican II. In the pages that follow we will use sections from key documents of the Council to better grasp the consequences of the Council. We will first draw on the Dogmatic Constitution on the Church (*Lumen Gentium*) and the Pastoral Constitution on the Church in the Modern World (*Gaudium et Spes*). These are the "big" documents of the Council, both in terms of sheer length and their consequences for the church as a believing community. The Constitution on the Sacred Liturgy, the Declaration on the Relationship of the Church to Non-Christian Religions, and the Declaration on Religious Freedom are shorter texts, but their impact likewise has been enormous. They radically altered the way Catholics worship, as well as their relationship to other religions and the secular world. These documents are still the subject of analysis and intense debate about their meaning and implications. It is no small matter to change forms of worship codified in the sixteenth century and seemingly immutable. The recognition that other religions contain insights into the truth and that people have a right to pursue the truth according to the dictates of their conscience is likewise a major shift, particularly in light of the church's refusal to accept the validity of other religions and resistance to the concept of religious freedom in general. As was the case with the Council of Nicea in the fourth century, it will probably take a century or more to unpack the meaning of Vatican II.

Phase One: Reform from the Inside

Most historians divide the work of the Council into two general phases, although it was ultimately a single process. Documents evolved as the ideas behind them took on new and unexpected trajectories. It was as if an airplane pilot caught in a very long holding pattern were suddenly given permission by the control tower to glide, hover, land, or do whatever seemed appropriate — short of crashing, of course! When the Council opened in 1962 the bishops focused most of their attention on the internal life of the church. They wanted to help Catholics better understand their beliefs and connection to each other as members of a believing community rather than as discrete believers sitting in their own pews caught up entirely in personal prayer and devotion. Drawing on pioneering work done in biblical and liturgical history in the 1930s and 1940s in Europe and the United States, they wanted to reinvigorate the idea of the church as a sacramental family that celebrated its faith in a collective way that others could also understand and appreciate. Prior to the Council the self-understanding of the church was still predicated on the polemics of the Reformation and the struggle with secular modernity in the eighteenth and nineteenth centuries. It was triumphal in tone, hostile to any criticism, and focused heavily on the hierarchy, particularly the pope as an absolute monarch and arbiter of every truth. At best, the laity was seen as a mass of foot soldiers in the church's struggle with a hostile world. By the mid-twentieth century, however, this top-down, "follow your orders" or "pray, pay, and obey" mentality no longer worked, and one of the first tasks the bishops faced in the Council was to forge a new and inclusive understanding of the church.

Given his age and conservative nature, many issues had been put on a back burner by Pius XII during the final years of his papacy. He was wary of theological innovation, but it was taking place anyway. The young theologians we alluded to, like Rahner and others, were working tenaciously to update theological thought despite a near total lack of support from the hierarchical church. So-called worker-priests in France were doing their best to win back men and women in factories who had long since ceased being Catholic. Foreign missionaries in developing countries were working tirelessly to create strong local churches, and native bishops, priests, and members of the laity were beginning to take the reins. The wherewithal for a new theology of the church was at the bishops' disposal. After many drafts and committee reports, in 1963 the bishops voted in favor of one of the Council's most important and uplifting texts, *Lumen Gentium*, the Dogmatic Constitution on the Church. A bit lengthy and naturally laced with theological language, *Lumen Gentium* nonetheless lays out an exciting vision of Catholicism. It set the tone for the remainder of the Council. No longer defined as a "perfect society" as it had been up until the 1950s, the church is described as the "people of God," a community of believers involved in a journey toward God meant to be experienced within the church for sure, but also in relationship to the larger human family. *Lumen Gentium* likens the church to a group of pilgrims. It is a dynamic community of people. Its leaders are guides and servants rather than a feudal aristocracy. As people on a journey, Christians necessarily require sustenance, and in the same year that *Lumen Gentium* was published the bishops issued the Constitution on the Sacred Liturgy, which we will analyze in greater detail in a few pages. The somewhat abstract language of *Lumen Gentium* was translated in a highly visible way by reforming and simplifying the liturgical life of the Catholic community, particularly the Mass, or Eucharist.

The implications of the new ecclesiology were impossible to miss. In the course of a few years local languages replaced Latin. The altar was turned around so the priest could face the people. Members of the laity as well as the priest read from the Hebrew Bible and New Testament. These liturgical changes were made possible by the new ecclesiology of *Lumen Gentium.* The shifts that had taken place were psychological as well as theological. The self-understanding of the Catholic community had been changed. It is laid out as it was in early Christianity: as fundamentally egalitarian rather than intrinsically hierarchical. Every member is responsible for each other and all are responsible for living the Gospel in ways that transform the surrounding world. The church is not a self-contained institution. Its primary purpose is to go beyond itself and spread the Gospel. The purpose of *Lumen Gentium* was to provide the church with the internal strength and self-confidence necessary to spread its message to the human community "joined together more closely than ever before by social, technical, and cultural bonds."[13]

Phase Two: Reform on the Outside

The second phase of the Council, from 1963 to 1965, was conducted under the leadership of John XXIII's successor, Paul VI. A highly gifted intellectual with an expansive knowledge of the institutional church and the international community, Giovanni Montini was one of the progressive movers and shakers from the outset of the Council. He was elected to the papacy to maintain the momentum begun by John and move the focus of the Council from internal reform to better relations with the non-Catholic world. He was the first pope to address the General Assembly of the United Nations, laying out the Catholic Church's position on social justice and understanding of the common good. Paul's speech at the United Nations in 1965 contained many of the points elaborated in *Gaudium et Spes,* a conciliar document that is arguably as important as *Lumen Gentium* in terms of the overall impact of the Council. During this second phase of conciliar work the bishops had a larger audience in mind than the Catholic community. They addressed their message to other Christians, Muslims, Jews, and nonbelievers. They wanted to do what had heretofore been discouraged: enter into conversation with those outside the institutional church. It was not a question of diluting the church's message or religious relativism as much as a recognition that God's word has always transcended the church as an institution. The preamble to the collected documents of the Council speaks about the "pleasure" the bishops experienced "in sending to all men [sic] and nations a message

---

13. *Lumen Gentium,* no. 1.

concerning that well-being, love, and peace which were brought into the world by Christ Jesus." But as *Gaudium et Spes*, the Declaration on the Relationship of the Church to Non-Christian Religions, and the Declaration on Religious Freedom make clear, God's word is found in the Hebrew Bible, the Qur'an, and even among nonbelieving people of good will. The bishops naturally wanted to proclaim the Gospel and had assembled to do so more effectively, but they were clear that the Gospel is not exclusionary nor should it ever to be used in ways that deprecate other people's beliefs and values.

Gaudium et Spes:
The Mission of the Church in the World

Gaudium et Spes was a hotly debated document. It went through various drafts and was voted on the day before the Council ended in 1965. The vast majority of the Council's participants approved it despite grumbles from more conservative bishops who felt that such enthusiastic openness to the modern world was a recipe for disaster. The hopefulness of the opening paragraph is still palpable, perhaps overly so in light of historical events after the conclusion of the Council:

> The joy and hope, the grief and anguish of the people of our time, especially of those who are poor or afflicted in any way, are the joy and hope, the grief and anguish of the followers of Christ as well. Nothing that is genuinely human fails to find an echo in their hearts. For theirs is a community of people united in Christ and guided by the holy Spirit in their pilgrimage towards the Father's kingdom, bearers of a message of salvation for all of humanity. That is why they cherish a feeling of deep solidarity with the human race and its history.[14]

The opening of *Gaudium et Spes* is disconcertingly effusive and poetic — not exactly what most people would expect from a church known for its wariness about the larger world. The style, in fact, is quite deliberate. It was intended to show the human and passionate side of the church. It is a declaration of solidarity with people of good will committed to human betterment, regardless of their religion or lack thereof. When Leo XIII published *Rerum novarum* in 1891 he recognized the efforts of non-Catholics to achieve greater social justice, but he felt that their efforts were necessarily deficient because they were not guided by Catholic principles. *Gaudium et Spes* is premised on the assumption that Catholics and non-Catholics alike can collaborate in the creation of a better world

---

14. *Gaudium et Spes*, no. 1.

with their respective insights. There are diverse ways of defining social justice and the common good, and usually they complement rather than contradict each other. Beyond the question of John XXIII's irrepressible optimism, there was reason to hope that humanity might be able to learn from its mistakes. Although people in Eastern Europe and China suffered under Marxist regimes, fascism had been defeated and Western Europe was once again flourishing on an economic and sociopolitical level. Lively, democratic societies had emerged out of the ashes of totalitarian regimes. Newly independent countries in Africa and Asia had thrown off decades if not centuries of colonial rule, and there was great hope that their leaders could create just societies that reflected their own cultural values. In many countries, the Catholic and Protestant churches were at the forefront of discussions about social justice. Hence the "joy" *Gaudium et Spes* refers to is especially about emerging ecclesial possibilities in the developing world. The bishops themselves felt it at the Council. Many referred to the energy in the air brought on by an experience of true Catholic diversity symbolized by the multilingual and cultural liturgies at the altar of St. Peter's. There were, however, "anxieties," of frightening proportions. In 1963, the year the Council opened, the United States and the Soviet Union came precariously close to nuclear annihilation. Proxy wars were being fought in the so-called Third World as the super powers vied for global hegemony. The bishops wanted to encourage and counsel a world that teetered between hope and despair by offering it Jesus' vision and value system — the Reign of God. The purpose of the Council, particularly the second half, was to explain what that vision was about for Catholics and non-Catholics alike. *Gaudium et Spes* is about the church's role in society and the transformation of social structures in ways that can make them more life-giving. It pays special attention of those who are poor and marginalized, not as the objects of charity but as the victims of injustice whose voices must be heard. But *Gaudium et Spes* makes clear the church wants to engage in respectful conversation. The old days of "take it or leave it" had come to an end.

Gaudium et Spes put to rest Augustine's Two Kingdom model of church and state — the foundational premise of Christendom and the medieval world that we looked at in previous chapters. In fact, the old symbiotic relationship between the institutional church and those who exercise political and social power is seen as an impediment to the church's mission. The institutional church must be free to preach the Gospel in an unencumbered way, and its lay members who are part of secular society need not carry around a sign that proclaims their Catholic identity. The church no longer needs the special protection afforded it by the concordats it had signed with Italy and Germany only a few decades before. It need not be recognized as an official entity. The only thing it requires is the right to proclaim its message and the rights of Catholics to live out their values in society in an unencumbered way. The rest will take care of itself. *Gaudium et Spes* states unequivocally that the church has no particular economic or political model. Such issues transcend its sphere of competence. It does, however, have its own expertise and message — the humanization and sanctification of human beings as the *Imago Dei*, the image of God. This is particularly true of the most vulnerable members of society, the poor and the oppressed who were Jesus' special concern. Just societies must go out of their way to protect those at risk, particularly the victims of injustice. *Gaudium et Spes* points to the enigma of a world in which we enjoy "an abundance of wealth, resources, and economic well-being" yet enormous numbers of people are "plagued by hunger and extreme need."[15] Because the Christian message is so antithetical to the day-to-day world we inhabit with its built-in, systemic injustices, the autonomy of the church is vitally important. To the extent that it is enmeshed in a given sociopolitical arrangement, it is limited in its ability to be a prophetic voice that challenges the inevitable deficiencies we create because of our individual and collective greed and myopia.

As *Gaudium et Spes* makes clear, the church is not about party politics or economic theories. It is about humanization, justice, and the recognition of God's presence in history. The church's task is to proclaim the Gospel and the transcendent dimension of every human person. So many of the horrors perpetrated in the twentieth century were the result of human beings succumbing to political idolatry in a futile effort to avoid hopelessness. They had succumbed to the blandishments of Marxism, Nazism, and free market capitalism as all-encompassing solutions to the human condition. *Gaudium et Spes*, however, sees the answer to our deeper questions as human beings in the mysterious ways in which we share life with each other and God. There is complete recognition of the fact that the church, as an institution, has itself failed to proclaim this message of human transcendence adequately. The treatment of skepticism and atheism in *Gaudium et Spes* is remarkably candid. At the same time, there is tangible optimism about the possibility of humanity achieving the necessary insight to change the course of history. Self-destruction need not be the final word, although as human beings we can always make that tragic choice. *Gaudium et Spes* points to the multiple resources at our disposal. It accepts the validity of non-Christian religions and secular philosophies in the search for truth. The stress on community found in so many non-Western cultures is another asset that it points to as a source of encouragement, especially in the capitalist world where individualism and consumerism have diminished our sense of the common good.

---

15. Ibid., no. 4.

Although some members of the hierarchy who had read too much Augustine refused to let go of their obsession with human sinfulness, *Gaudium et Spes* makes it clear that we have the means at our disposal to be hopeful about the future.

The Constitution on the Sacred Liturgy

Vatican II was meant to reinvigorate the Catholic Church on every level, and each of the sixteen documents it issued addressed a specific need, including the rituals and sacraments of the church. Although church ceremonies could be beautiful, they were relics of the Tridentine and the Baroque eras. Years of scholarship and campaigning for liturgical updating paid off when the bishops took up the question of liturgical reform and issued the decree on the liturgy, profoundly changing the sacramental life of Catholics in the process.[16] Although *Lumen Gentium* and *Gaudium et Spes* were groundbreaking documents they are long, theoretical texts that few people would read from beginning to end. The Constitution on the Sacred Liturgy, however, was different in the sense that it had an almost immediate impact on the entire church. It led to noticeable differences in the daily life of Catholics who were suddenly hearing and seeing the rituals they had known from childhood celebrated in a different way. Unchanged since the Council of Trent in 1565 the congregation made the sign of the cross from time to time, stood, kneeled, or sat, but otherwise had very little to do with the celebration of a sacrament, particularly the Mass. Rituals were the domain of the clergy, who were privileged people with nearly magical powers. If someone wanted to receive communion she or he approached a communion rail meant to create s physical and spiritual barrier between what went on in the main body of the church and the altar. Although everything in the church was part of a sacred space, some spaces were more sacred than others. The biblical texts in the first part of the Mass were read in Latin with only the Gospel translated into the local language. Little effort, obviously, was invested in creating biblical literacy. Sermons tended to be short and sometimes were omitted. The second part of the Mass, in which the priest consecrated the bread and wine in the great mystery of transubstantiation, was clearly the most important part of the ritual, everything else being preliminary to this sacred event. The word of God found in the Bible and the celebration of Jesus' presence in the Eucharist were only tenuously connected.

---

16. The official title of the document is the Constitution on the Sacred Liturgy. The newly elected Paul VI issued it in late 1963. Liturgical changes were implemented in rapid sequence, sometimes causing confusion and provoking resistance on the part of more conservative members of the Catholic community, clerical and lay alike.

The decree on the liturgy attempted to balance out what had become a lopsided ritual with excessive stress on the otherworldliness of the sacraments, particularly the ritual Catholics participated in on a weekly and sometimes even daily basis. Drawing on the liturgical heritage of the early Christian church, liturgists created simplified but beautiful ceremonies. The altar was turned around, the priest faced the people, and the readings were done in the language of the local community. These changes were not just cosmetic. They were profoundly psychological and theological. Suddenly you knew what was going on and why. All of this occurred in a period of about five years, the equivalent of a nanosecond in the Catholic scheme of things. The reformed liturgy was meant to be participatory. The Constitution makes it clear that the priest's role is that of a committed leader who presides over the Eucharist in the name of the community. The priest celebrates what the community already has in its possession — the presence of Jesus. Readings from the Hebrew Bible often speak of a covenant between God and the Hebrew people based on equality and justice. The epistles of the New Testament frequently focus on the ethical responsibilities of individual members of the community, its internal dynamics and relationship with those outside it. The Gospel readings speak about Jesus and his all-consuming passion for the Reign of God. Everyone was now called upon to think about the readings and apply them to her or his life, the priest included. Finally, some balance had been achieved between the so-called Proclamation of the Word and the celebration of Jesus' presence made possible by the act of consecrating bread and wine. In the Tridentine Mass parishioners often sat by themselves or with their immediate families. Eucharistic piety was personal and private for the most part. There was little stress on the parish as a community. That changed after 1965 when the Mass was reformed in such a way as to stress its nature as a meal, a source of sustenance for believing people who share a common faith. Because we inhabit a world that is functionally agnostic and materialistic, the celebration of the Eucharist is in many ways countercultural and subverts the assumptions behind the status quo. The social dynamism of the Eucharist had been rediscovered.

The reform of the liturgy had inter-Christian consequences as well. The reformed liturgy helped ease the tension between Catholics and Protestants, especially those who followed the so-called Magisterial Reformation of Luther, Calvin, and the Anglican Church. Although the Council did not resolve theological differences between the churches about the meaning of the Eucharist, it became easier to see some common ground. Even non-believers could grasp what was going on at a Catholic Mass. It was no longer a strange ritual celebrated in an incomprehensible language by a priest who hid his face from the congregation most of the time. Perhaps the most striking example of the attractiveness of the reformed liturgy is to see the varied ways in which the Mass is celebrated in the world today. Although the core structure of the Eucharist still follows a common rite set forth by Rome, there is enormous cultural variation in the way the Mass is celebrated. The Constitution on the Liturgy deliberately encouraged people to incorporate into the Eucharist those aspects of their culture and history that would make the Eucharist more joyful and meaningful. We now enjoy a situation in which diverse forms of catholicism create varied types of eucharistic celebrations, all reflecting a common belief in the Incarnation but recognizing the mysterious diversity of God's presence in human beings.

The Declaration on the Relationship of the Church to Non-Christian Religions and the Declaration on Religious Freedom

Since the Council came to an end more than forty years ago, there has been a debate as to how much it changed the inner core of Catholicism. The bishops did not assemble to discuss doctrinal issues. Ostensibly, they had been settled in prior councils, particularly Trent and Vatican I. Their challenge was to update and revitalize the church in light of events in the twentieth century and the emergence of new forms of Catholicism outside the Western world. But one can argue that by expressing traditional doctrine in a more contemporary way, the bishops changed the way it was understood and lived out by the Catholic community. The either/or, black and white theological discourse that had been so prevalent before 1962 gave way to a more open-ended, contextual approach to Catholic belief. In terms of theology itself, the era of rigid Thomism had come to an end. There were other equally valid ways of "doing" theology. Theological pluralism was seen as an asset rather than a liability and, as we will see in the next chapter, there was a flurry of theological creativity in the developing world. Furthermore, given the wide variation of cultural and sociopolitical systems, the social teaching of the church would have to be crafted to fit each one. This could be done properly only by committed Catholics working on a local level, from bishops to members of the laity interacting with each other and also taking into account the ideas and values of non-Catholics in their respective environments. They, too, had truthful and valuable insights. One of the key words that emerged from Vatican II was that of "dialogue" along theological and social lines. It assumes that no one has a monopoly on the truth.

Two short conciliar documents published in the fall of 1965 had far-reaching implications for the self-understanding of Catholics, their approach to other religions, and their relationship to the social order. They are still being debated today and have created fault lines between liberals, moderates, and conservatives with their respective interpretations of the Council. The first document is the Declaration on the Relationship of the Church to Non-Christian Religions. It was an unprecedented attempt to reach out in a fraternal way to the members of the world's major faith traditions — Hindus, Buddhists, Muslims, and especially Jews. Prior to the Council conversion to Catholicism entailed a complete break with a person's former religious identity. Some cultural elements might be carried over, but everything else had to go. The situation after Vatican II was far more nuanced since, as will we see, there is recognition that other religions contain their own God-given wisdom. What, then, does conversion entail? If a Hindu decides to become a Catholic, what is wrong with incorporating the insights and wisdom of the Vedas into this person's new faith? Is Catholic Christianity exclusive or inclusive? For conservatives the answer was and is an essential break with the past, including much of the worldview associated with a person's previous religious identity. Liberals, however, drawing on explicit paragraphs from the Declaration on the Relationship of the Church to Non-Christian Religions, have drawn different conclusions. Accepting the Gospel does not entail rejecting one's cultural heritage or even aspects of a person's former religious identity. Christianity is about Jesus' vision of the Reign of God and the reality of God's incarnation in human history. It is all for the better if the teachings of the Buddha provide additional insight into these central Christian beliefs. During the seventeenth century Jesuit missionaries in Asia had pushed for the same sort of acceptance, only to be punished by Rome for their openness to other religions. In 1965, however, they were vindicated.

The second document, and the one that has produced even greater tension, was the Declaration on Religious Freedom. It is predicated on the assumption that people have an inherent right to believe or not believe in a particular religion, as well as to follow the dictates of conscience to their fullest. No state or social order has the right to dictate belief or behavior so long as it is in the best interests of society. This is a God-given and therefore universal human right that should be enshrined and protected in the legal framework of every society. There is no way around the fact that Vatican II's perspective on non-Christian religions, religious freedom, and the freedom of conscience is in contradiction with that of the nineteenth-century and twentieth-century church's exclusivist point of view on theological and most social issues. There was the "Catholic Way" and the "wrong way." One need only think back to Pius XI's *Syllabus of Errors* to appreciate what a radical shift has taken place.

For most of us today religious freedom is a nonnegotiable right that we extend to everyone. At least in the Western world where religion and society are separate entities, we assume that we can believe as our conscience dictates. But right up to the Council many in the church resisted such ideas and some rigid conservatives still do. Admitting that others might have their own insights into truth and ethical behavior at variance with traditional ideas seemed like a concession to theological heterodoxy and moral deviance. Conservatives were still committed to the Christendom model of the church and insisted that it be granted special status. They were convinced that the best social arrangement was one in which the church was officially recognized and could guide those in charge of society in light of Catholic teaching. This was particularly true in the field of education. Steeped in a Catholic ethos, young people who would eventually take up the reins of political and social power would be more likely to act in accord with the principles they had absorbed as students. As late as 1952 the Vatican signed a concordat with the wily Spanish dictator Francisco Franco. The church was recognized as "the only religion of the Spanish nation,"[17] and priests and bishops were paid salaries by the state. In turn, Franco was granted veto power over aspects of the church's internal life, particularly the appointment of bishops. The public practice of other religions in Spain, even Protestant worship, was prohibited despite this restriction being in direct violation of the 1948 United Nations Universal Declaration of Human Rights.

Yet others in the church were thinking in diametrically opposite ways, convinced that concordats were an anachronism that now tarnished the church's credibility. In the 1950s the Jesuit legal and political scholar John Courtney Murray had done innovative work on the relationship between church and state, drawing on his experience in the United States. Murray argued that the separation of church and state was actually a positive arrangement that helped the church avoid the inevitable compromises it would have to make as a politically established entity. The church would be better off in a "free market" of religious traditions. To the extent that people chose a religious and ethical code they would be more likely to live in conformity with it. During the last years of Pius XII's papacy conservatives in the Vatican had Murray "silenced." He could not write or lecture about his ideas. Although the strength of the Catholic Church in the United States was undeniable, many in the Vatican considered theologians like Murray, and even some North American bishops, as far too liberal. To the dismay of Roman bureaucrats many interacted publicly with Protestants and encouraged Catholics to integrate fully into the American economic and political system. Ironically, the American Catholic Church in the 1950s was bursting at the seams with vocations to the priesthood

---

17. Constitution of the Spaniards, article 6, appendix 7, as cited in the *New Catholic Encyclopedia*, 2nd ed., vol. 13, 397.

and religious life, and Catholicism was no longer a barrier to "making it" in America, as evidenced by Kennedy's election to the presidency in 1960. For several years the most popular show on the new medium of television was hosted by Bishop Fulton J. Sheen, who would walk around the stage prop in his flamboyant episcopal robes, chalk in hand and a large crucifix in the background, lecturing an audience of millions about Catholic beliefs and behavior. Although there were differences among them, the American bishops at the Council formed a sizeable bloc, and their successful experience of integration in a multireligious country could not be overlooked. Furthermore, they had enormous financial resources at their disposal, and generously subsidized the Council itself. The same was true of bishops from Canada, the Commonwealth countries, and Germany, where Catholics were also successful minorities in tolerant democracies.

Although the word "globalization" was not yet in vogue, it was obvious that cultural, geopolitical, and religious barriers were breaking down. Fortress Catholicism had seen its last days. Furthermore, if the church wanted to be respected it, too, had to respect the right of others to hold different ideas as long as they were compatible with the common good. The vast majority of the bishops in attendance at the final session of the Council in 1965 voted in favor of the Declaration on the Relationship of the Church to Non-Christian Religions and the Declaration on Religious Freedom, but there was considerable resistance on the part of a conservative minority who felt that the Council was dangerously close to altering long-held theological premises that were nonnegotiable aspects of the Catholic tradition.[18] Furthermore, safe and predictable alliances with autocrats like Franco would be put in jeopardy. Would Spain remain "Catholic" if Murray's ideas prevailed? What about Ireland and Québec, where the church exercised enormous power through various political parties it was allied to? In effect, the question revolved around whether people in pluralistic democracies would make the right decisions without the formal guidance of the institutional church. The conservatives at the Council were not power-hungry men, although some were certainly autocratic and expected to be deferred to. They might be compared to overly protective parents who refuse to let their child take the training wheels off her bicycle. They doubted that a secular, nonsectarian social system could maintain its balance for long without taking a painful fall. Cognizant of the cyclical chaos that had enveloped Europe since the French Revolution, they longed for the supposed stability of the past. They were enveloped in nostalgia for a homogenous and harmonious Catholic world, although it had never existed.

---

18. As O'Malley and others point out, this rapid about-face raises the question about how continuous or discontinuous Vatican II is in terms of prior councils.

The Declaration on the Relationship of the Church to non-Christian Religions begins with a remarkably positive assessment of other faiths. After recognizing that all religions seek the truth to common human questions, and specifically mentioning Hinduism and Buddhism, Asian religions predicated on assumptions very different from Christianity, it says the following in paragraph 2:

> The Catholic Church rejects nothing of what is true and holy in these religions. It has a high regard for the manner of life and conduct, the precepts and doctrines which, although differing in many ways from its own teaching, nevertheless reflect a ray of that truth which enlightens all men and women.

The recognition that there is something "true and holy" in Hinduism, Buddhism, Islam, and Judaism clearly speaks to an expansive understanding of the human search for meaning. In many ways, it was facilitated by the crisis of meaning in the West and the breakup of the colonial world. The era of religious tribalism seemed to be coming to an end, replaced by a culture of tolerance that had its roots in the Enlightenment and the secular world it helped create. At the beginning of the twenty-first century, of course, the opening of the Declaration on Religious Freedom, like that of *Gaudium et Spes,* seems overly optimistic given the resurgence of religious fundamentalism in many parts of the world. But most of the bishops were already aware of the religious pluralism of the world around them, particularly those from Africa and Asia, where Christians constantly interacted with non-Christians, often as tiny minorities. They were anxious to encourage interreligious dialogue and diminish tension between different believers. In fact, there was a flurry of religious dialogue after the Council between Catholics, Protestants, Jews, Muslims, and even Marxists. Exhausted by the dangerous ideological struggle of the Cold War and trying to address the growing poverty in developing countries, socially responsible believers and nonbelievers were looking for common solutions to problems they were grappling with. Fights over theology and political theory helped no one. Many of the bishops were aware of the church's long history of assimilating the insights of other philosophical and religious traditions as long as they were not fundamentally incompatible with Christian truth and encouraged interreligious dialogue and contact with secular thinkers. If Christians had used Platonism to explain and expand their ideas in the second-century Roman Empire, why not do the same in the twentieth by trying to create parallels between the life of the Buddha and Jesus. Were not some of Marx's ideas about capitalist society true? Was his criticism of institutional Christianity totally off the mark, or could believers learn something from him despite his general hostility to religion?

There was a growing recognition that Catholicism is like a sponge that soaks up its cultural and even sociopolitical environment. Furthermore, the Declaration on the Relationship of the Church to Non-Christian Religions makes it clear that truth and revelation are expansive. No religious tradition is self-contained or static. If it is, it will begin to atrophy and die. All religious people are involved in an ongoing search for the truth and the insights they garner are a type of shared wisdom. The Declaration on the Relationship of the Church to Non-Christian Religions in no way minimizes the incisiveness of Catholic belief, but it stresses the obvious fact that God's hands are not tied when it come to religious inspiration. The document had an immediate and positive impact on non-Western Catholics. They no longer needed to cut themselves off from a vital source of sustenance — their own non-Christian cultures. They could enter into a conversation with those around them as fellow citizens with a different experience of truth and God. Although conservative critics of the declaration felt that it promoted relativism, its purpose was to foster religious dialogue in an increasingly global world. Suddenly Benedictine monks were visiting Hindu ashrams and gaining new insights from a different form of monastic life. Catholic theologians were taught Torah by rabbis who, in turn, were taught about Augustine and Aquinas. The conversation went beyond purely religious issues. It entailed ethical concerns as well. No two religions define the common good in precisely the same way, which is why the social values of every religious tradition provide useful insights into the social order that are invariably beneficial.

One of the most sensitive and painful topics the declaration deals with is Judaism and the Jewish community. The Holocaust cast its grisly shadow over the Council just as it did throughout the Western world. Had the church done enough in the 1930s and 1940s to protect the Jewish community? Had institutional self-interest taken precedence over moral principles? The Vatican was not alone in its soul-searching. Why had Churchill and Roosevelt said so little about the persecution of European Jews? Was there a type of "subterranean" anti-Semitism behind their lack of support for the Jewish community in Europe? As a preeminently moral institution, however, the church faced a particular challenge in the post-war era. Soon after he was elected pope and had summoned the Council John XXIII made it clear that he wanted an explicit statement to be made by the bishops on Judaism that would emphasize the common heritage of Jews and Christians, put an end to the ancient accusation that Jews were responsible for the death of Jesus, and explicitly condemn anti-Semitism as a sin. John was uncharacteristically forceful about the so-called "Jewish Question" and would brook no compromise with members of the hierarchy who counseled a less direct approach. Although his preference for a separate document on Judaism was not fulfilled, the Declaration on non-Christians Religions nonetheless devotes special attention to Jewish-Christian relations, more so than any other religious tradition. Paragraph 4 makes it clear that Judaism is part of God's plan for humanity. The declaration is careful to avoid an old trap based on a misreading of Paul's letter to the Romans, especially chapter 4. Of all of Paul's letters, Romans 4 is the most frequently used and abused text in the history of Christian anti-Semitism. The bishops carefully avoid creating a dichotomy between Judaism and Christianity, as if the former were inferior and the latter superior, which is a serious misreading of what Paul was actually saying in his convoluted and tortured discussion about Judaism and the Law in Romans. In fact, the bishops make it clear that Judaism is a foundational dimension of Christianity itself. Neither Jesus nor Christianity can be understood without a clear recognition of the Jewish ground in which they were born and took root. To put an end to centuries of Christian anti-Semitism, the bishops call for "brotherly dialogues" between Jews and Christians and encourage the exchange of ideas between biblical and theological scholars. This may all seem innocuous, but using the term "brotherly" was a conscious and telling choice meant to put an end to Christianity's superiority complex in terms of the Jewish tradition and community. Perhaps the most important aspect of the declaration is the explicit repudiation of the idea that the Jews as a people were responsible in any way for the death of Jesus. Those at fault were the priestly class in Jerusalem who controlled the Temple and acted as imperial agents, and the Roman procurator Pontius Pilate who was the official representative of the empire. Jesus was a victim of an oppressive imperial system like countless other Jews, thousands of whom were likewise crucified. In the concluding paragraphs, the declaration once and for all condemns anti-Semitism and religious intolerance as incompatible with Christian values:

> Indeed, the church reproves every form of persecution against whomever it may be directed. Remembering, then, its common heritage with the Jews and moved not by any political consideration, but solely by the motivation of Christian charity, it deplores all hatreds, persecutions, displays of anti-semitism leveled at any time or from any source against the Jews.[19]

Religious bias and persecution are condemned as a violation of God-given freedom and the universal right of a person to respond to the truth, as she or he perceives it. The Hebrew Bible is a source of revelation, and Judaism a valid path to the truth. The same applies to Hinduism, Buddhism, and Islam. For Christians Jesus is the incarnation of God and the definitive form of revelation. But this central tenet of Christianity can

---

19. Declaration on the Relationship of the Church to Non-Christian Religions, no. 4.

never be forced on people. It has to be explained respectfully and affirmed in a reasonable and voluntary way by those who see it as true. This precludes any bias toward other religions and a clear recognition that they contain a "ray of that truth that enlightens all men and women." Religions once deemed deviant or at best defective were recognized as part of God's plan for humankind. Vatican II marked the end of an era of Catholic "exclusivism" — the long-held notion that salvation depended on being a member of the Catholic Church to be saved. This in no way minimizes the truthfulness of Catholicism, however. It simply means that being a Catholic is not a first-class ticket to heaven. Anyone of good will can board the train. But Catholics still have to explain what they believe and why they act the way they do. There is something specific about Jesus and his vision of the Reign of God that has to be shared with one's fellow travelers.

The Declaration on Religious Freedom was even more controversial than the Declaration on the Relationship of the Church to Non-Christian Religions. It passed in the final days of the Council, forever altering the relationship between the Catholic Church and the social order. It remains an incomplete discussion of the relationship between church and society, leaving many questions unanswered. What is a good social order? What should believers do when they are confronted with social policies and laws that violate their nonnegotiable values? What about abortion, gay rights, grotesque economic injustice, the neocolonialism of some developed countries? The declaration fails to answer these questions, which have only become more intense since the Council ended almost half a century ago. That said, the Declaration on Religious Freedom is arguably the most innovative and radical document of Vatican II. It states unequivocally that people have a nonnegotiable right to believe as their conscience dictates and act accordingly, with the obvious caveat that their behavior be responsible and respectful. In effect, it calls for the separation of church and state. Murray's ideas are the cornerstones of the document and historians have little doubt that he wrote large sections of the text itself. His realization that religious pluralism was an asset rather than a liability for the Catholic Church led him to similar conclusions about church-state relations and discussion about the best social order. A healthy social system necessarily allows different points of view about how to achieve the greatest good for its citizens. No institution should control discussion or be in a privileged position. And although this may entail tension and even heated debates, a democratic, pluralistic society is invariably the best one. The Latin title for the declaration, *Dignitatis humanae,* has traditionally been translated as the Declaration on Religious Freedom, but its scope is far more ample than religious freedom alone. The document is actually about our God-given right, in fact, our obligation, to follow the dictates of our conscience. This entails a process of rigorous analysis about what is right and wrong and how we should act in the most responsible way, but once we have arrived at that point no religious entity or state has the right to tell us what to believe or how to act if doing so violates our conscience. Of course, what we believe and do invariably has an impact on others, and an informed conscience must always work from that premise.

Freedom of conscience is a foundational aspect of Christian thought, but it is one that has often been violated in practice. With its legalization toward the end of the fourth century, Christianity in the Greco-Roman world ran the risk of intolerance toward other religions and even toward forms of Christianity deemed heterodox by those who exercised power in the institutional church. On a theoretical level Augustine believed in free will but he had no compunction about making people in his diocese believe in the "right" form of Christianity, as *he* understood it. Aquinas was more optimistic about humanity's ability to discern and affirm the truth through revelation and the use of reason, but he also felt that in worst-case scenarios church and state should act synergistically to suppress beliefs and behaviors that threatened the common good. Despite their stress on the power of grace and Christian freedom, Luther and Calvin were not much better than their Catholic predecessors. Calvin stood by as the physician and theologian Michael Servetus was burned to death for questioning the doctrine of the Trinity. Although "rediscovered" in the Enlightenment and now an intrinsic part of most countries' legal systems, religious freedom and the right to follow the dictates of conscience in a reasonable way have been grossly violated in the twentieth century in particular, invariably by idolatrous political regimes of both right- and left-wing persuasions that demand complete submission to their totalizing understanding of the social order. The Declaration on Religious Freedom is actually about our human right to engage in prophetic honesty and courageous dissent, be it religious or otherwise. Truth transcends any and every social order, and this fundamental biblical principle is clearly laid out in the prophetic texts of the Hebrew Bible and Jesus' annunciation of the Reign of God.

The Declaration on Religious Freedom is predicated on the premise that we can know the truth, never completely but well enough to live our lives meaningfully and create societies that are just and capable of accommodating an array of beliefs and value systems. God provides us with the power to perceive and respond to the truth, be it through the revelation contained in nature or through an adult and critical reading of the scriptural texts used by our respective faith traditions. But nature is endlessly complex, and a Christian who thinks the texts of the Hebrew Bible or New Testament can be read at face value has grossly underestimated their complexity. Furthermore, we can never achieve clear insight into the truth and a truly mature conscience entirely on our own. For those of us who identify with a faith tradition, achieving a well-formed conscience requires being challenged by other members of our faith community, as well as those outside of it. This is why the Council advocated interreligious dialogue and honest interaction with the secular world. In terms of the Catholic community, there is an obvious specificity to what it believes and the way it acts, but it should never engage in hyperbole or triumphalism. The Catholic sociologist Andrew Greeley refers to the special quality of Catholicism as a "sacramental imagination."[20] This imagination is characterized by a celebration of God's concrete presence everywhere, in our fellow human beings of course, but also in the natural world that we must also treat respectfully. Naturally, acquiring such an expansive, "incarnational" imagination and ethical framework takes most of a lifetime, but as Greeley points out, it is possible. People do it all the time. In Catholicism we call such men and women saints — those who reach out to others as an expression of God's love that they feel in themselves and perceive in others. They are moving examples of the power of truth and goodness. They refuse to give in to cynicism and evil and by doing so play a powerful social role. One only need think of Dorothy Day, who founded the Catholic Worker movement, the American Trappist monk Thomas Merton, who courageously denounced his own country's oppressive and violent geopolitical policies, and John Paul II, who had no compunction about demanding justice and freedom for everyone, be it the prisoners of conscience of communist countries or the poor in the developing world victimized by the greed of the already wealthy.

The church's grasp of the truth is necessarily limited. Furthermore, the way the church's beliefs and values are articulated is subject to constant revision. Historical contexts constantly change, and given the growing catholicity of the church itself, the message of the Gospel must be readjusted on an ongoing basis if it is to make sense in the multicultural Catholicism of the twenty-first century. Our understanding of the truth should become progressively more nuanced. This is key to a truly free social order in which people's right to believe and behave in conformity with their conscience is fully respected. Conservative critics of Vatican II, and specifically the Declaration on Religious Freedom, have accused its authors of being naïve about the darker side of human nature, but there is a realistic acknowledgment of sin and the way it limits the development of our conscience. We often suffer from bouts of individual and collective arrogance born of delusion that we are right and everyone else is wrong. We have an innate tendency to fall down on our knees and worship ourselves in a mirror. Sometimes we want to impose the truth in another

---

20. Greeley, *The Catholic Myth.*

person's "best interests," assuming that discovering what the truth is and responding to it in a conscientious way is a simple proposition. This is the very recipe for intolerance and the violation of other's religious and ethical liberties that the Council wants Christians to transcend and nation-states to renounce. Discussions about religious values and what constitutes the best social order certainly are time-consuming and enervating at times, but they are part of what it means to be a mature believer and citizen in pluralistic, modern societies.

Had it not been for the insistence of Paul VI the Declaration on Religious Freedom may well have been pushed aside as too hot to handle.[21] He realized, however, that the credibility of the church in the secular world, as well as the rights of Christians in many communist countries, was at stake. It was not clear if it would be possible to pass the Declaration on Religious Freedom without the bishops splitting down conservative and liberal lines. Nonetheless, an overwhelming majority voted in favor of the document during the final days of the fourth session. One of the major "sticking-points" that characterized the church's struggle with modernity, freedom of religion, and conscience had been resolved. The declaration, however, was not a blanket endorsement of every aspect of modernity. In fact, the Council itself was consistently critical of the materialistic, consumption-driven individualism that we erroneously associate with freedom in the Western world. The declaration is based on a different assumption, namely, that true freedom and a just social order can be achieved only when we respond to others' needs and well-being as much as our own. Particularly in capitalist societies we tend to think of religious freedom and questions of conscience as primarily personal matters exercised by discrete individuals. *I* choose to believe and do what *I* consider appropriate with no particular need to explain the reason or consequences of my beliefs or behavior so long as they have no adverse effect on you. All too often we act like atoms circling in our own orbits. We may bump into each other on rare occasions but our paths are largely autonomous. The Declaration on Religious Freedom is predicated on a far more collective understanding of truth and ethical behavior. Freedom does not reside primarily in the fact that I am an individual; rather it resides in the fact that I am a member of a community that strives to achieve the greatest good for all its members.[22] What I believe and do, whatever it may be, must be based on respect for every member of the community, not just my own narrow interests. As a citizen of a democratic society, I can and sometimes must try to influence the social order in ways that I consider ethically imperative. I cannot, however, engage in any form of coercion or

---

21. Rynne, *Vatican Council II.*
22. O'Malley et al., *Vatican II.*

violence in the process. The Declaration on Religious Freedom marks the formal renunciation of this type of intolerance on the part of the church. It is also a plea for tolerance on the part of the secular world, particularly in those countries in which people have been unable to exercise their religious and ethical freedom. It marks the end of the Christendom model of church-state relations and a long overdue recognition that secular democracy is perfectly compatible with the beliefs and values of the Catholic Church.

Vatican II: A Brief Assessment

Vatican II ended almost a half century ago, but there are still varied interpretations of its meaning. There is a "minimalist" school of thought that construes the Council as an exercise in fine-tuning that only led to a slightly updated understanding of the church. A "maximalist" train of thought sees Vatican II as a watershed event in which much of the past was left behind, creating a new form of Catholicism. Both are minority opinions and the truth, as always, lies someplace in between. Nonetheless, the Council changed the self-understanding of the church and especially its social role in significant ways. A once profoundly medieval institution became open and democratic in nearly every way. Although strong episcopal leadership has remained part and parcel of the Catholic Church, members of the laity have assumed greater levels of responsibility, particularly at a local level where Catholic life is most important. That said, there was and is considerable resistance on the part of some conservative members of the hierarchy to a truly inclusive and democratic church. Nothing could be more emblematic of this resistance than the institutional Church's ongoing reluctance to allowing women to exercise true leadership within its ranks, although they have always been its de facto pillars from its very inception. After all, the clergy have never made up much more than 1 percent of the church's total population and are unrepresentative of the community as a whole despite their commitment to the communities they serve. But there has been significant progress in transforming the church from the old model of a Perfect Society to that of a community of equals that collectively makes up the People of God. Throughout the world parishes are being administered by the laity, and married men and women play a de facto role in the governance of the church despite their exclusion from sacramental ministry. Although part of this shift is due to the decline in the number of vocations to the priesthood and religious life, it is also a product of a new understanding of the church itself as a community of equals. Vatican II put an end of centuries of "clericalism," giving the laity voice and vote in a church that is now their own. Certainly, the church's social teaching articulated by the hierarchy is crucial, but without an active laity responding to the church's views and values, it would have no real social presence. The "Age of the Laity" has dawned and despite occasional tensions — that are sometimes actually beneficial — the church is much more of a grassroots social institution than ever before. We will examine this profound shift in the next chapter.

Living out the church's commitment to the Gospel internally and externally has been made considerably easier by the reform of the liturgy. The Mass is now an unequivocal sign of the believing community's faith and inner strength. It nourishes it members while it proclaims their responsibility to others outside of the community. There are multiple references in the new liturgy to the concept of covenant and the Reign of God that few would have caught when the Mass was still celebrated in Latin. By and large, the transition from the preconciliar Mass to the postconciliar Mass has gone smoothly. For those still attached to the Tridentine Mass, the Vatican has allowed them to continue celebrating the Eucharist in a more traditional way. By its nature, Catholicism is the proverbial "big tent" that allows for an array of religious expression. For most contemporary Catholics, however, the Mass has become a moving ritual in which people can draw on their culture and language to express their faith in God and Jesus, something that was not possible in the fixed, "decontextualized" Tridentine ritual. There is a natural flow from the readings, the consecration of the eucharistic bread and wine, and the call at the end of the liturgy to go out and live Jesus' vision of discipleship in one's personal and social life. With the exception of the clergy and a small number of dedicated laity, few postconciliar Catholics have worked their way through the documents of Vatican II. But the meaning of the Council as a call to renewal and recommitment to the larger world is driven home time and again through a revitalized approach to the church that has altered the self-understanding and vocation of Catholics throughout the world. Given the scarcity of priests, an increasing number of communities now celebrate communion services conducted by women and men drawn from the laity. Unfortunately, these committed Catholics are excluded from formal ministry, with the exception of male deacons, but the quality of their pastoral efforts is usually excellent. Ipso facto, the collective and sacramental life of the church is being changed for the better.

The amount of theological creativity and imagination unleashed by Vatican II is incalculable. After decades of excessive caution and even occasional repression of innovative thinking, Catholic theologians, clerics and laity alike, burst out with innovative ideas about the church's theological assumptions and social role. This theological renewal that continues to the present entails engaging discourse about Jesus' meaning and message, the best structures for the church, and the social role of Christians in society. To use the categories of traditional theology, there has been an explosion of Christological and ecclesiological thinking that has had a profound impact on the way Christians understand their social responsibilities. Although much of the innovative preconciliar theological thinking had come from Europeans and North Americans, suddenly there was a flood of new ideas coming from men *and* women in the developing world. The issues they faced were quite different from those faced by Christians in Belgium or Australia. They were facing exponential population growth, poverty at unprecedented levels, and growing social violence. It soon became apparent that a new ethical and theological category was necessary — structural sin. There was something deeply wrong and even antihuman about the way societies in the developing world were put together. Sin was just not a personal phenomenon; it was societal and systemic as a cursory glance at the suffering of so many people made clear.

People in developing countries were living in enormous slums, not because they wanted to, obviously, but because that was the fate they were forced to accept by economic and sociopolitical forces beyond their control. This misery was also a breeding ground for all sorts of political pathology, be it of a right- or left-wing variety. It was clear that the church had a moral obligation to be a spokesperson for the poor and oppressed, to make an option on the behalf of the voiceless and oppressed in light of a vocation that had its roots in the Hebrew Bible and Jesus' action in first-century Palestine. The theological axis of the Catholic community had moved from the developed to the developing world. In Latin America, Asia, and Africa a new generation of Catholic thinkers had emerged. Although well aware of the theological genius of their predecessors, they were also ready to stand on their own two feet with context-specific approaches to Catholic ethics and theology. At the beginning of the twenty-first century there is a new twist to things. We have become increasingly aware that there are oppressed communities within the so-called developed world — pockets of immigrants and impoverished people who are the victims of unjust economic and political policies in countries that we once considered fairly equitable. There is something profoundly wrong with the ethical values, or lack thereof, that shape social discourse in the developed world, and it is the task of ethical people of many persuasions to raise hard questions about what is really going on.

On an institutional level, the church became one of the most significant advocates for justice and peace after the Council. Just before his death in 1963 John XXIII had published *Mater et Magister,* undoubtedly his most important encyclical letter. He argued for an end to the Cold War, unequivocally denouncing the damage it was doing to the human community as a whole and the developing countries in particular that were caught in the web of superpowers that cynically lined them up in two geopolitical rows playing one off the other. In 1965 Paul VI spoke before the United Nations, the first pope to do so, in a speech that would be reformulated in his encyclical *Populorum progressio*, which called for the end of the economic exploitation of developing countries. A well-traveled diplomat and a skilled pastor prior to his election to the papacy, Paul VI would set the tone for Catholic social teaching up to the present. He was also deeply committed to interreligious dialogue and was a man of deep inner strength and equanimity. But his own term in office would lead to fierce controversy as he attempted to spell out Catholic teaching on the complex issues of birth control and human sexuality. Although he had convened a commission to examine the issues involved, he decided that the best course of action was to reaffirm the church's traditional teaching on natural law and the illicit nature of using contraceptive devices to impede conception. Because his decision contravened the overwhelming majority of the commission he had convoked, it appeared to many that Paul VI, otherwise a theological moderate and staunch proponent of conciliar reform, was acting in ways that contradicted the spirit of the Council itself. From Paul VI's vantage point, however, he had to defend the traditional teaching of the church on natural law, which insists that sexuality should always be open to the possibility of procreation.

From those who looked at things from a more contextual vantage point, and in light of the commission's own findings, he had displayed an unwillingness to see the new situation in which Catholics found themselves, especially in developing countries with burgeoning populations. It was easy, from their perspective, to praise family life as Paul VI had done, but another thing for a woman in an impoverished country to face pregnancy after pregnancy with a husband whose chances of a stable job were less than promising. Something of a false polarity was set up after 1968 that bedevils the Catholic Church to the present. Paul VI's approach to reproductive issues was amazing positive and pointed to the beauty of conjugal love in unprecedented ways. And he was certainly not unaware of the pressures faced by people in developing countries. He had spent considerable time in many of them. The publication of *Humanae vitae*, nonetheless, led to a controversy about reproductive and sexual issues that remain white hot to this day. A significant percentage of the laity simply defied papal teaching, along with a considerable number of priests and a few bishops. Many decided to pay no attention to church teaching on certain ethical issues, particularly in the area of human sexuality, citing the primacy of conscience as the justification for their dissent. Although it seemed that matters could not be worse, the clerical sexual abuse crises of the late 1990s and first decade of the twenty-first century has only made the church's lack of credibility on ethical questions even more acute. The church has suffered through an enormous crisis of confidence in the last forty or more years, much to the detriment of its overall message. Unfortunately, we humans tend to lump things together despite knowing that doing so is often an example of sloppy thinking.

But in spite of this incredible mess, and that may be the best albeit prosaic word for what has happened, the church continues to be one of the most stalwart and consistent promoters of the inherent value of human life and defenders of social justice. In the name of Jesus' vision of the Reign of God Christians, Catholics and non-Catholics alike, have given their lives in large numbers over the last half-century counteracting many of the deficiencies of the institutional church by fighting for the rights of workers, immigrants, and the most vulnerable members of society. After the Council the question of social justice for Catholics is once again central to their identity, especially in a global economic system in which disparity is so rank and violence so pervasive. Although it is a cliché, it bears repetition: economies and political systems are not accidents. They are the result of decisions that we all make as members of a given social order. Precisely what should be done in a particular context is open to different interpretations, and even fierce debate is sometimes unavoidable, but there is no question that something must be done. As a teacher the institutional church lays out criteria for the best course of action in light of the Gospel and contemporary circumstances. As "practitioners" Catholic women and men, however, are the most important part of the picture. They must live out a social vision that maximizes the common good in light of their own best judgments, supported by the context-specific wisdom of the faith communities they belong to. Vatican II is a wonderful example of a mysterious, transcendent force moving a plodding, tradition-bound institution beyond itself in ways that no one could have anticipated. The church no longer instinctually forges alliances with politically and socially conservative groups. In many instances, it is actually their greatest critic and has paid a high price in some countries for taking a prophetic stance. As we asserted previously, Vatican II did not change Catholic doctrines, but it did alter both the way they are understood and the role of the Catholic community in the social order in a profound way. The drawbridge raised by Trent and Vatican I has been lowered and traffic is now flowing both ways.

Chapter Eight

Dialectical Engagement
The Church and Society after Vatican II

Contextualization and Restructuring

After decades of near repression by authorities in the Vatican there was a tremendous burst of contextual theological activity after the Council. The institutional church was now more open to local expression of Catholicism, and many bishops were committed to creating a church in which the laity would be key players rather than passive observers. In Latin America, Africa, and Asia, theologians went to work creating new approaches to Christology and ecclesiology that reflected the insights of the Council as well as the universal challenge of social justice that believers faced in those often tumultuous environments. In Europe and North America black, feminist, and Latino theologies took shape, soon followed by discussion about ecological issues. Bishops throughout the world took up the issue of injustice and oppression, along with priests, religious women, and especially the laity. In the 1971 Synod of Bishops held in Rome the participants committed themselves to the struggle for social justice, equating the oppression of the poor with an affront to God, in other words, a type of social or structural sin that committed Christians must face head on:

> Action on behalf of justice and participation in the transformation of the world fully appear to us as a constitutive dimension of the preaching of the Gospel, or, in other words, of the Church's mission for the redemption of the human race and its liberation from every oppressive situation. (*Justice in the World*, 6)[1]

Theologians used the experiences of Christians struggling for justice as the framework for their books, creating a new type of socially oriented theology. Theology was no longer an ivory tower discipline imported from Europe or North America. It had become a type of strategic, homegrown discourse about the meaning of discipleship and the role of faith in social

---

1. Gremillion, *The Gospel of Peace and Justice.*

223

transformation. Much as the earliest Christians had understood it, theology was recast as a type of food for the soul, a spirituality or wisdom meant to sustain a person committed to living the Gospel in the real world.

Theologians worked intensely to help people better understand the person and message of Jesus, hoping to move beyond the rigid Christology of the past that had made Jesus such an intimidating and inaccessible figure. Feminist theologians explored Jesus' meaning for women, as well as pointing out the patriarchal distortions of the institutional church that contradicted the egalitarian ethos of early Christianity. Jesus was not a celestial king or God's chief of staff on earth. His gender had nothing to do with his role in God's redemptive plan. He was the greatest expression of God's compassion and desire for human liberation, and this alone made his life and vision of God's Reign a saving reality. The incarnation was about this world as much as it was about the next and as such a real source of hope for those whose lives were lived on the margins of society. Theologians in developing countries pointed to the relationship between Jesus' life, death, and resurrection and the experience of the poor and oppressed in the developing world where poverty was growing at an exponential rate. Christians of all denominations were struggling for life, experiencing persecution and death at the hands of repressive regimes, but likewise experiencing their own form of resurrection in the small victories they achieved in their struggle for justice. New theological approaches to Jesus and the Christian community were a source of hope in what were otherwise desperate circumstances. As Gustavo Gutiérrez made clear in one of his best books, the poor and oppressed could now "drink from their own wells."[2] There was an abundance of cultural and religious resources that could be tapped to strengthen people's faith and commitment. It was time to explore the connections between the Andean cultures of Latin America and traditional Catholicism. In Asia it was now possible to look for the similarities between Christianity, Hinduism, and Buddhism rather than stressing their differences and creating unnecessary tensions between religious communities. Vatican II unleashed the forces of a contextualized church whose power no one could have anticipated. Although marginalized, the poor were taking responsibility for the church, not as objects of charity but as God's chosen ones. Because of Vatican II and a series of meetings held throughout the world by committed bishops, the institutional church began to sever its connections with the oppressive elites and the oligarchies that supported them.

Bishops, priests, women religious, and lay leaders have always had a clearly defined task: to guide people in the journey toward deep and consequential discipleship through the sacraments and preaching. But after

---

2. Gutiérrez, *We Drink from Our Own Wells.*

Vatican II that task was given a more social orientation. It required helping the poor understand the mechanisms used to oppress them and effectively organize themselves in ways that would change the social order. Many members of the church made what would be called a "preferential option for the poor." In other words, they allied themselves with the victims of injustice. This was not predicated on a romantic notion of poverty or the poor themselves, who are as capable of malice and ill will as anyone else, but rather on the biblical notion that God has a special compassion and love for those who suffer injustice. This same God likewise condemns those who inflict injustice with their unbridled greed and power. In the New Testament, there is no greater example of the preferential option for the poor than Matthew 25, in which those who reach out to the poor are saved while those who ignore or oppress them are condemned. Many bishops, priests, and nuns left their secluded and comfortable houses and took up residence in the slums of Lima, São Paulo, and Nairobi. Tremendous energy was invested in creating base Christian communities, small groups of lay people, fifteen to twenty-five at the most, who were neighbors and shared not only a common faith but also the same challenges in poor and often dangerous neighborhoods. Informal meetings involved a reading from scripture, group reflection on its meaning, and ways the passage from the Hebrew Bible or New Testament could be applied to immediate challenges in the neighborhood and even the nation. What does the fifth chapter of the Gospel of Mark have to say about the sick and the suffering on the block we live on? What does the lack of decent health care say about the country we are citizens of? What should we do as believers? Although usually started by religious sisters and parish priests, these small communities were designed to function on their own. The hierarchical nature of the church was affirmed as central to Catholic identity, but the grassroots aspect of the church was given new emphasis. What emerged might be called a "micro-ecclesiology" predicated on the notion that *we* are the church — all of us without distinction. As Christians *we* are also charged with living in ways that reflect Jesus' vision of the Reign of God. This is *our* responsibility as well as the primary way we make a contribution to the societies that we are part of.

In the late 1960s and early 1970s there was a great deal of euphoria in the Latin American church, as well as in Africa and Asia. What would soon be called liberation theology — with local variations that reflected the cultural and historical diversity of Catholics and other Christians in the developing world — generated tremendous interest. In Africa, where the Christian community was just coming out of a long period of colonial exploitation, theologians faced the challenge of creating a form of indigenous Catholicism that went beyond the work of European missionaries, as innovative as some of those efforts had been. The fact that many countries were multilingual and multiethnic was a particular challenge. In Asia the minority status of the Christianity community, along with the deep roots of major non-Christian religions, was a catalyst for significant thought about the meaning of Jesus and the role of the church in an overwhelmingly non-Christian environment. But not everyone was enthusiastic about what was happening in the church. When the bishops described the economies and sociopolitical structures of Latin American countries as examples of "structural sin," those in power took offense. So too in Africa when members of the Christian community condemned the neocolonialism that emerged after independence and the malfeasance of dictatorial politicians who were often more ruthless than their colonial predecessors. Conservative members of the church hierarchy were also displeased and unsupportive, often questioning the orthodoxy of the various forms of liberation theology that were emerging. They were reluctant to rock the sociopolitical boat, and many were hostile to the notion of an open, egalitarian church.

Until the mid-twentieth century few Latin American countries were truly democratic, and even today in many African and Asian countries democracy remains elusive. Repressive regimes are still commonplace. Power has tended to reside in a few oligarchic families that control economic policy and manipulate the political system in their favor. Cooptation, intimidation, and brute force continue to be used to suppress any form of dissent. With the push for democratization in the 1960s, a wave of repressive violence was unleashed throughout Latin America as the military took over in one country after another. In the name of "fighting communism" and "defending Christianity" and free market capitalism dictators used every means at their disposal to suppress all forms of dissent. In the last twenty years the situation in Africa has become even worse with repressive regimes wreaking havoc on their countries' economies and people's lives. The genocidal slaughter in Rwanda, the millions of dead in the Democratic Republic of the Congo, and the current suffering of the people of Zimbabwe are cases in point. But as always, there were and are courageous individuals who denounce what is going on. Trying to fulfill its mission in the midst of political oppression, the church often serves as a crucially important spokesperson for human rights in developing countries, helping the victims of political repression. In many countries the church is the only institution people trust. Lawyers and human rights advocates, Catholic and otherwise, often defend peoples' civil liberties, locate prisoners, and determine the fate of "disappeared" men and women.

The church does not side with the political left or the right. Neutrality is maintained at all times because the church is not a political institution in the traditional sense. It should have nothing to do with the quagmire of party politics. But the church is not neutral in its defense of the innate dignity of the poor and oppressed. When attempts at cooptation or intimidation failed to silence the members of the church, violence became inevitable. Bishops, priests, and religious women were tortured, raped, and assassinated. Their names are now part of a proud history of martyrdom in Latin America and elsewhere — Oscar Romero, Ignacio Ellacuría, Ita Ford, and many others. Just as important are the tens of thousands of anonymous martyrs who were lay pastors, catechists, and leaders of base Christian communities.

The church in South Africa played a courageous role in fighting against the apartheid regime that was predicated on a variety of racism and economic exploitation akin to colonial slavery. If it were not for the help of the church today in Africa, thousands infected with HIV/AIDS would suffer even more than they do. Often the churches, Catholic and Protestant, offer support that would otherwise be unavailable because dysfunctional and often corrupt political systems pay no attention to the most vulnerable members of society. In some cases, the churches have shamed government authorities into taking action they would otherwise have avoided by setting up clinics, community kitchens, and neighborhood schools. These very actions help the poor realize that they can exercise control over their lives and avoid the trap of fatalism. To use the title of a book written by Gustavo Gutiérrez in the early 1980s, this is the "power of the poor in history."[3]

The Dialectics of Sin and Hope

For many Catholics the institutional and local churches' commitment to reform after the Council seemed to promise a new form of Catholicism. Conservatives in the Vatican, however, were beginning to reassert their former powers, trying to micromanage the church from Rome as they had since at least the nineteenth century. What had once been a small group of people who expressed their reservations about Vatican II grew in number, sometimes provoked by advocates of reform with their own hidden, sometimes angry agendas. In addition, the departure of large numbers of priests and religious women in the postconciliar period opened up new opportunities for theological and social conservatives to criticize what they considered an excessively liberal interpretation of what had taken place from 1962 to 1965. Vatican II remained the norm, but many now interpreted it in a minimalist way, accusing more liberal theologians of misconstruing its meaning to fit their own skewed theology. Certainly, the church is not a liberal democracy in the modern sense of the word. Its

---

3. Gutiérrez, *The Power of the Poor in History*.

day-to-day behavior and values are determined by the Gospel, not mere consensus politics. At the same time, it is radically egalitarian in the sense that every member, from the laywoman in the pews to the diocesan bishop, share the same Christian identity as baptized members of the community. All of its members are spokespersons for a radically egalitarian social vision predicated on the dignity of every human life. From the outset of the Council, there was growing concern about the seeming naïveté of some members of the church and fear about the high price being exacted for taking a prophetic stance against structural injustices. For centuries, the institutional church had been a bastion of social conservatism. As Alberigo and O'Malley point out in their multiple books, the conservatives at the Council were nostalgic for the topheavy Christendom model of the church that had survived right up to the papacy of Pius XII. They saw the modern world as hopelessly poisoned and any efforts to engage in conversation with its foundational ideas and intellectual figures a fool's errand. Certainly, the world outside of the church was hardly tranquil. There was growing political violence in Latin America and the church was under attack on multiple levels. In Africa one dictatorship after another emerged and those members of the church who were courageous enough to denounce what was going on could expect persecution and sometimes a gruesome death. In Asia interreligious dialogue and cooperation were proving more arduous in an atmosphere of growing fundamentalism that has only grown more intense in the twenty-first century. Yet the progressive spirit of the Council survived conservative criticism, some of which may have been warranted. It is perfectly legitimate to interpret the sixteen documents of Vatican II in different ways. Provided it is carried on respectfully, theological debate only enriches the life of the Catholic community. But we must be honest about the tensions at play in the contemporary church. The divisions are both theological and sociopolitical and reflect deep and potentially destructive tensions.[4]

In 1973 a brilliant young Peruvian theologian, Gustavo Gutiérrez, wrote one of the most important theological texts of the postconciliar period entitled *A Theology of Liberation,* in which he laid out a theological vision rooted in Jesus' vision and the demands of Christian discipleship in a world being split apart by economic and social injustice.[5] Gutiérrez was a priest of the archdiocese of Lima who lived in one of the city's oldest slums. He also worked with Catholic university students, who often came from privileged backgrounds but were nonetheless committed to

---

4. O'Malley et al., *Vatican II.* In typically masterful form, O'Malley provides an incisive description of the tensions between conservatives and liberals at Vatican II that helps explain the tensions in twenty-first-century Catholicism.

5. Gutiérrez, *A Theology of Liberation.*

social change. He wanted to help them better understand their responsibilities as Catholics to address the sufferings of their fellow Peruvians. He drew on biblical materials, the best European theology of the 1960s and 1970s, and a selective use of social science to explain what must be done on an economic, political, and especially religious level to address the suffering of the poor in Peru and elsewhere. Of course, much has changed since the publication of the book, but its basic message remains valid. As human beings we are faced with a fundamental choice — personal and social self-deception, what Gutiérrez and others often refer to as ideology, or a truthful and hopeful understanding of who we are as children of God called to struggle for a more human and just world, what he calls utopia. These are not concepts that Gutiérrez invented or, as his sometimes disingenuous critics assert, a sort of Marxism in Christian disguise. They are the basic ideas of the Hebrew Prophets, Jesus, Paul, and the early Christian community. Although somewhat quickly, we will explore their meaning to avoid any confusion as to what they actually entail for believing people, hopefully clarifying some of the key principles behind what would come to be known as liberation theology in the process.

Society's Original Sin: Ideology

Why do most of us accept the social order we are part of with few if any questions? What is it that allows us to overlook the inequality and injustice that are part and parcel of the modern world order with its nearly cosmic gap between developed and developing countries or between the mansions of the rich in Los Angeles and the slums of its inner city? A concept many theologians use for our myopia is ideology. The word itself has its origins in Marx's rather muddled discussion of mid-nineteenth-century capitalism and the worldview behind it. Theologians, however, use the word primarily to get at the heart of the sinful and destructive social structures that are integral to the societies they live in. There are, of course, empirical and social scientific explanations that are useful in explaining the affluence and poverty that surround us, but a theological analysis provides another perspective. We are dealing with social pathology whose origin lies in self-serving, self-deceptive sin. Too often we think of sin, if we think of it at all, as an individual matter. But in fact entire social systems can be built and sustained by sinful assumptions. Ideology is the force that blinds us to the obvious. It is something poured into our brains even before grade one. We absorb it at the hands of our parents, or teachers, and often our religious leaders. This is the way things are — accept them and make do with the situation. Ideological institutions, from education to organized religion, legitimate what often should not be legitimated. In the now largely defunct Marxist system the Party always knew best. In the capitalist West Adam Smith's notion of the invisible hand of free market capitalism is assumed to produce the greatest degree of well-being for the largest number of people. To think otherwise is to be a nonconformist and heretic, subject to ridicule and even persecution. Ideology is a type of useful naïveté that absolves us from responsibility for the social order we are all part of. Often the wealthy fall back on useful rationalizations about their affluence. They are more intelligent or more disciplined — hence their success in life. The poor can succumb to self-destructive fatalism, convinced that there is nothing they can do about their lot in life. But, of course, we must be careful to avoid simplistic dualisms. Regardless of our place in the social order, we can dispel the ideological fog that envelops us. There are conscientious people of means who use their resources to create more just social structures. Also, some of the most effective resistance to injustice comes from the poor who have the courage to organize themselves and create alternative structures that challenge the supposed inevitability of the poverty they are subjected to.

Ideological systems invariably have a quasi-religious quality to them. Those who control them often claim to possess a sort of secular infallibility. They are deferred to and revered as omniscient high priests. This type of hubris has produced most of the suffering of the twentieth century, leading to the deaths of millions of human beings in the name of some vaunted worldview embodied in a Hitler, a Stalin or a Mao. Useful categories are deployed to explain away the discrepancies and downright horrors these delusional systems produce. Party membership in the old Marxist world or the superiority of an Ivy League education in North America have proven wonderfully useful in explaining and rationalizing systems of privilege with few beneficiaries but numberless victims. Certainly, race, class, and gender were and still are the common categories used to explain away injustice and suffering. They were central to the colonial violence of the past and the ongoing exploitation we see in many facets of the global economy today. These classic categories still have an almost metaphysical quality in the minds of some people — as if these variations on being human were somehow God-given rather than human constructs. To stress the obvious, however, all races are the same, none is more nor less intelligent than another, social class is the result of economic and political structures that can be changed and made more just, there is nothing inevitable about them at all, and women and men complement each other in their humanity as the biblical narrative in Genesis makes abundantly clear. Vatican II lays out these central tenets of Catholicism in unequivocal terms. Catholics, who put so much stress on the incarnation as the central dynamic of their faith, have to put the lie to ideological distortions. Faith requires prophetic courage, much like Jesus overturning the tables of the moneychangers in the Temple. Naturally, this is a risky proposition. Those who wield power, the Romans and Sadducees of our own day, are not about to tolerate a challenge to their power and will react with predictable defensiveness and frequently with violence. Being truthful, however, is an inherent aspect of belief. It is only in this way that Christians can provide "a service to the history of freedom, or more precisely, as a service to human liberation."[6] Certainly, the Christian community should not be in the business of proposing specific economic and political models for society. Nonetheless, as the preamble of *Gaudium et Spes* points out, members of the church are to be honest witnesses regarding the social systems they participate in, criticizing deficiencies and celebrating signs of progress.

Utopia as Faith-Filled and Hope-Full Antithesis

We have all seen the pictures of emaciated refugees in Darfur and the shantytowns of Johannesburg. We have heard the news reports about the latest violence in the cities we live in even if we are sheltered in the suburbs. Perhaps we have actually been in a developing country or driven by a crime scene with the telling ribbons used by the police to cordon off the area. Hope in a better social order can be elusive. We are prone to become numb and pull into a shell to protect ourselves from the seemingly intractable social problems caused by greed and violence. The power of human sinfulness sometimes seems invincible. If we are lucky enough to "have it," we will be tempted to take it for granted, and if we are poor or marginalized, we may be tempted to reach out for anything that can anesthetize us to reality: alcohol, drugs, violence — whatever works. Of course, these forms of pathology are not class-specific. Fatalism and self-destructive behaviors transcend social class and status. The acquisitiveness of modern capitalism is perhaps the most salient example of isolation and hopelessness. The question is not rhetorical: Why not give up and surrender to the moment? To hell with it all, *carpe diem,* or whatever aphorism works best. In the Christian tradition, and that of every other religion, however, that sort of despair is the greatest of sins, not only because it harms us as individuals, but because it harms others as well. We are now increasingly aware that the deranged materialism that has come to rule so many people's lives is wreaking terrible damage on the natural world as well. Some scientists and theologians have begun to use a new term: "ecocide." The trap we have fallen into is simply unsustainable, it leads to destructive hopelessness and has reached a level in which other life forms are threatened by our uncontrolled materialism.

---

6. Ibid., 128.

In his first letter to the Corinthians, those shaky early Christians Paul had such a hard time with, he tried to help them understand that we are hard-wired by God to refute the fatalism of what he referred to as "the world" — the ideological systems that say that what is simply is. For Paul we are called to "faith, hope, and love" — a way of being human that is profoundly anti-ideological (1 Cor. 13:13). This is our true nature revealed in Jesus and part of God's design for humankind. These are not docile virtues but subversive ones that often seem totally illogical in the world we live in. But that was Paul's very point. He wanted the members of this quarrelsome and confused community to challenge the Greco-Roman world they were part off, a port city on the way to Rome infamous for its prostitutes, thieves, and corrupt officials. Hoping, believing, and acting in a loving way in that sort of environment must have seemed frankly stupid, but for Paul such "stupidity," what is often more politely translated from the Greek as "folly," was the very essence of the Gospel. It was the core of Jesus' message about the Reign of God and the driving force behind his relentless efforts to spread it to as many people as possible. In 1994 a wonderfully gifted photojournalist, Mev Puleo, did a series of interviews with people in Brazil, primarily poor women and men, but also theologians and members of the clergy working among and committed to the poor.[7] All of these people exude energy. Their faith, hope, and love are palpable. They have transformed their lives in light of the Gospel and Vatican II and are intensely committed to reshaping their neighborhoods and Brazilian society in ways the reflect Jesus' vision of the Reign of God. Their optimism is a result of their experience as members of Christian communities and their efforts to transform the social order. They have gained insight from the Bible, each other, and the institutional church. They support each other with prayer, reflection, action, and celebration. In light of the fact that Brazilians suffered under the hands of a repressive military government and endured economic chaos from 1964 to 1985 their optimism is all the more astounding. Most impressive of all is that most of the people interviewed were women speaking their minds and acting on behalf of other women in a country noted for its sexism or *machismo.* Many were Afro-Brazilians committed to racial equality in a country in which nearly half the population has African blood because of centuries of slavery but continues to exclude black Brazilians from the mainstream of society. Mev Puleo gave considerable thought to the title of her book — *The Struggle Is One.* It is meant to unite Christians in the developed and developing world, Catholics and non-Catholics, in what might be called a utopian spirit, a concept that is vitally important in the struggle for justice but one that is frequently misunderstood.

---

7. Puleo, *The Struggle Is One.*

Theologians in developing countries put great stress on the term "utopia." They understand it as the antithesis of ideology, a counterweight to the fatalistic assumption that nothing can be done about the present, and the future is already set in stone. Particularly in our materialistic, empirical world, we are conditioned to think of utopia as a sort of useless daydream. Thomas More, the courageous chancellor of England who was executed by Henry VIII for refusing to compromise his faith and values to suit the king's political ambitions, coined the word in the early sixteenth century. In *Utopia* More describes a society that does not exist but one that he clearly wants to exist. It is predicated on justice and respect. There is an operative government but its sole purpose is to serve the common good. Everyone enjoys the fruits of citizenship. It is a telling indication of our contemporary cynicism that we consider such a society impossible, an absurd illusion entertained only by people on the psychological and social fringe. Economic, social, and gender-based equality are simply impossible to achieve. That, of course, is the ideological message we have absorbed from our earliest days. But the utopian message of More and the Christian tradition says something quite different. We need to recall the short passage in Galatians 3:28: "There is neither Jew nor Greek, slave nor free, there is neither male nor female; for you are all one in Christ Jesus." Some biblical scholars believe that this formula was actually part of the baptismal ritual of the earliest Christian communities. Whether it was or not, it is indicative of the powerfully utopian imagination of Jesus' first followers who employed his vision of the Reign of God to create communities that were devoid of distinctions and characterized by a commitment to harmony and justice, not only in the community itself, but ultimately in the surrounding social order. As Paul's letters make clear, there is bound to be a gap between the real and ideal, but the whole point of his letters was to encourage the members of the communities he established to live up to the egalitarian vision he introduced them to and in whose name he baptized them. A utopian imagination has always been an indispensable part of being a committed Christian, and that is especially true in the modern world.[8] A utopian value system, in other words, is a belief system based on faith, hope, and love. It helps believing people juxtapose what is with what can be. It helps them tap their imaginations and draw on their hope for the future. It provides them with a plan for action that will change the social order. They can provide reasonable alternatives that will actually change things. It likewise gives them the courage to endure the hostility they will encounter from those who wield economic and political power unjustly and sometimes even from members of the institutional church. Finally, it allows them to celebrate little victories knowing that they have

---

8. Sobrino, *No Salvation outside the Poor.*

changed the social order and made the Reign of God something more real in their lives and other people's as well. Again, we should paraphrase the titles of two of Gustavo Gutiérrez's books. Utopia is the water the poor drink from their own wells. It is also the power the poor exercise in history, not as its objects but as its subjects.

Liberation and Contextualization: Jesus and the Church in a World of Injustice

From the Reformation to the opening of the Council, the Roman Catholic Church was a model of bureaucratic centralization and doctrinal uniformity. Popes insisted on the "Romanization" of the church, assuming that the total conformity of the church's members would be the best defense against the hostile forces pitted against it. There was a price to be paid for such excessive homogeneity, however. Many members of the clergy lost sight of the cultural specificity of the people they were serving. The theology they learned in seminaries was highly abstract and generally unrelated to the day-to-day lives of ordinary people. Bishops sent their best students to Rome to think as the Romans thought about theology and the institutional church, and often these students replaced the bishops who sent them. They were steeped in a high Christology that paid scant attention to Jesus' humanity and an ecclesiology that put excessive stress on the hierarchical and papal nature of the church. The social dimensions of Jesus' message were given little emphasis. By and large, he was portrayed as a celestial king and judge, much as he is in Byzantine and medieval Catholic art. The problem with this magnificent art, however, is that it has little to do with the historical Jesus — the powerless Galilean Jew who displayed compassion and forgiveness toward those whom the religious authorities of his day considered sinners and dangerous rabble. The monarchical ecclesiology of the preconciliar period was likewise off the mark. As we see in the Acts of the Apostles, the early Christian community was essentially egalitarian. The apostles were respected but they were not understood as qualitatively different from other members of the community. In the description of Pentecost found in Acts the spirit descends on everyone without distinction. Much of traditional Christology and ecclesiology prior to the Council needed to be revised in order to more accurately reflect the New Testament and the history of the early Christian church.

Contextual Christology

The first efforts at reformulating Christology were launched in Latin America, but they would soon spread to Africa and Asia. Nor were they confined entirely to the developing world. Superb work was being done in Europe and would eventually take shape in North America as well. A type of theological cross-fertilization was under way that linked the developing and developed worlds. A particular challenge in Latin America was undoing the "colonial Christology" brought by the Spanish and Portuguese. In their efforts to baptize as many people as possible and thus save them from what they considered inevitable damnation, missionaries often Christianized people in a superficial way and conveyed an image of Jesus that was harsh and imperious. To this day many Spanish-speaking Latin Americans still refer to Jesus as the *justo juez*, the "just judge" who needs to be mollified and sometimes even bribed, much like colonial and even modern-day authorities. These distortions obviously needed correction if the Gospel was going to have a liberating impact on people's lives. In the late 1970s Leonardo Boff, a leading theologian in Brazil, published a major work in Christology entitled *Jesus Christ Liberator*. A decade later, the Salvadoran Jesuit Jon Sobrino published *Jesus in Latin America*. Both of these seminal Christological books were written in the midst of growing poverty and political turmoil. The process of hyper-urbanization had filled Brazil's cities with millions of poor people who were leaving rural areas in search of a better life. In El Salvador, a vicious civil war was beginning that would eventually take the lives of at least seventy thousand people. The questions were obvious. What does Jesus have to say to people who have moved from rural to urban areas only to find themselves isolated and jobless? What does he have to say to people who are detained, tortured, and "disappeared" for questioning the injustice of a given social order? Theologians were anxious to point out that Jesus and the Christian community did, in fact, have answers to these questions. They could be found in the Bible, the tradition of the Christian community, and the past and present experience of those struggling for justice.

Boff, Sobrino, African and Asian theologians, along with their counterparts in the developed world, tried to point out the connection between the historical Jesus and the challenges believers faced in the modern world. In Mark 5 Jesus heals a "madman" who is diabolically possessed, in modern terms someone suffering from a severe form of mental illness. Although Jesus asks him not to do so, this newly healthy person cannot help but tell others what has happened to him. His faith in God and Jesus has restored him. He has returned to society as a healthy member. This same centrifugal dynamic is part of the modern Christian community as well. Its members are consumed by a passion to explain what has happened to them and how their experience can change society as a whole. In all four of the Gospels there are various versions of the "miracle" of the loaves and fishes, but this miracle is replicated every day in soup kitchens throughout the world. Belief in Jesus clearly has real social consequences, not in the sense of creating sophisticated socioeconomic programs, but through the modest efforts of Christians to reach out to their neighbors. As believers this is their principal joy *and* responsibility. Living the Gospel, therefore, leads to incremental social change. In the grinding poverty of the developing world, where life is so cheap and violence so pervasive, living out Jesus' utopian values is a profoundly subversive response to injustice. In *The Future of Christology* the American Jesuit Roger Haight makes the connection between the person of Jesus as savior and liberator and the social responsibility of the Christian community.

> Instead of considering his earthly career as a particular transaction with God, one may regard it is as concrete symbol revealing the intrinsic character of the primal relation between God and human existence. From this perspective, one would read in the actual teaching, ministry, and final outcome of Jesus a pattern revelatory of God, human existence, and the relationship between them. Jesus saves by revealing what is going on generally in the world and in history from the very beginning.[9]

The Brazilians Mev Puleo interviewed share a common trait, a passionate belief in Jesus and the possibility of transforming their country in light of their faith. Maria, a grandmother who only recently has learned how to read, composes poetry, works intensely in her base Christian community, and is deeply involved in improving the *favela*, or slum, she lives in. Tonya, a young Afro-Brazilian woman, fights for racial justice in a country that still considers whites beautiful and blacks ugly. Leonardo Boff writes books on Christology and ecclesiology, but his inspiration is derived from those places where he himself finds Jesus — among the poor and oppressed. Pedro Casaldáliga, a bishop in one of the poorest parts of Brazil, makes sure the door of his house is always open so anyone can come in. This is liberating Christology in action. It is found in books, poetry, song, and dance, as well as in neighborhood meetings.

Contextual Ecclesiology

As paragraph 58 of *Gaudium et Spes* makes clear, the Catholic Church has been and always will be a "poly-cultural" form of Christianity. The ritual uniformity imposed by Trent did not eliminate the cultural and historical specificity of the varied peoples who make up the Catholic community. The roots of the church are always watered by local water with its own chemistry. After the Council, this diversity was celebrated in an open

---

9. Haight, *The Future of Christology*, 69.

fashion. The multicultural nature of the church was more evident than ever. It was time for a more ample understanding of the church, a more accepting and contextual approach to ecclesiology. More accurately, it was time for new *ecclesiologies*. In the secular Western world the church faced the challenge of growing indifference and disbelief. It was increasingly clear that the church had to explain itself anew to people who thought of it largely as a remnant from the past rather than a vital institution that could enrich their lives. Churches were seen by many as museums that might contain beautiful art but had no existential connection with ordinary life. In the developing world, the challenges were different. The rapid growth of the Catholic community made new Christians anxious to incorporate their culture into their understanding of the church. Vatican II gave them free reign to contextualize their faith, something that was looked askance at prior to the Council. The church was becoming less Roman and more catholic and in the process insuring itself a healthy future in diverse cultural environments. Missionaries were leaving churches that were often more vibrant and culturally rooted than the ones that had sent them. And the incredibly peripatetic John Paul II did everything in his power to encourage the growth of local churches, even if his ecclesiological vision tended to be on the conservative side. As the historian and religious scholar Philip Jenkins has pointed out, a new Christendom is beginning to emerge in the southern hemisphere, but it is different from its medieval counterpart. It is not centralized or uniform. It is diverse and exuberant.[10]

The liturgical and ecclesiological changes made possible by Vatican II may seem like anthropological or theological window-dressing to some, but a specific example will help us grasp just how significant they were to the inner and outer life of the Catholic community. When the Spanish arrived in Peru in the 1530s they went about doing what they had done two decades before in Mexico and a half century before in Spain: destroying local cultures and replacing native people's religious worldview with Catholicism. It was a nonnegotiable proposition. Andean peoples were told that their language, culture, and history were inferior, that their religious beliefs were diabolical. Everything about their humanness was denigrated. Tragically, Spanish Catholicism formed the cornerstone of an imperial ideology in which everything European and Western was deemed superior while all things Andean were deemed inferior. Mass was celebrated in Latin and homilies, if they were given at all to presumably stupid and savage people, were usually in Spanish. This began to change after the Council. Think of yourself as an Andean peasant who goes to Mass and hears it celebrated in the local language for the first time in

---

10. Jenkins, *The Next Christendom*.

her or his memory. Aspects of the local culture are incorporated into the liturgy — in the case of Andean peoples the use of a pardon ceremony that replaces a rather abstract act of contrition in the old Tridentine ritual. A lay leader whose command of the language is a breath of fresh air and whose social status is not a cause for concern may give the homily. He is a peasant, too. Suddenly, the church assumes a different meaning. But the situation is not so tranquil as it might sound nor the transition so fluid. Spanish-speaking landowners are less than thrilled by what is going on. Although most are only nominal Catholics, they consider the church "theirs." The use of the local language and the incorporation of Andean culture into the Eucharistic liturgy is an affront to their sense of superiority. The Mass now irritates them. Some are actually enraged by what has happened to "their" variety of Catholicism. A contextualized ecclesiology has become a line in the sand. But after Vatican II, the church really had no choice but to run this risk. It was morally imperative to side with the victims of oppression in their cultural and historical specificity. After nearly a half a millennium of silence and hobnobbing with oppressive elites, the institutional church in Latin America began to make amends for its own sins of omission. Analogous processes would take place in Africa and Asia, although the history of the institutional church was different on those continents and often less onerous. Africans had endured roughly a century of European colonialism, and the great religions of Asia had made the imposition of Christianity impossible. Africans were less inflicted with a Eurocentric church tradition, while Catholics in Asia were accustomed to being a powerless minority. African ecclesiology therefore, could more easily take up the issue of ecclesiological contextualization;[11] the Catholic community in Asia was now free to focus on the issue of interreligious dialogue and the contribution the Christian community might make as a tiny minority in an immense, non-Christian continent.[12]

Unlike Trent and Vatican I, which focused on dogmatic issues and the hierarchical nature of the church, the Second Vatican Council was about the believing community as a whole and its relationship with the larger world. Some perfectly obvious but overlooked math was finally factored in to the church's self-understanding — 99 percent of its membership was made up of men and women who were neither members of the clergy nor vowed religious women. The church could no longer simply tell people what to do and expect unquestioned obedience. The contradictions of the institutional church in the twentieth century led many people, even those who were committed Catholics, to raise questions about their church and

---

11. Orobator, *Theology Brewed in an African Pot.*
12. Pieris, *An Asian Theology of Liberation.*

faith that would have been considered disloyal and impertinent in prior decades. The publication of *Humanae vitae* in 1968 made many Catholics question whether members of the hierarchy really understood the demands of modern family life, and the clergy sexual abuse scandals that followed only made matters worse. The Council had encouraged members of the Catholic community to stand on their own two feet — to dig more deeply into their faith and assimilate it in a more adult way in order to be effective agents of evangelization. The message was clear: study the Bible, participate in the liturgy, take responsibility for your parish and Catholic community. You have voice and vote by virtue of your baptism. Respect the leaders of the church but do not hesitate to ask them questions. They have a particular expertise in theology or biblical studies. Ask them to share their insights and knowledge. In fact, they are required to do so. But remember that you have insights as well. You know the effects of economic injustice, racism, and sexism in ways that may be more concrete and insightful than the church's ordained leadership. This gives you a strategic advantage when it comes to creating a more just and humane social order. This shift was long overdue, and in fact the old clerical system predicated on a caste-like distinction between clergy and laity was coming to a rapid end. For an array of complex reasons, the number of vocations to the priesthood and religious life declined precipitously in the late 1960s. In Europe and North America the number of young men and women entering seminaries and convents declined by up to 90 percent, and there is no indication that this free-fall will be reversed in the near future. In the developing world, the situation generally has been less dramatic, but the large number of Catholics virtually guarantees that there will never be enough priests or sisters to go around. Vatican II unleashed new forms of pent-up energy. The age of clerical control is over. What has emerged is an ecclesiological model based on collaboration. The celebration of the sacraments, of course, remains an indispensable part of Catholic life, but it has become clear that lay Catholics are also very good at evangelizing the surrounding world as well.

Why Small Is Better Than Big

Before the process of "imperialization" set in at the beginning of the fourth century, the catholic community attracted new members because it offered people a supportive, loving environment in an otherwise savagely unjust world. Its members taught each other the meaning of their faith by their actions toward each other and their unconditional willingness to help anyone in need, not just members of the community. There was little formal theological discourse until the end of the second century. The beliefs and values of Christianity were taught very effectively, however, in the celebration of baptism and the Eucharist accompanied by the varied works of the community, including mutual support and assistance to those in need, particularly the enormous number of poor who inhabited the cities of the empire. Christians learned what they believed and how they should act from each other. At their baptism, new Christians recited the creed, which that was understood both as a profession of faith and a great "equalizer." No longer neophytes, they had adult responsibilities. Leaders were chosen by acclamation and duly respected because their ability to guide the community was perceived as a gift of the Holy Spirit, but they did not "lord it over" other members of the community. The "Constantinian Shift" subverted this inclusive spirit. Constantine granted bishops senatorial status and flooded dioceses with money from the state treasury. Bishops and priests enjoyed unprecedented prestige, but they paid a price in terms of integrity. They were also expected to support the reigning emperor in every possible way. Monasticism, the Franciscan movement of the thirteenth century, and modern-day lay groups like the Catholic Worker movement in North America or the St. Egidio community in Italy and other parts of Europe were founded to re-create the original, egalitarian, and socially "proactive" spirit of early Christianity. All of these movements have made a strenuous effort to keep structures to a minimum for the simple reason that we are prone to rely on them to the detriment of our creativity. Decisions are arrived at through discussion and consensus. It may take longer to figure out what do, but when that happens people understand the reasons behind their decisions and will be the more intent on the course of action they have chosen. Although it is a challenge, it is possible to be Catholic and a bit anarchistic at the same time.

These past and present movements were affirmed unconditionally by the Council as the best way to address the challenges faced by the church in the modern world. There are specific ecclesiological reasons behind the Council's support. We will discuss two of the more obvious ones. First, grace and the liberation from sin are more than vertical, individual experiences. The bishops at the Council were trying to correct the erroneous but pervasive theological notion that God "sends" down grace that is subsequently channeled by the institutional church to individual Catholics when they participate in the church's sacramental life. This simplistic, "post office" understanding of grace is obviously something of a caricature, but it was a pervasive misperception prior to Vatican II. It encouraged both clericalism and a magical understanding of the sacraments. In reality, grace is ineffable and all-pervasive. It affects the entire community that shares in its benefits. It is available through the sacraments of the institutional church, but it is also found in the community as a whole. It is even present in other religions and the natural world. The Council documents on non-Christian religions and religious freedom are explicit about this. Grace pushes us outward toward other members of the communities we belong to as well as the non-Christian world.

The second ecclesiological premise that emerged from the Council was based on a reaffirmation of a very Catholic organizational principle — subsidiarity. This technical term simply means doing things as contextually and simply as possible. The people who are best equipped to understand and live out the Christian message are those who inhabit a specific neighborhood, town, or city. They can evangelize each other and their environment in the most effective way — with a minimum of complexity and a straightforward mode of belief and behavior that others will grasp quickly. Put in another way, you do not need a degree in theology to "do" theology. A willingness to learn and refine your insights is sufficient. Theology in the best sense of the word is about commitment and growing wisdom and no one has the corner on the market, not even theologians with doctoral degrees. Equipped with a basic but solid knowledge of the Bible provided by their parishes and dioceses, analytical tools to better understand the social structures around them, along with the support of their fellow Christians, the men and women Mev Puleo interviewed had become powerful agents of evangelization and social change. They were committed to supporting and transforming each other, and doing everything possible to transform their neighborhoods and even the national political and social system of Brazil. For all of them acting in this way was understood as an obvious and inherent part of being a Christian, a challenge but also a privilege. They have not wasted their time. Today Brazil enjoys a flourishing democracy. There is a newfound willingness to discuss racism, classism, and sexism. Although it is impossible to measure, certainly Brazilian Christians have played a role in what has happened. This change has been effected in a bottom-up rather than a top-down way by intensely committed people with an incredible amount of "street smarts."

Reactions: From Secular Hostility to Ecclesiastical Wariness

It is easy to understand why those who exercise economic and political power in antidemocratic and exploitative ways would feel threatened by the people Mev Puleo interviewed. They have no formal sociopolitical power, of course, but they embody something more important — integrity and commitment to justice that flows from indomitable faith. They articulate a responsible critique and give shape to an alternative vision of society that they themselves live out on a daily basis, from their activities in neighborhood associations to their political activity on behalf of marginalized black Brazilians. In the eyes of those accustomed to a colonial, docile church willing to cut a deal for a place in society, these grassroots Catholics are a dangerous group of people. They know too much and refuse to be manipulated. After the Council the cautious conservative position on social issues that had prevailed in the church during the nineteenth century and for the first half of the twentieth was no longer viable. It was morally imperative to side with the poor, wake up middle-class Catholics to what was going on and challenge those who were wealthy to use their resources in ways that were compatible with the Catholic values they espoused. Neutrality was no longer possible. Catholics had to ask themselves hard questions about where they stood in terms of the societies they inhabited. Suddenly, a once quiescent religious institution was at the forefront of the struggle for justice and human dignity.[13] Many of these bishops were, and are, socially and theologically cautious men, but the level of injustice and suffering on their respective continents was and generally continues to be so grotesque that Paul VI in *Populorum progressio,* one of his most important encyclical letters, characterized it as an economic arrangement "whose injustice cries to heaven."[14]

As soon as the church articulated a critique of a particular leader or country the reaction was usually swift and hostile. This was especially true in Latin America where those in power were accustomed to a compliant church that said little about justice and human rights since the European invasion of the sixteenth century. Suddenly the church was acting in unprecedented and, in their minds, treasonous ways. When Catholics in South Africa joined forces with Protestants to opposed apartheid, they were branded as subversives. Ferdinand Marcos, an incredibly corrupt and oppressive dictator, persecuted progressive Catholics in the Philippines until he was forced to flee the country by a nonviolent, grassroots movement in which Catholics were among the most active participants. When Cardinal Kim denounced the brutality of the military regime that had taken over Korea he was swiftly denounced as a menace to national security and constantly harassed. His "crime" was pointing to the suffering of his fellow Koreans caused by a regime that ran roughshod over human rights and brutalized workers in its efforts to create a modern, capitalist economy. We tend to forget just how violent the developing world was from the 1960s to the early 1990s, and even today it is hardly tranquil, particularly in sub-Saharan Africa. But we need to keep our memories sharp, not only because tremendous suffering marked this period, but also because it

---

13. This commitment to the poor and oppressed was reaffirmed in 2007 by the Latin American bishops meeting in Aparecida, Brazil. This same commitment has been reiterated by the African bishops who met in the fall of 2009.

14. Gremillion, *The Gospel of Peace and Justice,* citing *Populorum progressio,* "On the Progress of Peoples," paragraph 30, 396.

was a time in which the seeds of struggle would come to fruition. We need to pose some nearly rhetorical questions. Could the churches' "ordinary" but actually extraordinary members have endured persecution and martyrdom without the support of the communities that nourished their faith and provided them with a justice-oriented spirituality? Could Catholics have stood their ground as Oscar Romero did in El Salvador if the Catholic Church had not made an option for the poor and oppressed?

One of the most erudite historians and theologians of the nineteenth century, John Henry Newman, a convert from the Anglican Church who would eventually become a cardinal, often mentioned in his books and correspondence that the decisions of church councils required decades to sink into the fabric of the church. As a participant in Vatican I, he was aware that despite the seeming unanimity of the bishops, there would be heated discussion and dissent after they signed the conciliar documents and left Rome. Newman worried about the intense centralization of the church set in motion by Vatican I as well as the timeliness of the doctrine of papal infallibility. Pius IX and Vatican I drove some brilliant people from the church and further alienated non-Catholics. For years Newman was on Rome's black list, someone Vatican officials viewed with a wary eye, although he was eventually recognized as a loyal member of the church. Vatican II has likewise produced its own forms of ambiguity and tension. As indicated, there are "minimalists" and "maximalists," those who insist that the Council changed little of the inner core of the church and those who see it as a Copernican revolution that changed it in fundamental ways. The divisions are theological in nature, but they are also based on diverse interpretations of the church's role vis-à-vis the social order. Conservatives are cautious about approaching society in ways that are too galvanizing and blunt. They are often concerned about alienating middle- and upper-class Catholics who, despite being a small percentage of the Catholic community, provide the church with a great deal of the financial resources it needs to carry out its mission. And, certainly, many of these more comfortable Catholics are people of good will with refined consciences. Liberal Catholics, on the other hand, are more inclined toward direct action on behalf of the marginalized members of their societies. Their critique of the economic and sociopolitical injustices of societies they are part of is sometimes quite sharp. As always, most people are someplace in the center of things, but there is some truth to the right- and left-wing dichotomies of modern-day Catholicism. It is evident in the episcopacy, theological circles, and the laity.

The Catholic Church is now a multifaceted entity in terms of its theological self-understanding and the way it approaches the secular world. Diversity can provide greater agility, and given the "de-Westernization" of the church that has been taking place since the mid-point of the twentieth century, this is all for the good. Roger Haight captures the challenges the church faces in the twenty-first century in an insightful way:

> Fragmentation within the church in the modern and postmodern periods, especially at the present time when the majority of Christians live in the developing world, requires rethinking the dynamics of the organizational structures of the church. Institutional boundaries help maintain the unity of the church and preserve the integrity of diverse traditions. They also set barriers that divide churches. How should these two lines of forces relate to each other?[15]

In many respects, this is a very old question in Catholicism. It is about the unavoidable tension between the church as a universal institution and a contextualized expression of the Gospel. But there is no need to play King Solomon and threaten to cut the baby in two. It is a question of balancing out these two inherent aspects of catholicity. Since the Council there has been enormous energy invested in contextualizing the church for an array of reasons. Among them is the fact that a contextualized explanation of Catholic belief helps people understand what it is that they affirm by virtue of their baptism. It also helps them to better understand what their obligations as Catholics are to the social order they are part of. This entails understanding the person of Jesus and the nature of the church in light of a person's culture and social situation rather than on the basis of abstract definitions drawn from a catechism with no points of reference to the world a person inhabits. But the pioneering work in Christology and ecclesiology that we have been discussing has been perceived by some officials in the Vatican as a threat to the integrity and universality of the church. Theologians from developing countries and liberal Catholic thinkers from the developed world have been called to Rome to explain their positions on innumerable occasions. By and large these tensions have been worked out amicably, but there is still a fair amount of misunderstanding in the air. There is a silver lining in this dialectical cloud, however. No one, conservative or liberal, disagrees about the egregious injustices of the modern economic and social order. There is a shared sense of moral outrage at the injustices inflicted on the people of the developing world and the growing number of poor in affluent countries, particularly in the last twenty to thirty years with the imposition of neoliberal economic policies that have exacerbated poverty on a global level. Liberation theologians like Gustavo Gutiérrez pointed out the inherently exploitative nature of unfettered global capitalism almost forty years ago. That has been the position of the institutional church as well, as even a cursory glance at the writings of

---

15. Haight, *Christian Community in History*, vol. 3, *Ecclesial Existence*, 53.

Paul VI, John Paul II, and Benedict XVI makes clear. Despite their theological conservatism, their approach to social issues is remarkably similar to the point of view found in the writings of Latin American, African, and Asian theologians. As Vatican II pointed out and recent popes have affirmed on many occasions, the church does not propose economic or political models. But it does and must express its point of view about the human consequences of the social orders we are part of. They can be life-giving or death-dealing, compatible with Christian values or a frank negation of the Gospel.

The Magisterium and the Modern Social Order

The word magisterium comes from the Latin word for a teacher — *magister*. In terms of the institutional church, it refers to the teaching role of its leaders who are called upon to explain to Catholics what it is they believe and how they should act in light of particular historical and social challenges. It is closely associated with the role of the pope as the church's most important pastor and teacher, but it is an integral aspect of a bishop's job as well. The teaching responsibilities of popes and bishops go beyond the church itself. Often they are required to explain to non-Catholics and non-Christians what it is that the Catholic community believes and why it is required to act in a specific way that may run against the grain of convention. The principal vehicle for papal teaching is through encyclical letters, and there have been many of them issued that focused specifically on social issues, beginning with Leo XIII's groundbreaking *Rerum novarum* of 1891, which we examined previously. John XXIII and Paul VI wrote letters that specifically focused on the economic and sociopolitical injustices and tensions produced by the Cold War. They were unequivocal in their denunciations of the power mongering associated with both the Soviet Union and the United States, along with their respective allies. They were well aware that a neocolonial system had emerged on a global level, much to the detriment of people in developing countries who were being forced to make artificial choices between two superpowers, neither of which really had the best interests of developing countries in mind. When John Paul II was elected in 1978 he continued the tradition of writing incisive, socially oriented letters, particularly in the first decade of his papacy. Benedict XVI has followed up on his predecessor's concern for social justice. In his travels to developed and developing countries since his election in 2005, he has displayed an increasingly sharp knowledge of economic and sociopolitical issues. Both John Paul and Benedict have been highly critical of the materialistic premises behind the modern global economic system that has left so many devastated people in its wake: vast numbers of people living in poverty and millions in developed countries who are economically well off but psychologically and spiritually miserable. It is well worth our time to take a quick look at the ideas behind John Paul II's social encyclicals, as well as those of Benedict XVI. We are dealing with intellectuals with a firm grasp of Western philosophical, social, and theological thought. We are also dealing with men consumed by pastoral compassion for the poor and oppressed. Their option for the poor has been stated clearly and repeatedly.

John Paul II

It is always important to understand the family background and sociocultural environment from which popes emerge. Despite the white cassocks and trappings of papal ceremonies, they are no different from the rest of us. An array of factors shape their self-understanding, approach to the church, and reaction to the world at large. In the case of Karol Wojtyla, who took the name of John Paul II when elected pope in 1978, a long tradition of electing Italian popes with either an aristocratic background or a history of service in the Vatican and its diplomatic corps was finally broken. As a child Wojtyla grew up in a loving family of modest means that was staunchly Catholic and deeply patriotic. The songs, dances, tragedies, and triumphs of his people were part and parcel of his self-understanding: although he lost his parents at a young age, he found sustenance in the faith he had inherited from them. It sustained Wojtyla and his fellow Poles as they suffered the horrors of a savage Nazi occupation during the Second World War only to be followed by the imposition of a hard-line, Stalinist regime controlled by the Soviet Union. One nightmare followed another. Under the Nazis Polish intellectuals and members of the clergy were summarily executed as threats to their absolute control. Under the communist regime that followed, the church was persecuted relentlessly because it threatened the power of a Marxist state that demanded unconditional loyalty from its citizens. As a student, priest, bishop, and eventually the cardinal-archbishop of Krakow, he consistently managed to outmaneuver his Marxist foes, never blinking in a high-stakes poker game. Although it was the Polish people who ultimately brought down the communist regime in 1989, there can be no doubt that the constancy and strategic ability of John Paul II played a key part in the fall of a repressive regime that had dominated nearly every facet of Polish society for forty years.

But John Paul was more than an astute politician. He was also a highly refined intellectual who understood the deficiencies of Marxism and capitalism. He laid them out in black and white. After his election to the papacy in 1978 he published a series of incisive encyclical letters in which he attacked the materialistic premises behind Marxism and the unbridled consumerism of the capitalist world. In no way was he a reactionary or antimodern, but he was convinced that there were deep flaws in the model behind modernity that needed to be challenged and corrected. In themselves neither system could answer the deeper questions we face as human beings, in large measure because both denied the transcendent dimension of existence. In the name of a workers' paradise whose design only elite members of the communist party could create and implement, millions of people were brutalized in prison camps and forced to watch their every step and guard their every word in order to stay out of them. Communism enslaved the very people it promised to free. In the thinking of John Paul II, free market capitalism was no less flawed. Adam Smith's "invisible hand" was like the Wizard of Oz. Behind the thunderous voice and awesome demands for obedience there was a small group of powerful and wealthy people pulling strings and levers, doing everything in their power to convince the majority of the population that the free market was, and is, some sort of supernatural force. A less than subtle inference has always been part and parcel of capitalist ideology. Those with wealth and power have earned their place in society while those who are at the bottom of the economic and social system deserve to be there. The poor are intellectually and often morally flawed — their own worst enemies. Both ideological systems desensitize those in power to the suffering of the victims of the respective systems. Workers are turned into cogs in a machine whose sole purpose is to crank out wealth — for the state in Marxist societies and in the capitalist system for those who own the means of production. Human beings are "reified," turned into things of no ultimate importance. In 1981 John Paul II issued *Laborem exercens,* roughly translated as On Doing Work. This is arguably one of John Paul's most important social encyclicals. He correctly points out the major flaws in these two systems. Marxism is predicated on the absolute power of the state while capitalism is based on the relentless pursuit of wealth for its own sake. The former leads to repression, ironically in the name of freedom, while the latter results in destructive class stratification and pathological acquisitiveness. Both are "reductionistic" and materialistic systems that have distorted our approach to what it means to be a human being and an active member of society. Although John Paul points to signs of progress, he also makes it clear that many of the unjust dynamics of nineteenth-century capitalism have persisted to the end of the twentieth century:

> This Christian "gospel of work" had to oppose the *materialistic* and *economistic* thought of the modern age. Work was understood as "merchandise" sold by the workers to the employer, the one who owned everything necessary for production. These nineteenth-century ideas have given way to a more human thinking about work, but the danger of treating work as "merchandise" — or an impersonal

"work force" — remains as long as economics is understood in a materialistic way.... The worker is treated as a tool whereas the worker ought to be treated as the *subject* of work, its maker and creator.[16]

Constantly monitored and frequently abused, workers are expected to be obedient and passive. This may sound like the stuff of a Dickens novel, but anyone who knows how the economies of developing countries work will recognize these dynamics. Even in developed, affluent countries workers and even members of the middle-class are now living on the edge, victims of economic and political systems that have made them increasingly vulnerable to economic forces beyond their control. Although there have always been economic differences between people and there always will be to some degree, we now inhabit a world in which the rich live in opulence while the poor live in squalor. To us a colloquial expression, we inhabit a world of "parallel universes" that provides superb education and health care to a minority while it denies these same human rights to the vast majority, primarily because these basic needs have been "commodified." Rich you live, poor you die.

There are three points that John Paul made consistently in his social encyclicals: the priority of labor over capital, the dignity and necessity of work, and the right of workers to organize and act as the subjects of history rather than as objects at the beck and call of those in power. Albeit succinctly, we will explore these three points because they are the foundations of Catholic social teaching in the twenty-first century.

In the capitalist West we are conditioned to think of the free market as some sort of self-regulating entity that produces the greatest good for the largest number of people. Certainly, that notion is key to Adam Smith's classic work published in 1776, *The Wealth of Nations*. But Smith was not talking about unregulated capitalism. He had a strong sense of the common good. His conviction that capitalism would ultimately benefit the largest number of people was sincere, as well as correct *if* the market is regulated in light of collective needs. Smith, however, could not foresee the savage industrial capitalism of the nineteenth century or the lightning-fast processes of the global market that dictates most aspects of our lives today. Today's economic moguls, be they on Wall Street or the Tokyo Stock Exchange, work for their own interests and those of their clients. And, as we have seen in economic meltdown of 2008 and 2009, there is often little sense of ethical responsibility among those with such staggering power. Most of us feel powerless when it comes to economic and sociopolitical affairs. Whole nations in the developing world likewise experience this sense of impotence when multinational corporations, banking consortia,

---

16. John Paul II, *The Encyclicals in Everyday Language*, 62 (*Laborem exercens*, 7).

and entities like the International Monetary Fund and World Bank dictate national economic and political policies, demanding that education and health care be privatized, or whatever policy they deem fit. Although these entities may have the best interests of people at heart on a theoretical level, they ipso facto ride roughshod over people's rights as subjects as well as over the sovereignty of the countries they ostensibly want to assist.

By asserting the priority of labor over capital, admittedly a somewhat abstract expression, John Paul is insisting that the dignity of workers and nations be respected. People have an inherent right to determine the shape of their own lives. They know what is in their best interests and must be allowed to determine the shape of their societies through democratic means. When multinational entities, even those with good intentions, dictate the conditions of labor and the political structures of other societies, they invariably do violence to the people and country they purportedly want to help. And all too often such good intentions are a ruse for exploitation, in other words, maximizing profit and with little regard for the price paid by workers and the societies they are part of. John Paul is challenging the pervasive assumption that profit takes priority over people. He insists that this principle has to be turned on its head. He is not condemning capitalism as such, but he is highly critical of the unregulated, profit-driven capitalism that has led to so much dehumanization and suffering from the nineteenth century to the present. The acquisition of money for its own sake is a destructive aberration and ultimately a sin of violence against those who are rendered poor and powerless. Furthermore, it negates a long-held Catholic belief that there is a "social mortgage" attached to wealth itself. Excessive wealth creates unnecessary poverty and it is only by finding a more reasonable economic model that we will be able to work our way out of the destructive gap that separates the rich from the poor in the world today.

John Paul II makes it clear in *Laborem exercens* that work is crucial for our sense of personal worth and the overall well-being of society. Not only do we have a right to work, we must work. Work allows us to raise families, participate in society as citizens, and make a contribution to the common good. We must use our talents on behalf of those around us. If we fail to do so we will drown in a sea of egocentric selfishness, never grasping that who *I* am is who *we* are. When people are denied this basic right to work their humanity is diminished. Few realize, however, that those with economic and political power sometimes use unemployment in a calculated way. By maintaining an unemployment rate of 5 percent or higher, those who manipulate national and international economies can keep workers in a defensive position, often competing against each other for stable jobs rather than joining forces to challenge the way a given economy works. Managers and workers often fight with each other, the former trying to maximize profit and the latter trying to minimize exploitation. In John Paul II's thinking this dichotomy has destructive consequences for everyone concerned. Rather than thinking of themselves as parts of a whole and participants in a creative process, negative energy is expended as one group tries to thwart the other. The boss easily becomes a tyrant and the worker an angry man or woman who hates the drudgery and dehumanizing aspects of labor. As a priest and bishop in Poland, Karol Wojtyla was aware of how tyrannical the Community Party was. It dictated the hours and the conditions of labor with little regard for the needs of workers themselves. So too in capitalist countries in which, even today, workers' moves are often monitored and adult women and men are forced to ask permission to go to the bathroom, and then only for a specific and brief period of time. A type of low-intensity class warfare develops that can easily lead to confrontation and violence.

Perhaps a bit romantically, John Paul II like Leo XIII recalls the guild model of the Middle Ages in which members took great pride in their work and were recognized and appreciated by society. Craftsmanship was a source of satisfaction for those with special talents, and these gifts were understood as a contribution to the common good. In the modern capitalist system, however, most people are relegated to being disposable parts in a machine that mass produces commodities they neither design nor take much pride in. There is little that is graceful in an assembly line, especially if you are making minimum wage with a boss who is likewise under a microscope. In some developing countries working conditions are so bad and the pay so miserable that some social scientists talk about "the new slavery."[17] When profit takes precedence over creativity and involvement, work ceases to be humanizing. What John Paul proposes is an inclusive, mixed economic model in which workers and managers act in a collaborative way, maximizing creativity and a sense of responsibility while minimizing the alienating drudgery of modern labor practices. For John Paul there is a simple solution that would quickly remedy what is wrong with contemporary economic models — allow workers to become vested owners with voice and vote in the industries they jointly own. What he is proposing is a blend of socialism and capitalism, collective responsibility coupled with due regard for efficiency and productivity.

Finally, workers have an inherent right to form unions and, if all other means have been exhausted, to go on a nonviolent strike to assert their right to a just wage and decent working conditions. Ironically, this right to form free unions was forbidden in the communist world. Since the Party presumably had the best interests of the workers at heart, why would they need unions to begin with? The unions that were allowed essentially

---

17. Bales, *Disposable People.*

were a stage-front that rubberstamped the economic and political policies of corrupt bureaucrats. In capitalist countries, of course, there is a long history of resistance to unions on the part of those who dominate the financial and industrial sectors. "Union busting" became part and parcel of nineteenth-century capitalism. Workers' struggle for recognition and just wages required many years of effort and thousands died in the process in Europe, North America, and elsewhere. In the modern global economy unionization is still resisted, often with tremendous violence, by those who control capital and own factories. And if unionization succeeds, there is often a concerted effort on the part of those in power to co-opt and manipulate union leaders. But unions can play an enormously positive role, not just in terms of wages and working conditions, but also with regard to the overall nature of society. When he was elected pope in 1978 Karol Wojtyla obviously had to leave his native Poland, but that did not mean cutting off contact. He remained actively involved in Polish life, primarily through his support of an illegal union known as Solidarity, which soon became an inclusive, anticommunist social movement. When he visited his native country, and he did so nine times, he was unequivocal in his support of Solidarity. This broad-based coalition did the seemingly impossible. In 1989 the Communist Party was forced to cede power in a free and fair election. The postwar Iron Curtain began to crumble, starting in Poland and moving quickly to other parts of now defunct Soviet bloc. A union, with the help of a pope, had caused a geopolitical earthquake.

What Solidarity and John Paul were tapping was the desire of the Polish people for real freedom and justice, rights denied to them by a totalitarian regime. The desire for freedom and basic human rights was the motor force behind what happened in 1989. The leaders of Solidarity and John Paul simply tapped this deep-seated desire in the Polish people. Their genius lay in pushing the right buttons at the right time. A seemingly serendipitous series of events changed the course of history. A secular social movement had a transcendent dimension to it. John Paul defended unions and strikes because, if properly formed and undertaken, they can be powerful tools in resisting injustice and affirming the common good.

> To secure these rights, the workers need the right to association in labor or trade unions. . . . Catholic social teaching does not see unions as reflecting only a "class" structure, and even less as engaged in a "class" struggle. They are indeed engaged in the struggle for social justice, but this is a struggle *for* the common good, and not *against* others. . . . One of the methods used by unions is the strike, or work stoppage — a means that is recognized by Catholic social teaching as legitimate under the proper conditions and within proper

limits. Workers should be assured of the right to strike without fear of penalty.[18]

These limits always entail prior negotiation and a willingness to make reasonable concessions in everyone's best interests. The Marxist-Leninist tradition that John Paul II experienced firsthand in his native Poland was based on the notion of class warfare. It used hatred and envy to pit one social class against another. The result was tremendous violence and injustice coupled with corruption and eventually social stagnation. Nothing could be more antithetical to a Christian vision of a just and healthy society. Reasonable economic differences are acceptable and can actually play a positive social role. Exaggerated economic differences, however, are another question. They create a spiral of injustice and oppression.

One of the lessons John Paul learned in Poland and emphasized as pope is that unions should remain independent of political parties. Party politics too often requires compromises and maneuvers that can diminish the credibility and effectiveness of the unions themselves. Sooner or later someone will try to stuff the pockets of union leaders with a wad of cash. A degree of autonomy, therefore, is indispensable. If they are turned into political puppets, unions rarely act on behalf of the common good. They must consider the rights of *all* workers, not just those of their members or the myopic interests of a political party. They are crucial for creating a sense of collective responsibility — challenging those with power to act justly as well as encouraging workers to organize and use their collective power responsibly. John Paul's message is that in terms of the social order we are all "connected vessels," and keeping this interconnectedness in mind is an indispensable aspect of moral behavior.

Benedict XVI

Josef Ratzinger was born in 1927 in a small Bavarian town. Like Karol Wojtyla's, his middle-class parents were devout Catholics. As a teenager he was inscribed in the Hitler Youth Corps and eventually drafted into the German army, a universal experience for young German males during the war. He had learned from his father, however, to detest everything about Nazism. Furthermore, the Nazis euthanized one of his cousins with Down's syndrome. Germans who were deemed mentally or physically defective were rounded up and injected with lethal drugs in the name of genetic purity. In 1951 Ratzinger was ordained to the priesthood. Given his obvious intellectual gifts, his bishop sent him on for advanced studies in theology. His doctoral dissertation explored the implications of

---

18. John Paul II, *The Encyclicals in Everyday Language*, 62–63 (*Laborem exercens*, 20).

Augustine's theology. Soon he would become equally versed in medieval authors such as Aquinas and Bonaventure. The next step in his intellectual journey would entail an in-depth study of the Enlightenment and modernity. These are not tangential considerations. Scholars look at the world through a set of lenses provided them by their intellectual mentors, living and dead, and the fact that Josef Ratzinger has been steeped in Augustine and medieval theology explains a great deal about his approach to the church and secular modernity. Augustine's concept of an inherently flawed earthly city that must be understood in light of its heavenly counterpart is the foundation of his theology and is the premise behind his most important work, the *City of God.* As a student Josef Ratzinger achieved an amazing grasp of this long, complex work, alone with other Augustinian texts. The priest/scholar, who would become a cardinal and eventually pope, has been correctly identified as a neo-Augustinian. Josef Ratzinger has always subscribed to what might be called an "eschatological reservation" about any given social order just as Augustine did. No social system, not even the institutional church, is able to achieve perfection or satisfy our deepest human needs. God alone can do that. But there is no need for a paralyzing depression or a sense of doom. We can contribute to a better social order and despite its limitations the church provides the grace and support we need as human beings.

There is a Thomistic side to Josef Ratzinger as well. He is a firm believer that a properly balanced relationship between church and state can lead to a more humane and just world. Church and state should never be fused, but they should be in contact and communication with each other. He is hardly advocating a return to Christendom, but he insists that the church be allowed a role in modern society. Its message is too important to be pushed to the side. As he reflected on the Enlightenment and European modernity, he drew the conclusion that much of what had gone wrong since the eighteenth century was predictable. Without the moral compass of Christian values, Western society had been set adrift, the victim of what he has often referred to as a culture of relativism. Relying on a materialistic philosophy and a Darwinian approach to society, the twin traps of Marxism and fascism were bound to ensnare many Europeans. When God was removed as a point of ethical and social reference, people predictably turned to the state or material possessions that they deified and worshiped. The young priest and scholar was not given a pastoral assignment by his bishop. He was sent, rather, to study and then teach in German universities where he was known as a conservative scholar, but always a sophisticated and respectful one. Ratzinger participated in Vatican II as the theological advisor to the archbishop of Munich. He was a strong supporter of the Council and continues to be to this day, but his interpretation of what transpired from 1962 to 1965 is predicated on the assumption that the Council was about fine-tuning the church rather than changing any of its major parts. After the Council his rise through the ranks of the institutional church was meteoric. In 1977 Paul VI named him the archbishop of Cologne. In 1981 John Paul II invited him to Rome to head the Congregation for the Doctrine of the Faith, once known as the Holy Office, or Inquisition. He became the guardian of Catholic orthodoxy and would hold this post until his election to the papacy in 2005.[19]

The twenty-four years Cardinal Ratzinger spent as one of the most important people in the Vatican provide us with tremendous insight into how the man who is the bishop of Rome understands the Catholic Church and its role in the social order. Benedict XVI is a conservative man, but his conservatism is intellectually solid. He knows where he stands and why he takes the positions that he does. There is no doubt that many events in the postconciliar church were deeply troubling for him, especially when some people tried to turn the church on its head, sometimes out of sheer anger. The preconciliar church was like an overly rigid parent trying to monitor every aspect of a child's behavior. Eventually, however, children leave home, and if they have been subjected to excessive control will most likely rebel soon after they are out the door. This happened in the Catholic Church after the Council. Otherwise reasonable adults sometimes acted like adolescents. As a university professor in Germany Benedict lived through the student revolution of 1968. At times things were utterly chaotic, not to mention occasionally idiotic. Students attacked everything associated with the past, just as some Catholics lashed out at every aspect of their tradition and the institutional church after the Council. The professor who would become pope was appalled by what he witnessed. The words "change" and "revolution" took on an ambiguous connotation for him. In some ways they became synonyms for self-indulgent destructiveness, at least in their more extreme forms. As prefect of the Congregation for the Doctrine of the Faith Ratzinger was open to new ideas, provided that they were properly explained and did not threaten the core doctrine of the Catholic Church. He is too skilled a scholar to deny that the way we understand faith and tradition is subject to constant reformulation. But change must be implemented prudently. For Benedict XVI the truth is the truth. Although it must be articulated in ways that make sense to people in a specific culture and historical moment, its essence is immutable because its source is God's own self revealed in the person of Jesus Christ.

As the head of the Vatican congregation in charge of doctrinal orthodoxy, the otherwise shy and scholarly Cardinal Ratzinger was often on the front pages of some of the world's most prominent newspapers. In 1984 he issued a document that was extremely critical of many aspects of liber-

---

19. Allen, *Pope Benedict XVI.*

ation theology. It was followed in 1986 by a document on the same theme that was a bit less negative, although still highly critical of certain theological ideas coming out of developing countries. Latin American, African, and Asian theologians were under scrutiny. Some were required to explain their ideas again and again in what proved to be a tense stand-off at times. A few were silenced, that is, told they could not write, teach, or lecture until the Vatican was certain that their ideas conformed with Catholic orthodoxy as Rome understood it. A few European and North America theologians suffered the same fate. Clearly, Rome frowned on what it considered intemperate theological writing, particularly when the topic at hand dealt with Jesus, the structure of the church, or the way Christians should confront social injustice. Liberal Catholics began to talk about pre–Vatican II "restorationism," as if John Paul and his associate Cardinal Ratzinger were intent on creating a church more in tune with the vision of Pius XII than John XXIII. When Benedict was elected in 2005 many feared a sort of theological bloodbath that would rival the modernist crisis unleashed by Pius X at the beginning of the twentieth century, in which liberal theologians were systematically harassed and silenced. In fact, some conservatives were frankly licking their chops in anticipation of a long overdue "comeuppance." It has not happened, nor is it likely to. The pluralism of the modern church is indispensable for its future well-being. From the first Pauline communities to the present there have been diverse ways of understanding Jesus, the church, and the best way to approach the world at large. This diversity can lead to occasional tensions, but it is ultimately a source of richness and a key to survival. As a knowledgeable theologian with a keen sense of history, Benedict XVI knows this. The social and intellectual challenges the Catholic Church faces today preclude any one answer, particularly when it comes to the person and message of Jesus and the nature and mission of the church.

Christology has always been one of the most sensitive topics in Christian theology. At times it is akin to an exposed nerve that sends shivers of pain in every direction when it is accidentally touched. This is reasonable since definitions of Jesus have a profound effect on the way we understand Christianity as a whole. Since at least the fourth century, the Gospel of John has held sway over the catholic churches, both in the Orthodox East and Roman West. Mark, Matthew, and Luke are cherished as well, but the portrait of Jesus painted by John has won the most votes over the centuries. Benedict's reliance on the Fourth Gospel is striking. His Christology is deeply Johannine, just as his approach to the church and social order is profoundly Augustinian. The Johannine Jesus descends from heaven and ascends back to his Father after a brief earthly stay. There is an ethereal, otherworldly quality to him that is quite distinct from the Jesus of the synoptic Gospels, who touches and is touched, weeps in empathy for those in pain, and experiences utter desolation as he dies on the cross. In an effort to "reinvigorate" the person and message of Jesus, modern theologians have written extensively about the historical Jesus of the synoptic tradition — the Jewish prophet who preached about the Reign of God and was tortured and murdered for doing so. In his 1984 and 1986 critiques of liberation theology, the then Cardinal Ratzinger accused liberation theologians of reducing Jesus to a political revolutionary, losing sight of the central importance of his divinity. Most likely he had the early Christological works of Leonardo Boff and Jon Sobrino in mind. But in all fairness, neither of these theologians is in the least bit "reductionistic." Neither understands Jesus in purely political or social terms. Jesus' divinity is non-negotiable for them as well, but Jesus' divinity is mediated through his historical humanity, most evident in his commitment to the poor and oppressed of Jewish Palestine. To the extent that the then Cardinal Ratzinger might favor John, they were inclined to favor Mark, whose Jesus experiences anxiety, disappointment, and pain like all normal people do. We need to keep in mind that there are four Gospels and you can pick the one you like the most. You can even mix and match if that suits your fancy.

Benedict's ecclesiology is much like his Christology. It is fundamentally hierarchical. He puts great stock in the apostolic origins of the church, even if many biblical scholars and historians question the accuracy of such an assertion in its most literal form. Of course, he recognizes that the institutional church has evolved over time and that there are many aspects of it that are quite peripheral to its mission in the world, but he has no doubt that the church is an expression of Jesus' saving will for humanity and the message it proclaims about salvation is therefore infallible. The Catholic Church is and always will be guided by the Holy Spirit. It is the task of the bishop of Rome as pope, and the magisterium of the church made up of the pope's advisors and bishops in their respective dioceses, to interpret and apply these truths in such a way that members of the Catholic community can understand and live out their Catholic faith in its fullness. The chain of command in the Catholic Church is not an accident. It exists to clarify the truth and to help people affirm it. Obedience is incumbent on all members of the church, not as a knee-jerk reaction or a fearful response to authority, but as an expression of informed assent to the truth that the church proclaims and lives out, in other words, the Gospel. This is the reason people in the hierarchical church are granted power: not for the sake of self-aggrandizement but for the sake of the well-being of the Catholic community and the message it is required to proclaim.

The church has often failed to measure up to these lofty standards, as Vatican II states. Both John Paul II and Benedict XVI have pointed to the sins of the institutional church. We all have egos and can be myopic at times. But the ecclesiology that emerged after Vatican II is predicated on a more ample vision of what it means to be Catholic. The church is still understood as a hierarchical institution, but Vatican II makes it clear that all baptized members of the church share in the priesthood of the faithful and are responsible for the well-being of the Catholic community. Soon after the Council ended there was a concerted effort on the part of theologians to take the next step forward and create models of the church that were more appropriate for the cultures and social arrangements of the people they were trying to empower as full-fledged members of the church. The assumption behind Vatican II is that everyone in the church should be held accountable to each other. At times, there has been considerable anger created by residual traditionalism and foot dragging that some members of the hierarchy continue to engage in. This was evident in the years after the publication of *Humanae vitae* and is a factor behind some of the hostility toward the institutional church generated by the clerical sexual abuse nightmare that began at the beginning of this century. There are still people in the hierarchy who insist on blind obedience and are not forthcoming with the truth. In what was something of a broadside published nearly a quarter of a century ago, the Brazilian theologian Leonardo Boff accused certain members of the hierarchy, especially in the Vatican, of minimizing and even betraying the spirit of Vatican II in one of his most famous books, *Church, Charism and Power.* Some of his criticisms are valid, others a result of his frustration with Rome. There are vestiges of medieval Christendom that are hard to explain and border on the ridiculous. Calling a cardinal Your Eminence, coats of arms for bishops, why? It is important to realize, however, that people who work in the Vatican have the nearly impossible task of trying to maintain cohesion in the world's most diverse religious community.

In a more upbeat book, *Ecclesiogenesis,* Boff proposed the base Christian community model as a way to make the church more meaningful for its members, as well as socially consequential. He pointed out the deficiencies of diocesan governance and the parish-based model of the church, in the mega-cities of Brazil as well as in the country's vast rural areas. Because of outmoded, historically anachronistic structures, the church was failing to preach the Gospel in the way it should. It remained addicted to the past, as well as too subservient to a powerful social oligarchy. There is considerable merit in his thesis, but there is also value in dioceses and parishes that are more traditional models but socially engaged. Much like the Gospels, however, it is perfectly legitimate to pick and choose different models of the church, as long as they conform with evangelical values and the vision of Vatican II. At the moment, unfortunately, there is probably more tension over ecclesiological issues in the Catholic Church than there is about the more abstract issue of Christology. Benedict insists on a hierarchical model of the church and he has many allies in both the developing and developed world. John Paul II and Benedict have shown what many consider excessive openness to conservative and ultra-conservative Catholic groups, among them Opus Dei and the Legionnaires of Christ. These groups are theologically traditionalist and socially conservative, recruiting a high percentage of their members from the middle and upper social classes.[20] Although they are not insensitive to the plight of the poor, they are almost always opposed to the structural change needed to alleviate social inequality. At the same time, many long for a less dogmatic and more democratic church in which their voices truly will be heard. Some have left out of sheer exasperation. This is tragic in itself, but what is just as tragic is that internal divisions threaten the contribution the church can make to the world at large.

Benedict sees a fundamental flaw at the heart of modernity — an idolatrous materialism that renders us numb to the suffering of those around us and ethically neutered as we contend for our piece of the pie. In his opinion we are sinking in a culture of relativism in which ethical and religious values are understood as private matters at best, but certainly irrelevant in the real, Darwinian world of winners and losers. Benedict sees this as a root cause of amoral behavior and social fragmentation. As pope, Benedict has made trips to his native Germany and other European countries, as well as Australia and the United States, in an effort to stem the tide of secularization that has emptied churches at a breath-taking pace. But his attention goes beyond affluent societies. In recent documents he has shown an astute knowledge of how the global economic system works. In itself, globalization is neither good nor bad. It certainly is an unavoidable fact of life in the twenty-first century. The ethical challenge is to focus on the common good of the entire human community and to use the advantages offered by globalization to this end. Developed countries continue to bully poorer nations using national elites to do their neocolonial dirty work. In Benedict's *Message for the Celebration of the World Day of Peace* in January 2009, he lays out the responsibilities incumbent on all members of the global community:

> In order to govern globalization, however, there needs to be a strong sense of *global solidarity* between rich and poor countries.... Effective means to redress the marginalization of the world's poor through globalization will only be found if people everywhere feel personally outraged by the injustices in the world and by the concomitant violations of human rights. The church which is the "sign and instrument

---

20. Allen, *Opus Dei*, 15–42.

of communion with God and of the unity of the entire human race" will continue to offer her contribution so that injustices and misunderstandings may be resolved, leading to a world of greater peace and solidarity.[21]

A phrase like "personally outraged" does not come to mind readily when one thinks of an academic, not to mention a pope. Supposedly, they are beyond such intense emotions. Fortunately, the current pope is not. Benedict also displays a keen understanding of the recent catastrophic meltdown of the world financial system that began in 2008. He correctly attributes its origins to greed and immorality. "The recent crisis demonstrates how financial activity can at times be completely turned in on itself, lacking any consideration of the common good."[22] Put another way, the amoral culture that now drives global markets was bound to lead to the meltdown that has produced so much misery. In developed countries people's pension funds have been decimated, but in developing countries whole national economies face the possibility of collapse and the social chaos that inevitably follows.

Speaking to the Catholic community in *Sacramentum caritatis* (The Sacrament of Love), an encyclical letter issued in 2007, Benedict points to the indispensable nourishment of the sacraments, particularly the Eucharist, in Catholics' struggle for social justice. It unites them in a common cause with others and provides them with the strength that is required in the long, hard struggle that invariably ensues when we attempt to create a society that reflects the values laid out in the Gospel.

> In the memorial of his sacrifice, the Lord strengthens our fraternal communion and, in a particular way, urges those in conflict to hasten their reconciliation by opening themselves to dialogue and a commitment to justice. Certainly, the restoration of justice, reconciliation and forgiveness are the conditions for building true peace. The recognition of this fact leads to a determination to transform unjust structures and to restore respect for the dignity of all men and women, created in God's image and likeness. Through the concrete fulfillment of this responsibility, the Eucharist becomes in life what it signifies in its celebration. As I have had occasion to say, it is not the proper task of the Church to engage in the political work of bringing about the most just society possible; nonetheless she cannot and must not remain on the sidelines in the struggle for justice.[23]

---

21. Benedict XVI, *Message for the Celebration of the World Day of Peace 2009*, paragraph 8.
22. Ibid., paragraph 10.
23. Benedict XVI, *Sacramentum caritatis*, paragraph 89.

To synthesize Benedict's assertions, the Eucharist is an eminently social sacrament. It breaks down barriers between people. Catholics should be open to people of good will who are likewise concerned about the common good. Although conversation and sometimes debate are inevitable, there is a shared passion for a just social order that we all can appreciate and celebrate. And although the church as an institution should not be in the business of telling people how to vote or side in any way whatsoever with political parties, it nonetheless must articulate its message in clear terms about what social values are in the best interest of the human community. In short, it is called to be the spokesperson for Jesus' vision of the Reign of God. This is its one and only task, but it is certainly no easy one in the modern world we inhabit.

A Frantic Conclusion

There are multiple ways in which to summarize this lengthy chapter; none is perfect. Perhaps we should begin with the obvious point that the Catholic Church has yet to settle down after the Second Vatican Council. There are competing theological models as well as diverse approaches to social issues. The church as a whole has undergone enormous change since 1965, too much for some, too little for others. There have been more "liberal" popes as well as more "conservative" ones, although these terms have limited utility. All of this has been coupled with incredibly rapid social and technological change. In 1965 a computer was a room-filling apparatus that only engineers could understand. The Internet was a pipedream, as was e-mail. Developing countries were casting off the last vestiges of colonial rule, sometimes chaotically, but there was a sense of optimism about the future. At the beginning of the twenty-first century, however, that optimism is more tenuous. The Cold War has been over now for two decades yet the structural discrepancies and injustices of the 1960s are just as acute today as they were a half-century ago, perhaps more so. They have simply mutated. The near absolute power of global capital has made people more vulnerable rather than less, a fact driven home by the economic crisis that began in 2008. Today vast numbers of people move within the boundaries of their countries as economic and political refugees. Many cross international borders illegally in search of work. The global economic system is pushing people like cattle from one place to another. Economic disparity in developed and developing countries is more pronounced than any time since the outset of industrialization in the mid-nineteenth century. The challenges for the Catholic Church and the Christian community as a whole are daunting. The overwhelming majority of Christians of all denominations are now poor, as well as socio-politically marginalized. As we have mentioned several times, the era of

Eurocentric, bourgeois Christianity has come to an end and the churches must grapple with this fact or suffer the consequences. The statistics point to a paradigm shift of fundamental importance:

> By 2025, according to one estimate, Africa and Latin America will together account for at least 50 per cent of the world Christian population, underlying their status as the new heartlands of the faith. This southward "shift," which has seen the emergence of Christianity as a non-Western religion, represents one of the most profound religious transformations in the world within the last half a century.[24]

This shift has a special dimension when it comes to Catholicism. The juggling act between the universal and local expressions of the church will be more complicated than ever. At the same time, this added complexity is a welcome turn of events. The Catholic Church is becoming more catholic. It is returning to its roots as a multicultural form of Christianity. The homogeneity imposed by Trent and the monarchical hierarchy that developed after the First Vatican Council are a thing of the past. In fact, they have become an impediment to the catholic nature of the church. The "threats" of Protestantism and the dangers of modernity are no longer salient issues. The question at hand is how to solidify the church's option for the poor. This entails letting the members of the church define Catholicism in light of their own contexts and experiences. Being a Catholic in Kenya is not exactly the same as being a Catholic in the United States. It is now time to savor this diversity.

By encouraging the laity to take responsibility for their church, the bishops at Vatican II altered the way the church is governed. Although there are still pockets of resistance, the age of "clericalism" is coming to an end. Officials in the Vatican, diocesan bishops, and parish priests have special expertise and play a vital role in the life of the church, but ultimately they are members of a community of equals. They are called to a life of service and, to the extent that they fulfill their duties faithfully, deserve great respect. But the laywoman or layman who does the same is equally important. Paul's metaphor about the Christian community found in 1 Corinthians 12:12 needs to be reemphasized. The church is one body with many members. Furthermore, the laity has an obvious advantage in terms of implementing the church's social vision in a grassroots way. Be it on a national or neighborhood level, an informed and empowered laity is the most effective force for raising questions about the social order as well as proposing reasonable alternatives in light of what needs to be done. The institutional church provides insights and guidelines while the laity

---

24. Walls and Ross, *Mission in the Twenty-First Century*, 126.

applies them on a personal and social level. In an age characterized by ethical indifference, Catholics should be at the forefront of those people who are outraged by what is going on in the world today, as Pope Benedict insists. How is it possible to be silent about the economic injustices that continue to this day, pitting the developed world against developing nations? How can Catholics remain silent while those who wield economic and political power in the United States and European Union wreak havoc with the lives of people in developing countries and, increasingly, their fellow citizens? Why are basic nutrition and health care treated as commodities when they are basic human rights? Responsible nonconformity is ethically imperative in the modern world order, just as it was in the earliest days of Christianity when Jesus' followers had the dangerous audacity to tell the truth. The church's loss of power that began in the eighteenth century should not be seen as a tragedy but as a gift. Now the church can be as prophetic as it wants to be. It no longer has a vested interest in the status quo. Freed from the vestiges of Christendom the women and men who make up the Catholic Church can now speak the truth to power as never before despite the timidity and excessive caution of some of their leaders. There are innumerable examples of catholic people who have done so through the ages — the first martyrs, Augustine, Francis, Dorothy Day, Oscar Romero. The list is very long. We need to remember these amazing people, and that is one of the reasons behind this book. But we also need to look around us. We are not alone. We form a community of Catholics, other Christians, and people of good will who are just as passionate about changing the social order in ways that will make our world more just, humane, and sustainable. We must break out of the pattern of economic and social exploitation, just as we must stop abusing the ecosystem that we are part of. We no longer have the resources or the time to do otherwise. Progress is usually very slow, but that makes even the tiniest victory a source of joy and celebration. The struggle for justice should never be somber. Jesus encouraged the poor and oppressed to enjoy each other, to sit down and savor a bit of wine and a modest meal. Today we can learn a valuable lesson from Christians in the slums of Nairobi and São Paulo. They know how to gather together to share their loaves and fishes and enjoy each other in the struggle for a new social order. As they teach each other, they also teach us. They go to the heart and soul of what it means to be a Catholic and, as Jon Sobrino has put it, "there is no salvation outside of the poor."[25]

It is only in relationship to one another and in a common effort on behalf of the Reign of God that we will achieve the peace and salvation we deeply long for.

---

25. Sobrino, *No Salvation outside the Poor.*

Works Cited

Alberigo, Giuseppe. *A Brief History of Vatican II.* Maryknoll, N.Y.: Orbis Books, 2006.

Alberigo, Giuseppe, and Joseph A. Komonchak, eds. *History of Vatican II.* Vol. 1 *Announcing and Preparing Vatican Council II: Toward a New Era in Catholicism.* Maryknoll, N.Y.: Orbis Books; Leuven: Peeters, 1995.

Allen, John L. *Opus Dei: The First Objective Look behind the Myths and Reality of the Most Controversial Force in the Catholic Church.* New York: Doubleday, 2005.

———. *Pope Benedict XVI: A Biography of Joseph Ratzinger.* New York: Continuum, 2005.

Aristotle. *The Politics, and the Constitution of Athens.* Rev. student ed. Ed. Stephen Everson. Cambridge Texts in the History of Political Thought. Cambridge and New York: Cambridge University Press, 1996.

Augustine. *The Confessions, The Works of Saint Augustine.* Trans. Maria Boulding, John E. Rotelle, and Augustinian Heritage Institute. Hyde Park, N.Y.: New City Press, 1997.

Augustine. *City of God.* Trans. Marcus Dos. New York: Random House, 1993.

Bales, Kevin. *Disposable People: New Slavery in the Global Economy.* Rev. ed. Berkeley: University of California Press, 2004.

Boff, Leonardo. *Jesus Christ Liberator: A Critical Christology for Our Time.* Maryknoll, N.Y.: Orbis Books, 1978.

———. *Church, Charism, and Power: Liberation Theology and the Institutional Church.* New York: Crossroad, 1985.

———. *Ecclesiogenesis: The Base Communities Reinvent the Church.* Maryknoll, N.Y.: Orbis Books, 1986.

Bokenkotter, Thomas. *Church and Revolution: Catholics in the Struggle for Democracy and Social Justice.* New York: Doubleday Image Books, 1998.

Borg, Marcus J. *Jesus, a New Vision: Spirit, Culture, and the Life of Discipleship.* San Francisco: HarperSanFrancisco, 1991.

———. *Jesus: Uncovering the Life, Teachings, and Relevance of a Religious Revolutionary.* New York: HarperOne, 2008.

Brown, Peter Robert Lamont. *The Body and Society: Men, Women, and Sexual Renunciation in Early Christianity.* Lectures on the History of Religions. New ser., no. 13. New York: Columbia University Press, 1988.

———. *Augustine of Hippo: A Biography.* New ed. Berkeley: University of California Press, 2000.

Bühlmann, Walbert. *The Church of the Future: A Model for the Year 2001.* Maryknoll, N.Y.: Orbis Books, 1986.

Carroll, James. *Constantine's Sword: The Catholic Church and the Jews.* Boston: Houghton Mifflin, 2001.

Cook, William, and Ronald B. Herzman. *The Medieval World View: An Introduction.* New York: Oxford University Press, 2004.

Cooke, Bernard J. *The Distancing of God: The Ambiguity of Symbol in History and Theology.* Minneapolis: Fortress Press, 1990.

Cornwell, John. *Hitler's Pope: The Secret History of Pius XII.* Boston: Houghton Mifflin, 1999.

Crossan, John Dominic. *The Historical Jesus: The Life of a Mediterranean Jewish Peasant.* San Francisco: HarperSanFrancisco, 1992.

Doyle, William. *The Oxford History of the French Revolution.* New York: Oxford University Press, 1989.

Drake, H. A. *Constantine and the Bishops: The Politics of Intolerance.* Ancient Society and History. Baltimore: Johns Hopkins University Press, 2000.

Duffy, Eamon. *The Voices of Morebath: Reformation and Rebellion in an English Village.* New Haven: Yale University Press, 2001.

Dunn, Geoffrey D. *Tertullian.* The Early Church Fathers. New York: Routledge, 2004.

Eusebius of Caesarea. *The Life of Constantine.* Clarendon Ancient History Series. Trans. Averil Cameron and Stuart George Hall. Oxford: Clarendon Press, 1999.

Evans, G. R. *The First Christian Theologians: An Introduction to Theology in the Early Church,* The Great Theologians. Malden, Mass.: Blackwell, 2004.

Finnis, John. *Aquinas: Moral, Political, and Legal Theory.* Founders of Modern Political and Social Thought. New York: Oxford University Press, 1998.

Flannery, Austin O.P., ed. *Vatican Council II: The Basic Sixteen Documents.* Northport, N.Y.: Costello Publishing Company, 2007. Original ed., 1996.

González, Justo L. *The Story of Christianity.* 2 vols. San Francisco: Harper & Row, 1984.

Greeley, Andrew M. *The Catholic Myth: The Behavior and Beliefs of American Catholics.* New York: Simon & Schuster, 1997.

Gremillion, Joseph. *The Gospel of Peace and Justice: Catholic Social Teaching since Pope John.* Maryknoll, N.Y.: Orbis Books, 1976.

Gutiérrez, Gustavo. *The Power of the Poor in History.* Maryknoll, N.Y.: Orbis Books, 1983.

———. *We Drink from Our Own Wells: The Spiritual Journey of a People.* Maryknoll, N.Y.: Orbis Books, 1984.

———. *A Theology of Liberation: History, Politics, and Salvation.* Maryknoll, N.Y.: Orbis Books, 1988.

———. *Las Casas: In Search of the Poor of Jesus Christ.* Maryknoll, N.Y.: Orbis Books, 1993.

Haight, Roger. *Jesus, Symbol of God.* Maryknoll, N.Y.: Orbis Books, 1999.

———. *The Future of Christology.* New York: Continuum, 2007.

———. *Christian Community in History.* Vol. 3: *Ecclesial Existence.* New York: Continuum, 2008.

Hampson, Norman, Malcolm Crook, William Doyle, and Alan I. Forrest. *Enlightenment and Revolution: Essays in Honour of Norman Hampson.* Aldershot, Hampshire, England; Burlington, Vt.: Ashgate, 2004.

Horsley, Richard A. *The Sociology of the Jesus Movement.* New York: Crossroad, 1994.

————. *Galilee: History, Politics, People.* Philadelphia: Trinity Press, 1995.

————. *Archaeology, History, and Society: The Social Context of Jesus and the Rabbis.* Philadelphia: Trinity Press International, 1996.

Horsley, Richard A., and Neil Asher Silberman. *The Message and the Kingdom: How Jesus and Paul Ignited a Revolution and Transformed the Ancient World.* Minneapolis: Fortress Press, 2002.

House, Adrian. *Francis of Assisi.* New York: HiddenSpring, 2001.

Ignatius of Loyola. *Personal Writings.* Trans. and ed. Joseph A. Munitiz and Philip Endean. New York: Penguin Group, 1996.

James, William. *The Varieties of Religious Experience: A Study in Human Nature.* New York: Simon & Schuster, 1997.

Jenkins, Philip. *The Next Christendom: The Coming of Global Christianity.* Oxford: Oxford University Press, 2002.

John Paul II. *The Encyclicals in Everyday Language.* Ed. Joseph G. Donders. New updated ed. Maryknoll, N.Y.: Orbis Books, 2005.

Küng, Hans. *Infallible? An Inquiry.* Garden City, N.Y.: Doubleday, 1983.

Lilla, Mark. *The Stillborn God: Religion, Politics, and the Modern West.* New York: Albert A. Knopf, 2007.

MacCulloch, Diarmaid. *The Reformation: A History.* New York: Viking, 2003.

MacMullen, Ramsay, and Eugene N. Lane. *Paganism and Christianity: 100–425 C.E.* Minneapolis: Fortress Press, 1992.

Meeks, Wayne A. *The First Urban Christians: The Social World of the Apostle Paul.* New Haven, Conn.: Yale University Press, 1983.

Meissner, William. *Ignatius of Loyola: The Psychology of a Saint.* New Haven: Yale University Press, 1994.

Mich, Marvin. *Catholic Social Teachings and Movements.* Mystic, Conn.: Twenty-Third Publications, 1998.

Nichols, Aidan. *Discovering Aquinas: An Introduction to His Life, Work and Influence.* Grand Rapids, Mich.: William B. Eerdmans, 2003.

O'Donnell, James J. *Confessions.* Text and Commentary. New York: Oxford University Press, 1992.

————. *Augustine: A New Biography.* New York: HarperCollins, 2005.

O'Malley, John W., Joseph A. Komonchak, Stephen Schloessler, and Neil J. Ormero. *Vatican II: Did Anything Happen?* Ed. D. G. Schultenover. New York: Continuum, 2005.

Orobator, Agbonkhianmeghe E. *Theology Brewed in an African Pot.* Maryknoll, N.Y.: Orbis Books, 2008.

Pieris, Aloysius. *An Asian Theology of Liberation.* Faith Meets Faith Series. Maryknoll, N.Y.: Orbis Books, 1988.

Puleo, Mev. *The Struggle Is One: Voices and Visions of Liberation.* Albany: State University of New York Press, 1994.

Rynne, Xavier. *Vatican Council II.* Maryknoll, N.Y.: Orbis Books, 1999.

Sanders, E. P. *Paul (Past Masters).* New York: Oxford University Press, 1991.

Shannon, Thomas A. "Rerum novarum." In *Modern Catholic Social Teaching: Commentaries and Interpretations.* Ed. Kenneth B. Himes. Mystic, Conn.: Twenty-Third Publications, 2004.

Sobrino, Jon. *Jesus in Latin America.* Maryknoll, N.Y.: Orbis Books, 1987.

————. *No Salvation outside the Poor: Prophetic-Utopian Essays.* Maryknoll, N.Y.: Orbis Books, 2007.

Spence, Jonathan D. *The Memory Palace of Matteo Ricci.* New York: Viking Penguin, 1984.

Suetonius, and Michael Grant. *The Twelve Caesars.* Rev. ed. New York: Penguin Books, 1980.

Thomas Aquinas. *Political Writings.* Cambridge Texts in the History of Political Thought. Ed. R. W. Dyson. Cambridge and New York: Cambridge University Press, 2002.

Tuchman, Barbara Wertheim. *A Distant Mirror: The Calamitous Fourteenth Century.* New York: Knopf, 1978.

Walls, Andrew F., and Cathy Ross, eds. *Mission in the Twenty-First Century: Exploring the Five Marks of Global Mission.* Maryknoll, N.Y.: Orbis Books, 2008.

Weber, Max. *The Protestant Ethic and the Spirit of Capitalism.* Ed. and trans. Peter Baehr and Gordon C. Wells. New York: Penguin Books Twentieth Century Classics, 2002.

Wills, Gary. *St. Augustine.* New York: Lipper/Viking, 1999.

————. *Papal Sin: Structures of Deceit.* New York: Doubleday, 2000.

Index